OTHELLO

and

THE TRAGEDY OF MARIAM

Contents

**Othello *and* The Tragedy of Mariam *in Context: Tracts
on Marriage   274***

An *Excerpt from the First Biography of Elizabeth Cary*   293

Further Reading   307

List of Illustrations

About Longman
Cultural Editions

Reading always seems to vibrate with the transformations of the day—now, yesterday, and centuries ago, when the presses first put printed language into wide circulation. Correspondingly, literary culture has always been a matter of change: of new practices confronting established traditions; of texts transforming under the pressure of new techniques of reading and new perspectives of understanding; of canons shifting and expanding; of informing traditions getting reviewed and renewed, recast and reformed by emerging cultural interests and concerns; of culture, too, as a variable "text"—a conversation, quarrel and debate of languages available for critical reading. Inspired by the innovative *Longman Anthology of British Literature*, Longman Cultural Editions respond creatively to the changes, past and recent, by presenting key texts in contexts that illuminate the lively intersections of literature, tradition, and culture. A principal work is made more interesting by materials that place it in relation to its past, present, and future, enabling us to see how it may be reworking traditional debates and practices, how it appears amid the conversations and controversies of its own historical moment, how it gains new significances in subsequent eras of reading and reaction. Readers new to the work will discover attractive paths for exploration, while those more experienced will encounter fresh perspectives and provocative juxtapositions.

The Longman Cultural Editions serve not only several kinds of readers but also (appropriately) their several contexts, from various courses of study to independent adventure. Handsomely produced and affordably priced, our volumes offer appealing companions to the *Longman Anthology of British Literature*, in some cases enriching and expanding units originally developed for the *Anthology*, and in other cases presenting this wealth for the first time. The logic and composition of the contexts vary across the series: the constants are the complete text of an important literary work, reliably edited, headed by an inviting introduction, and supplemented by helpful annotation: a table of dates to track its composition, publication, and public reception in relation to biographical, cultural, and historical events: and a guide for further inquiry and study. With these common measures and uncommon assets, the Longman Cultural Editions encourage your literary pleasures with resources for lively reflection and adventurous inquiry.

Susan J. Wolfson
General Editor
Professor of English
Princeton University

About This Edition

The text of *Othello* printed here is based on David Bevington's edition of *Othello* in *The Complete Works of Shakespeare* (Longman, 1992). Bevington, like most editors, bases his text on the 1623 Folio (F), which he deems to be the fuller and more authoritative text. He makes substitutions from the First Quarto (Q1) when he decides these produce a better reading. Some of these readings from the Quarto are mentioned in the footnotes to the text. An appendix at the end of the text lists the variants.

The first printed Quarto of the play did not appear until 1622. There are many controversies among editors about how to solve the difficulties posed by the texts of the Quarto and the Folio. Many of these problems are still unsolved. Was the Quarto based on the "foul papers" of Shakespeare, which the compositor in the print shop could not clearly make out, and chose to alter not only in changing numerous details of punctuation but also in cutting some 160 lines? Or was the Quarto based on a performance from which the actors had cut the additional lines that appear in the Folio text?

It is impossible to reconstruct the texts of Shakespeare's plays exactly as he wrote them, given the absence of his manuscripts and, as is the case with *Othello* and many other plays, the conflicting readings of the different printed versions of the text. For further reading on the textual problem of *Othello*, see E. A. J. Honigmann, *The Texts of Othello and Shakespearean Revision* (1996) and Scott McMillin (ed.), *The First Quarto of Othello* (2001).

The text of *The Tragedy of Mariam* is based on the 1914 Malone Society Facsimile of the 1613 edition printed by Thomas Creede for Richard Hawkins. This facsimile is based on the copies of the 1613 edition in the British Museum and the Bodleian Library.

The text of Third Decade. Story 7. from Giraldi Cinthio's *Hecatommithi* (1565) is based on the translation by Geoffrey Bullough, printed in his *Narrative and Dramatic Sources of Shakespeare Volume VII: Major Tragedies* (London: Routledge and Kegan Paul. 1973). pp. 241–51.

The excerpts from Josephus's *The Antiquities of the Jews* are based on the University of Michigan Microfilm of *The Famous and Memorable Workes of Josephus . . . Faithfully translated out of the Latine. and French. by Tho. Lodge* (1620).

The excerpts from translator Richard Eden's *Decades of the New World . . . Written in Latin by Peter Martyr* (1555) is based on Edward Arber. ed.. *The First Three English Books on America* (1885: repr. 1971).

The excerpt from Pliny's *Historia Naturalis* is based on *The History of the World. Commonly Called the Naturall Historie of C. Plinius Secundus.* Translated into English by Philemon Holland (1601).

The excerpt from Leo Africanus' *A Geographical History of Africa* (1601) is based on Robert Brown. ed. *The History and Description of Africa . . . Written by Al-Hassan Ibn-Mohammed Al Wezaz Al-Fasi. . . . Done into English in the Year 1600 by John Pory.* 3 vols. (1896).

The excerpts from Edmund Spenser's *A View of the Present State of Ireland* is based on that in Henry Morley. ed.. *Ireland Under Elizabeth and James the First. Described by Edmund Spenser. Sir John Davies and Fynes Moryson* (1890).

The excerpt from Sir John Smith's *The General History of Virginia. New England. and the Summer Isles* (1614) is based on Philip L. Barbour. ed.. *The Complete Works of Sir John Smith* (1886).

The excerpt from *The Second Tome of Homilies* (1563) is based on the University of Michigan Microfilm series Early English Books 1475–1640. *STC (Short Title Catalogue) 13651.* Included here are: signatures Ttttv-Tttt2r: Tttt3r-Tttt4r: Tttt4v-Uuuuv.

The excerpt from Edmund Tilney's *The Flower of Friendship* is based on Valerie Wayne. ed.. *The Flower of Friendship: A*

Renaissance Dialogue Contesting Marriage (Ithaca and London: Cornell University Press, 1992).

The excerpt from Robert Cleaver's *A Godly Form of Household Government: for the ordering of private families, according to the direction of God's word* (1598) is based on the University of Michigan Microfilm series *Early English Books 1475–1640,* STC 5387. Included here are: 1: 189–92; 220–22.

The excerpt from William Perkins's *Christian Economy, translated by Thomas Pickering* (London, 1609) is based on the text in Joan Larsen Klein, ed., *Daughters, Wives, and Widows: Writings by Men about Women and Marriage in England, 1500–1640* (Urbana and Chicago: University of Illinois Press, 1992).

The excerpt from William Whatley's *A Bride-Bush* (1617) is based on the University of Michigan Microfilm series *Early English Books 1475–1640,* STC 25296, 42–43.

Spellings are modernized throughout.

Clare Carroll
Queens College,
City University of New York

Introduction

William Shakespeare's *The Tragedy of Othello, the Moor of Venice* and Elizabeth Cary's *The Tragedy of Mariam, The Fair Queen of Jewry* pose perplexing questions. Why is Desdemona's choice of Othello as husband viewed as a betrayal of her father and evidence of her capacity for deceit? How is it that the villain Iago can so successfully manipulate Othello to believe his wife Desdemona is unfaithful? Why does Othello view himself as wanting in his wife's eyes? Why does the hero liken himself to the Turkish enemy he has fought against at the moment he kills himself in grief over his murder of his innocent wife? Why is it that Desdemona does not defy her husband in his rage or choose to speak out against him even at the moment of her death? Why does Mariam's mother Alexandra view Herod as beneath her daughter? How can Mariam's husband, Herod, construe his wife's anger at his tyrannical actions and her refusal to feign love for him as evidence of her infidelity? How is it that Salome can convince Herod that Mariam is deceitful? Why are these chaste women, Mariam and Desdemona, murdered for adultery? This edition invites the reader to compare *Othello* and *Mariam* to one another and to set them in relation to contextual materials that reconstruct the cultural assumptions impinging on all of these questions. The narrative sources and a variety of early modern texts on race and marriage help develop a historical understanding of how each tragedy not only reflects but may also question these cultural assumptions.

The date of composition for both texts is uncertain. *Othello*, its first recorded performance in 1604, was not published until 1622 in Quarto, and then in the First Folio of 1623. *Mariam* may have circulated in manuscript earlier than its publication in 1613, which has led some critics to hypothesize that Shakespeare may have read Cary's work. Alternatively, she may have read or heard his,

Shakespeare's play was performed both at court and on the popular stage. Cary's play, so far as we know, was written for reading or recitation, in the genre of "closet drama," composed in imitation of the rhetorically set speeches of Senecan tragedy. Despite these differences, the two dramas resonate with one another in verbal echoes (as the footnotes show), as well as in plot and theme. The collateral texts assembled here deepen our understanding of what is at stake in these tragedies.

Both plays are about tragically mistaken jealousy that leads a husband to murder his wife. Both husbands are from backgrounds marked by cultural—even racial—difference. Othello is "the Moor," a North African, described repeatedly as "black"; Mariam's husband, Herod, is an "Edomite," a descendant of Esau, who had sold his birthright to Jacob; and he is deemed "base" for not being of the royal Jewish blood. Both women are in conflict with their parents over their marriages: Desdemona with her father, Mariam with her mother. Both women are subject to false accusation, and both husbands to manipulation by malignant enemies, Iago and Salome. Both women also suffer from the intense passion and rage that they arouse in their husbands. If Herod's ruthless ambition makes him far less sympathetic than Othello (when the play opens he has already killed Mariam's grandfather and brother in his rise to power), Mariam's outspokenness makes her in some respects more understandable than Desdemona.

Elements of Comparison to the Narrative Sources

Comparison of each tragedy to its narrative source reveals how the playwright has transformed the material to create drama and pathos and, in so doing, has also at times challenged inherited cultural assumptions. Both authors contract the timeframe of their sources. Shakespeare's compression of Giraldi Cinthio's more protracted tale of the Moorish captain from his *Hecatommithi* yields an emotionally overpowering sense of the sudden change from Othello's passionate love to rageful mistrust and hatred. Cary's conflation of different historical periods and locations from Josephus's *Antiquities of the Jews* and *History of the Jewish War* brings a cast of female characters together in one place and on one day. On the day they learn of Herod's death, a rumor soon proved false, their

conflicting views of how his power, patriarchal and tyrannical, affects their lives, set the stage for the tragedy. Salome defiantly de-
fends divorce for women. Doris laments how she has been wronged
as a divorced wife and mother. Mariam, caught between her re-
membered love for and current anger at her husband, struggles to
defend her own integrity.

To create a more intensely dramatic sense of the conflict between good and evil, Shakespeare and Cary also reshape the characters from their sources. Whereas the thuggish and unrepentant
Moorish captain of Cinthio's tale becomes the ennobled and an-
guished hero Othello, the manipulative Mariam of ancient history
becomes more thoroughly virtuous. Shakespeare suggests a new
motive for Iago: his resentment at having been passed over for a position Othello gives to Cassio. Iago's far subtler powers of manipulation and ability to insinuate himself into intimacy with everyone
make him a much more psychologically threatening villain than his
counterpart in the source. Similarly, in her early modern English in-
carnation, Salome acquires the character of a virago, killing off
husbands for new lovers. If Cinthio's Desdemona voices conventional upper class Venetian prejudice in blaming her troubles on
marrying a Moor, Shakespeare's Desdemona never regrets her love
for Othello. It is rather Iago who fixates on Othello's race, circulat-
ing slurs against Othello as "a lascivious Moor," and it is Iago who
makes Othello suspicious of the sexual mores of Venetian women.
Shakespeare's addition of Iago's sexually demonized portrayal of
Othello, and his bestially obscene representation of the union of
Desdemona and Othello present a palpable sense of the evil racism
that Othello, in his tortured insecurity, later turns in upon himself
when led by Iago to doubt Desdemona's faithfulness.

Cultural and Racial Difference in Context

Since both plays are concerned in varying degrees with the cultural
otherness of Othello and Herod, and describe cultural and racial
difference in their allusions and imagery, a variety of texts in the
genre of ethnography, that is, writing about a nation or cultural
group, has been included in this volume. With the new and increasing exploration and colonization of the globe in the early modern

period. accounts of cultural difference are motivated by an increased concern to justify European domination. Some early modern texts, although they are staged as eyewitness accounts, contain a residue of the fantastical mythology of monstrous otherness descending from such ancient texts as Pliny's *Historia Naturalis*, translated by Philemon Holland in 1601. *Historia Naturalis*, for instance, was Shakespeare's source for the description of freakish creatures in Othello's account of his travels.

Other texts excerpted in this volume concern the figure of African and Moor. *Decades of the New World* (Richard Eden's 1555 translation of Peter Martyr) and Sir John Smith's 1624 account of his visit to Barbary show the instability of the term "Moor" as a racial and cultural category. John Pory's translation of *A Geographical History of Africa* (1600) is by a North African Moor, Leo Africanus, whose life history bears comparison to that of Othello. Leo gives a much more detailed sense of African cultures than do Eden and Smith. True to the genre of early modern ethnography, however, Leo's depictions of peoples contain stereotypes, including the depiction of Numidians who "by reason of jealousy" are "the death and destruction of one another" and "will by no means match themselves unto a harlot." This is just one example, among many, of how the discourse on race and marriage interact. At times gendered and racial difference become metaphorically allied with one another; at other times they come into conflict.

Marriage in Context

The cultural importance of a wife's chastity, as it is portrayed in both *Othello* and *Mariam*, can be pieced together from sermons and tracts on marriage from Elizabethan and Jacobean England. Early modern texts on marriage express the notion that women were expected not just to be sexually faithful to their husbands, but also not even to converse with other men. As Robert Cleaver writes in *A Godly Form of Household Government* (1598): "this modesty and government ought to be in a wife; namely, that she should not speak but to her husband or by her husband." The conservative Chorus castigates Mariam for not living up to this ideal of chastity: "Her mind if not peculiar is not chaste / For in a wife it is no worse to find / A common body than a common mind." In contrast, Othello at first refuses to allow that Desdemona's friendly sociability and charm could be taken as signs of the dishonesty of which Iago accuses her.

In addition to being chaste and silent, a woman was counseled to be obedient to her husband's will, even when it contradicted her own, because the husband was the head of his wife as Christ was of the Church, and as the king was of his subjects. A woman was thus held to the conflicting standard of being completely true to her husband, and yet out of necessity, dissembling her emotions in order to maintain harmony in the household. Desdemona conceals the full extent of her fear and distress at Othello's rage, which she reveals to Emilia. Mariam, however, cannot dissemble. Knowing of Herod's order that she must be killed should he die first, she refuses to acquiesce to her husband's desire for her, even when that could have saved her from his wrath. Emilia questions the misogynist double sexual standard, which, as both plays show, has destructive consequences for men as well as women. In different ways, Iago and Salome deploy the misogynistic view of women as deceitful and uncontrollable to slander the wife and to manipulate the husband's obsessive fears of being cuckolded—not only betrayed but subjected to public shame and ridicule.

If early modern texts on marriage demand the wife's "shamefastness," they do not condone a husband's jealousy, but often caution against it. As Edmund Tilney's *Flower of Friendship* puts it: "There is no greater torment than the vexation of a jealous mind, which, even as the moth fretteth the cloth, doth consume the heart that is vexed therewith." While clearly more restrictive for women than for men, marriage was a matter of mutual responsibilities. The tracts on marriage also speak to the duties of husbands in marriage, among which were forbearance with the wife. Both Herod and Othello would fall short of the gentleness recommended of the husband toward his wife in the "Sermon of the State of Matrimony" in the *Second Tome of Homilies*, which was a standard reading in early modern English wedding ceremonies. Here we read that the husband should be "the leader and author of love, in cherishing and increasing concord, which then shall take place if he will use measurableness and not tyranny." Herod, with his power as patriarch and king controlling the lives of all his subjects, is clearly cast in the role of a tyrant. But all husbands in this period could be thought of as potential benevolent kings or cruel tyrants. English law presented the relationship between monarch and subjects on the analogy of husband and wife, so that a wife who killed her husband was implicitly guilty of petit treason. Similarly, members of the community, if not the law, would deem a violently abusive husband to be a petit tyrant. Relationships between husbands and wives thus formed part of the legal, political, and theological hierarchical order of early modern society.

The emphasis in this Longman Cultural Edition upon the cultural contexts of racial difference and the relations between the sexes in marriage is meant to provoke reflection on what these contexts may illuminate, without implying the full explanatory capacities and limits of such an approach. Such questions as, "Why is Desdemona so submissive?" and "Why is Othello so self-hating?" can in part be more fully, if never entirely, explained by reference to these discourses in early modern English culture. The roles that these contextual discourses play in shaping the meaning of each tragedy need to be read against the language and the action of the plays themselves, which in turn may modify our interpretation of what we read in the collateral texts. In the end, this process of contextual interpretation should produce more historically informed and more textually sensitive questions about both the primary and collateral texts, which exist in a lively literary dialogue and ideological tension with one another. At the same time, this reading of early modern texts and culture should produce questions about our own cultural assumptions as they impinge upon our inquiry into the past and our relation to it in the present.

Table of Dates

1554   First black men brought to England as a result of an English trade expedition to Africa.

1555   Richard Eden's *Decades of the New World* (a translation of Peter Martyr's *De Orbe Novo Decades*) published.

1558   Elizabeth I becomes Queen of England.

1563   *Second Tome of Homilies* is printed.

1564   William Shakespeare is born in Stratford-on-Avon, England.

1565   Publication of Giraldi Cinthio's *Hecatommithi*.

1568   First edition of Edmund Tilney's *The Flower of Friendship* is published.

1571   Turkish forces take over Famagusta in Cyprus, August 2. European Holy League defeats the Turks at the Battle of Lepanto, October 2.

1582   William Shakespeare marries Anne Hathaway.

1583   Susanna Shakespeare is born to William and Anne.

1585   Elizabeth Tanfield is born at Burford Priory, Oxfordshire.
        Shakespeare's children Hamnet and Judith are born.

1588   The Spanish Armada is launched and routed.

1589   George Peele writes *The Battle of Alcazar*, which features a black villain.

1592   Shakespeare is mentioned for the first time in print as an actor and playwright in London in a pamphlet by Robert Greene.

1594   Shakespeare becomes a Charter Member of the Chamberlain's Men, a theatrical company that, in 1603, became the King's Men.
Shakespeare's *Titus Andronicus*, which features the black villain Aaron, is performed.

1596   Publication of Edmund Spenser's *The Faerie Queene*.

1597   Michael Drayton publishes England's *Heroical Epistles*, dedicated to Elizabeth Tanfield.

1598   Edmund Spenser's *A View of the Present State of Ireland* is entered in the Stationer's Register.
Robert Cleaver's *A Godly Form of Household Government* is printed.

1600   *The History and Description of Africa* (John Pory's translation of Leo Africanus) is published.

1600–01   The Moorish ambassador of the King of Barbary visits London.

1601   Elizabeth issues a royal proclamation for the transportation of Negroes out of England.
Publication of Holland's translation of Pliny's *History of the World*.

1602   Marriage of Elizabeth Tanfield to Sir Henry Cary.
Publication of Thomas Lodge's *The Famous and Most Memorable Works of Josephus*.

1603   Death of Elizabeth I and accession of James VI of Scotland, son of Mary, Queen of Scots, as James I of England.
Hamlet is printed in Quarto, and again in 1604.

1604   First recorded performance of Shakespeare's *Othello*.

1604–09   Possible dates of composition for Elizabeth Cary's *The Tragedy of Mariam*.

1605   The Gunpowder Plot to blow up the Parliament is discovered. The apprehension of Catholic conspirators.

motivated by religious persecution, had disastrous consequences for English and Irish Catholics for the next 200 years.

Introduction to
William Shakespeare and
The Tragedy of Othello, the Moor of Venice

William Shakespeare (1564–1616)

Ben Jonson's praise of Shakespeare as a writer "not of an age, but for all time!" expresses the enormous popularity of his works during his life and beyond. From Francis Mere's *Palladis Tamia* (1598), in which, of all playwrights of the age, only Shakespeare merits the mention of his works by title, to any current video catalogue that lists the many recent film adaptations, we have proof that Shakespeare was—and is—box office. Our appreciation of the lasting power of Shakespeare, however, need not be divorced from an appreciation of him as a man of his age. We can get a better sense of what contributed to his becoming such a complex and popular playwright by taking into account what we know of his life and times. In the case of his great tragedy *Othello*, we can better understand what made and continues to make it so arresting by setting it in the context of a whole network of cultural beliefs and practices in early modern England.

Shakespeare was the oldest son of John Shakespeare, glove manufacturer and seller, as well as alderman and bailiff, and Mary Arden, daughter of a Catholic farm owner who left property to her. As a member of one of the leading families of the market town of Stratford-on-Avon, Shakespeare most likely attended the local grammar school. The classical allusions and mastery of rhetoric in his plays show that he read the Latin poets Ovid and Virgil, and the playwrights Plautus and Seneca, all part of the standard humanist curriculum. He left school around the age of fifteen, at which point he may have had to help his father, who was having

1

financial difficulties. (There are records of his continuing to suffer from debt in later years.)

A few years after leaving school. Shakespeare wed Anne Hathaway. whose family his parents had known for a long time. While Shakespeare and his wife grew up in what biographer Park Honan calls "the shadow of the old faith" (Roman Catholicism). he and his wife conformed to the Church of England. His marriage at age eighteen was early for a man of his time: Hathaway's age. twenty-six. was the average for a woman to be married. If they had promised marriage to one another at any point in their courtship. the Church of England would have viewed the promise as binding. Like many women of her time. Hathway was pregnant when the marriage license was issued in November 1582: their first child Susanna was christened on May 26. 1583. Their twins. Judith and Hamnet. were born in 1585: the boy lived only to eleven. Shakespeare was to spend much of his married life away from home. in London and working in the theater. and retired to Stratford in 1610.

Shakespeare's Career

There is a tradition that after leaving school. Shakespeare. under the name "Shakeshafte." served as a schoolmaster and acted in plays for the Hoghtons. a Catholic family in Lancashire. It may have been through the Hoghtons that Shakespeare encountered their friend Ferdinando Stanley. Lord Strange. who denounced his own father's papistry. The Hoghtons sponsored an acting troupe that performed at least two of Shakespeare's plays. Members of this troupe. under the patronage of Lord Strange. would become the Chamberlain's Men. one of the most successful London theatrical companies. Shakespeare became a shareholder in 1594. jointly owning and managing the company.

At this same time. through his connection with Richard Field. a Stratford man who had set up as a printer in London. Shakespeare published his first serious poetical works. *Venus and Adonis* (1593) and *The Rape of Lucrece* (1594). both dedicated to the Earl of Southampton. Shakespeare most likely wrote these works during 1592–93. when the plague compelled city authorities to close the London theaters. in an attempt to prohibit contagion in such crowded public gathering spots.

That Shakespeare did not go on to university, which at the time prepared young men for service in the government or church, may have been a blessing in disguise. He had to work to survive, and during the 1590s, he was quite busy in the London theater world writing plays and acting in them. He soon attracted the scorn of playwright Robert Greene, who referred to Shakespeare in 1592 as "an upstart crow, beautified with our feathers, that with his tiger's heart wrapped in a player's hide . . . is in his own conceit the only Shake-scene in a country."

Although we don't know for certain which roles Shakespeare played, legend has it that these included the ghost of Hamlet's father and a part in Ben Jonson's *Every Man in His Humor*. Already the object of envy and derision by Greene's account, Shakespeare became so popular that after 1598, even plays that were not written by him were printed with his name on them. The first complete edition of Shakespeare's *Comedies, Histories and Tragedies* did not appear until seven years after his death in the Folio of 1623. (See page 4.)

Scholars have constructed a chronology of Shakespeare's plays based on recorded performances, the printing of individual Quarto editions, and the internal evidence of the plays themselves. By this reckoning, his output in the 1590s was staggering. Using Holinshed's *Chronicles* as his chief source, Shakespeare wrote his first four history plays, culminating in one of his most often-performed works, *The Tragedy of Richard III*, celebrating the defeat of Richard's tyranny by Elizabeth I's grandfather Henry VII, who began the reign of the Tudors. These history plays would be followed by four more, including one meditating on the dangers of absolute monarchy, *Richard II*, performed at the Globe at the prompting of Essex's faction to incite a revolt on the eve of their failed rebellion. Shakespeare also wrote two Roman plays, *The Tragedy of Julius Caesar*, which again concerns tyranny, this time in relation to the responsibilities of freedom demanded in the Roman republic; and *Titus Andronicus*, which portrays a world of horrendous violence—mutilation, murder, and cannibalism.

In the genre of comedy, his staggering output in the 1590s includes: *The Comedy of Errors, The Taming of the Shrew, Two Gentlemen of Verona, Love's Labor's Lost, A Midsummer Night's Dream, The Merchant of Venice, The Merry Wives of Windsor, Much Ado About Nothing, As You Like It* and *Twelfth Night*. These

Portrait of Shakespeare. title page of the Shakespeare First Folio (London. 1623). Courtesy of The Library of Congress.

plays pursue themes that he would later take up in his romantic tragedy *Romeo and Juliet*, the dark comedies (or problem plays) *Measure for Measure* and *Troilus and Cressida*, and his first two great tragedies, *Hamlet* and *Othello*—treating respectively, the disastrous effects of revenge and the self-deceptions of love. By the time *Othello* was performed, he had written twenty-seven of his thirty-eight plays.

Othello

The first recorded performance of *Othello* was on November 1, 1604, before King James I and his guests at Whitehall Palace. The Chamberlain's Men were now the King's Men, and as such, their duties at times even included waiting on the king, as Shakespeare and eleven of his troupe did earlier in August of that year. The play would be performed again at court as part of the marriage celebrations for the king's daughter, Princess Elizabeth in 1612–13. A notation on the title page of the Quarto gives evidence of the play's popularity: "As it hath been diverse times acted at the Globe and Black Friers, by his Maiesties Servants." A man from an Oxford college who had seen one of these productions wrote an account of how the boy actor who played Desdemona "acted her part supremely, yet when she was killed was even more moving, for when she fell back upon the bed she implored the pity of the spectators by her very face." Contemporary audiences were clearly moved to pity by Othello as well, as can be seen in an elegy for Richard Burbage, the star of Shakespeare's troupe:

> But let me not forget one chiefest part
> Wherein beyond the rest, he mov'd the heart.
> The grieved Moor, made jealous by a slave,
> Who sent his wife to fill a timeless grave,
> Then slew himself upon the bloody bed.

The Play's Treatment of Race

The above poem sympathetically echoes the play's reversal of the audience's expectations. It is Iago, who speaks of Othello in racist language, who is the "slave" and "villain," not Othello, who had been "sold to slavery." Othello is "The grieved Moor." As the collateral texts in the *Othello in Context* show, the term "Moor" has various

English actress Peggy Ashcroft as Desdemona and American singer and actor Paul Robeson as Othello in a production of the play by Shakespeare at the Savoy Theater in London. 1929. © Hulton-Deutsch Collection/CORBIS.

connotations in the early modern period. It is often synonymous with "black Moor," as in Windham's account of his voyage to Benin in *Decades of the New World*, or it can be identified with the "tawny" inhabitants of Barbary, as in Sir John Smith's account of his visit there. At least one recent editor of *Othello*, E. A. J. Honigmann, has questioned the identification of "the noble Moor" as "black." Honigmann hypothesizes that the play was inspired by the visit to Elizabeth's court by the Moorish ambassador from the King of Barbary (see the illustration on page 12), whom Shakespeare would have witnessed when performing at court with the Chamberlain's Men during Christmastime in 1601. The vast majority of Shakespeare's audience, however, would not have seen this very aristocratic Moorish diplomat. The identification between "Moor" and a specific complexion is perhaps less important than the notion that Moors were seen as culturally alien and could be subject to racist practices. There were blacks in England, a result of the capture of slaves from Spanish and Portuguese vessels by English seamen. These Africans, brought into the country by force, were in turn expelled by force. In 1601, Elizabeth I issued a proclamation for the transportation of all "Negroes and blackamoors" out of England.

Shakespeare's audience would have known at least three black characters on the popular stage, all monstrous villains. Muly Hamet in George Peele's revenge tragedy *The Battle of Alcazar* (1589) seeks to destroy his own family; though given to bombastic rants, he proves cowardly and underhanded. Shakespeare's first black character, Aaron, in *Titus Andronicus* (1594), may have a redeeming concern for his son, but he is possessed by a motiveless and unrepentant drive to commit evil: He boasts of having "done a thousand dreadful things / As willingly as one would kill a fly." Eleazar in *Lust's Dominion* (ca. 1600) embodies the sexual stereotype of the "black devil," manipulating his erotic hold over a white woman of royal blood to gain power.

It is against this network of racial exclusion, in both political practice and dramatic representation, that the play's persistent references to Othello's race need to be read. Othello's bravery and passionate love for Desdemona confound the stereotype of the black villain, and his Italian name and loyal service to the state suggest his assimilation to and identification with Venice. Yet to a certain degree, Othello shares some of his dramatic ancestors' traits—rhetorical bombast. an intense sexuality and uncontrollable violence. Iago voices sexually demonized portrayals of Othello's blackness. calling him "an old black ram." a "Barbary horse." "a lascivious Moor." "an erring Barbarian." However. Othello. too. is haunted by his own "blackness." as when he expresses his fear that Iago's claims of Desdemona's infidelity are true and that she has left him for another man: "Haply for I am black . . . she's gone." Through imagining Othello's internalization of the stereotype of racial inferiority. Shakespeare adds to our understanding of his vulnerability and the fatal consequences of such self-hatred.

The Play's Treatment of Sex and Marriage

Shakespeare's thinking both in his time and ahead of his time emerges in his complex representation of race in relation to marriage. sexuality. and love. From his rather more schematic narrative source. Giraldi Cinthio's *Hecatommithi* (1565). an Italian Renaissance tale of lust. brutality and banal moralization. Shakespeare creates a tragedy. A brief synopsis of the Italian novella will make the point. The Ensign (Iago) to a Moorish Captain (Othello) lusts after his wife Desdemona. and when she will not return his advances. the Ensign decides it is because she is in love with the Corporal (Cassio). Filled with hate and a desire to kill her lest even her husband enjoy her. the Ensign sets about convincing the Captain of his wife's infidelity. When Desdemona is confronted with her husband's jealous suspicions. she concludes that she should never have married a Moor. The Ensign plots with the Moor to kill Desdemona. Bludgeoning her to death with sandbags. they then pull the plaster down from the ceiling to make it look like an accident. Afterwards realizing that his wicked Ensign has cost him the joy of his life. the Captain demotes him: in turn. the Ensign accuses the Captain of murdering his own wife. The Moorish Captain denies everything under torture. but Desdemona's relatives eventually get their revenge upon him.

In the narrative source. the protagonist is merely a cultural marker. "the Moor." whom the heroine can dismiss as an inappropriate choice for marriage—a warning to other young women. Shakespeare transforms the Ensign's frustrated lust for Desdemona into the complex homoeroticism of Iago's sexual jealousy of and manipulative intimacy with both Cassio and Othello. Whereas the tales in Cinthio's *Hecatommithi* as a whole do not deny the validity of Iago's cynical views of sexuality and love. Desdemona's combination of passion and faithful devotion exposes how sickly twisted and hatefully vengeful such a view is. The ruling emotion of Cinthio's Moor. a compound of mere jealousy and unrepentant hatred. becomes. in Shakespeare's conception. the tormented self-hatred that leads the tragic hero to doubt his worthiness to be loved and to shoulder the unbearable responsibility that leads him to take his life. The Moor's uncontrollable desire to punish his wife for her supposed sexual transgression in the tale is allied in the tragedy with Othello's obsession with punishing himself for his racial difference: "My name that was as fresh / As Dian's visage is now begrimed and black / As my own face."

At the same time. Othello's identification of his public honor with his wife's chastity demonstrates Shakespeare's understanding of how the need to control women's sexuality in early modern conceptions of marriage functions as a microcosm of the larger theological and political order. Iago's accusations of Desdemona's infidelity stir up the male fear of uncontrollable female sexuality. causing Othello to lament: "O curse of marriage / That we can call these delicate creatures ours / And not their appetites." Renaissance tracts on marriage present women as "the weaker vessel." requiring control by fathers and husbands. The sermons on marriage echoed St. Paul in stating that men should be "the head of the woman. as Christ is the head of the Church." This male authority demanded the woman's obedience to her husband. just as subjects owed obedience to their sovereign. In eloping with Othello. Desdemona has already transgressed the authority of her father. who taunts Othello with Desdemona's potential for future disobedience: "She has deceived her father and may thee." Although she defies her father in her unswerving loyalty and love for her husband. like that recommended in early modern tracts on marriage. Desdemona is simultaneously compromised as disobedient and furtive. According to William Whatley's sermon. *The Bride-Bush.* women had to submit to their husband's wills especially when they contradicted their own: "this declares conscionable submission. when she chooseth to do what herself would not. because her husband wills it."

While the play celebrates the passionate love of Desdemona for Othello, it also reveals the terrible costs of her submission. Such submission also informs Emilia's desire to please Iago. By obeying Iago's desire that she steal the handkerchief that becomes the circumstantial evidence of Desdemona's betrayal. Emilia becomes an unwitting accomplice in her mistress's murder. In telling the truth at the end of the play. Emilia defies her husband's command that she be silent. acknowledging how shocking such defiance would seem: "Let heaven and men and devils. let them all. / All. all. cry shame against me. yet I'll speak." In giving her this defiant speech. the play speaks volumes about the silent obedience demanded of women. a silence that Elizabeth Cary's Mariam would also defy with tragic consequences.

In multiple and sometimes contradictory ways. Shakespeare's *Othello* reproduces the discourses of racism and sexism in early modern English culture and contests them. defying audience expectations by creating sympathy for a black hero and a disobedient daughter. and placing this sympathy against a hero's sexism and a wife's too willing submission. Iago's manipulation of these discourses in preying upon Othello's self-hatred of his "blackness" and fear of Desdemona's passionate independence lead him to murder her. To protect her husband. even as he kills her. Desdemona persists in her loyalty by claiming responsibility for her own death. But may she also be acknowledging her acquiescence in her murder? At the end of the play. Othello acknowledges how he has allowed himself to be blinded. but maintains that he was "not easily jealous but. being wrought. / Perplexed in the extreme." Witnessing to his wife's faithful love. he describes his crime in racially charged terms: "one whose hand / Like the base Indian. threw a pearl away / Richer than all his tribe." The unbearable guilt he suffers for her death leads him to take his own life. Othello's self-description as "one who loved not wisely. but too well." may more accurately describe Desdemona's self-sacrifice and suffering for love. To what extent either she or Othello achieves self-knowledge are questions the audience must answer in relation to themselves and their own world. as well as the world in which Shakespeare lived and created.

THE TRAGEDY OF OTHELLO,

the Moor of Venice

[by William Shakespeare]

The Moorish Ambassador to Queen Elizabeth. 1600–1. This portrait represents one early seventeenth-century English impression of what a Moor looked like—one which some critics claim Shakespeare would have seen in person at court. Although the term "Moor" was racially unstable, allowing the possibility of white or black skin color, Shakespeare clearly depicts his hero as black. (Original portrait owned by The Shakespeare Institute, The University of Birmingham. Image © The Shakespeare Institute.)

The Tragedy of Othello, the Moor of Venice

The Names of the Actors

OTHELLO, *the Moor*
BRABANTIO, *a senator,*
  father to Desdemona
CASSIO, *an honorable lieutenant*
  to Othello
IAGO, *Othello's ancient, a villain*
RODERIGO, *a gulled gentleman*
DUKE OF VENICE
SENATORS *of Venice*
MONTANO, *Governor of Cyprus*
GENTLEMEN *of Cyprus*
LODOVICO AND GRATIANO,
  kinsmen to Brabantio, two
  noble Venetians

SAILORS
CLOWN
DESDEMONA, *daughter to*
  Brabantio and wife to Othello
EMILIA, *wife to Iago*
BIANCA, *a courtesan and mistress*
  to Cassio
A MESSENGER
A HERALD
A MUSICIAN
SERVANTS, ATTENDANTS,
  OFFICERS, SENATORS,
  MUSICIANS, GENTLEMEN

[*Scene: Venice: a seaport in Cyprus*]

ACT 1
SCENE 1

[*Location: Venice. A street. Enter* RODERIGO *and* IAGO.]

RODERIGO. Tush, never tell me! I take it much unkindly
  That thou, Iago, who hast had my purse
  As if the strings were thine, shouldst know of this.[1]
IAGO. 'Sblood,[2] but you'll not hear me.
  If ever I did dream of such a matter,   5
  Abhor me.

---

1. this Desdemona's elopement.   **2. 'Sblood** by His (Christ's) blood.

From *The Complete Works of Shakespeare* 4th ed. by David Bevington. Copyright ©
1992 by HarperCollins Publishers. Reprinted by permission of Pearson Education, Inc.

RODERIGO. Thou toldst me thou didst hold him in thy hate.
IAGO. Despise me
    If I do not. Three great ones of the city.
    In personal suit to make me his lieutenant.   10
    Off-capped to him:[3] and by the faith of man.
    I know my price. I am worth no worse a place.
    But he. as loving his own pride and purposes.
    Evades them with a bombast circumstance[4]
    Horribly stuffed with epithets of war.   15
    And. in conclusion.
    Nonsuits[5] my mediators. For. "Certes."[6] says he.
    "I have already chose my officer."
    And what was he?
    Forsooth. a great arithmetician.[7]   20
    One Michael Cassio. a Florentine.
    A fellow almost damned in a fair wife.[8]
    That never set a squadron in the field
    Nor the division of a battle knows
    More than a spinster[9]—unless the bookish theoric.[10]   25
    Wherein the togaed consuls[11] can propose[12]
    As masterly as he. Mere prattle without practice
    Is all his soldiership. But he. sir. had th'election:
    And I. of whom his[13] eyes had seen the proof
    At Rhodes. at Cyprus. and on other grounds   30
    Christened[14] and heathen. must be beleed and calmed[15]
    By debitor and creditor.[16] This countercaster.[17]
    He. in good time.[18] must his lieutenant be.
    And I—God bless the mark![19]—his Moorship's ancient.[20]

---

3. him: Othello.   **4. bombast circumstance** wordy evasion. *Bombast* is cotton padding.   **5. Nonsuits** rejects.   **6. "Certes."** certainly.   **7. arithmetician** a man whose military knowledge is merely theoretical. based on books of tactics.   **8. fellow . . . wife** Cassio does not seem to be married. but his counterpart in Shakespeare's source does have a woman in his house.   **9. spinster** a housewife. one whose regular occupation is spinning.   **10. theoric** theory.   **11. consuls** senators.   **12. propose** discuss   **13. his** Othello's.   **14. Christened** Christian.   **15. beleed and calmed** left to leeward without wind. becalmed (a sailing metaphor).   **16. debitor and creditor** a name for a system of bookkeeping. here used as a contemptuous nickname for Cassio.   **17. countercaster** bookkeeper. one who tallies with counters. or "metal disks." Said contemptuously.   **18. in good time** opportunely.   **19. God . . . mark!** Perhaps originally a formula to ward off evil; here an expression of impatience.   **20. ancient** ensign.

RODERIGO. By heaven, I rather would have been his hangman.   35
IAGO. Why, there's no remedy. 'Tis the curse of service:
    Preferment[21] goes by letter and affection.[22]
    And not by old gradation,[23] where each second
    Stood heir to th' first. Now, sir, be judge yourself
    Whether I in any just term[24] am affined[25]   40
    To love the Moor.
RODERIGO.   I would not follow him then.
IAGO. O sir, content you.[26]
    I follow him to serve my turn upon him.
    We cannot all be masters, nor all masters
    Cannot be truly[27] followed. You shall mark   45
    Many a duteous and knee-crooking knave
    That, doting on his own obsequious bondage,
    Wears out his time, much like his master's ass,
    For naught but provender,[28] and when he's old, cashiered.[29]
    Whip me[30] such honest knaves. Others there are   50
    Who, trimmed in forms and visages of duty,[31]
    Keep yet their hearts attending on themselves,
    And, throwing but shows of service on their lords,
    Do well thrive by them, and when they have lined their
        coats,[32]
    Do themselves homage.[33] These fellows have some soul,   55
    And such a one do I profess myself. For, sir,
    It is as sure as you are Roderigo,
    Were I the Moor I would not be Iago.[34]
    In following him, I follow but myself—
    Heaven is my judge, not I for love and duty,   60
    But seeming so for my peculiar[35] end.
    For when my outward action doth demonstrate

21. **preferment** promotion.   22. **letter and affection** personal influence and fa-
voritism.   23. **old gradation** step-by-step seniority, the traditional way.   24. **just
term** respect.   25. **affined** bound.   26. **content you** don't you worry about that.
27. **truly** faithfully.   28. **provender** food.   29. **cashiered** dismissed.   30. **whip
me** whip, as far as I'm concerned.   31. **forms and visages of duty** dressed up in the
mere form and show of dutifulness.   32. **lined their coats** stuffed their purses.
33. **do themselves homage** attend to self-interest solely.   34. **Were . . . Iago** if I
were able to assume command, I certainly would not choose to remain a subordinate,
or I would keep a suspicious eye on a flattering subordinate.   35. **peculiar** particular.

The native[36] act and figure[37] of my heart
In compliment extern.[38] 'tis not long after
But I will wear my heart upon my sleeve   65
For daws[39] to peck at. I am not what I am.[40]
RODERIGO. What a full[41] fortune does the thick-lips[42] owe[43]
If he can carry 't thus![44]
IAGO.   Call up her father.
Rouse him. make after him. poison his delight.
Proclaim him in the streets: incense her kinsmen.   70
And. though he in a fertile climate dwell.
Plague him with flies.[45] Though that his joy be joy.[46]
Yet throw such changes of vexation[47] on 't
As it may lose some color.[48]
RODERIGO. Here is her father's house. I'll call aloud.   75
IAGO. Do. with like timorous[49] accent and dire yell
As when. by night and negligence. the fire
Is spied in populous cities.
RODERIGO. What ho. Brabantio! Signor Brabantio. ho!
IAGO. Awake! What ho. Brabantio! Thieves. thieves. thieves!   80
Look to your house. your daughter. and your bags!
Thieves. thieves!

[BRABANTIO *enters above at a window.*][50]

BRABANTIO. What is the reason of this terrible summons?
    What is the matter[51] there?
RODERIGO. Signor. is all your family within?   85
IAGO. Are your doors locked?
BRABANTIO.   Why. wherefore ask you this?
IAGO. Zounds.[52] sir. you're robbed. For shame. put on your
    gown!

---

36. native innate.   **37. figure** intent.   **38. extern** outward show (conforming in this case to the inner workings and intention of the heart).   **39. daws** small crowlike birds. proverbially stupid and avaricious.   **40. I . . . am** I am not one who wears his heart on his sleeve.   **41. full** swelling.   **42. thick-lips** Elizabethans often applied the term "Moor" to men of African descent.   **43. owe** own.   **44. carry't thus!** carry this off.   **45. though . . . flies** though he seems prosperous and happy now. vex him with misery.   **46. Though . . . joy** although he seems fortunate and happy.   **47. changes of vexation** vexing changes.   **48. As . . . color** that may cause it to lose some of its fresh gloss.   **49. timorous** frightening.   **50. [Brabantio . . . window]** this stage direction. from the Quarto. probably calls for an appearance on the gallery above and rearstage.   **51. matter** your business.   **52. Zounds** by His (Christ's) wounds.

Your heart is burst: you have lost half your soul.
Even now, now, very now, an old black ram
Is tupping your white ewe.[53] Arise, arise!   90
Awake the snorting[54] citizens with the bell,
Or else the devil[55] will make a grandsire of you.
Arise, I say!
BRABANTIO.   What, have you lost your wits?
RODERIGO. Most reverend signor, do you know my voice?
BRABANTIO. Not I. What are you?   95
RODERIGO. My name is Roderigo.
BRABANTIO.   The worser welcome.
    I have charged thee not to haunt about my doors.
    In honest plainness thou hast heard me say
    My daughter is not for thee: and now, in madness,
    Being full of supper and distempering[56] drafts,   100
    Upon malicious bravery[57] dost thou come
    To start[58] my quiet.
RODERIGO. Sir, sir, sir—
BRABANTIO.   But thou must needs be sure
    My spirits and my place[59] have in[60] their power
    To make this bitter to thee.   105
RODERIGO.   Patience, good sir.
BRABANTIO. What tell'st thou me of robbing? This is Venice:
    My house is not a grange.[61]
RODERIGO.   Most grave Brabantio,
    In simple[62] and pure soul I come to you.
IAGO. Zounds, sir, you are one of those that will not serve God
    if the devil bid you. Because we come to do you service and 110
    you think we are ruffians, you'll have your daughter cov-
    ered with a Barbary[63] horse; you'll have your nephews[64]
    neigh to you; you'll have coursers for cousins and jennets
    for germans.[65]
BRABANTIO. What profane wretch art thou?   115

53. **tupping . . . ewe** covering, copulating with (said of sheep).   54. **snorting** snor-
ing.   55. **devil** the devil was conventionally pictured as black.   56. **distempering**
intoxicating.   57. **malicious bravery** with hostile intent to defy me.   58. **start** dis-
rupt.   59. **My . . . place** my temperament and my authority of office.   60. **have in**
have it in.   61. **grange** country house.   62. **simple** sincere.   63. **Barbary** from
northern Africa (and hence associated with Othello).   64. **nephews** i.e., grandsons.
65. **coursers . . . germans** you'll have stallions for kinsmen and ponies for relatives.

IAGO. I am one, sir, that comes to tell you your daughter and
    the Moor are now making the beast with two backs.
BRABANTIO. Thou art a villain.
IAGO.   You are—a senator.[66]
BRABANTIO. This thou shalt answer.[67] I know thee. Roderigo.
RODERIGO. Sir, I will answer anything. But I beseech you.   120
    If't be your pleasure and most wise[68] consent—
    As partly I find it is—that your fair daughter,
    At this odd-even[69] and dull watch o' the night,
    Transported with[70] no worse nor better guard
    But with a knave of common hire,[71] a gondolier,   125
    To the gross clasps of a lascivious Moor—
    If this be known to you and your allowance[72]
    We then have done you bold and saucy[73] wrongs.
    But if you know not this, my manners tell me
    We have your wrong rebuke. Do not believe   130
    That, from[74] the sense of all civility,[75]
    I thus would play and trifle with your reverence.[76]
    Your daughter, if you have not given her leave,
    I say again, hath made a gross revolt,
    Tying her duty, beauty, wit,[77] and fortunes   135
    In an extravagant[78] and wheeling[79] stranger[80]
    Of here and everywhere. Straight[81] satisfy yourself.
    If she be in her chamber or your house,
    Let loose on me the justice of the state
    For thus deluding you.   140
BRABANTIO. Strike on the tinder,[82] ho!
    Give me a taper! Call up all my people!
    This accident[83] is not unlike my dream.
    Belief of it oppresses me already.
    Light, I say, light!   *[Exit above.]*

---

66. You . . . senator said with mock politeness, as though the word itself were an insult. **67. answer** be held accountable. **68. wise** well-informed. **69. odd-even** between one day and the next, i.e., about midnight. **70. with** by. **71. But with a knave of common hire** than by a low fellow, a servant. **72. allowance** permission. **73. saucy** insolent. **74. from** contrary to. **75. civility** decency. **76. reverence** the respect due to you. **77. wit** intelligence. **78. extravagant** expatriate. **79. wheeling** vagabond. **80. stranger** foreigner. **81. straight** straightway. **82. tinder** charred linen ignited by a spark from flint and steel, used to light torches or *tapers*. **83. accident** event.

IAGO.   Farewell, for I must leave you.
    It seems not meet[84] nor wholesome to my place[85]
    To be producted[86]—as, if I stay, I shall—
    Against the Moor. For I do know the state,
    However this may gall[87] him with some check.[88]
    Cannot with safety cast[89] him, for he's embarked[90]   150
    With such loud reason[91] to the Cyprus wars,
    Which even now stands in act,[92] that, for their souls,[93]
    Another of his fathom[94] they have none
    To lead their business; in which regard,[95]
    Though I do hate him as I do hell pains,   155
    Yet for necessity of present life[96]
    I must show out a flag and sign of love,
    Which is indeed but sign. That you shall surely find him,
    Lead to the Sagittary[97] the raisèd search.[98]
    And there will I be with him. So farewell.   160

                                                              [*Exit*]

[*Enter below,* BRABANTIO *in his nightgown*[99] *with servants and
torches.*]

BRABANTIO. It is too true an evil. Gone she is;
    And what's to come of my despisèd time[100]
    Is naught but bitterness. Now, Roderigo,
    Where didst thou see her?—O unhappy girl!—
    With the Moor, sayst thou?—Who would be a father!—   165
    How didst thou know 'twas she?—O, she deceives me
    Past thought!—What said she to you?—Get more tapers.
    Raise all my kindred.—Are they married, think you?
RODERIGO. Truly, I think they are.

84. **meet** fitting.   85. **place** position.   86. **producted** produced (as a witness).
87. **gall** oppress.   88. **check** rebuke.   89. **cast** dismiss.   90. **embarked** engaged.
91. **loud reason** unanimous shout of confirmation (in the Senate).   92. **stands in
act** are going on.   93. **for their souls** to save themselves.   94. **fathom** i.e., ability,
depth of experience.   95. **in which regard** out of regard for which.   96. **life** liveli-
hood.   97. **Sagittary** an inn or house where Othello and Desdemona are staying,
named for its sign of Sagittarius, or Centaur.   98. **raised search** search party
roused out of sleep.   99. **nightgown** dressing gown. (This costuming is specified in
the Quarto text.).   100. **time** i.e., remainder of life.

BRABANTIO. O heaven! How got she out? O treason of the   170
    blood!
    Fathers. from hence trust not your daughters' minds
    By what you see them act. Is there not charms[101]
    By which the property[102] of youth and maidhood
    May be abused?[103] Have you not read. Roderigo.
    Of some such thing?   175
RODERIGO.   Yes. sir. I have indeed.
BRABANTIO. Call up my brother.—O. would you had had her!—
    Some one way. some another.—Do you know
    Where we may apprehend her and the Moor?
RODERIGO. I think I can discover[104] him. if you please
    To get good guard and go along with me.   180
BRABANTIO. Pray you. lead on. At every house I'll call:
    I may command[105] at most.—Get weapons. ho!
    And raise some special officers of night.—
    On. good Roderigo. I will deserve[106] your pains.

                                          [*Exeunt.*]

                          SCENE 2

[*Location: Venice. Another street. Before Othello's lodgings.
Enter* OTHELLO. IAGO. *attendants with torches.*]

IAGO. Though in the trade of war I have slain men.
    Yet do I hold it very stuff[1] o' the conscience
    To do no contrived[2] murder. I lack iniquity
    Sometimes to do me service. Nine or ten times
    I had thought t' have yerked[3] him[4] here under the ribs.   5
OTHELLO. 'Tis better as it is.
IAGO.   Nay. but he prated.
    And spoke such scurvy and provoking terms
    Against your honor
    That. with the little godliness I have.
    I did full hard forbear him.[5] But. I pray you. sir.   10

---

101. charms spells. **102. property** nature. **103. abused** deceived.
104. discover reveal. **105. command** demand aid. **106. deserve** reward.
1. stuff essence. basic. material (continuing the metaphor of *trade* from line 1).
2. contrived premeditated. **3. yerked** stabbed. **4. him** Roderigo. **5. forbear
him** I restrained myself with great difficulty from assaulting him.

Are you fast married? Be assured of this,
That the magnifico[6] is much beloved.
And hath in his effect[7] a voice potential[8]
As double as the Duke's. He will divorce you,
Or put upon you what restraint or grievance   15
The law, with all his might to enforce it on,
Will give him cable.[9]
OTHELLO.   Let him do his spite.
My services which I have done the seigniory[10]
Shall out-tongue his complaints. 'Tis yet to know[11]
Which, when I know that boasting is an honor,   20
I shall promulgate—I fetch my life and being
From men of royal siege,[12] and my demerits[13]
May speak unbonneted[14] to as proud a fortune
As this that I have reached. For know, Iago,
But that I love the gentle Desdemona,   25
I would not my unhousèd[15] free condition
Put into circumscription and confine[16]
For the sea's worth.[17] But look, what lights come yond?

[*Enter* CASSIO *and certain officers[18] with torches.*]

IAGO. Those are the raisèd father and his friends.
You were best go in.   30
OTHELLO.   Not I. I must be found.
My parts, my title, and my perfect soul[19]
Shall manifest me rightly. Is it they?
IAGO. By Janus,[20] I think no.
OTHELLO. The servants of the Duke? And my lieutenant?
The goodness of the night upon you, friends!   35
What is the news?
CASSIO.   The Duke does greet you, General,

---

6. magnifico Venetian grandee, i.e., Brabantio.   **7. effect** command.   **8. potential** powerful.   **9. cable** scope.   **10. seigniory** government.   **11. 'Tis . . . know** not yet known.   **12. siege** rank.   **13. demerits** deserts.   **14. unbonneted** without removing the hat, i.e., on equal terms (or "with hat off," "in all due modesty").   **15. unhoused** unconfined.   **16. confine** confinement.   **17. For . . . worth** all the riches at the bottom of the sea.   **18. Cassio . . . officers** the Quarto text calls for "Cassio with lights, officers with torches."   **19. My . . . soul** my natural gifts, my position or reputation, and my unflawed conscience.   **20. Janus** Roman two-faced god of beginnings.

And he requires your haste-post-haste appearance
Even on the instant.
OTHELLO.   What is the matter.[21] think you?
CASSIO. Something from Cyprus. as I may divine.[22]
It is a business of some heat.[23] The galleys   40
Have sent a dozen sequent[24] messengers
This very night at one another's heels.
And many of the consuls.[25] raised and met.
Are at the Duke's already. You have been hotly called for:
When. being not at your lodging to be found.   45
The Senate hath sent about[26] three several[27] quests
To search you out.
OTHELLO.   'Tis well I am found by you.
I will but spend a word here in the house
And go with you.   [*Exit.*]
CASSIO.   Ancient. what makes[28] he here?
IAGO. Faith. he tonight hath boarded[29] a land carrack.[30]   50
If it prove lawful prize.[31] he's made forever.
CASSIO. I do not understand.
IAGO.   He's married.
CASSIO.   To who?

[*Enter* OTHELLO.]

IAGO. Marry.[32] to—Come. Captain. will you go?
OTHELLO. Have with you.[33]
CASSIO. Here comes another troop to seek for you.   55

[*Enter* BRABANTIO. RODERIGO. *with officers and torches.*][34]

IAGO. It is Brabantio. General. be advised.[35]
He comes to bad intent.
OTHELLO.   Holla! Stand there!

21. **matter** business.   22. **divine** guess.   23. **heat** urgency.   24. **sequent** successive.   25. **consuls** senators.   26. **sent about** all over the city.   27. **several** separate   28. **makes** does.   29. **boarded** gone aboard and seized as an act of piracy (with sexual suggestion).   30. **carrack** merchant ship.   31. **prize** booty.   32. **marry** an oath. originally "by the Virgin Mary": here used with wordplay on *married.*   33. **Have with you** let's go.   34. [**Enter ... torches.**] the Quarto text calls for "others with lights and weapons."   35. **be advised** be on your guard.

RODERIGO. Signor. it is the Moor.
BRABANTIO.   Down with him. thief!

[*They draw on both sides.*]

IAGO. You. Roderigo! Come. sir. I am for you.
OTHELLO. Keep up[36] your bright swords. for the dew will rust   60
    them.
    Good signor. you shall more command with years
    Than with your weapons.
BRABANTIO. O thou foul thief. where hast thou stowed my
        daughter?
    Damned as thou art. thou hast enchanted her!
    For I'll refer me to all things of sense.[37]   65
    If she in chains of magic were not bound
    Whether a maid so tender. fair. and happy.
    So opposite to marriage that she shunned
    The wealthy curlèd darlings of our nation.
    Would ever have. t' incur a general mock.   70
    Run from her guardage[38] to the sooty bosom
    Of such a thing as thou—to fear, not to delight.
    Judge me the world if 'tis not gross in sense[39]
    That thou hast practiced on her with foul charms.
    Abused her delicate youth with drugs or minerals[40]   75
    That weakens motion.[41] I'll have 't disputed on:[42]
    'Tis probable and palpable to thinking.
    I therefore apprehend and do attach[43] thee
    For an abuser of the world. a practicer
    Of arts inhibited[44] and out of warrant.[45]   80
    Lay hold upon him! If he do resist.
    Subdue him at his peril.
OTHELLO.   Hold your hands.
    Both you of my inclining[46] and the rest.
    Were it my cue to fight. I should have known it

36. **keep up** sheath.   37. **For . . . sense** submit my case to creatures possessing
common sense.   38. **guardage** my guardianship of her.   39. **gross in sense** obvious.   40. **minerals** poisons.   41. **weakens motion** impair the vital faculties.
42. **disputed on** argued in court by professional counsel. debated by experts.
43. **attach** arrest.   44. **arts inhibited** black magic.   45. **out of warrant** illegal.
46. **inclining** following.

Without a prompter.—Whither will you that I go   85
    To answer this your charge?
BRABANTIO.   To prison. till fit time
    Of law and course of direct session[47]
    Call thee to answer.
OTHELLO.   What if I do obey?
    How may the Duke be therewith satisfied.   90
    Whose messengers are here about my side
    Upon some present business of the state
    To bring me to him?
OFFICER.   'Tis true. most worthy signor.
    The Duke's in council. and your noble self.
    I am sure. is sent for.   95
BRABANTIO.   How? The Duke in council?
    In this time of the night? Bring him away.[48]
    Mine's not an idle[49] cause. The Duke himself.
    Or any of my brothers of the state.
    Cannot but feel this wrong as 'twere their own:
    For if such actions may have passage free.[50]   100
    Bondslaves and pagans shall our statesmen be.

                                              [*Exeunt.*]

                        SCENE 3

[*Location: Venice. A council chamber. Enter* DUKE *and*
SENATORS *and sit at a table. with lights. and* OFFICERS. *The*
DUKE *and* SENATORS *are reading dispatches.*][1]

DUKE. There is no composition[2] in these news
    That gives them credit.
FIRST SENATOR. Indeed. they are disproportioned.[3]
    My letters say a hundred and seven galleys.
DUKE. And mine. a hundred forty.   5
SECOND SENATOR.   And mine. two hundred.

47. **direct session** regular or specially convened legal proceedings.   48. **away** right
along.   49. **idle** trifling.   50. **may have passage free** are allowed to go unchecked.
1. [**Location . . . dispatches.**] the Quarto text calls for the Duke and senators to "sit
at a table with lights and attendants."   2. **composition** consistency.   3. **disproportioned** inconsistent.

But though they jump[4] not on a just[5] account—
As in these cases, where the aim[6] reports
'Tis oft with difference—yet do they all confirm
A Turkish fleet, and bearing up to Cyprus.
DUKE. Nay, it is possible enough to judgment.   10
    I do not so secure me in the error
    But the main article I do approve[7]
    In fearful sense.
SAILOR. [*within*]   What ho, what ho, what ho!

    [*Enter* SAILOR.]

OFFICER. A messenger from the galleys.
DUKE. Now, what's the business?   15
SAILOR. The Turkish preparation[8] makes for Rhodes.
    So was I bid report here to the state
    By Signor Angelo.
DUKE. How say you by[9] this change?
FIRST SENATOR.   This cannot be
    By no assay[10] of reason. 'Tis a pageant[11]   20
    To keep us in false gaze.[12] When we consider
    Th' importancy of Cyprus to the Turk,
    And let ourselves again but understand
    That, as it more concerns the Turk than Rhodes,
    So may he with more facile question bear it,[13]   25
    For that[14] it stands not in such warlike brace,[15]
    But altogether lacks th' abilities[16]
    That Rhodes is dressed in[17]—if we make thought of this,
    We must not think the Turk is so unskillful[18]
    To leave that latest[19] which concerns him first,   30
    Neglecting an attempt of ease and gain
    To wake[20] and wage[21] a danger profitless.

4. jump agree. 5. just exact. 6. aim conjecture. 7. But ... approve I do not take such (false) comfort in the discrepancies that I fail to perceive the main point, i.e., that the Turkish fleet is threatening. 8. Turkish preparation fleet prepared for battle. 9. by about. 10. assay test. 11. pageant mere show. 12. false gaze looking the wrong way. 13. So may ... it so also he (the Turk) can more easily capture it (Cyprus). 14. for that since. 15. brace state. 16. abilities means of defense. 17. dressed in equipped with. 18. unskillful careless. 19. latest last. 20. wake stir up. 21. wage risk.

DUKE. Nay. in all confidence. he's not for Rhodes.
OFFICER. Here is more news.

[*Enter a* MESSENGER.]

MESSENGER. The Ottomites. reverend and gracious.   35
  Steering with due course toward the isle of Rhodes.
  Have there injointed them[22] with an after[23] fleet.
FIRST SENATOR. Ay. so I thought. How many. as you guess?
MESSENGER. Of thirty sail: and now they do restem
  Their backward course.[24] bearing with frank[25]
    appearance   40
  Their purposes toward Cyprus. Signor Montano.
  Your trusty and most valiant servitor.[26]
  With his free duty[27] recommends[28] you thus.
  And prays you to believe him.
DUKE. 'Tis certain then for Cyprus.   45
  Marcus Luccicos. is not he in town?
FIRST SENATOR. He's now in Florence.
DUKE. Write from us to him. post-post-haste. Dispatch.
FIRST SENATOR. Here comes Brabantio and the valiant Moor.

[*Enter* BRABANTIO. OTHELLO. CASSIO. IAGO. RODERIGO. *and*
officers.]

DUKE. Valiant Othello. we must straight[29] employ you   50
  Against the general enemy[30] Ottoman.
  [*To* BRABANTIO.] I did not see you: welcome. gentle[31] signor.
  We lacked your counsel and your help tonight.
BRABANTIO. So did I yours. Good Your Grace. pardon me:
  Neither my place[32] nor aught I heard of business   55
  Hath raised me from my bed. nor doth the general care
  Take hold on me. for my particular[33] grief
  Is of so floodgate[34] and o'erbearing nature
  That it engluts[35] and swallows other sorrows

22. injointed them joined themselves. 23. after following. 24. restem ...
course retrace their original course. 25. frank undisguised. 26. servitor officer.
27. free duty freely given and loyal service. 28. recommends commends himself
and reports to. 29. straight straightway. 30. general enemy universal enemy to
all Christendom. 31. gentle noble. 32. place official position. 33. particular
personal. 34. floodgate overwhelming (as when floodgates are opened).
35. engluts engulfs.

And it is still itself.[36]   60
DUKE.   Why, what's the matter?
BRABANTIO. My daughter! O, my daughter!
DUKE AND SENATORS.   Dead?
BRABANTIO.   Ay, to me.
    She is abused,[37] stol'n from me, and corrupted
    By spells and medicines bought of mountebanks:
    For nature so preposterously to err,
    Being not deficient,[38] blind, or lame of sense,   65
    Sans[39] witchcraft could not.
DUKE. Whoe'er he be that in this foul proceeding
    Hath thus beguiled your daughter of herself,
    And you of her, the bloody book of law
    You shall yourself read in the bitter letter   70
    After your own sense[40]—yea, though our proper[41] son
    Stood in your action.[42]
BRABANTIO.   Humbly I thank Your Grace.
    Here is the man, this Moor, whom now it seems
    Your special mandate for the state affairs
    Hath hither brought.   75
ALL.   We are very sorry for 't.
DUKE. [to OTHELLO]
    What, in your own part, can you say to this?
BRABANTIO. Nothing, but this is so.
OTHELLO. Most potent, grave, and reverend signors,
    My very noble and approved[43] good masters:
    That I have ta'en away this old man's daughter,   80
    It is most true; true, I have married her,
    The very head and front[44] of my offending
    Hath this extent, no more. Rude[45] am I in my speech,
    And little blessed with the soft phrase of peace:
    For since these arms of mine had seven years' pith,[46]   85

---

36. still itself remains undiminished.   **37. abused** deceived.   **38. deficient** defective.   **39. Sans** without.   **40. After . . . sense** according to your own interpretation.
41. proper my own.   **42. Stood . . . action** were under your accusation.
43. approved esteemed.   **44. head and front** height and breadth, entire extent.
45. Rude unpolished.   **46. seven years' pith** since I was seven.

Till now some nine moons wasted.[47] they have used
Their dearest[48] action in the tented field:
And little of this great world can I speak
More than pertains to feats of broils and battle.
And therefore little shall I grace my cause   90
In speaking for myself. Yet, by your gracious patience.
I will a round[49] unvarnished tale deliver
Of my whole course of love—what drugs. what charms.
What conjuration. and what mighty magic.
For such proceeding I am charged withal.[50]   95
I won his daughter.
BRABANTIO.   A maiden never bold:
    Of spirit so still and quiet that her motion
    Blushed at herself:[51] and she. in spite of nature.
    Of years.[52] of country. credit.[53] everything.
    To fall in love with what she feared to look on!   100
    It is a judgment maimed and most imperfect
    That will confess[54] perfection so could err
    Against all rules of nature. and must be driven
    To find out practices[55] of cunning hell
    Why this should be. I therefore vouch[56] again   105
    That with some mixtures powerful o'er the blood.[57]
    Or with some dram conjured to this effect.[58]
    He wrought upon her.
DUKE.   To vouch this is no proof.
    Without more wider[59] and more overt test[60]
    Than these thin habits[61] and poor likelihoods[62]   110
    Of modern seeming[63] do prefer[64] against him.
FIRST SENATOR. But Othello. speak.
    Did you by indirect and forcèd courses[65]

---

47. nine moons wasted until some nine months ago (since when Othello has evidently not been on active duty. but in Venice). **48. dearest** most valuable. **49. round** plain. **50. withal** with. **51. Blushed at herself** She blushed easily at herself. (Motion can suggest the impulse of the soul or of the emotions. or physical movement.). **52. years** i.e. difference in age. **53. credit** reputation. **54. confess** concede (that). **55. practices** plots. **56. vouch** assert. **57. blood** passions. **58. dram . . . effect** dose made by magical spells to have this effect. **59. wider** fuller. **60. test** testimony. **61. habits** garments. i.e.. appearances. **62. likelihoods** weak inferences. **63. modern seeming** commonplace assumption. **64. prefer** bring forth. **65. forced courses** means used against her will.

Subdue and poison this young maid's affections?
Or came it by request and such fair question[66]   115
As soul to soul affordeth?
OTHELLO.   I do beseech you.
  Send for the lady to the Sagittary
  And let her speak of me before her father.
  If you do find me foul in her report,
  The trust, the office I do hold of you   120
  Not only take away, but let your sentence
  Even fall upon my life.
DUKE.   Fetch Desdemona hither.
OTHELLO. Ancient, conduct them. You best know the place.

                          [*Exeunt* IAGO *and attendants.*]

  And, till she come, as truly as to heaven
  I do confess the vices of my blood.[67]   125
  So justly[68] to your grave ears I'll present
  How I did thrive in this fair lady's love,
  And she in mine.
DUKE.   Say it, Othello.
OTHELLO. Her father loved me, oft invited me,
  Still[69] questioned me the story of my life   130
  From year to year—the battles, sieges, fortunes
  That I have passed.
  I ran it through, even from my boyish days
  To th' very moment that he bade me tell it.
  Wherein I spoke of most disastrous chances,   135
  Of moving accidents[70] by flood and field,
  Of hairbreadth scapes i' th' imminent deadly breach,[71]
  Of being taken by the insolent foe
  And sold to slavery, of my redemption thence,
  And portance[72] in my travels' history,   140
  Wherein of antres[73] vast and deserts idle,[74]
  Rough quarries,[75] rocks, and hills whose heads touch
     heaven,

---

66. question conversation.   **67. blood** passions.   **68. justly** accurately.   **69. Still**
continually.   **70. accidents** stirring happenings.   **71. deadly breach** death-threat-
ening gaps made in a fortification.   **72. portance** conduct.   **73. antres** caverns.
74. idle barren.   **75. quarries** rock formations.

It was my hint[76] to speak—such was my process—
And of the Cannibals that each other eat.
The Anthropophagi.[77] and men whose heads   145
Do grow beneath their shoulders. These things to hear
Would Desdemona seriously incline:
But still the house affairs would draw her thence.
Which ever as she could with haste dispatch
She'd come again. and with a greedy ear   150
Devour up my discourse. Which I. observing.
Took once a pliant[78] hour. and found good means
To draw from her a prayer of earnest heart
That I would all my pilgrimage dilate.[79]
Whereof by parcels[80] she had something heard.   155
But not intentively.[81] I did consent.
And often did beguile her of her tears.
When I did speak of some distressful stroke
That my youth suffered. My story being done.
She gave me for my pains a world of sighs.   160
She swore. in faith. 'twas strange. 'twas passing[82] strange.
'Twas pitiful. 'twas wondrous pitiful.
She wished she had not heard it. yet she wished
That heaven had made her[83] such a man. She thanked me.
And bade me. if I had a friend that loved her.   165
I should but teach him how to tell my story.
And that would woo her. Upon this hint[84] I spake.
She loved me for the dangers I had passed.
And I loved her that she did pity them.
This only is the witchcraft I have used.   170
Here comes the lady. Let her witness it.

[*Enter* DESDEMONA. IAGO. *and attendants.*]

DUKE. I think this tale would win my daughter too.
Good Brabantio.
Take up this mangled matter at the best.[85]

---

76. hint opportunity.   **77. Anthropophagi** man-eaters (a term from Pliny's *Nat-ural History*).   **78.   pliant** well-suiting.   **79.   dilate** relate   in   detail.
80. parcels piecemeal.   **81. intentively** continuously.   **82. passing** exceedingly.
83. made her created her to be or made for her.   **84. hint** opportunity.   **85. mat-ter . . . best** make the best of a bad bargain.

Men do their broken weapons rather use   175
  Than their bare hands.
BRABANTIO.   I pray you, hear her speak.
  If she confess that she was half the wooer.
  Destruction on my head if my bad blame
  Light on the man! —Come hither, gentle mistress.
  Do you perceive in all this noble company   180
  Where most you owe obedience?
DESDEMONA.   My noble Father.
  I do perceive here a divided duty.
  To you I am bound for life and education;[86]
  My life and education both do learn[87] me
  How to respect you. You are the lord of duty;[88]   185
  I am hitherto your daughter. But here's my husband.
  And so much duty as my mother showed
  To you, preferring you before her father,
  So much I challenge[89] that I may profess
  Due to the Moor my lord.   190
BRABANTIO. God be with you! I have done.
  Please it Your Grace, on to the state affairs.
  I had rather to adopt a child than get[90] it.
  Come hither, Moor. [*He joins the hands of* OTHELLO *and*
    DESDEMONA.]
  I here do give thee that with all my heart[91]   195
  Which, but thou hast already, with all my heart[92]
  I would keep from thee.—For your sake,[93] jewel.
  I am glad at soul I have no other child.
  For thy escape[94] would teach me tyranny,
  To hang clogs[95] on them.—I have done, my lord.   200
DUKE. Let me speak like yourself,[96] and lay a sentence[97]
  Which, as a grice[98] or step, may help these lovers
  Into your favor.
  When remedies[99] are past, the griefs are ended

---

86. education upbringing. **87. learn** teach. **88. duty** to whom duty is due.
89. challenge claim. **90. get** beget. **91. all my heart** wherein my whole affection
has been engaged. **92. all my heart** gladly. **93. For your sake** on your account.
94. escape elopement. **95. clogs** blocks of wood fastened to the legs of criminals or
convicts to inhibit escape. **96. like yourself** as you would, in your proper temper.
97. lay a sentence apply a maxim. **98. grice** step. **99. remedies** hopes of remedy.

By seeing the worst, which late on hopes depended.[100] 205
To mourn a mischief[101] that is past and gone
Is the next[102] way to draw new mischief on.
What[103] cannot be preserved when fortune takes,
Patience her injury a mockery makes.[104]
The robbed that smiles steals something from the thief; 210
He robs himself that spends a bootless grief.[105]
BRABANTIO. So let the Turk of Cyprus us beguile,
We lose it not, so long as we can smile.
He bears the sentence well that nothing bears
But the free comfort which from thence he hears, 215
But he bears both the sentence and the sorrow
That, to pay grief, must of poor patience borrow.[106]
These sentences, to sugar or to gall,
Being strong on both sides, are equivocal.[107]
But words are words, I never yet did hear 220
That the bruisèd heart was piercèd through the ear.[108]
I humbly beseech you, proceed to th' affairs of state.
DUKE. The Turk with a most mighty preparation makes for
Cyprus. Othello, the fortitude[109] of the place is best known
to you; and though we have there a substitute[110] of most al- 225
lowed[111] sufficiency, yet opinion, a sovereign mistress of ef-
fects, throws a more safer voice on you.[112] You must there-
fore be content to slubber[113] the gloss of your new fortunes
with this more stubborn[114] and boisterous expedition.
OTHELLO. The tyrant custom, most grave senators, 230
Hath made the flinty and steel couch of war

100. **which . . . depended** which griefs were sustained until recently by hopeful an-
ticipation. 101. **mischief** misfortune. 102. **next** nearest. 103. **What** whatever.
104. **Patience . . . makes** patience laughs at the injury inflicted by fortune (and thus
eases the pain). 105. **He . . . grief** indulges in unavailing grief. 106. **That . . .
borrow** a person well bears out your maxim who can enjoy its platitudinous comfort,
free of all genuine sorrow, but anyone whose grief bankrupts his poor patience is left
with your saying and his sorrow, too. (*Bears the sentence* also plays on the meaning,
"receives judicial sentence.") 107. **equivocal** these fine maxims are equivocal, either sweet or bitter in their application. 108. **was piercèd . . . ear** i.e., surgically
lanced and cured by mere words of advice. 109. **fortitude** strength.
110. **substitute** deputy. 111. **allowed** acknowledged. 112. **opinion . . . you**
general opinion, an important determiner of affairs, chooses you as the best man.
113. **slubber** soil, sully. 114. **stubborn** harsh, rough.

My thrice-driven[115] bed of down. I do agnize[116]
A natural and prompt alacrity
I find in hardness,[117] and do undertake
These present wars against the Ottomites.   235
Most humbly therefore bending to your state,[118]
I crave fit disposition for my wife,
Due reference of place and exhibition.[119]
With such accommodation[120] and besort[121]
As levels[122] with her breeding.[123]   240
DUKE. Why, at her father's.
BRABANTIO.   I will not have it so.
OTHELLO. Nor I.
DESDEMONA.   Nor I. I would not there reside.
  To put my father in impatient thoughts
  By being in his eye. Most gracious Duke,
  To my unfolding[124] lend your prosperous[125] ear,   245
  And let me find a charter[126] in your voice,
  T' assist my simpleness.
DUKE. What would you, Desdemona?
DESDEMONA. That I did love the Moor to live with him.
  My downright violence and storm of fortunes[127]   250
  May trumpet to the world. My heart's subdued
  Even to the very quality of my lord.[128]
  I saw Othello's visage in his mind,
  And to his honors and his valiant parts[129]
  Did I my soul and fortunes consecrate.   255
  So that, dear lords, if I be left behind
  A moth[130] of peace, and he go to the war,
  The rites[131] for why I love him are bereft me,
  And I a heavy interim shall support

---

115. thrice-driven thrice sifted. **116. agnize** know in myself, acknowledge.
117. hardness hardship. **118. bending ... state** bowing to your authority.
119. Due ... exhibition provision of appropriate place to live and allowance of
money. **120. accommodation** provision. **121. besort** attendance. **122. levels**
suits. **123. breeding** upbringing. **124. unfolding** proposal. **125. prosperous**
propitious. **126. charter** authorization. **127. My ... fortunes** my plain and total
breach of social custom, taking my future by storm and disrupting my whole life.
128. Even ... lord My heart is brought wholly into accord with Othello's virtues; I
love him for his virtues. **129. parts** qualities **130. moth** i.e., one who consumes
merely. **131. rites** rites of love (with a suggestion, too, of "rights," sharing).

By his dear[132] absence. Let me go with him.   260
OTHELLO. Let her have your voice.[133]
   Vouch with me. heaven. I therefor beg it not
   To please the palate of my appetite.
   Nor to comply with heat[134]—the young affects[135]
   In me defunct—and proper[136] satisfaction.   265
   But to be free[137] and bounteous to her mind.
   And heaven defend[138] your good souls that you think[139]
   I will your serious and great business scant
   When she is with me. No. when light-winged toys
   Of feathered Cupid seel[140] with wanton dullness   270
   My speculative and officed instruments.[141]
   That my disports corrupt and taint my business.[142]
   Let huswives make a skillet of my helm.
   And all indign[143] and base adversities
   Make head[144] against my estimation![145]   275
DUKE. Be it as you shall privately determine.
   Either for her stay or going. Th' affair cries haste.
   And speed must answer it.
A SENATOR.   You must away tonight.
DESDEMONA. Tonight. my lord?
DUKE.   This night.
OTHELLO.   With all my heart.
DUKE. At nine i' the morning here we'll meet again.   280
   Othello. leave some officer behind.
   And he shall our commission bring to you.
   With such things else of quality and respect[146]
   As doth import[147] you.
OTHELLO.   So please Your Grace. my ancient:
   A man he is of honesty and trust.   285
   To his conveyance I assign my wife.

---

132. **dear** heartfelt. Also. costly.   133. **voice** consent.   134. **heat** sexual passion.
135. **affects** desires.   136. **proper** personal.   137. **free** generous.   138. **defend** forbid.   139. **think** should think.   140. **seel** i.e.. make blind (as in falconry. by sewing up the eyes of the hawk during training).   141. **instruments** eyes and other faculties used in the performance of duty.   142. **That . . . business** so that my sexual pastimes impair my work.   143. **indign** unworthy. shameful.   144. **Make head** rise up.   145. **estimation** reputation.   146. **quality and respect** of importance and relevance.   147. **import** concern.

With what else needful Your Good Grace shall think
To be sent after me.
DUKE.   Let it be so.
Good night to everyone. [*To* BRABANTIO.] And, noble signor,
If virtue no delighted[148] beauty lack.   290
Your son-in-law is far more fair than black.
FIRST SENATOR. Adieu, brave Moor. Use Desdemona well.
BRABANTIO. Look to her, Moor, if thou hast eyes to see.
She has deceived her father, and may thee.

       [*Exeunt* DUKE, BRABANTIO, CASSIO, SENATORS, *and officers.*]

OTHELLO. My life upon her faith! Honest Iago.   295
My Desdemona must I leave to thee.
I prithee, let thy wife attend on her.
And bring them after in the best advantage.[149]
Come, Desdemona, I have but an hour
Of love, of worldly matters and direction,[150]   300
To spend with thee. We must obey the time.[151]

                                        [*Exit with* DESDEMONA.]

RODERIGO. Iago—
IAGO. What sayst thou, noble heart?
RODERIGO. What will I do, think'st thou?
IAGO. Why, go to bed and sleep.   305
RODERIGO. I will incontinently[152] drown myself.
IAGO. If thou dost, I shall never love thee after. Why, thou silly
       gentleman?
RODERIGO. It is silliness to live when to live is torment; and then
       have we a prescription[153] to die when death is our physician.
IAGO. O villainous![154] I have looked upon the world for four   310
       times seven years, and, since I could distinguish betwixt a
       benefit and an injury, I never found man that knew how to
       love himself. Ere I would say I would drown myself for the

---

148. delighted delightful.   **149. best advantage** at the most favorable opportunity.
150. direction instructions.   **151. time** the urgency of the present crisis.   **152. incontinently** immediately.   **153. prescription** right based on long-established custom. Also, doctor's prescription.   **154. O villainous!** i.e., what perfect nonsense.

love of a guinea hen.[155] I would change my humanity with
a baboon.   315
RODERIGO. What should I do? I confess it is my shame to be so
fond.[156] but it is not in my virtue[157] to amend it.
IAGO. Virtue? A fig![158] 'Tis in ourselves that we are thus or
thus. Our bodies are our gardens, to the which our wills
are gardeners: so that if we will plant nettles or sow let-   320
tuce. set hyssop[159] and weed up thyme. supply it with one
gender[160] of herbs or distract it with[161] many. either to
have it sterile with idleness[162] or manured with industry—
why. the power and corrigible authority[163] of this lies in
our wills. If the beam[164] of our lives had not one scale of   325
reason to poise[165] another of sensuality. the blood[166] and
baseness of our natures would conduct us to most prepos-
terous conclusions. But we have reason to cool our raging
motions.[167] our carnal stings. our unbitted[168] lusts. whereof I take this that you call love to be a sect or scion.[169]   330
RODERIGO. It cannot be.
IAGO. It is merely a lust of the blood and a permission of the
will. Come. be a man. Drown thyself? Drown cats and blind
puppies. I have professed me thy friend. and I confess me
knit to thy deserving with cables of perdurable[170] tough-   335
ness. I could never better stead[171] thee than now. Put
money in thy purse. Follow thou the wars: defeat thy
favor[172] with an usurped[173] beard. I say. put money in thy
purse. It cannot be long that Desdemona should continue
her love to the Moor—put money in thy purse—nor he his   340
to her. It was a violent commencement in her. and thou
shalt see an answerable sequestration[174]—put but money

155. guinea hen a slang term for a prostitute.   156. fond infatuated.   157. virtue
strength. nature.   158. A fig! to give a fig is to thrust the thumb between the first
and second fingers in a vulgar and insulting gesture.   159. hyssop an herb of
the mint family.   160. gender kind.   161. distract it with divine it among.
162. idleness want of cultivation.   163. authority power to correct.   164. beam
balance.   165. poise counterbalance.   166. blood natural passions.   167. raging
motions natural passions.   168. unbitted unbridled. uncontrolled.   169. scion
cutting or offshoot.   170. perdurable very durable.   171. stead assist.
172. defeat thy favor disguise your face.   173. usurped the suggestion is that
Roderigo is not man enough to have a beard of his own.   174. sequestration a corresponding separation or estrangement.

in thy purse. These Moors are changeable in their wills[175]—
fill thy purse with money. The food that to him now is as
luscious as locusts[176] shall be to him shortly as bitter as   345
coloquintida.[177] She must change for youth: when she is
sated with his body, she will find the error of her choice. She
must have change, she must. Therefore put money in thy
purse. If thou wilt needs damn thyself, do it a more delicate
way than drowning. Make[178] all the money thou canst. If   350
sanctimony[179] and a frail vow betwixt an erring[180] barbarian and a supersubtle Venetian be not too hard for my wits
and all the tribe of hell, thou shalt enjoy her. Therefore
make money. A pox of drowning thyself! It is clean out of
the way.[181] Seek thou rather to be hanged in compassing[182]   355
thy joy than to be drowned and go without her.

RODERIGO. Wilt thou be fast[183] to my hopes if I depend on the
issue?[184]

IAGO. Thou art sure of me. Go, make money. I have told thee
often, and I retell thee again and again, I hate the Moor.   360
My cause is hearted;[185] thine hath no less reason. Let us be
conjunctive[186] in our revenge against him. If thou canst
cuckold him, thou dost thyself a pleasure, me a sport.
There are many events in the womb of time which will be
delivered. Traverse,[187] go, provide thy money. We will   365
have more of this tomorrow. Adieu.

RODERIGO. Where shall we meet i' the morning?

IAGO. At my lodging.

RODERIGO. I'll be with thee betimes.[188] *[He starts to leave.]*

IAGO. Go to, farewell.—Do you hear, Roderigo?   370

RODERIGO. What say you?

IAGO. No more of drowning, do you hear?

RODERIGO. I am changed.

IAGO. Go to, farewell. Put money enough in your purse.

---

175. wills carnal appetites.   **176. locusts** fruit of the carob tree (see Matthew 3:4),
or perhaps honeysuckle.   **177. coloquintida** colocynth or bitter apple, a purgative.
178. Make raise, collect.   **179. sanctimony** sacred ceremony.   **180. erring** wandering, vagabond, unsteady.   **181. clean . . . way** entirely unsuitable as a course of
action.   **182. in compassing** encompassing, embracing.   **183. fast** true.
184. issue successful outcome.   **185. hearted** fixed in the heart, heartfelt.
186. conjunctive united.   **187. Traverse** a military marching term.   **188. betimes**
early.

RODERIGO. I'll sell all my land. [*Exit.*]

IAGO. Thus do I ever make my fool my purse:
For I mine own gained knowledge should profane
If I would time expend with such a snipe[189]
But for my sport and profit. I hate the Moor:
And it is thought abroad[190] that twixt my sheets   380
He's done my office.[191] I know not if 't be true:
But I. for mere suspicion in that kind.
Will do as if for surety.[192] He holds me well:[193]
The better shall my purpose work on him.
Cassio's a proper[194] man. Let me see now: 385
To get his place and to plume[195] up my will
In double knavery—How. how?—Let's see:
After some time. to abuse[196] Othello's ear
That he[197] is too familiar with his wife.
He hath a person and a smooth dispose[198]   390
To be suspected. framed to make women false.
The Moor is of a free[199] and open[200] nature.
That thinks men honest that but seem to be so.
And will as tenderly[201] be led by the nose
As asses are.   395
I have 't. It is engendered. Hell and night
Must bring this monstrous birth to the world's light.

[*Exit.*]

ACT 2
SCENE 1

[*A seaport in Cyprus. An open place near the quay. Enter
MONTANO and two GENTLEMEN.*]

MONTANO. What from the cape can you discern at sea?
FIRST GENTLEMAN. Nothing at all. It is a high-wrought flood.[1]

---

189. snipe woodcock. i.e.. fool.   **190. thought abroad** rumored.   **191. office** my
sexual functions as husband.   **192. Will . . . surety** act as if on certain knowledge.
193. holds me well regards me favorably.   **194. proper** handsome.   **195. plume**
put a feather in the cap of. i.e.. glorify. gratify.   **196. abuse** deceive.   **197. he** Cassio.   **198. dispose** disposition.   **199. free** frank.   **200. open** unsuspicious.
201. tenderly readily.   **1. high-wrought flood** agitated sea.

I cannot. twixt the heaven and the main.[2]
Descry a sail.
MONTANO. Methinks the wind hath spoke aloud at land: 5
  A fuller blast ne'er shook our battlements.
  If it hath ruffianed[3] so upon the sea.
  What ribs of oak. when mountains[4] melt on them.
  Can hold the mortise?[5] What shall we hear of this?
SECOND GENTLEMAN. A segregation[6] of the Turkish fleet.   10
  For do but stand upon the foaming shore.
  The chidden[7] billow seems to pelt the clouds:
  The wind-shaked surge. with high and monstrous mane,[8]
  Seems to cast water on the burning Bear[9]
  And quench the guards of th' ever-fixèd pole.   15
  I never did like molestation[10] view
  On the enchafèd[11] flood.
MONTANO.   If that[12] the Turkish fleet
  Be not ensheltered and embayed.[13] they are drowned:
  It is impossible to bear it out.[14]

[*Enter a (Third) Gentleman.*]

THIRD GENTLEMAN. News. lads! Our wars are done.   20
  The desperate tempest hath so banged the Turks
  That their designment[15] halts.[16] A noble ship of Venice
  Hath seen a grievous wreck[17] and sufferance[18]
  On most part of their fleet.
MONTANO. How? Is this true?   25
THIRD GENTLEMAN.   The ship is here put in.
  A Veronesa:[19] Michael Cassio.

---

2. main ocean. 3. ruffianed raged. 4. mountains mountains of water. 5. Can
... mortise hold their joints together. 6. segregation dispersal. 7. chidden i.e.
rebuked. repelled (by the shore). and thus shot into the air. 8. wind-shaked ...
mane the surf is like the mane of a wild beast. 9. Bear the constellation of Ursa Minor or the Little Bear. which includes the polestar (and hence regarded as *the guards
of th' ever-fixed pole* in the next line; sometimes the term *guards* is applied to the two
"pointers" of the Big Bear or Dipper. which may be intended here.).
10. molestation such a disturbance. 11. enchafed angry. 12. If that if.
13. embayed in a harbor. 14. bear it out survive. 15. designment enterprise.
16. halts is lame. 17. wreck shipwreck. 18. sufferance damage. 19. Veronesa
fitted out in Verona for Venetian service, or possibly *Verennessa* (the Folio spelling).
i.e.. *verrinessa*, a cutter (from *verrinare*. "to cut through").

Lieutenant to the warlike Moor Othello.
Is come on shore: the Moor himself at sea.
And is in full commission here for Cyprus.
MONTANO. I am glad on 't. 'Tis a worthy governor.   30
THIRD GENTLEMAN. But this same Cassio, though he speak of
    comfort
Touching the Turkish loss, yet he looks sadly[20]
And prays the Moor be safe, for they were parted
With foul and violent tempest.
MONTANO.   Pray heaven he be.
For I have served him, and the man commands   35
Like a full[21] soldier. Let's to the seaside, ho!
As well to see the vessel that's come in
As to throw out our eyes for brave Othello.
Even till we make the main and th' aerial blue[22]
An indistinct regard.[23]   40
THIRD GENTLEMAN.   Come, let's do so.
For every minute is expectancy[24]
Of more arrivance.[25]

    [Enter CASSIO.]

CASSIO. Thanks, you the valiant of this warlike isle,
    That so approve[26] the Moor! O, let the heavens
    Give him defense against the elements,   45
    For I have lost him on a dangerous sea.
MONTANO. Is he well shipped?
CASSIO. His bark is stoutly timbered, and his pilot
    Of very expert and approved allowance:[27]
    Therefore my hopes, not surfeited to death,[28]   50
    Stand in bold cure.[29]
                        [A cry within:] "A sail, a sail, a sail!"
CASSIO. What noise?
A GENTLEMAN. The town is empty. On the brow o' the sea[30]

---

20. **sadly** gravely.   21. **full** perfect.   22. **main . . . blue** the sea and the sky.
23. **indistinct regard** indistinguishable in our view.   24. **expectancy** gives expectation.   25. **arrivance** arrival.   26. **approve** honor.   27. **approved allowance**
tested reputation.   28. **surfeited to death** overextended, worn thin through repeated application or delayed fulfillment.   29. **bold cure** in strong hopes of fulfillment.   30. **brow o' the sea** cliff-edge.

Stand ranks of people, and they cry "A sail!"

CASSIO. My hopes do shape him for[31] the governor.   55

[*A shot within.*]

SECOND GENTLEMAN. They do discharge their shot of courtesy:[32]
    Our friends at least.

CASSIO.   I pray you, sir, go forth,
    And give us truth who 'tis that is arrived.

SECOND GENTLEMAN. I shall.   [*Exit.*]

MONTANO. But, good Lieutenant, is your general wived?   60

CASSIO. Most fortunately. He hath achieved a maid
    That paragons[33] description and wild fame,[34]
    One that excels the quirks[35] of blazoning[36] pens,
    And in th' essential vesture of creation
    Does tire the enginer.[37]   65

[*Enter* SECOND GENTLEMAN.][38]

                    How now? Who has put in?[39]

SECOND GENTLEMAN. 'Tis one Iago, ancient to the General.

CASSIO. He's had most favorable and happy speed.
    Tempests themselves, high seas, and howling winds,
    The guttered[40] rocks and congregated sands—
    Traitors ensteeped[41] to clog the guiltless keel—   70
    As[42] having sense of beauty, do omit[43]
    Their mortal[44] natures, letting go safely by
    The divine Desdemona.

MONTANO.   What is she?

CASSIO. She that I spake of, our great captain's captain,
    Left in the conduct of the bold Iago,   75
    Whose footing[45] here anticipates our thoughts
    A se'nnight's[46] speed. Great Jove, Othello guard,

---

31. My . . . for I hope it is.   **32. discharge . . . courtesy** fire a salute in token of respect and courtesy.   **33. paragons** surpasses.   **34. wild fame** rumor.   **35. quirks** witty conceits.   **36. blazoning** setting forth as though in heraldic language.   **37. enginer** in her real, God-given, beauty, (she) defeats any attempt to praise her. The enginer [engineer] is the poet, one who devises.   **38. [Enter . . . Gentleman.]** so identified in the Quarto text here and in lines 56, 59, 66 and 94; the Folio calls him a gentleman.   **39. put in** to harbor.   **40. guttered** jagged.   **41. ensteeped** lying under water.   **42. As** as if.   **43. omit** suspend.   **44. mortal** deadly.   **45. footing** landing.   **46. se'nnight's** week's.

And swell his sail with thine own powerful breath.
That he may bless this bay with his tall[47] ship.
Make love's quick pants in Desdemona's arms.   80
Give renewed fire to our extincted spirits.
And bring all Cyprus comfort!

[*Enter* DESDEMONA. IAGO. RODERIGO. *and* EMILIA.]

                              O. behold.
The riches of the ship is come on shore!
You men of Cyprus. let her have your knees.

[*The gentlemen make curtsy to* DESDEMONA.]

Hail to thee. lady! And the grace of heaven   85
Before. behind thee. and on every hand
Enwheel thee round!
DESDEMONA.   I thank you. valiant Cassio.
What tidings can you tell me of my lord?
CASSIO. He is not yet arrived. nor know I aught
But that he's well and will be shortly here.   90
DESDEMONA. O. but I fear—How lost your company?
CASSIO. The great contention of the sea and skies
Parted our fellowship.

[*Within: "A sail. a sail!" A shot.*]

                              But hark. A sail!
SECOND GENTLEMAN. They give their greeting to the citadel.
This likewise is a friend.   95
CASSIO.   See for the news.

                    [*Exit* SECOND GENTLEMAN.]

Good Ancient. you are welcome. [*Kissing* EMILIA.]
Welcome. mistress.
Let it not gall your patience. good Iago.
That I extend[48] my manners: 'tis my breeding[49]
That gives me this bold show of courtesy.   100
IAGO. Sir. would she give you so much of her lips

---

47. tall splendid.   **48. extend** give scope to.   **49. breeding** training in the niceties
of etiquette.

As of her tongue she oft bestows on me.
You would have enough.
DESDEMONA. Alas, she has no speech![50]
IAGO.   In faith, too much.
I find it still,[51] when I have list[52] to sleep.   105
Marry, before your ladyship, I grant,
She puts her tongue a little in her heart
And chides with thinking.[53]
EMILIA.   You have little cause to say so.
IAGO. Come on, come on. You are pictures out of doors,[54]
Bells[55] in your parlors, wildcats in your kitchens,[56]   110
Saints[57] in your injuries, devils being offended,
Players[58] in your huswifery,[59] and huswives[60] in your beds.
DESDEMONA. O, fie upon thee, slanderer!
IAGO. Nay, it is true, or else I am a Turk.[61]
You rise to play, and go to bed to work.   115
EMILIA. You shall not write my praise.
IAGO.   No, let me not.
DESDEMONA. What wouldst write of me, if thou shouldst praise me?
IAGO. O gentle lady, do not put me to 't,
For I am nothing if not critical.[62]
DESDEMONA. Come on, essay.[63]—There's one gone to the   120
   harbor?
IAGO. Ay, madam.
DESDEMONA. I am not merry, but I do beguile
The thing I am by seeming otherwise.
Come, how wouldst thou praise me?
IAGO. I am about it, but indeed my invention   125
Comes from my pate as birdlime[64] does from frieze—[65]
It plucks out brains and all. But my Muse labors,[66]
And thus she is delivered:

50. **Alas . . . speech!** She's not a chatterbox, as you allege. 51. **still** always.
52. **list** desire. 53. **thinking** in her thoughts only. 54. **pictures . . . doors** silent
and well-behaved in public. 55. **Bells** jangling, noisy, and brazen. 56. **wildcats
. . . kitchens** in domestic affairs. (Ladies would not do the cooking.) 57. **Saints**
martyrs. 58. **Players** idlers. 59. **huswifery** housekeeping. 60. **huswives**
hussies (i.e., women are "busy" in bed, or unduly thrifty in dispensing sexual favors).
61. **Turk** an infidel, not to be believed. 62. **critical** censorious. 63. **essay** try.
64. **birdlime** sticky substance used to catch small birds. 65. **frieze** coarse cloth.
66. **labors** exerts herself. Also, prepares to deliver a child (with a following pun on
"*delivered*" in line 128).

If she be fair and wise. fairness and wit.
The one's for use. the other useth it.[67]   130
DESDEMONA. Well praised! How if she be black[68] and witty?
IAGO. If she be black. and thereto have a wit.
   She'll find a white[69] that shall her blackness fit.[70]
DESDEMONA. Worse and worse.
EMILIA. How if fair and foolish?   135
IAGO. She never yet was foolish that was fair.
   For even her folly[71] helped her to an heir.[72]
DESDEMONA. These are old fond[73] paradoxes to make fools
   laugh i' th' alehouse. What miserable praise hast thou for
   her that's foul[74] and foolish?   140
IAGO. There's none so foul and foolish thereunto.[75]
   But does foul[76] pranks which fair and wise ones do.
DESDEMONA. O heavy ignorance! Thou praisest the worst best.
   But what praise couldst thou bestow on a deserving
   woman indeed. one that. in the authority of her merit. did   145
   justly put on the vouch[77] of very malice itself?
IAGO. She that was ever fair. and never proud.
   Had tongue at will. and yet was never loud.
   Never lacked gold and yet went never gay.[78]
   Fled from her wish. and yet said. "Now I may."[79]   150
   She that being angered. her revenge being nigh.
   Bade her wrong stay[80] and her displeasure fly.
   She that in wisdom never was so frail
   To change the cod's head for the salmon's tail.[81]
   She that could think and ne'er disclose her mind.   155
   See suitors following and not look behind.
   She was a wight. if ever such wight were—
DESDEMONA. To do what?
IAGO. To suckle fools and chronicle small beer.[82]

67. If . . . it Her cleverness will make use of her beauty.   **68. black** dark-complex-
ioned. brunette.   **69. white** a fair person (with wordplay on "wight." a person).
70. fit with sexual suggestion of mating.   **71. folly** with added meaning of "lechery.
wantonness."   **72. an heir** to bear a child.   **73. fond** foolish.   **74. foul** ugly.
75. thereunto in addition.   **76. foul** sluttish.   **77. vouch** compel the approval.
78. gay extravagantly clothed.   **79. Fled . . . may** avoided temptation where the
choice was hers.   **80. Bade . . . stay** resolved to put up with her injury patiently.
81. To . . . tail to exchange a lackluster husband for a sexy lover(?) (*Cod's head* is
slang for "penis.")   **82. To . . . beer** to nurse babies and keep petty household accounts.

DESDEMONA. O most lame and impotent conclusion! Do not   160
learn of him, Emilia, though he be thy husband. How say
you, Cassio? Is he not a most profane and liberal[83] counselor?
CASSIO. He speaks home,[84] madam. You may relish[85] him
more in[86] the soldier than in the scholar.   165

[CASSIO *and* DESDEMONA *stand together, conversing intimately.*]

IAGO. [*aside*] He takes her by the palm. Ay, well said,[87] whisper. With as little a web as this will I ensnare as great a fly
as Cassio. Aye, smile upon her, do; I will gyve[88] thee in
thine own courtship.[89] You say true;[90] 'tis so, indeed. If
such tricks as these strip you out of your lieutenantry, it   170
had been better you had not kissed your three fingers so
oft, which now again you are most apt to play the sir[91] in.
Very good; well kissed! An excellent courtesy! 'Tis so, indeed. Yet again your fingers to your lips? Would they were
clyster pipes[92] for your sake! [*Trumpet within.*] The   175
Moor! I know his trumpet.
CASSIO. 'Tis truly so.
DESDEMONA.   Let's meet him and receive him.
CASSIO. Lo, where he comes!

[*Enter* OTHELLO *and attendants.*]

OTHELLO. O my fair warrior!
DESDEMONA.   My dear Othello!
OTHELLO. It gives me wonder great as my content   180
To see you here before me. O my soul's joy,
If after every tempest come such calms,
May the winds blow till they have weakened death,
And let the laboring bark climb hills of seas
Olympus-high, and duck again as low   185
As hell's from heaven! If it were now to die,
'Twere now to be most happy, for I fear

---

83. liberal ribald and licentious.   **84. home** right to the target (a term from fenc-
ing).   **85. relish** appreciate.   **86. in** in the character of.   **87. well said** well done.
88. gyve fetter, shackle.   **89. courtship** courtesy, show of courtly manners.
90. true that's right, go ahead.   **91. sir** the fine gentleman.   **92. clyster pipes**
tubes used for enemas and douches.

My soul hath her content so absolute
That not another comfort like to this
Succeeds in unknown fate.[93]   190
DESDEMONA.   The heavens forbid
But that our loves and comforts should increase
Even as our days do grow!
OTHELLO.   Amen to that, sweet powers!
I cannot speak enough of this content.
It stops me here: it is too much of joy.
And this, and this, the greatest discords be   195

[*They kiss.*][94]

That e'er our hearts shall make!
IAGO. [*aside*]   O, you are well tuned now!
But I'll set down[95] the pegs that make this music,
As honest as I am.[96]
OTHELLO.   Come, let us to the castle.
News, friends! Our wars are done, the Turks are drowned.
How does my old acquaintance of this isle?—   200
Honey, you shall be well desired[97] in Cyprus:
I have found great love amongst them. O my sweet,
I prattle out of fashion,[98] and I dote
In mine own comforts.—I prithee, good Iago,
Go to the bay and disembark my coffers.[99]   205
Bring thou the master[100] to the citadel:
He is a good one, and his worthiness
Does challenge[101] much respect.—Come, Desdemona.—
Once more, well met at Cyprus!

[*Exeunt* OTHELLO *and* DESDEMONA *and all but* IAGO *and* RODERIGO.]

IAGO. [*to an attendant*] Do thou meet me presently at the har-   210
bor. [*To* RODERIGO.] Come hither. If thou be'st valiant—as,
they say, base men[102] being in love have then a nobility in
their natures more than is native to them—list[103] me. The

---

93. Succeeds . . . fate can follow in the unknown future.   **94. [They kiss.]** The direction is from the Quarto.   **95. set down** loosen (and hence untune the instrument).   **96. As . . . am** for all my supposed honesty.   **97. well desired** welcomed.
98. out of fashion incoherently.   **99. coffers** chests.   **100. master** ship's captain.
101. challenge deserve.   **102. base men** even lowly born men.   **103. list** listen to.

Lieutenant tonight watches on the court of guard.[104] First.
I must tell thee this: Desdemona is directly in love with him.   215
RODERIGO. With him? Why, 'tis not possible.
IAGO. Lay thy finger thus,[105] and let thy soul be instructed.
Mark me with what violence she first loved the Moor, but[106]
for bragging and telling her fantastical lies. To love him
still for prating? Let not thy discreet heart think it. Her eye   220
must be fed; and what delight shall she have to look on the
devil? When the blood is made dull with the act of sport,[107]
there should be, again to inflame it and to give satiety a
fresh appetite, loveliness in favor,[108] sympathy[109] in years,   225
manners, and beauties—all which the Moor is defective in.
Now, for want of these required conveniences,[110] her delicate tenderness will find itself abused,[111] begin to heave
the gorge,[112] disrelish and abhor the Moor. Very nature[113]
will instruct her in it and compel her to some second choice.
Now, sir, this granted—as it is a most pregnant[114] and un-   230
forced position—who stands so eminent in the degree[115] of
this fortune as Cassio does? A knave very voluble,[116] no
further conscionable[117] than in putting on the mere form of
civil and humane[118] seeming for the better compassing of
his salt[119] and most hidden loose affection.[120] Why, none,   235
why, none. A slipper[121] and subtle knave, a finder out of
occasions, that has an eye can stamp[122] and counterfeit
advantages,[123] though true advantage never present itself:
a devilish knave. Besides, the knave is handsome, young,
and hath all those requisites in him that folly[124] and   240
green[125] minds look after. A pestilent complete knave, and
the woman hath found him[126] already.

---

104. court of guard guardhouse (Cassio is in charge of the watch.)   **105. thus** i.e.,
on your lips.   **106. but** only.   **107. act of sport** sex.   **108. favor** appearance.
109. sympathy correspondence, similarity.   **110. conveniences** things conducive
to sexual compatibility.   **111. abused** cheated, revolted.   **112. heave the gorge**
experience nausea.   **113. Very nature** her very instincts.   **114. pregnant** evident,
cogent.   **115. eminent . . . degree** as next in line for.   **116. voluble** facile, glib.
117. conscionable conscientious, conscience-bound.   **118. humane** polite, courteous.   **119. salt** licentious.   **120. affection** passion.   **121. slipper** slippery.
122. eye . . . stamp an eye that can coin, create.   **123. advantages** favorable op-
portunities.   **124. folly** wantonness. **125. green** immature.   **126. found him** sized
him up, perceived his intent.

RODERIGO. I cannot believe that in her. She's full of most blessed condition.[127]

IAGO. Blessed fig's end! The wine she drinks is made of grapes. 245 If she had been blessed, she would never have loved the Moor. Blessed pudding![128] Didst thou not see her paddle with the palm of his hand? Didst not mark that?

RODERIGO. Yes, that I did; but that was but courtesy.

IAGO. Lechery, by this hand. An index[129] and obscure prologue 250 to the history of lust and foul thoughts. They met so near with their lips that their breaths embraced together. Villainous thoughts, Roderigo! When these mutualities[130] so marshal the way, hard at hand[131] comes the master and main exercise, th' incorporate[132] conclusion. Pish! But, sir, 255 be you ruled by me. I have brought you from Venice. Watch you[133] tonight: for the command, I'll lay 't upon you.[134] Cassio knows you not. I'll not be far from you. Do you find some occasion to anger Cassio, either by speaking too loud, or tainting[135] his discipline, or from what other course you 260 please, which the time shall more favorably minister.[136]

RODERIGO. Well.

IAGO. Sir, he's rash and very sudden in choler,[137] and haply[138] may strike at you. Provoke him that he may, for even out of that will I cause these of Cyprus to mutiny,[139] whose quali- 265 fication[140] shall come into no true taste[141] again but by the displanting of Cassio. So shall you have a shorter journey to your desires by the means I shall then have to prefer[142] them, and the impediment most profitably removed, without the which there were no expectation of our prosperity. 270

RODERIGO. I will do this, if you can bring it to any opportunity.

IAGO. I warrant[143] thee. Meet me by and by[144] at the citadel. I must fetch his necessaries ashore. Farewell.

RODERIGO. Adieu.   [Exit.]

---

127. condition disposition.   **128. pudding** sausage.   **129. index** table of contents.
130. mutualities exchanges, intimacies.   **131. hard at hand** closely following.
132. incorporate carnal.   **133. Watch you** stand watch.   **134. I'll lay't . . . you**
I'll arrange for you to be appointed, given orders.   **135. tainting** disparaging.
136. minister provide.   **137. choler** wrath.   **138. haply** perhaps.   **139. mutiny**
riot.   **140. qualification** appeasement.   **141. true taste** acceptable state.
142. prefer advance.**143. warrant** assure.   **144. by and by** immediately.

IAGO. That Cassio loves her, I do well believe 't;   275
That she loves him, 'tis apt[145] and of great credit.[146]
The Moor, howbeit that I endure him not,
Is of a constant, loving, noble nature,
And I dare think he'll prove to Desdemona
A most dear husband. Now, I do love her too,   280
Not out of absolute lust—though peradventure
I stand accountant[147] for as great a sin—
But partly led to diet[148] my revenge
For that I do suspect the lusty Moor
Hath leaped into my seat, the thought whereof   285
Doth, like a poisonous mineral, gnaw my innards:
And nothing can or shall content my soul
Till I am evened with him, wife for wife,
Or failing so, yet that I put the Moor
At least into a jealousy so strong   290
That judgment cannot cure. Which thing to do,
If this poor trash of Venice, whom I trace[149]
For[150] his quick hunting, stand[151] the putting on,
I'll have our Michael Cassio on the hip.[152]
Abuse[153] him to the Moor in the rank garb[154]   295
For I fear Cassio with my nightcap[155] too—
Make the Moor thank me, love me, and reward me
For making him egregiously an ass
And practicing upon[156] his peace and quiet
Even to madness. 'Tis here, but yet confused,   300
Knavery's plain face is never seen till used.   *[Exit.]*

SCENE 2

[Location: Cyprus. A street. Enter Othello's HERALD *with a proclamation.]*

---

145. apt probable. **146. credit** credibility. **147. accountant** accountable. **148. diet** feed. **149. trace** train, or follow (?), or perhaps trash, a hunting term, meaning to put weights on a hunting dog to slow him down. **150. For** to make more eager. **151. stand** respond properly when I incite him to quarrel. **152. on the hip** at my mercy, where I can throw him (a wrestling term). **153. Abuse** slander. **154. rank garb** coarse manner. **155. nightcap** as a rival in my bed, as one who gives me cuckold's horns. **156. practicing upon** plotting against.

HERALD. It is Othello's pleasure. our noble and valiant general.
that. upon certain tidings now arrived. importing the mere
perdition[1] of the Turkish fleet. every man put himself into
triumph:[2] some to dance. some to make bonfires. each man
to what sport and revels his addiction[3] leads him. For. be-   5
sides these beneficial news. it is the celebration of his nuptial. So much was his pleasure should be proclaimed. All offices[4] are open. and there is full liberty of feasting from this
present hour of five till the bell have told eleven. Heaven
bless the isle of Cyprus and our noble general Othello!   10

[Exit.]

SCENE 3

[Location: Cyprus. The citadel. Enter OTHELLO. DESDEMONA.
CASSIO. *and attendants.]*

OTHELLO. Good Michael. look you to the guard tonight.
Let's teach ourselves that honorable stop[1]
Not to outsport[2] discretion.
CASSIO. Iago hath direction what to do.
But notwithstanding. with my personal eye   5
Will I look to 't.
OTHELLO.   Iago is most honest.
Michael. good night. Tomorrow with your earliest[3]
Let me have speech with you. [*To* DESDEMONA.] Come. my
dear love.
The purchase made. the fruits are to ensue:
That profit's yet to come 'tween me and you.[4]   10
Good night.

[*Exit* OTHELLO. *with* DESDEMONA *and attendants.*]

[*Enter* IAGO.]

CASSIO. Welcome. Iago. We must to the watch.

---

1. perdition complete destruction.   **2. triumph** public celebration.   **3. addiction**
inclination.   **4. offices** rooms where food and drink are kept.   **1. stop** restraint.
2. outsport celebrate beyond.   **3. with . . . earliest** at your earliest convenience.
4. That . . . you Though married. we haven't yet consummated our love.

IAGO. Not this hour.[5] Lieutenant: 'tis not yet ten o' the clock.
Our general cast[6] us thus early for the love of his Desdemona: who[7] let us not therefore blame. He hath not yet   15
made wanton the night with her, and she is sport for Jove.

CASSIO. She's a most exquisite lady.

IAGO. And, I'll warrant her, full of game.

CASSIO. Indeed, she's a most fresh and delicate creature.

IAGO. What an eye she has! Methinks it sounds a parley[8] to   20
provocation.

CASSIO. An inviting eye, and yet methinks right modest.

IAGO. And when she speaks, is it not an alarum[9] to love?

CASSIO. She is indeed perfection.

IAGO. Well, happiness to their sheets! Come, Lieutenant, I have
a stoup[10] of wine, and here without[11] are a brace[12] of   25
Cyprus gallants that would fain have a measure[13] to the
health of black Othello.

CASSIO. Not tonight, good Iago. I have very poor and unhappy
brains for drinking. I could well wish courtesy would invent
some other custom of entertainment.   30

IAGO. O, they are our friends. But one cup! I'll drink for you.[14]

CASSIO. I have drunk but one cup tonight, and that was craftily
qualified[15] too, and behold what innovation[16] it makes
here.[17] I am unfortunate in the infirmity and dare not task
my weakness with any more.   35

IAGO. What, man? 'Tis a night of revels. The gallants desire it.

CASSIO. Where are they?

IAGO. Here at the door. I pray you, call them in.

CASSIO. I'll do't, but it dislikes me.[18]   [*Exit.*]

IAGO. If I can fasten but one cup upon him,   40
With that which he hath drunk tonight already,
He'll be as full of quarrel and offense[19]

---

5. Not ... hour not for an hour yet. **6. cast** dismissed. **7. who** Othello.
8. parley calls for a conference, issues an invitation. **9. alarum** signal calling men
to arms (continuing the military metaphor of *parley*, line 20). **10. stoup** measure
of liquor, two quarts. **11. without** outside. **12. brace** pair. **13. have a measure**
gladly drink a toast. **14. I'll ... you** in your place. (Iago will do the steady drinking to keep the gallants company while Cassio has only one cup.) **15. qualified** di-
luted. **16. innovation** disturbance, insurrection. **17. here** i.e. in my head.
18. dislikes me I'm reluctant. **19. offense** readiness to take offense.

As my young mistress' dog. Now. my sick fool Roderigo.
Whom love hath turned almost the wrong side out.
To Desdemona hath tonight caroused[20]   45
Potations pottle-deep:[21] and he's to watch.[22]
Three lads of Cyprus—noble swelling[23] spirits.
That hold their honors in a wary distance.[24]
The very elements[25] of this warlike isle—
Have I tonight flustered with flowing cups.   50
And they watch[26] too. Now. 'mongst this flock of drunkards
Am I to put our Cassio in some action
That may offend the isle.—But here they come.

[*Enter* CASSIO. MONTANO. *and gentlemen: servants following
with wine.*]

If consequence do but approve my dream.[27]
My boat sails freely both with wind and stream.[28]   55
CASSIO. 'Fore God. they have given me a rouse[29] already.
MONTANA. Good faith. a little one: not past a pint. as I am a soldier.
IAGO. Some wine. ho!
    [*He sings.*] "And let me the cannikin[30] clink. clink.
And let me the cannikin clink.   60
A soldier's a man.
O. man's life's but a span:[31]
Why. then. let a soldier drink."

    Some wine. boys!
CASSIO. 'Fore God. an excellent song.   65
IAGO. I learned it in England. where indeed they are most potent
    in potting.[32] Your Dane. your German. and your swag-bel-
    lied Hollander—drink. ho!—are nothing to your English.
CASSIO. Is your Englishman so exquisite in his drinking?

---

20. caroused drunk off. **21. pottle-deep** to the bottom of the tankard. **22. to
watch** stand watch. **23. swelling** proud. **24. wary distance** are extremely sensitive of their honor. **25. elements** typical sort. **26. watch** are on guard. **27. If . . .
dream** if subsequent events will only substantiate my scheme. **28. stream** current.
29. rouse large drink. **30. cannikin** cup. **31. span** brief span of time. (Cf. Psalm
39.5 as rendered in the Book of Common Prayer: "Thou hast made my days as it
were a span long.") **32. potting** drinking.

IAGO. Why, he drinks you,[33] with facility, your Dane dead   70
drunk: he sweats not[34] to overthrow your Almain:[35] he gives
your Hollander a vomit ere the next pottle can be filled.
CASSIO. To the health of our general!
MONTANO. I am for it, Lieutenant, and I'll do you justice.[36]
IAGO. O sweet England! [*He sings.*]   75

"King Stephen was and-a worthy peer,
His breeches cost him but a crown:
He held them sixpence all too dear,
With that he called the tailor lown.[37]

He was a wight of high renown,   80
And thou art but of low degree.
'Tis pride[38] that pulls the country down:
Then take thy auld[39] cloak about thee."

Some wine, ho!
CASSIO. 'Fore God, this is a more exquisite song than the other.   85
IAGO. Will you hear 't again?
CASSIO. No, for I hold him to be unworthy of his place that does
those things. Well, God's above all: and there be souls must
be saved, and there be souls must not be saved.
IAGO. It's true, good Lieutenant.   90
CASSIO. For mine own part—no offense to the General, nor any
man of quality[40]—I hope to be saved.
IAGO. And so do I too, Lieutenant.
CASSIO. Ay, but, by your leave, not before me: the lieutenant is
to be saved before the ancient. Let's have no more of this: 95
let's to our affairs.—God forgive us our sins!—Gentlemen,
let's look to our business. Do not think gentlemen, I am
drunk. This is my ancient: this is my right hand, and this is
my left. I am not drunk now. I can stand well enough, and
speak well enough.   100
GENTLEMEN. Excellent well.
CASSIO. Why, very well then: you must not think then that I am
drunk.   [*Exit.*]

---

33. **drinks you** drinks.   34. **sweats not** need not exert himself.   35. **Almain** German.   36. **I'll . . . justice** I'll drink as much as you.   37. **lown** lout.   38. **pride** extravagance in dress.   39. **auld** old.   40. **quality** rank.

MONTANO. To th' platform. masters. Come. let's set the watch.[41]

[*Exeunt* GENTLEMEN.]

IAGO. You see this fellow that is gone before.
He's a soldier fit to stand by Caesar   105
And give direction: and do but see his vice.
'Tis to his virtue a just equinox.[42]
The one as long as th' other. 'Tis pity of him.
I fear the trust Othello puts him in.
On some odd time of his infirmity.   110
Will shake this island.
MONTANO.   But is he often thus?
IAGO. 'Tis evermore the prologue to his sleep.
He'll watch the horologe a double set.[43]
If drink rock not his cradle.
MONTANO.   It were well
The General were put in mind of it.   115
Perhaps he sees it not. or his good nature
Prizes the virtue that appears in Cassio
And looks not on his evils. Is not this true?

[*Enter* RODERIGO.]

IAGO. [*aside to him*] How now. Roderigo?
I pray you. after the Lieutenant: go.   [*Exit* RODERIGO.]
MONTANO. And 'tis great pity that the noble Moor
Should hazard such a place as his own second
With[44] one of an engraffed[45] infirmity.
It were an honest action to say so
To the Moor.   125
IAGO.   Not I. for this fair island.
I do love Cassio well and would do much
To cure him of this evil. [*Cry within:* "Help! Help!"]
But. hark! What noise?

[*Enter* CASSIO. *pursuing* RODERIGO.][46]

---

41. set . . . watch mount the guard.   **42. equinox** exact counterpart. (*Equinox* is an equal length of days and nights.)   **43. watch . . . set** stay awake twice around the clock or *horologe*.   **44. With** risk giving such an important position as his second in command to.   **45. engraffed** inveterate.   **46. [Enter . . . Roderigo.]** the Quarto text reads. "driving in."

CASSIO. Zounds, you rogue! You rascal!

MONTANO. What's the matter, Lieutenant?

CASSIO. A knave teach me my duty? I'll beat the knave into a   130
twiggen[47] bottle.

RODERIGO. Beat me?

CASSIO. Dost thou prate, rogue? [*He strikes* RODERIGO.]

MONTANO. Nay, good Lieutenant. [*Restraining him.*] I pray you,
sir, hold your hand.

CASSIO. Let me go, sir, or I'll knock you o'er the mazard.[48]

MONTANO. Come, come, you're drunk.   135

CASSIO. Drunk? [*They fight.*]

IAGO. [*aside to* RODERIGO] Away, I say, Go out and cry a mutiny.[49]

[*Exit* RODERIGO.]

Nay, good Lieutenant—God's will, gentlemen—
Help, ho!—Lieutenant—sir—Montano—sir—
Help, masters![50]—Here's a goodly watch indeed   140

[*A bell rings.*][51]

Who's that which rings the bell?—Diablo,[52] ho!
The town will rise.[53] God's will, Lieutenant, hold!
You'll be ashamed forever.

[*Enter* OTHELLO *and attendants with weapons.*]

OTHELLO. What is the matter here?

MONTANO.   Zounds, I bleed still.
I am hurt to th' death. He dies! [*He thrusts at* CASSIO.]   145

OTHELLO.   Hold, for your lives!

IAGO. Hold, ho! Lieutenant—sir—Montano—gentlemen—
Have you forgot all sense of place and duty?
Hold! The General speaks to you. Hold, for shame!

OTHELLO. Why, how now, ho! From whence ariseth this?   150
Are we turned Turks, and to ourselves do that

---

47. twiggen wicker-covered. (Cassio vows to assail Roderigo until his skin resembles wickerwork or until he has driven Roderigo through the holes in a wickerwork.) **48. mazard** head (literally, a drinking vessel). **49. mutiny** riot. **50. masters** sirs. **51. [A . . . rings.]** This direction is from the Quarto, as are *Exit Roderigo* at line 137, *They fight* at line 136, and *with weapons* at line 143. **52. Diablo** the devil. **53. rise** grow riotous

Which heaven hath forbid the Ottomites?[54]
For Christian shame, put by this barbarous brawl!
He that stirs next to carve for[55] his own rage
Holds his soul light:[56] he dies upon his motion.[57]
Silence that dreadful bell. It frights the isle   155
From her propriety.[58] What is the matter, masters?
Honest Iago, that looks dead with grieving,
Speak. Who began this? On thy love, I charge thee.

IAGO. I do not know. Friends all but now, even now,
In quarter[59] and in terms[60] like bride and groom   160
Devesting them[61] for bed; and then, but now—
As if some planet had unwitted men—
Swords out, and tilting one at others' breasts
In opposition bloody. I cannot speak[62]
Any beginning to this peevish odds;[63]   165
And would in action glorious I had lost
Those legs that brought me to a part of it!

OTHELLO. How comes it, Michael, you are thus forgot?[64]

CASSIO. I pray you, pardon me. I cannot speak.

OTHELLO. Worthy Montano, you were wont[65] be civil;   170
The gravity and stillness[66] of your youth
The world hath noted, and your name is great
In mouths of wisest censure.[67] What's the matter
That you unlace[68] your reputation thus
And spend your rich opinion[69] for the name   175
Of a night-brawler? Give me answer to it.

MONTANO. Worthy Othello, I am hurt to danger.
Your officer, Iago, can inform you—
While I spare speech, which something[70] now offends[71]
    me—

---

54. Are ... Ottomites inflict on ourselves the harm that heaven has prevented the Turks from doing (by destroying their fleet). **55. carve for** indulge, satisfy with his sword. **56. Holds ... light** places little value on his life. **57. motion** if he moves. **58. propriety** proper state. **59. In quarter** in friendly conduct, within bounds. **60. in terms** on good terms. **61. Devesting them** undressing. **62. speak** explain. **63. odds** quarrel. **64. forgot** have forgotten yourself thus. **65. wont** accustomed to be. **66. stillness** sobriety. **67. censure** judgment. **68. unlace** undo, lay open (as one might loose the strings of a purse containing reputation). **69. opinion** reputation. **70. something** somewhat. **71. offends** pains.

Of all that I do know; nor know I aught   180
By me that's said or done amiss this night,
Unless self-charity be sometimes a vice,
And to defend ourselves it be a sin
When violence assails us.
OTHELLO.   Now, by heaven,
My blood[72] begins my safer guides[73] to rule,   185
And passion, having my best judgment collied,[74]
Essays[75] to lead the way. Zounds, if I stir,
Or do but lift this arm, the best of you
Shall sink in my rebuke. Give me to know
How this foul rout[76] began, who set it on;   190
And he that is approved in[77] this offense,
Though he had twinned with me, both at a birth,
Shall lose me. What? In a town of[78] war
Yet wild, the people's hearts brim full of fear,
To manage[79] private and domestic quarrel?   195
In night, and on the court and guard of safety?[80]
'Tis monstrous. Iago, who began 't?
MONTANO. [*to* IAGO] If partially affined,[81] or leagued in office,[82]
Thou dost deliver more or less than truth,
Thou art no soldier.   200
IAGO.   Touch me not so near.
I had rather have this tongue cut from my mouth
Than it should do offense to Michael Cassio:
Yet, I persuade myself, to speak the truth
Shall nothing wrong him. Thus it is, General.
Montano and myself being in speech,   205
There comes a fellow crying out for help,
And Cassio following him with determined sword
To execute[83] upon him. Sir, this gentleman [*indicating*
      MONTANO.]
Steps in to Cassio and entreats his pause.[84]

---

72. blood passion (of anger). **73. guides** i.e., reason. **74. collied** darkened.
75. Essays undertakes. **76. rout** riot. **77. approved in** found guilty of. **78. town
of** town garrisoned for. **79. manage** undertake. **80. In . . . safety** at the main
guardhouse or headquarters and on watch. **81. partially affined** made partial by
some personal relationship. **82. leagued in office** in league as fellow officers.
83. execute give effect to (his anger). **84. pause** him to stop.

Myself the crying fellow did pursue.   210
Lest by his clamor—as it so fell out—
The town might fall in fright. He. swift of foot.
Outran my purpose. and I returned. the rather[85]
For that I heard the clink and fall of swords
And Cassio high in oath. which till tonight   215
I ne'er might say before. When I came back—
For this was brief—I found them close together
At blow and thrust. even as again they were
When you yourself did part them.
More of this matter cannot I report.   220
But men are men: the best sometimes forget.[86]
Though Cassio did some little wrong to him.
As men in rage strike those that wish them best.[87]
Yet surely Cassio. I believe. received
From him that fled some strange indignity.   225
Which patience could not pass.[88]

OTHELLO.   I know. Iago.
Thy honesty and love doth mince this matter.
Making it light to Cassio. Cassio. I love thee.
But nevermore be officer of mine.

[*Enter* DESDEMONA. *attended.*]

Look if my gentle love be not raised up.   230
I'll make thee an example.

DESDEMONA. What is the matter. dear?

OTHELLO.   All's well now. sweeting:
Come away to bed. [*To* MONTANO.] Sir. for your hurts.
Myself will be your surgeon.[89]—Lead him off.

[MONTANO *is led off.*]

Iago. look with care about the town   235
And silence those whom this vile brawl distracted.
Come. Desdemona. 'Tis the soldiers' life
To have their balmy slumbers waked with strife.

---

85. rather sooner. **86. forget** forget themselves. **87. those . . . best** even those who are well disposed. **88. pass** overlook. **89. surgeon** make sure you receive medical attention.

[*Exit with all but* IAGO *and* CASSIO.]

IAGO. What, are you hurt, Lieutenant?

CASSIO. Ay, past all surgery.   240

IAGO. Marry, God forbid!

CASSIO. Reputation, reputation, reputation! O, I have lost my
reputation! I have lost the immortal part of myself, and
what remains is bestial. My reputation, Iago, my reputation!

IAGO. As I am an honest man, I thought you had received some   245
bodily wound; there is more sense in that than in reputation. Reputation is an idle and most false imposition,[90] oft
got without merit and lost without deserving. You have lost
no reputation at all, unless you repute yourself such a
loser. What, man, there are more ways to recover[91] the   250
General again. You are but now cast in his mood[92]—a
punishment more in policy[93] than in malice, even so as one
would beat his offenseless dog to affright an imperious
lion.[94] Sue[95] to him again and he's yours.

CASSIO. I will rather sue to be despised than to deceive so good   255
a commander with so slight,[96] so drunken, and so indis-
creet an officer. Drunk? And speak parrot?[97] And squab-
ble? Swagger? Swear? And discourse fustian with one's
own shadow? O thou invisible spirit of wine, if thou hast
no name to be known by, let us call thee devil!   260

IAGO. What was he that you followed with your sword? What
had he done to you?

CASSIO. I know not.

IAGO. Is 't possible?

CASSIO. I remember a mass of things, but nothing distinctly: a   265
quarrel, but nothing wherefore.[98] O God, that men should
put an enemy in their mouths to steal away their brains!
That we should, with joy, pleasance, revel, and applause[99]
transform ourselves into beasts!

---

90. imposition thing artificially imposed and of no real value.   **91. recover** regain
favor with.   **92. cast . . . mood** dismissed in a moment of anger.   **93. in policy**
done for expediency's sake and as a public gesture.   **94. beat . . . lion** would make
an example of a minor offender to deter more important and dangerous offenders.
95. Sue petition.   **96. slight** worthless.   **97. speak parrot** talk nonsense, rant.
(*Discourse fustian*, in the next line, has much the same meaning.)   **98. wherefore**
why.   **99. applause** desire for applause.

IAGO. Why, but you are now well enough. How came you thus   270
recovered?

CASSIO. It hath pleased the devil drunkenness to give place to
the devil wrath. One unperfectness shows me another, to
make me frankly despise myself.

IAGO. Come, you are too severe a moraler.[100] As the time, the   275
place, and the condition of this country stands, I could
heartily wish this had not befallen; but since it is as it is,
mend it for your own good.

CASSIO. I will ask him for my place again; he shall tell me I am
a drunkard. Had I as many mouths as Hydra,[101] such an   280
answer would stop them all. To be now a sensible man, by
and by a fool, and presently a beast! O, strange! Every inordinate cup is unblessed, and the ingredient is a devil.

IAGO. Come, come, good wine is a good familiar creature, if it
be well used. Exclaim no more against it. And, good Lieu-   285
tenant, I think you think I love you.

CASSIO. I have well approved[102] it, sir. I drunk!

IAGO. You or any man living may be drunk at a time,[103] man.
I'll tell you what you shall do. Our general's wife is now the
general—I may say so in this respect, for that[104] he hath   290
devoted and given up himself to the contemplation, mark,
and denotement[105] of her parts[106] and graces. Confess
yourself freely to her; importune her help to put you in
your place again. She is of so free,[107] so kind, so apt, so
blessed a disposition, she holds it a vice in her goodness   295
not to do more than she is requested. This broken joint between you and her husband entreat her to splinter;[108] and,
my fortunes against any lay[109] worth naming, this crack of
your love shall grow stronger than it was before.

CASSIO. You advise me well.   300

IAGO. I protest,[110] in the sincerity of love and honest kindness.

---

100. moraler moralizer.   **101. Hydra** the Lernaean Hydra, a monster with many
heads and the ability to grow two heads when one was cut off, slain by Hercules as
the second of his twelve labors.   **102. approved** proved.   **103. at a time** at one
time or another.   **104. for that** in view of this fact, that.   **105. mark . . . denotement** both words mean "observation."   **106. parts** qualities.   **107. free** generous.
108. splinter bind with splints.   **109. lay** stake, wager.   **110. protest** insist, declare.

CASSIO. I think it freely;[111] and betimes in the morning I will
　beseech the virtuous Desdemona to undertake for me. I am
　desperate of my fortunes if they check[112] me here.
IAGO. You are in the right. Good night, Lieutenant. I must to　305
　the watch.
CASSIO. Good night, honest Iago.　　　　　　　　　[*Exit* CASSIO.]
IAGO. And what's he then that says I play the villain,
　When this advice is free[113] I give, and honest,
　Probal[114] to thinking, and indeed the course　　　　　310
　To win the Moor again? For 'tis most easy
　Th' inclining[115] Desdemona to subdue[116]
　In any honest suit; she's framed as fruitful[117]
　As the free elements.[118] And then for her
　To win the Moor—were 't to renounce his baptism,　315
　All seals and symbols of redeemèd sin—
　His soul is so enfettered to her love
　That she may make, unmake, do what she list,
　Even as her appetite[119] shall play the god
　With his weak function.[120] How am I then a villain,　320
　To counsel Cassio to this parallel[121] course
　Directly to his good? Divinity of hell![122]
　When devils will the blackest sins put on,[123]
　They do suggest[124] at first with heavenly shows,
　As I do now. For whiles this honest fool　　　　325
　Plies Desdemona to repair his fortune,
　And she for him pleads strongly to the Moor,
　I'll pour this pestilence into his ear,
　That she repeals him[125] for her body's lust;
　And by how much she strives to do him good,　330
　She shall undo her credit with the Moor.
　So will I turn her virtue into pitch,[126]

---

111. freely unreservedly.　**112. check** repulse.　**113. free** free from guile. Also, freely given.　**114. Probal** reasonable.　**115. inclining** willing.　**116. subdue** persuade.　**117. framed . . . fruitful** created as generous.　**118. elements** i.e., earth, air, fire, and water, unrestrained and spontaneous.　**119. appetite** her desire, or, perhaps, his desire for her.　**120. weak function** exercise of faculties (weakened by his fondness for her.)　**121. parallel** corresponding to these facts and to his best interests.　**122. Divinity . . . hell!** inverted theology of hell (which seduces the soul to its damnation).　**123. put on** instigate.　**124. suggest** tempt.　**125. repeals him** attempts to get him restored.　**126. pitch** foul blackness. Also a snaring substance.

And out of her own goodness make the net
That shall enmesh them all.

[*Enter* RODERIGO.]

How now, Roderigo?

RODERIGO. I do follow here in the chase, not like a hound that   335
hunts, but one that fills up the cry.[127] My money is almost
spent; I have been tonight exceedingly well cudgeled; and I
think the issue will be I shall have so much[128] experience
for my pains, and so, with no money at all and a little more
wit, return again to Venice.   340

IAGO. How poor are they that have not patience!
What wound did ever heal but by degrees?
Thou know'st we work by wit, and not by witchcraft,
And wit depends on dilatory time.
Does 't not go well? Cassio hath beaten thee,   345
And thou, by that small hurt, hast cashiered[129] Cassio.
Though other things grow fair against the sun,
Yet fruits that blossom first will first be ripe.[130]
Content thyself awhile. By the Mass, 'tis morning!
Pleasure and action make the hours seem short.   350
Retire thee: go where thou art billeted.
Away, I say! Thou shalt know more hereafter.
Nay, get thee gone.   [*Exit* RODERIGO.]
Two things are to be done.
My wife must move[131] for Cassio to her mistress: 355
I'll set her on;
Myself the while to draw the Moor apart
And bring him jump[132] when he may Cassio find
Soliciting his wife. Ay, that's the way.
Dull not device[133] by coldness[134] and delay.   [*Exit.*]

ACT 3
SCENE 1

[*Location: Before the chamber of* OTHELLO *and* DESDEMONA.
Enter CASSIO *and* MUSICIANS.]

127. fills . . . cry merely takes part as one of the pack.   128. so much just so much
and no more.   129. cashiered dismissed.   130. Yet . . . ripe Plans that are well
prepared and set expeditiously in motion will sooner ripen into success.   131. move
plead.   132. jump precisely.   133. device plot.   134. coldness lack of zeal.

CASSIO. Masters, play here—I will content your pains[1]—
    Something that's brief, and bid "Good morrow, General."
      [*They play.*]

    [*Enter* CLOWN.]

CLOWN. Why, masters, have your instruments been in Naples,
    that they speak i' the nose[2] thus?
A MUSICIAN. How, sir, how?   5
CLOWN. Are these, I pray you, wind instruments?
A MUSICIAN. Ay, marry, are they, sir.
CLOWN. O, thereby hangs a tail.
A MUSICIAN. Whereby hangs a tale, sir?
CLOWN. Marry, sir, by many a wind instrument[3] that I know.   10
    But, masters, here's money for you. [*He gives money.*] And
    the General so likes your music that he desires you, for
    love's sake,[4] to make no more noise with it.
A MUSICIAN. Well, sir, we will not.
CLOWN. If you have any music that may not[5] be heard, to 't   15
    again; but, as they say, to hear music the General does not
    greatly care.
A MUSICIAN. We have none such, sir.
CLOWN. Then put up your pipes in your bag, for I'll away.[6] Go,
    vanish into air, away!   [*Exeunt* MUSICIANS.]
CASSIO. Dost thou hear, mine honest friend?
CLOWN. No, I hear not your honest friend; I hear you.
CASSIO. Prithee, keep up[7] thy quillets.[8] There's a poor piece of
    gold for thee. [*He gives money.*] If the gentlewoman that at-
    tends the General's wife be stirring, tell her there's one Cas-   25
    sio entreats her a little favor of speech.[9] Wilt thou do this?
CLOWN. She is stirring, sir. If she will stir[10] hither, I shall seem[11]
    to notify unto her.

---

1. **content ... pains** reward your efforts. 2. **speak ... nose** sound nasal. Also
sound like one whose nose has been attacked by syphilis. (Naples was popularly supposed to have a high incidence of venereal disease.) 3. **Whereby ... instrument**
with a joke on flatulence. The *tail* that hangs nearby the *wind instrument* suggests
the penis. 4. **for love's sake** out of friendship and affection. Also, for the sake of
lovemaking in Othello's marriage. 5. **may not** cannot. 6. **I'll away** (possibly a
misprint, or a snatch of song?). 7. **keep up** do not bring out. 8. **quillets** quibbles,
puns. 9. **favor of speech** the favor of a brief talk. 10. **stir** bestir herself (with a
play on stirring, "rousing herself from rest"). 11. **seem** deem it good, think fit.

CASSIO. Do. good my friend.   [*Exit* CLOWN.]

  [*Enter* IAGO.]

                    In happy time.[12] Iago.
IAGO. You have not been abed. then?   30
CASSIO. Why. no. The day had broke
  Before we parted. I have made bold. Iago.
  To send in to your wife. My suit to her
  Is that she will to virtuous Desdemona
  Procure me some access.   35
IAGO. I'll send her to you presently:
  And I'll devise a means to draw the Moor
  Out of the way. that your converse and business
  May be more free.
CASSIO. I humbly thank you for 't.   [*Exit* IAGO.]
                    I never knew
  A Florentine[13] more kind and honest.

  [*Enter* EMILIA.]

EMILIA. Good morrow. good Lieutenant. I am sorry
  For your displeasure:[14] but all will sure be well.
  The General and his wife are talking of it.
  And she speaks for you stoutly.[15] The Moor replies   45
  That he you hurt is of great fame[16] in Cyprus
  And great affinity.[17] and that in wholesome wisdom
  He might not but refuse you: but he protests[18] he loves you
  And needs no other suitor but his likings
  To take the safest occasion by the front[19]   50
  To bring you in again.
CASSIO.   Yet I beseech you.
  If you think fit. or that it may be done.
  Give me advantage of some brief discourse
  With Desdemon alone.
EMILIA.   Pray you. come in.

---

12. In happy time well met.   **13. Florentine** i.e. even a fellow Florentine. (Iago is a Venetian: Cassio is a Florentine.)   **14. displeasure** fall from favor.   **15. stoutly** spiritedly.   **16. fame** importance.   **17. affinity** family connection.   **18. protests** insists.   **19. To . . . front** opportunity by the forelock.

I will bestow you where you shall have time   55
To speak your bosom[20] freely.
CASSIO. I am much bound to you.   [*Exeunt.*]

SCENE 2

[*Location: The citadel. Enter* OTHELLO, IAGO, *and* GENTLEMEN.]

OTHELLO. [*giving letters*] These letters give, Iago, to the pilot,
And by him do my duties[1] to the Senate.
That done, I will be walking on the works:[2]
Repair[3] there to me.
IAGO.   Well, my good lord, I'll do 't.
OTHELLO. This fortification, gentlemen, shall we see 't?   5
GENTLEMEN. We'll wait upon[4] your lordship.   [*Exeunt.*]

SCENE 3

[*Location: The garden of the citadel. Enter* DESDEMONA, CASSIO,
and EMILIA.]

DESDEMONA. Be thou assured, good Cassio, I will do
All my abilities in thy behalf.
EMILIA. Good madam, do. I warrant it grieves my husband
As if the cause were his.
DESDEMONA. O, that's an honest fellow. Do not doubt, Cassio,   5
But I will have my lord and you again
As friendly as you were.
CASSIO.   Bounteous madam,
Whatever shall become of Michael Cassio,
He's never anything but your true servant.
DESDEMONA. I know 't. I thank you. You do love my lord;   10
You have known him long, and be you well assured
He shall in strangeness[1] stand no farther off
Than in a politic[2] distance.
CASSIO.   Ay, but, lady,

---

20. bosom thoughts. **1. duties** give my respects. **2. works** fortifications.
3. Repair return. **4. wait upon** attend. **1. strangeness** aloofness. **2. politic** required by wise policy.

That policy may either last so long.
Or feed upon such nice and waterish diet.[3]   15
Or breed itself so out of circumstance.[4]
That, I being absent and my place supplied.[5]
My general will forget my love and service.
DESDEMONA. Do not doubt[6] that. Before Emilia here
I give thee warrant[7] of thy place. Assure thee.   20
If I do vow a friendship I'll perform it
To the last article. My lord shall never rest.
I'll watch him tame[8] and talk him out of patience:[9]
His bed shall seem a school, his board[10] a shrift:[11]
I'll intermingle everything he does   25
With Cassio's suit. Therefore be merry, Cassio.
For thy solicitor[12] shall rather die
Than give thy cause away.[13]

[*Enter* OTHELLO *and* IAGO *at a distance*].

EMILIA. Madam, here comes my lord.
CASSIO. Madam, I'll take my leave.   30
DESDEMONA. Why, stay, and hear me speak.
CASSIO. Madam, not now. I am very ill at ease.
Unfit for mine own purposes.
DESDEMONA. Well, do your discretion.[14]   [*Exit* CASSIO.]
IAGO. Ha? I like not that.   35
OTHELLO.   What dost thou say?
IAGO. Nothing, my lord; or if—I know not what.
OTHELLO. Was not that Cassio parted from my wife?
Iago. Cassio, my lord? No, sure. I cannot think it.
That he would steal away so guiltylike.
Seeing you coming.   40
OTHELLO.   I do believe 'twas he.
DESDEMONA. How now, my lord?

---

3. **Or . . . diet** or sustain itself at length upon such trivial and meager technicalities.
4. **Or . . . circumstance** continually renew itself so out of chance events, or yield so
few chances for my being pardoned. 5. **supplied** filled by another person.
6. **doubt** fear. 7. **warrant** guarantee. 8. **I'll . . . tame** tame him by keeping him
from sleeping (a term from falconry). 9. **out of patience** past his endurance.
10. **board** table. 11. **shrift** confessional. 12. **solicitor** advocate. 13. **away** up.
14. **do your discretion** act according to your own discretion.

I have been talking with a suitor here,
A man that languishes in your displeasure.
OTHELLO. Who is 't you mean?
DESDEMONA. Why, your lieutenant, Cassio. Good my lord,   45
    If I have any grace or power to move you,
    His present reconciliation take.[15]
    For if he be not one that truly loves you,
    That errs in ignorance and not in cunning.[16]
    I have no judgment in an honest face.   50
    I prithee, call him back.
OTHELLO.   Went he hence now?
DESDEMONA. Yes, faith, so humbled
    That he hath left part of his grief with me
    To suffer with him. Good love, call him back.
OTHELLO. Not now, sweet Desdemon. Some other time.   55
DESDEMONA. But shall 't be shortly?
OTHELLO.   The sooner, sweet, for you.
DESDEMONA. Shall 't be tonight at supper?
OTHELLO.   No, not tonight.
DESDEMONA. Tomorrow dinner,[17] then?
OTHELLO.   I shall not dine at home.
    I meet the captains at the citadel.
DESDEMONA.
    Why, then, tomorrow night, or Tuesday morn.   60
    On Tuesday noon, or night, on Wednesday morn.
    I prithee, name the time, but let it not
    Exceed three days. In faith, he's penitent;
    And yet his trespass, in our common reason[18]—
    Save that, they say, the wars must make example   65
    Out of her best[19]—is not almost[20] a fault
    T' incur a private check.[21] When shall he come?
    Tell me, Othello. I wonder in my soul
    What you would ask me that I should deny,

---

15. **His . . . take** Let him be reconciled to you right away.   16. **in cunning** wittingly.   17. **dinner** noontime.   18. **reason** judgments.   19. **Save . . . best** were it not that, as the saying goes, military discipline requires making an example of the very best men. (*Her* refers to *wars* as a singular concept.)   20. **almost** scarcely.   21. **private check** even a private reprimand.

Or stand so mammering on.[22] What? Michael Cassio.   70
That came a-wooing with you, and so many a time,
When I have spoke of you dispraisingly,
Hath ta'en your part—to have so much to do
To bring him in![23] By 'r Lady, I could do much—
OTHELLO. Prithee, no more. Let him come when he will;   75
I will deny thee nothing.
DESDEMONA.   Why, this is not a boon.
'Tis as I should entreat you wear your gloves,
Or feed on nourishing dishes, or keep you warm,
Or sue to you to do a peculiar[24] profit
To your own person. Nay, when I have a suit   80
Wherein I mean to touch[25] your love indeed,
It shall be full of poise[26] and difficult weight,
And fearful to be granted.
OTHELLO.   I will deny thee nothing.
Whereon,[27] I do beseech thee, grant me this,
To leave me but a little to myself.   85
DESDEMONA. Shall I deny you? No. Farewell, my lord.
OTHELLO. Farewell, my Desdemona. I'll come to thee straight.[28]
DESDEMONA. Emilia, come.—Be as your fancies[29] teach you:
    Whate'er you be, I am obedient.   [*Exit with* EMILIA.]
OTHELLO. Excellent wretch![30] Perdition catch my soul   90
    But I do love thee! And when I love thee not,
    Chaos is come again.[31]
IAGO. My noble lord—
OTHELLO.   What dost thou say, Iago?
IAGO. Did Michael Cassio, when you wooed my lady,
    Know of your love?   95
OTHELLO. He did, from first to last. Why dost thou ask?
IAGO. But for a satisfaction of my thought;
    No further harm.

22. **mammering on** wavering about.   23. **bring him in** restore him to favor.
24. **peculiar** personal.   25. **touch** test.   26. **poise** weight, heaviness; or equipoise,
delicate balance involving hard choice.   27. **Whereon** in return.   28. **straight**
straightway.   29. **fancies** inclinations.   30. **Excellent wretch!** a term of affectionate endearment.   31. **Chaos . . . again** i.e. my love for you will last forever, until the
end of time when chaos will return. (But with an unconscious, ironic suggestion that,
if anything should induce Othello to cease loving Desdemona, the result would be
chaos.)

OTHELLO.   Why of thy thought, Iago?
IAGO. I did not think he had been acquainted with her.
OTHELLO. O, yes, and went between us very oft.   100
IAGO. Indeed?
OTHELLO. Indeed? Ay, indeed. Discern'st thou aught in that?
   Is he not honest?
IAGO.   Honest, my lord?
OTHELLO.   Honest. Ay, honest.
IAGO. My lord, for aught I know.
OTHELLO. What dost thou think?   105
IAGO.   Think, my lord?
OTHELLO. "Think, my lord?" By heaven, thou echo'st me,
   As if there were some monster in thy thought
   Too hideous to be shown. Thou dost mean something,
   I heard thee say even now, thou lik'st not that,
   When Cassio left my wife. What didst not like?   110
   And when I told thee he was of my counsel[32]
   In my whole course of wooing, thou criedst "Indeed?"
   And didst contract and purse[33] thy brow together
   As if thou then hadst shut up in thy brain
   Some horrible conceit.[34] If thou dost love me,   115
   Show me thy thought.
IAGO. My lord, you know I love you.
OTHELLO.   I think thou dost;
   And, for[35] I know thou'rt full of love and honesty,
   And weigh'st thy words before thou giv'st them breath.
   Therefore these stops[36] of thine fright me the more;   120
   For such things in a false disloyal knave
   Are tricks of custom,[37] but in a man that's just
   They're close dilations,[38] working from the heart
   That passion cannot rule.[39]
IAGO.   For[40] Michael Cassio,
   I dare be sworn I think that he is honest.   125
OTHELLO. I think so too.

---

32. of my counsel in my confidence.   **33. purse** knit.   **34. conceit** fancy.   **35. for** because.   **36. stops** pauses.   **37. custom** customary.   **38. dilations** secret or involuntary expressions or delays.   **39. That . . . rule** i.e., that are too passionately strong to be restrained (referring to the workings), or that cannot rule its own passions (referring to the heart).   **40. For** as for.

IAGO.   Men should be what they seem;
   Or those that be not, would they might seem none![41]
OTHELLO. Certain, men should be what they seem.
IAGO. Why, then, I think Cassio's an honest man.
OTHELLO. Nay, yet there's more in this.   130
   I prithee, speak to me as to thy thinkings,
   As thou dost ruminate, and give thy worst of thoughts
   The worst of words.
IAGO.   Good my lord, pardon me.
   Though I am bound to every act of duty,
   I am not bound to that[42] all slaves are free to.[43]   135
   Utter my thoughts? Why, say they are vile and false,
   As where's that palace whereinto foul things
   Sometimes intrude not? Who has that breast so pure
   But some uncleanly apprehensions
   Keep leets and law days,[44] and in sessions sit   140
   With[45] meditations lawful?[46]
OTHELLO. Thou dost conspire against thy friend,[47] Iago,
   If thou but think'st him wronged and mak'st his ear
   A stranger to thy thoughts.
IAGO.   I do beseech you,
   Though I perchance am vicious[48] in my guess—   145
   As I confess it is my nature's plague
   To spy into abuses, and oft my jealousy[49]
   Shapes faults that are not—that your wisdom then,[50]
   From one[51] that so imperfectly conceits,[52]
   Would take no notice, nor build yourself a trouble   150
   Out of his scattering[53] and unsure observance.
   It were not for your quiet nor your good,
   Nor for my manhood, honesty, and wisdom,
   To let you know my thoughts.
OTHELLO.   What dost thou mean?

---

41. Or . . . none i.e., not to be men, or not seem to be honest.   **42. that** that which
43. free to free with respect to.   **44. Keep . . . days** i.e., hold court, set up their authority in one's heart. *Leets* are a kind of manor court; *law days* are the days courts sit in session, or those sessions.   **45. With** along with.   **46. lawful** innocent.
47. thy friend i.e., Othello.   **48. vicious** wrong.   **49. jealousy** suspicious nature.
50. then on that account.   **51. one** i.e., myself, Iago.   **52. conceits** conjectures.
53. scattering random.

IAGO. Good name in man and woman, dear my lord,　　　　155
　　Is the immediate[54] jewel of their souls.
　　Who steals my purse steals trash: 'tis something, nothing:
　　'Twas mine, 'tis his, and has been slave to thousands:
　　But he that filches from me my good name
　　Robs me of that which not enriches him　　　　　　160
　　And makes me poor indeed.
OTHELLO. By heaven, I'll know thy thoughts.
IAGO. You cannot, if[55] my heart were in your hand,
　　Nor shall not, whilst 'tis in my custody.
OTHELLO. Ha?　　　　　　　　　　　　　　　　165
IAGO.　　　　　O, beware, my lord, of jealousy.
　　It is the green-eyed monster which doth mock
　　The meat it feeds on.[56] That cuckold lives in bliss
　　Who, certain of his fate, loves not his wronger:[57]
　　But O, what damnèd minutes tells[58] he o'er
　　Who dotes, yet doubts, suspects, yet fondly loves!　　170
OTHELLO. O misery!
IAGO. Poor and content is rich, and rich enough,[59]
　　But riches fineless[60] is as poor as winter
　　To him that ever fears he shall be poor.
　　Good God, the souls of all my tribe defend　　　　175
　　From jealousy!
OTHELLO.　　　　　Why, why is this?
　　Think'st thou I'd make a life of jealousy,
　　To follow still the changes of the moon
　　With fresh suspicions?[61] No! To be once in doubt
　　Is once[62] to be resolved.[63] Exchange me for a goat　　180
　　When I shall turn the business of my soul
　　To such exsufflicate and blown[64] surmises

---

54. immediate essential.　**55. if** even if.　**56. mock . . . on** mocks and torments the heart of its victim, the man who suffers jealousy.　**57. wronger** i.e., his faithless wife. (The unsuspecting cuckold is spared the misery of loving his wife only to discover she is cheating on him.)　**58. tells** counts.　**59. Poor . . . enough** to be content with what little one has is the greatest wealth of all (proverbial).　**60. fineless** boundless.　**61. To . . . suspicions** to be constantly imagining new causes for suspicion, changing incessantly like the moon.　**62. once** once and for all.　**63. resolved** free of doubt, having settled the matter.　**64. To . . . blown** inflated and blown up, rumored about, or, spat out and flyblown, hence loathsome, disgusting.

Matching thy inference.[65] 'Tis not to make me jealous
To say my wife is fair, feeds well, loves company,
Is free of speech, sings, plays, and dances well: 185
Where virtue is, these are more virtuous.
Nor from mine own weak merits will I draw
The smallest fear or doubt of her revolt.[66]
For she had eyes, and chose me. No, Iago,
I'll see before I doubt; when I doubt, prove;   190
And on the proof, there is no more but this—
Away at once with love or jealousy.
IAGO. I am glad of this, for now I shall have reason
To show the love and duty that I bear you
With franker spirit. Therefore, as I am bound,   195
Receive it from me. I speak not yet of proof.
Look to your wife: observe her well with Cassio.
Wear your eyes thus, not[67] jealous nor secure.[68]
I would not have your free and noble nature,
Out of self-bounty,[69] be abused.[70] Look to 't.   200
I know our country disposition well:
In Venice they do let God see the pranks
They dare not show their husbands; their best conscience
Is not to leave 't undone, but keep 't unknown.
OTHELLO. Dost thou say so?   205
IAGO. She did deceive her father, marrying you;
And when she seemed to shake and fear your looks,
She loved them most.
OTHELLO.   And so she did.
IAGO.   Why, go to[71] then!
She that, so young, could give out such a seeming,[72]
To seel[73] her father's eyes up close as oak,[74]   210
He thought 'twas witchcraft! But I am much to blame.
I humbly do beseech you of your pardon
For too much loving you.

---

65. **inference** allegation.   66. **The . . . revolt** fear of her unfaithfulness.   67. **not** neither.   68. **secure** certain.   69. **self-bounty** inherent or natural goodness and generosity.   70. **abused** deceived.   71. **go to** an expression of impatience.   72. **seeming** false appearance.   73. **seel** blind (a term from falconry).   74. **oak** a close-grained wood.

OTHELLO.   I am bound[75] to thee forever.

IAGO. I see this hath a little dashed your spirits.

OTHELLO. Not a jot, not a jot.   215

IAGO.   I' faith, I fear it has.
 I hope you will consider what is spoke
 Comes from my love. But I do see you're moved.
 I am to pray you not to strain my speech
 To grosser issues[76] nor to larger reach[77]
 Than to suspicion.   220

OTHELLO. I will not.

IAGO.   Should you do so, my lord,
 My speech should fall into such vile success[78]
 Which my thoughts aimed not. Cassio's my worthy friend.
 My lord, I see you're moved.

OTHELLO.   No, not much moved.
 I do not think but Desdemona's honest.[79]   225

IAGO. Long live she so! And long live you to think so!

OTHELLO. And yet, how nature erring from itself—

IAGO. Ay, there's the point! As—to be bold with you—
 Not to affect[80] many proposèd matches
 Of her own clime, complexion, and degree,[81]   230
 Whereto we see in all things nature tends—
 Foh! One may smell in such a will[82] most rank,
 Foul disproportion,[83] thoughts unnatural.
 But pardon me. I do not in position[84]
 Distinctly speak of her, though I may fear   235
 Her will, recoiling[85] to her better[86] judgment,
 May fall to match you with her country forms[87]
 And happily repent.[88]

OTHELLO.   Farewell, farewell!
 If more thou dost perceive, let me know more.
 Set on thy wife to observe. Leave me, Iago.   240

---

75. **bound** indebted (but perhaps with the ironic sense of "tied").   76. **issues** significance.   77. **reach** scope.   78. **success** effect.   79. **honest** chaste.   80. **affect** prefer.   81. **Of ... degree** country, color, and social position.   82. **will** sensuality.   83. **disproportion** abnormality.   84. **position** argument.   85. **recoiling** reverting.   86. **better** i.e., more natural and reconsidered.   87. **May ... forms** undertake to compare you with Venetian norms of handsomeness.   88. **repent** perhaps repent her marriage.

IAGO. [*going*] My lord. I take my leave.
OTHELLO. Why did I marry? This honest creature doubtless
    Sees and knows more. much more. than he unfolds.
IAGO. [*returning*] My Lord. I would I might entreat your honor
    To scan[89] this thing no farther. Leave it to time.   245
    Although 'tis fit that Cassio have his place—
    For. sure. he fills it up with great ability—
    Yet. if you please to hold him off awhile.
    You shall by that perceive him and his means.[90]
    Note if your lady strain his entertainment[91]   250
    With any strong or vehement importunity:
    Much will be seen in that. In the meantime.
    Let me be thought too busy[92] in my fears—
    As worthy cause I have to fear I am—
    And hold her free.[93] I do beseech your honor.   255
OTHELLO. Fear not my government.[94]
IAGO.   I once more take my leave.

                              [*Exit.*]

OTHELLO. This fellow's of exceeding honesty.
    And knows all qualities.[95] with a learnèd spirit.
    Of human dealings. If I do prove her haggard.[96]
    Though that her jesses[97] were my dear heartstrings.   260
    I'd whistle her off and let her down the wind[98]
    To prey at fortune.[99] Haply. for[100] I am black
    And have not those soft parts of conversation[101]
    That chamberers[102] have. or for I am declined
    Into the vale of years—yet that's not much—   265
    She's gone. I am abused.[103] and my relief
    Must be to loathe her. O curse of marriage.
    That we can call these delicate creatures ours

---

89. scan scrutinize.   **90. means** the method he uses (to regain his post).   **91. Note
. . . entertainment** urge his reinstatement.   **92. busy** interfering.   **93. hold . . .
free** regard her as innocent.   **94. government** conduct.   **95. qualities** natures.
96. haggard wild (like a wild female hawk).   **97. jesses** straps fastened around the
legs of a trained hawk.   **98. I'd . . . wind** I'd let her go forever. (To release a hawk
downwind was to invite it not to return).   **99. To . . . fortune** fend for herself in the
wild.   **100. for** perhaps because.   **101. soft . . . conversation** pleasing graces of social behavior.   **102. chamberers** gallants.   **103. abused** deceived.

And not their appetites! I had rather be a toad
And live upon the vapor of a dungeon   270
Than keep a corner in the thing I love
For others' uses. Yet, 'tis the plague of great ones:
Prerogatived[104] are they less than the base.[105]
'Tis destiny unshunnable, like death.
Even then this forkèd[106] plague is fated to us   275
When we do quicken.[107] Look where she comes.

[*Enter* DESDEMONA *and* EMILIA.]

If she be false, O, then heaven mocks itself!
I'll not believe 't.
DESDEMONA.   How now, my dear Othello?
Your dinner, and the generous[108] islanders
By you invited, do attend[109] your presence.   280
OTHELLO. I am to blame.
DESDEMONA.   Why do you speak so faintly?
Are you not well?
OTHELLO. I have a pain upon my forehead here.
DESDEMONA. Faith, that's with watching.[110] 'Twill away again.

[*She offers her handkerchief.*]

Let me but bind it hard, within this hour   285
It will be well.
OTHELLO.   Your napkin[111] is too little.
Let it alone.[112] Come, I'll go in with you.

[*He puts the handkerchief from him, and it drops.*]

DESDEMONA. I am very sorry that you are not well.

[*Exit with* OTHELLO.]

EMILIA. [*picking up the handkerchief*]

---

104. Prerogatived privileged (to have honest wives).   **105. base** ordinary citizens.
(Socially prominent men are especially prone to the unavoidable destiny of being
cuckolded and to the public shame that goes with it.)   **106. forked** an allusion to
the horns of the cuckold.   **107. quicken** receive life. *Quicken* may also mean to
swarm with maggots as the body festers, in which case these lines suggest that *even
then*, in death, we are cuckolded by *forked* worms. **108. generous** noble
109. attend await **110. watching** too little sleep **111. napkin** handkerchief
112. Let it alone never mind.

I am glad I have found this napkin.
This was her first remembrance from the Moor.   290
My wayward[113] husband hath a hundred times
Wooed me to steal it, but she so loves the token—
For he conjured her she should ever keep it—
That she reserves it evermore about her
To kiss and talk to. I'll have the work ta'en out.[114]   295
And give 't Iago. What he will do with it
Heaven knows, not I;
I nothing but to please his fantasy.[115]

[Enter IAGO.]

IAGO. How now? What do you here alone?
EMILIA. Do not you chide. I have a thing for you.   300
IAGO. You have a thing for me? It is a common thing[116]—
EMILIA. Ha?
IAGO. To have a foolish wife.
EMILIA. O, is that all? What will you give me now
      For that same handkerchief?   305
IAGO. What handkerchief?
EMILIA. What handkerchief?
      Why, that the Moor first gave to Desdemona;
      That which so often you did bid me steal.
IAGO. Hast stolen it from her?   310
EMILIA. No, faith. She let it drop by negligence,
      And to th' advantage[117] I, being here, took 't up.
      Look, here 'tis.
IAGO.   A good wench! Give it me.
EMILIA. What will you do with 't, that you have been so earnest
      To have me filch it?   315
IAGO. [snatching it]   Why, what is that to you?
EMILIA. If it be not for some purpose of import,
      Give 't me again. Poor lady, she'll run mad
      When she shall lack[118] it.

---

113. wayward capricious.   **114. I'll ... out** design of the embroidery copied.
115. fantasy whim.   **116. common thing** with bawdy suggestion: *common* suggests
coarseness and availability to all comers, and *thing* is a slang term for the genitals.
117. advantage taking the opportunity.   **118. lack** miss.

IAGO.   Be not acknown on 't.[119]
   I have use for it. Go, leave me.   [*Exit Emilia.*]
   I will in Cassio's lodging lose[120] this napkin   320
   And let him find it. Trifles light as air
   Are to the jealous confirmations strong
   As proofs of Holy Writ. This may do something.
   The Moor already changes with my poison.
   Dangerous conceits[121] are in their natures poisons,   325
   Which at the first are scarce found to distaste,[122]
   But with a little act[123] upon the blood
   Burn like the mines of sulfur.

   [*Enter* OTHELLO.]
                         I did say so.
   Look where he comes! Not poppy nor mandragora[124]
   Nor all the drowsy syrups of the world   330
   Shall ever medicine thee to that sweet sleep
   Which thou owedst[125] yesterday.
OTHELLO.   Ha, ha, false to me?
IAGO. Why, how now, General? No more of that.
OTHELLO. Avaunt! Begone! Thou hast set me on the rack.
   I swear 'tis better to be much abused   335
   Than but to know 't a little.
IAGO.   How now, my lord?
OTHELLO. What sense had I of her stolen hours of lust?
   I saw 't not, thought it not, it harmed not me.
   I slept the next night well, fed well, was free[126] and merry;
   I found not Cassio's kisses on her lips.   340
   He that is robbed, not wanting[127] what is stolen,
   Let him not know 't and he's not robbed at all.
IAGO. I am sorry to hear this.
OTHELLO. I had been happy if the general camp,
   Pioners[128] and all, had tasted her sweet body,   345

---

119. Be . . . on't Do not confess knowledge of it.   **120. lose** the Folio spelling, *loose*, is a normal spelling for "lose," but it may also contain the idea of "let go," "release." **121. conceits** ideas. **122. distaste** be distasteful. **123. act** action. **124. mandragora** an opiate made of the mandrake root. **125. owedst** you did own. **126. free** carefree. **127. wanting** missing. **128. Pioners** diggers of mines, the lowest grade of soldiers.

So[129] I had nothing known. O. now. forever
Farewell the tranquil mind! Farewell content!
Farewell the plumèd troops and the big[130] wars
That makes ambition virtue! O. farewell!
Farewell the neighing steed and the shrill trump.   350
The spirit-stirring drum. th' ear-piercing fife.
The royal banner. and all quality.[131]
Pride.[132] pomp. and circumstance[133] of glorious war!
And O. you mortal engines.[134] whose rude throats
Th' immortal Jove's dread clamors[135] counterfeit.   355
Farewell! Othello's occupation's gone.

IAGO. Is 't possible. my lord?

OTHELLO. Villain. be sure thou prove my love a whore!
Be sure of it. Give me the ocular proof.
Or. by the worth of mine eternal soul.   360
Thou hadst been better have been born a dog
Than answer my waked wrath!

IAGO.   Is 't come to this?

OTHELLO. Make me to see 't. or at the least so prove it
That the probation[136] bear no hinge nor loop
To hang a doubt on. or woe upon thy life!   365

IAGO. My noble lord—

OTHELLO. If thou dost slander her and torture me.
Never pray more: abandon all remorse:[137]
On horror's head horrors accumulate:
Do deeds to make heaven weep. all earth amazed: 370
For nothing canst thou to damnation add
Greater than that.

IAGO.   O grace! O heaven forgive me!
Are you a man? Have you a soul or sense?
God b' wi' you: take mine office. O wretched fool.[138]
That lov'st to make thine honesty a vice![139]   375
O monstrous world! Take note. take note. O world.

---

129. So provided.   **130. big** stately.   **131. quality** character.   **132. Pride** display.
133. circumstance pageantry.   **134. mortal engines** cannon. (*Mortal* means
"deadly.")   **135. clamors** thunder.   **136. probation** proof.   **137. remorse** pity.
138. fool Iago addresses himself as a fool for having carried honesty too far.   **139.
vice** failing.

To be direct and honest is not safe.
I thank you for this profit.[140] and from hence[141]
I'll love no friend. sith[142] love breeds such offense.[143]
OTHELLO. Nay. stay. Thou shouldst be honest.[144]   380
IAGO. I should be wise. for honesty's a fool
      And loses that[145] it works for.
OTHELLO.   By the world.
      I think my wife be honest and think she is not:
      I think that thou art just and think thou art not.
      I'll have some proof. My name. that was as fresh   385
      As Dian's[146] visage. is now begrimed and black
      As mine own face. If there be cords. or knives.
      Poison. or fire. or suffocating streams.
      I'll not endure it. Would I were satisfied!
IAGO. I see, sir. you are eaten up with passion.   390
      I do repent me that I put it to you.
      You would be satisfied?
OTHELLO.   Would? Nay. and I will.
IAGO. And may: but how? How satisfied. my lord?
      Would you. the supervisor.[147] grossly gape on?
      Behold her topped?   395
OTHELLO.   Death and damnation! O!
IAGO. It were a tedious difficulty. I think.
      To bring them to that prospect. Damn them then.[148]
      If ever mortal eyes do see them bolster[149]
      More[150] than their own.[151] What then? How then?
      What shall I say? Where's satisfaction?   400
      It is impossible you should see this.
      Were they as prime[152] as goats. as hot as monkeys.
      As salt[153] as wolves in pride.[154] and fools as gross
      As ignorance made drunk. But yet I say.

---

140. **profit** instruction.   141. **from hence** henceforth.   142. **sith** since.
143. **offense** harm to the one who offers help and friendship.   144. **Thou . . . honest** It appears that you are. (But Iago replies in the sense of "ought to be.")
145. **that** what.   146. **Dian's** Diana. goddess of the moon and of chastity.
147. **supervisor** onlooker.   148. **Damn . . . then** They would have to be really incorrigible.   149. **bolster** go to bed together. share a bolster.   150. **More** other.
151. **own** own eyes.   152. **prime** wanton.   153. **salt** lustful.   154. **pride** heat.

If imputation[155] and strong circumstances 405
Which lead directly to the door of truth
Will give you satisfaction, you might have 't.
OTHELLO. Give me a living reason she's disloyal.
IAGO. I do not like the office.
But sith[156] I am entered in this cause so far. 410
Pricked[157] to 't by foolish honesty and love,
I will go on. I lay with Cassio lately,
And being troubled with a raging tooth
I could not sleep. There are a kind of men
So loose of soul that in their sleeps will mutter 415
Their affairs. One of this kind is Cassio.
In sleep I heard him say, "Sweet Desdemona,
Let us be wary, let us hide our loves!"
And then, sir, would he grip and wring my hand,
Cry "O sweet creature!", then kiss me hard, 420
As if he plucked up kisses by the roots
That grew upon my lips; then laid his leg
Over my thigh, and sighed, and kissed, and then
Cried, "Cursèd fate that gave thee to the Moor!"
OTHELLO. O monstrous! Monstrous! 425
IAGO.   Nay, this was but his dream.
OTHELLO. But this denoted a foregone conclusion.[158]
    'Tis a shrewd doubt,[159] though it be but a dream.
IAGO. And this may help to thicken other proofs
    That do demonstrate thinly.
OTHELLO.   I'll tear her all to pieces.
IAGO. Nay, but be wise. Yet we see nothing done; 430
    She may be honest yet. Tell me but this:
    Have you not sometimes seen a handkerchief
    Spotted[160] with strawberries in your wife's hand?
OTHELLO. I gave her such a one, 'Twas my first gift.
IAGO. I know not that; but such a handkerchief— 435
    I am sure it was your wife's—did I today
    See Cassio wipe his beard with.

---

155. imputation strong circumstantial evidence. 156. sith since. 157. Pricked spurred. 158. foregone conclusion concluded experience or action. 159. shrewd doubt suspicious circumstance. 160. Spotted embroidered.

OTHELLO.   If it be that—

IAGO. If it be that, or any that was hers.
   It speaks against her with the other proofs.

OTHELLO. O, that the slave[161] had forty thousand lives!   440
   One is too poor, too weak for my revenge.
   Now do I see 'tis true. Look here, Iago,
   All my fond[162] love thus do I blow to heaven.
   'Tis gone.
   Arise, black vengeance, from the hollow hell!   445
   Yield up, O love, thy crown and hearted[163] throne
   To tyrannous hate! Swell, bosom, with thy freight,[164]
   For 'tis of aspics'[165] tongues!

IAGO.   Yet be content.[166]

OTHELLO. O, blood, blood, blood!

IAGO. Patience, I say. Your mind perhaps may change.   450

OTHELLO. Never, Iago. Like to the Pontic Sea,[167]
   Whose icy current and compulsive course
   Ne'er feels retiring ebb, but keeps due on
   To the Propontic[168] and the Hellespont,[169]
   Even so my bloody thoughts with violent pace   455
   Shall ne'er look back, ne'er ebb to humble love,
   Till that a capable[170] and wide revenge
   Swallow them up. Now, by yond marble[171] heaven,
   [*Kneeling.*] In the due reverence of a sacred vow
   I here engage my words.   460

IAGO.   Do not rise yet.
   [*He kneels.*][172] Witness, you ever-burning lights above,
   You elements that clip[173] us round about,
   Witness that here Iago doth give up
   The execution[174] of his wit,[175] hands, heart,
   To wronged Othello's service. Let him command.   465

---

161. slave Cassio.   **162. fond** foolish (but also suggesting "affectionate").
163. hearted fixed in the heart.   **164. freight** burden.   **165. aspics'** venomous serpents.'   **166. content** calm.   **167. Pontic Sea** Black Sea.   **168. Propontic** Sea of Marmora, between the Black Sea and the Aegean.   **169. Hellespont** Dardanelles, straits where the Sea of Marmora joins with the Aegean.   **170. capable** ample.
171. marble i.e., gleaming like marble and unrelenting.   **172. [He kneels.]** In the Quarto text, Iago kneels here after Othello has knelt at line 459.   **173. clip** encompass.   **174. execution** exercise.   **175. wit** mind.

And to obey shall be in me remorse.[176]
What bloody business ever.[177] [*They rise.*]
OTHELLO.   I greet thy love.
Not with vain thanks. but with acceptance bounteous.
And will upon the instant put thee to 't.[178]
Within these three days let me hear thee say   470
That Cassio's not alive.
IAGO.   My friend is dead:
'Tis done at your request. But let her live.
OTHELLO. Damn her. lewd minx![179] O. damn her. damn her!
Come. go with me apart. I will withdraw
To furnish me with some swift means of death   475
For the fair devil. Now art thou my lieutenant.
IAGO. I am your own forever.   [*Exeunt.*]

SCENE 4

[*Location: Before the citadel. Enter* DESDEMONA. EMILIA. *and*
CLOWN.]

DESDEMONA. Do you know. sirrah.[1] where Lieutenant Cassio
lies?
CLOWN. I dare not say he lies[2] anywhere.
DESDEMONA. Why. man?
CLOWN. He's a soldier. and for me to say a soldier lies. 'tis stab-   5
bing.
DESDEMONA. Go to. Where lodges he?
CLOWN. To tell you where he lodges is to tell you where I lie.
DESDEMONA. Can anything be made of this?
CLOWN. I know not where he lodges. and for me to devise a   10
lodging and say he lies here. or he lies there. were to lie in
mine own throat.[3]
DESDEMONA. Can you inquire him out. and be edified by report?
CLOWN. I will catechize the world for him: that is. make ques-
tions. and by them answer.   15

---

176. remorse pity (for Othello's wrongs).   **177. ever** whatsoever.   **178. to't** to the
proof.   **179. lewd minx!** wanton.   **1. sirrah** a form of address to an inferior.
2. lies lodges. (But the Clown makes the obvious pun.)   **3. lie . . . throat** lie egregiously and deliberately. Also. use the windpipe to speak a lie.

DESDEMONA. Seek him, bid him come hither. Tell him I have
    moved[4] my lord on his behalf and hope all will be well.
CLOWN. To do this is within the compass of man's wit, and
    therefore I will attempt the doing it.   [*Exit* CLOWN.]
DESDEMONA. Where should I lose that handkerchief, Emilia?   20
EMILIA. I know not, madam.
DESDEMONA. Believe me, I had rather have lost my purse
    Full of crusadoes:[5] and but my noble Moor
    Is true of mind and made of no such baseness
    As jealous creatures are, it were enough   25
    To put him to ill thinking.
EMILIA.   Is he not jealous?
DESDEMONA. Who, he? I think the sun where he was born
    Drew all such humors[6] from him.
EMILIA.   Look where he comes.

    [*Enter* OTHELLO.]

DESDEMONA. I will not leave him now till Cassio
    Be called to him.—How is 't with you, my lord?   30
OTHELLO. Well, my good lady. [*Aside.*] O, hardness to dissemble!—
    How do you, Desdemona?
DESDEMONA.   Well, my good lord.
OTHELLO. Give me your hand. [*She gives her hand.*] This hand is
    moist, my lady.
DESDEMONA. It yet hath felt no age nor known no sorrow.
OTHELLO. This argues fruitfulness and liberal heart.[7]   35
    Hot, hot, and moist. This hand of yours requires
    A sequester[8] from liberty, fasting and prayer,
    Much castigation,[9] exercise[10] devout;
    For here's a young and sweating devil here
    That commonly rebels. 'Tis a good hand,   40
    A frank[11] one.
DESDEMONA.   You may indeed say so,
    For 'twas that hand that gave away my heart.

---

4. moved petitioned.   **5. crusadoes** gold coins.   **6. humors** refers to the four bodily fluids thought to determine temperament.   **7. liberal heart** gives evidence of
amorousness, fecundity, and sexual freedom.   **8. sequester** separation.   **9. casti-
gation** discipline.   **10. exercise** prayer.   **11. frank** generous, open (with sexual
suggestion).

OTHELLO. A liberal hand. The hearts of old gave hands.[12]
  But our new heraldry is hands, not hearts.[13]
DESDEMONA. I cannot speak of this. Come now, your promise.   45
OTHELLO. What promise, chuck?[14]
DESDEMONA. I have sent to bid Cassio come speak with you.
OTHELLO. I have a salt and sorry rheum[15] offends me:
  Lend me thy handkerchief.
DESDEMONA.   Here, my lord. [*She offers a*
  handkerchief.]
OTHELLO. That which I gave you.   50
DESDEMONA.   I have it not about me.
OTHELLO. Not?
DESDEMONA. No, faith, my lord.
OTHELLO.   That's a fault. That handkerchief
  Did an Egyptian to my mother give.
  She was a charmer,[16] and could almost read
  The thoughts of people. She told her, while she kept it   55
  'Twould make her amiable[17] and subdue my father
  Entirely to her love, but if she lost it
  Or made a gift of it, my father's eye
  Should hold her loathèd and his spirits should hunt
  After new fancies.[18] She, dying, gave it me,   60
  And bid me, when my fate would have me wived,
  To give it her.[19] I did so: and take heed on 't:
  Make it a darling like your precious eye,
  To lose 't or give 't away were such perdition[20]
  As nothing else could match.   65
DESDEMONA.   Is 't possible?
OTHELLO. 'Tis true. There's magic in the web[21] of it.
  A sibyl, that had numbered in the world
  The sun to course two hundred compasses.[22]

---

12. The . . . hands. In former times, people would give their hearts when they gave their hands to something.   **13. But . . . hearts.** In our decadent times, the joining of hands is no longer a badge to signify the giving of hearts.   **14. chuck** a term of endearment.   **15. rheum** distressful head cold or watering of the eyes.   **16. charmer** sorceress.   **17. amiable** desirable.   **18. fancies** loves.   **19. her** i.e., to my wife.   **20. perdition** loss.   **21. web** weaving.   **22. compasses** annual circlings. (The *sibyl,* or prophetess, was 200 years old.)

In her prophetic fury[23] sewed the work:[24]
The worms were hallowed that did breed the silk,   70
And it was dyed in mummy[25] which the skillful
Conserved of[26] maidens' hearts.
DESDEMONA.   I' faith! Is 't true?
OTHELLO. Most veritable. Therefore look to 't well.
DESDEMONA. Then would to God that I had never seen 't!
OTHELLO. Ha? Wherefore?   75
DESDEMONA. Why do you speak so startingly and rash?[27]
OTHELLO. Is 't lost? Is 't gone? Speak, is 't out o' the way?[28]
DESDEMONA. Heaven bless us!
OTHELLO. Say you?
DESDEMONA. It is not lost; but what an if[29] it were?   80
OTHELLO. How?
DESDEMONA. I say it is not lost.
OTHELLO.   Fetch 't, let me see 't.
DESDEMONA. Why, so I can, sir, but I will not now.
    This is a trick to put me from my suit.
    Pray you, let Cassio be received again.   85
OTHELLO. Fetch me the handkerchief! My mind misgives.
DESDEMONA. Come, come,
    You'll never meet a more sufficient[30] man.
OTHELLO. The handkerchief!
DESDEMONA.   I pray, talk[31] me of Cassio.
OTHELLO. The handkerchief!   90
DESDEMONA.   A man that all his time[32]
    Hath founded his good fortunes on your love,
    Shared dangers with you—
OTHELLO. The handkerchief!
DESDEMONA. I' faith, you are to blame.
OTHELLO. Zounds!   [*Exit* OTHELLO.]
EMILIA. Is not this man jealous?
DESDEMONA. I ne'er saw this before.

---

23. prophetic fury frenzy of prophetic inspiration.   **24. work** embroidered pattern.
25. mummy medicinal or magical preparation drained from mummified bodies.
26. Conserved of prepared or preserved out of.   **27. startingly and rash** disjoint-
edly and impetuously, excitedly.   **28. out o' the way** misplaced.   **29. an if** if.
30. sufficient able.   **31. talk** talk to.   **32. all his time** throughout his career.

Sure, there's some wonder in this handkerchief.
I am most unhappy in the loss of it.
EMILIA. 'Tis not a year or two shows us a man.[33]   100
    They are all but[34] stomachs, and we all but food;
    They eat us hungerly,[35] and when they are full
    They belch us.

[*Enter* IAGO *and* CASSIO.]

                    Look you, Cassio and my husband.
IAGO. [*to* CASSIO]
    There is no other way; 'tis she must do 't.
    And, lo, the happiness![36] Go and importune her.   105
DESDEMONA. How now, good Cassio? What's the news with you?
CASSIO. Madam, my former suit. I do beseech you
    That by your virtuous[37] means I may again
    Exist and be a member of his love
    Whom I, with all the office[38] of my heart,   110
    Entirely honor, I would not be delayed.
    If my offense be of such mortal[39] kind
    That nor[40] my service past, nor present sorrows,
    Nor purposed merit in futurity
    Can ransom me into his love again,   115
    But to know so must be my benefit;[41]
    So shall I clothe me in a forced content,
    And shut myself up in[42] some other course,
    To fortune's alms.[43]
DESDEMONA.   Alas, thrice-gentle Cassio,
    My advocation[44] is not now in tune.   120
    My lord is not my lord; nor should I know him,
    Were he in favor[45] as in humor[46] altered.
    So help me every spirit sanctified
    As I have spoken for you all my best

---

33. 'Tis ... man You can't really know a man even in a year or two of experience
(?), or, real men come along seldom (?).   **34. all but** nothing but.   **35. hungerly**
hungrily.   **36. happiness** in happy time, fortunately met.   **37. virtuous** effica-
cious.   **38. office** loyal service.   **39. mortal** fatal.   **40. nor** neither.   **41. But . . .
benefit** Merely to know that my case is hopeless will have to content me (and will be
better than uncertainty).   **42. shut ... in** confine myself to.   **43. fortune's alms**
throwing myself on the mercy of fortune.   **44. advocation** advocacy.   **45. favor**
appearance.   **46. humor** mood.

And stood within the blank[47] of his displeasure   125
For my free speech! You must awhile be patient.
What I can do I will, and more I will
Than for myself I dare. Let that suffice you.

IAGO. Is my lord angry?

EMILIA.   He went hence but now,
And certainly in strange unquietness.   130

IAGO. Can he be angry? I have seen the cannon
When it hath blown his ranks into the air,
And like the devil from his very arm
Puffed his own brother—and is he angry?
Something of moment[48] then. I will go meet him.   135
There's matter in 't indeed, if he be angry.

DESDEMONA. I prithee, do so.   *[Exit* IAGO.*]*
                     Something, sure, of state.[49]
Either from Venice, or some unhatched practice[50]
Made demonstrable here in Cyprus to him,
Hath puddled[51] his clear spirit; and in such cases   140
Men's natures wrangle with inferior things,
Though great ones are their object. 'Tis even so;
For let our finger ache, and it indues[52]
Our other, healthful members even to a sense
Of pain. Nay, we must think men are not gods,   145
Nor of them look for such observancy[53]
As fits the bridal.[54] Beshrew me[55] much, Emilia,
I was, unhandsome[56] warrior as I am,
Arraigning his unkindness with[57] my soul;
But now I find I had suborned the witness,[58]   150
And he's indicted falsely.

EMILIA.   Pray heaven it be
State matters, as you think, and no conception
Nor no jealous toy[59] concerning you.

---

47. within the blank within pointblank range. (The blank is the center of the target.) **48. moment** of immediate importance, momentous. **49. of state** state affairs. **50. unhatched practice** as yet unexecuted or undiscovered plot. **51. puddled** muddied. **52. indues** induces. **53. observancy** attentiveness. **54. bridal** wedding (when a bridegroom is newly attentive to his bride). **55. Beshrew me** a mild oath. **56. unhandsome** unskillful. **57. with** before the bar of. **58. suborned the witness** induced the witness to give false testimony. **59. toy** fancy.

DESDEMONA. Alas the day! I never gave him cause.
EMILIA. But jealous souls will not be answered so: 155
    They are not ever jealous for the cause.
    But jealous for[60] they're jealous. It is a monster
    Begot upon itself.[61] born on itself.
DESDEMONA. Heaven keep that monster from Othello's mind!
EMILIA. Lady. amen.   160
DESDEMONA. I will go seek him. Cassio. walk hereabout.
    If I do find him fit. I'll move your suit
    And seek to effect it to my uttermost.
CASSIO. I humbly thank your ladyship.

                                    [*Exit* DESDEMONA *with* EMILIA.]

    [*Enter* BIANCA.]

BIANCA. Save[62] you. friend Cassio!   165
CASSIO.   What make[63] you from home?
    How is 't with you. my most fair Bianca?
    I' faith. sweet love. I was coming to your house.
BIANCA. And I was going to your lodging. Cassio.
    What. keep a week away? Seven days and nights?
    Eightscore-eight[64] hours? And lovers' absent hours   170
    More tedious than the dial[65] eightscore times?
    O weary reckoning!
CASSIO.   Pardon me. Bianca.
    I have this while with leaden thoughts been pressed:
    But I shall. in a more continuate[66] time.
    Strike off this score[67] of absence. Sweet Bianca.   175

    [*Giving her* DESDEMONA's *handkerchief.*]

    Take me this work out.[68]
BIANCA.   O Cassio. whence came this?
    This is some token from a newer friend.[69]
    To the felt absence now I feel a cause.

---

60. for because.   **61. Begot . . . itself** generated solely from itself.   **62. Save** God save.   **63. make** do.   **64. Eightscore-eight** one hundred sixty-eight. the number of hours in a week.   **65. dial** a complete revolution of the clock.   **66. continuate** uninterrupted.   **67. Strike . . . score** settle this account.   **68. Take . . . out** Copy this embroidery for me.   **69. friend** mistress.

Is 't come to this? Well, well.

CASSIO.   Go to, woman!
Throw your vile guesses in the devil's teeth,   180
From whence you have them. You are jealous now
That this is from some mistress, some remembrance.
No, by my faith, Bianca.

BIANCA.   Why, whose is it?

CASSIO. I know not, neither. I found it in my chamber.
I like the work well. Ere it be demanded[70]   185
As like[71] enough it will—I would have it copied.
Take it and do 't, and leave me for this time.

BIANCA. Leave you? Wherefore?

CASSIO. I do attend here on the General,
And think it no addition,[72] nor my wish,   190
To have him see me womaned.

BIANCA. Why, I pray you?

CASSIO. Not that I love you not.

BIANCA. But that you do not love me.
I pray you, bring[73] me on the way a little,   195
And say if I shall see you soon at night.

CASSIO. 'Tis but a little way that I can bring you,
For I attend here; but I'll see you soon.

BIANCA. 'Tis very good. I must be circumstanced.[74]

                                   [*Exeunt omnes.*]

                              ACT 4
                              SCENE 1

[*Location: Before the citadel. Enter* OTHELLO *and* IAGO.]

IAGO. Will you think so?

OTHELLO.   Think so, Iago?

IAGO.   What,
To kiss in private?

OTHELLO.   An unauthorized kiss!

IAGO. Or to be naked with her friend in bed

---

70. demanded inquired for.   **71. like** likely.   **72. addition** i.e., addition to my
reputation.   **73. bring** accompany.   **74. be circumstanced** be governed by circumstance, yield to your conditions.

An hour or more, not meaning any harm?
OTHELLO. Naked in bed, Iago, and not mean harm?   5
It is hypocrisy against the devil.
They that mean virtuously and yet do so,
The devil their virtue tempts, and they tempt heaven.
IAGO. If they do nothing, 'tis a venial[1] slip.
But if I give my wife a handkerchief—   10
OTHELLO. What then?
IAGO. Why then, 'tis hers, my lord, and being hers,
She may, I think, bestow 't on any man.
OTHELLO. She is protectress of her honor too.
May she give that?   15
IAGO. Her honor is an essence that's not seen:
They have it[2] very oft that have it not.
But, for the handkerchief—
OTHELLO. By heaven, I would most gladly have forgot it.
Thou saidst—O, it comes o'er my memory   20
As doth the raven o'er the infectious house,[3]
Boding to all—he had my handkerchief.
IAGO. Ay, what of that?
OTHELLO.   That's not so good now.
IAGO.   What
If I had said I had seen him do you wrong?
Or heard him say—as knaves be such abroad,[4]   25
Who having, by their own importunate suit,
Or voluntary dotage[5] of some mistress,
Convincèd or supplied[6] them, cannot choose
But they must blab—
OTHELLO.   Hath he said anything?
IAGO. He hath, my lord; but, be you well assured,   30
No more than he'll unswear.
OTHELLO.   What hath he said?
IAGO. Faith, that he did—I know not what he did.
OTHELLO. What? What?

1. **venial** pardonable. 2. **They ... it** They enjoy a reputation for it. 3. **As ... house** allusion to the belief that the raven hovered over a house of sickness or infection, such as one visited by the plague. 4. **abroad** around about. 5. **dotage** willing infatuation. 6. **supplied** seduced or sexually gratified.

IAGO. Lie—
OTHELLO. With her?   35
IAGO.   With her, on her: what you will.
OTHELLO. Lie with her? Lie on her? We say "lie on her" when
     they belie[7] her. Lie with her? Zounds, that's fulsome.[8]
     —Handkerchief—confessions—handkerchief!—To confess
     and be hanged for his labor—first to be hanged and then to
     confess.[9]—I tremble at it. Nature would not invest herself in   40
     such shadowing passion without some instruction.[10] It is not
     words[11] that shakes me thus. Pish! Noses, ears, and lips.—
     Is 't possible?—Confess—handkerchief!—O devil!

     [*Falls in a trance.*]

IAGO. Work on. My medicine, work! Thus credulous fools are
     caught,
     And many worthy and chaste dames even thus,   45
     All guiltless, meet reproach.—What, ho! My lord!
     My lord! I say! Othello!

     [*Enter* CASSIO.]

                         How now, Cassio?
CASSIO. What's the matter?
IAGO. My lord is fall'n into an epilepsy.
     This is his second fit. He had one yesterday.   50
CASSIO. Rub him about the temples.
IAGO.   No, forbear.
     The lethargy[12] must have his[13] quiet course.
     If not, he foams at mouth, and by and by
     Breaks out to savage madness. Look, he stirs.
     Do you withdraw yourself a little while.   55
     He will recover straight. When he is gone,
     I would on great occasion speak with you.

                              [*Exit* CASSIO.]

---

7. belie slander.   **8. fulsome** foul.   **9. To ... confess** Othello reverses the proverbial *confess and be hanged*: Cassio is to be given no time to confess before he dies.
10. Nature ... instruction i.e., without some foundation in fact, nature would not
have dressed herself in such an overwhelming passion that comes over me now and
fills my mind with images, or in such a lifelike fantasy as Cassio had in his dream of
lying with Desdemona.   **11. words** mere words.   **12. lethargy** coma.   **13. his** its.

How is it. General? Have you not hurt your head?
OTHELLO. Dost thou mock me?[14]
IAGO.   I mock you not. by heaven.
Would you would bear your fortune like a man!   60
OTHELLO. A hornèd man's a monster and a beast.
IAGO.There's many a beast then in a populous city.
    And many a civil[15] monster.
OTHELLO. Did he confess it?
IAGO.   Good sir. be a man.
    Think every bearded fellow that's but yoked[16]   65
    May draw with you.[17] There's millions now alive
    That nightly lie in those unproper[18] beds
    Which they dare swear peculiar.[19] Your case is better.[20]
O. 'tis the spite of hell. the fiend's arch-mock.
    To lip[21] a wanton in a secure couch   70
    And to suppose her chaste! No. let me know.
    And knowing what I am.[22] I know what she shall be.[23]
OTHELLO. O. thou art wise. 'Tis certain.
IAGO.   Stand you awhile apart:
    Confine yourself but in a patient list.[24]
    Whilst you were here o'erwhelmèd with your grief—   75
    A passion most unsuiting such a man—
    Cassio came hither. I shifted him away.[25]
    And laid good 'scuse upon your ecstasy.[26]
    Bade him anon return and here speak with me.
    The which he promised. Do but encave[27] yourself   80
    And mark the fleers.[28] the gibes. and notable[29] scorns
    That dwell in every region of his face:
    For I will make him tell the tale anew.
    Where. how. how oft. how long ago. and when
    He hath and is again to cope[30] your wife.   85

14. **mock me** Othello takes Iago's question about hurting his head to be a mocking reference to the cuckold's horns.   15. **civil** city-dwelling.   16. **yoked** married. Also. put into the yoke of infamy and cuckoldry.   17. **May . . . you** pull as you do. like oxen who are yoked. i.e.. share your fate as cuckold.   18. **unproper** shared.   19. **peculiar** their own.   20. **Your . . . better** i.e.. because you know the truth.   21. **lip** kiss.   22. **knowing . . . am** i.e.. a cuckold.   23. **know . . . be** will happen to her.   24. **patient list** within the bounds of patience.   25. **shifted . . . away** used a dodge to get rid of him.   26. **ecstasy** trance.   27. **encave** conceal.   28. **fleers** sneers.   29. **notable** obvious.   30. **cope** have sex with.

I say. but mark his gesture. Marry. patience!
Or I shall say you're all-in-all in spleen.[31]
And nothing of a man.

OTHELLO.   Dost thou hear. Iago?
I will be found most cunning in my patience:
But—dost thou hear?—most bloody.   90

IAGO.   That's not amiss:
But yet keep time[32] in all. Will you withdraw?

[OTHELLO *stands apart.*]

Now will I question Cassio of Bianca.
A huswife[33] that by selling her desires
Buys herself bread and clothes. It is a creature
That dotes on Cassio—as 'tis the strumpet's plague   95
To beguile many and be beguiled by one.
He, when he hears of her, cannot restrain[34]
From the excess of laughter. Here he comes.

[*Enter* CASSIO.]

As he shall smile. Othello shall go mad:
And his unbookish[35] jealousy must conster[36]   100
Poor Cassio's smiles. gestures, and light behaviors
Quite in the wrong.—How do you now. Lieutenant?

CASSIO. The worser that you give me the addition[37]
Whose want[38] even kills me.

IAGO. Ply Desdemona well and you are sure on 't.   105
[*Speaking lower.*] Now, if this suit lay in Bianca's power,
How quickly should you speed!

CASSIO. [*laughing*]   Alas, poor caitiff![39]

OTHELLO. [*aside*] Look how he laughs already!

IAGO. I never knew a woman love man so.

CASSIO. Alas, poor rogue! I think, i' faith, she loves me.   110

OTHELLO. Now he denies it faintly. and laughs it out.

IAGO. Do you hear. Cassio?

---

31. in spleen utterly governed by passionate impulses.   **32. keep time** keep yourself steady (as in music).   **33. huswife** hussy.   **34. restrain** refrain.
35. unbookish uninstructed.   **36. conster** construe.   **37. addition** title.
38. want the lack of which.   **39. caitiff** wretch.

OTHELLO.   Now he importunes him
   To tell it o'er. Go to!⁴⁰ Well said.⁴¹ well said.
IAGO. She gives it out that you shall marry her.
   Do you intend it?   115
CASSIO. Ha. ha. ha!
OTHELLO. Do you triumph. Roman?⁴² Do you triumph?
CASSIO. I marry her? What? A customer?⁴³ Prithee. bear some
   charity to my wit:⁴⁴ do not think it so unwholesome. Ha.
   ha. ha!   120
OTHELLO. So. so. so. so! They laugh that win.⁴⁵
IAGO. Faith. the cry goes that you shall marry her.
CASSIO. Prithee. say true.
IAGO. I am a very villain else.⁴⁶
OTHELLO. Have you scored me?⁴⁷ Well.   125
CASSIO. This is the monkey's own giving out. She is persuaded
   I will marry her out of her own love and flattery.⁴⁸ not out
   of my promise.
OTHELLO. Iago beckons⁴⁹ me. Now he begins the story.
CASSIO. She was here even now: she haunts me in every place.   130
   I was the other day talking on the seabank⁵⁰ with certain
   Venetians. and thither comes the bauble.⁵¹ and. by this
   hand.⁵² she falls me thus about my neck—

[*He embraces* IAGO.]

OTHELLO. Crying. "O dear Cassio!" as it were: his gesture im-
   ports it.   135
CASSIO. So hangs and lolls and weeps upon me. so shakes and
   pulls me. Ha. ha. ha!
OTHELLO. Now he tells how she plucked him to my chamber.
   O. I see that nose of yours. but not that dog I shall throw it
   to.⁵³

---

40. Go to! an expression of remonstrance.   41. Well said well done.   42. Do . . .
Roman The Romans were noted for their *triumphs* or triumphal processions.
43. customer prostitute.   44. Prithee . . . wit Be more charitable to my judgment.
45. They . . . win i.e.. they that laugh last laugh best.   46. I . . . else Call me a complete rogue if I'm not telling the truth.   47. scored me scored off me. beaten me.
made up my reckoning. branded me.   48. flattery self-flattery. self-deception.
49. beckons signals.   50. seabank seashore.   51. bauble plaything.   52. by . . .
hand I make my vow..   53. O . . . to Othello imagines himself cutting off Cassio's
nose and throwing it to a dog.

CASSIO. Well. I must leave her company.   140
IAGO. Before me.[54] look where she comes.

[*Enter* BIANCA *with* OTHELLO's *handkerchief.*]

CASSIO. 'Tis such another fitchew![55] Marry, a perfumed one.—
    What do you mean by this haunting of me?
BIANCA. Let the devil and his dam[56] haunt you! What did you
    mean by that same handkerchief you gave me even now? I   145
    was a fine fool to take it. I must take out the work? A likely
    piece of work.[57] that you should find it in your chamber
    and know not who left it there! This is some minx's token.
    and I must take out the work? There: give it your hobby-
    horse.[58] [*She gives him the handkerchief.*]   150
Wheresoever you had it. I'll take out no work on 't.
CASSIO. How now. my sweet Bianca? How now? How now?
OTHELLO. By heaven. that should be[59] my handkerchief!
BIANCA. If you'll come to supper tonight, you may: if you will
    not. come when you are next prepared for.[60]   [*Exit.*]
IAGO. After her. after her.   155
CASSIO. Faith. I must. She'll rail in the streets else.
IAGO. Will you sup there?
CASSIO. Faith. I intend so.
IAGO. Well. I may chance to see you. for I would very fain
    speak with you.   160
CASSIO. Prithee. come. Will you?
IAGO. Go to. Say no more.   [*Exit* CASSIO.]
OTHELLO. [*advancing*] How shall I murder him. Iago?
IAGO. Did you perceive how he laughed at his vice?
OTHELLO. O. Iago!   165
IAGO. And did you see the handkerchief?
OTHELLO. Was that mine?
IAGO. Yours, by this hand. And to see how he prizes the foolish
    woman your wife! She gave it him. and he hath given it his
    whore.   170

---

54. Before me on my soul.   **55. 'Tis . . . fitchew!** What a polecat she is! Just like all
the others. (Polecats were often compared with prostitutes because of their rank
smell and presumed lechery.)   **56. dam** mother.   **57. A . . . work** a fine story.
58. hobbyhorse harlot.   **59. should be** must be.   **60. if . . . for** when I'm ready for
you (i.e.. never).

OTHELLO. I would have him nine years a-killing. A fine
woman! A fair woman! A sweet woman!

IAGO. Nay, you must forget that.

OTHELLO. Ay, let her rot and perish, and be damned tonight,
for she shall not live. No, my heart is turned to stone: I   175
strike it, and it hurts my hand. O, the world hath not a
sweeter creature! She might lie by an emperor's side and
command him tasks.

IAGO. Nay, that's not your way.[61]

OTHELLO. Hang her! I do but say what she is. So delicate with   180
her needle! An admirable musician! O, she will sing the
savageness out of a bear. Of so high and plenteous wit and
invention![62]

IAGO. She's the worse for all this.

OTHELLO. O, a thousand, a thousand times! And then, of so   185
gentle a condition![63]

IAGO. Ay, too gentle.[64]

OTHELLO. Nay, that's certain. But yet the pity of it, Iago! O,
Iago, the pity of it, Iago!

IAGO. If you are so fond[65] over her iniquity, give her patent[66]   190
to offend, for if it touch not you it comes near nobody.

OTHELLO. I will chop her into messes.[67] Cuckold me?

IAGO. O, 'tis foul in her.

OTHELLO. With mine officer?

IAGO. That's fouler.   195

OTHELLO. Get me some poison, Iago, this night. I'll not expos-
tulate with her, lest her body and beauty unprovide[68] my
mind again. This night, Iago.

IAGO. Do it not with poison. Strangle her in her bed, even the
bed she hath contaminated.   200

OTHELLO. Good, good! The justice of it pleases. Very good.

IAGO. And for Cassio, let me be his undertaker.[69] You shall
hear more by midnight.

---

61. way i.e., the way you should think of her. 62. invention imagination. 63. so
... condition wellborn and well-bred. 64. gentle generous, yielding (to other
men). 65. fond foolish. 66. patent license. 67. messes portions of meat,
i.e., bits. 68. unprovide weaken, render unfit. 69. be his undertaker undertake
to dispatch him.

OTHELLO. Excellent good. [*A trumpet within.*] What trumpet
    is that same? 205
IAGO. I warrant, something from Venice.

    [*Enter* LODOVICO, DESDEMONA, *and attendants.*]

    'Tis Lodovico. This comes from the Duke.
    See, your wife's with him.
LODOVICO. God save you, worthy General!
OTHELLO.   With all my heart,
    sir.[70] 210
LODOVICO. [*giving him a letter*] The Duke and the senators of
    Venice greet you.
OTHELLO. I kiss the instrument of their pleasures.

    [*He opens the letter, and reads.*]

DESDEMONA. And what's the news, good cousin Lodovico?
IAGO. I am very glad to see you, signor.
    Welcome to Cyprus.
LODOVICO. I thank you. How does Lieutenant Cassio? 215
IAGO. Lives, sir.
DESDEMONA. Cousin, there's fall'n between him and my lord
    An unkind[71] breach; but you shall make all well.
OTHELLO. Are you sure of that?
DESDEMONA. My lord? 220
OTHELLO. [*reads*] "This fail you not to do, as you will—"
LODOVICO. He did not call; he's busy in the paper.
    Is there division twixt my lord and Cassio?
DESDEMONA. A most unhappy one. I would do much
    T' atone[72] them, for the love I bear to Cassio. 225
OTHELLO. Fire and brimstone!
DESDEMONA.   My lord?
OTHELLO.   Are you wise?
DESDEMONA. What, is he angry?
LODOVICO.   Maybe the letter moved him;
    For, as I think, they do command him home,
    Deputing Cassio in his government.[73]

---

70. with . . . sir I thank you most heartily.   **71. unkind** unnatural, contrary to their
natures; hurtful.   **72. atone** reconcile.   **73. government** office.

DESDEMONA. By my troth. I am glad on 't.[74]   230
OTHELLO.   Indeed?
DESDEMONA.   My lord?
OTHELLO. I am glad to see you mad.[75]
DESDEMONA.   Why. sweet Othello—
OTHELLO. [*striking her*] Devil!
DESDEMONA. I have not deserved this.
LODOVICO. My lord. this would not be believed in Venice.
     Though I should swear I saw 't. 'Tis very much.[76]   235
     Make her amends; she weeps.
OTHELLO.   O devil. devil!
     If that the earth could teem[77] with woman's tears.
     Each drop she falls[78] would prove a crocodile.[79]
     Out of my sight!
DESDEMONA.   I will not stay to offend you. [*Going.*]
LODOVICO. Truly. an obedient lady.   240
     I do beseech your lordship. call her back.
OTHELLO. Mistress!
DESDEMONA. [*returning*] My lord?
OTHELLO. What would you with her. sir?
LODOVICO.   Who. I. my lord?
OTHELLO.Ay. you did wish that I would make her turn.[80]   245
     Sir. she can turn. and turn. and yet go on
     And turn again; and she can weep. sir. weep;
     And she's obedient.[81] as you say. obedient.
     Very obedient.—Proceed you in your tears.—
     Concerning this. sir—O well-painted passion!—[82]   250
     I am commanded home.—Get you away;
     I'll send for you anon.—Sir. I obey the mandate
     And will return to Venice.—Hence. avaunt!

                         [*Exit* DESDEMONA.]

     Cassio shall have my place. And. sir. tonight

---

74. on't of it.   **75. I . . . mad** i.e.. I am glad to see that you are insane enough to rejoice in Cassio's promotion. (Othello bitterly plays on Desdemona's *I am glad.*).   **76.**
much outrageous.   **77. teem** breed.   **78. falls** lets fall.   **79. crocodile** Crocodiles
were supposed to weep hypocritical tears for their victims.   **80. Ay . . . turn** Othello
implies that Desdemona is pliant and will do a *turn* for any man.   **81. obedient**
with much the same sexual connotation as *turn*.   **82. passion** grief.

I do entreat that we may sup together.   255
    You are welcome, sir, to Cyprus.—Goats and monkeys![83]
LODOVICO. Is this the noble Moor whom our full Senate
    Call all in all sufficient? Is this the nature
    Whom passion could not shake? Whose solid virtue
    The shot of accident nor dart of chance   260
    Could neither graze nor pierce?
IAGO.   He is much changed.
LODOVICO. Are his wits safe? Is he not light of brain?
IAGO. He's that he is. I may not breathe my censure
    What he might be. If what he might he is not,
    I would to heaven he were![84]   265
LODOVICO.   What, strike his wife?
IAGO. Faith, that was not so well; yet would I knew
    That stroke would prove the worst!
LODOVICO.   Is it his use?[85]
    Or did the letters work upon his blood[86]
    And new-create his fault?
IAGO.   Alas, alas!
    It is not honesty in me to speak   270
    What I have seen and known. You shall observe him.
    And his own courses will denote[87] him so
    That I may save my speech. Do but go after.
    And mark how he continues.
LODOVICO. I am sorry that I am deceived in him.   [*Exeunt.*]

SCENE 2

[*Location: The Citadel. Enter* OTHELLO *and* EMILIA.]

OTHELLO. You have seen nothing then?
EMILIA. Nor ever heard, nor ever did suspect.
OTHELLO. Yes, you have seen Cassio and she together.
EMILIA. But then I saw no harm, and then I heard
    Each syllable that breath made up between them.   5
OTHELLO. What, did they never whisper?

---

83. Goats and monkeys! the most lustful animals.   **84. I . . . were** I dare not venture an opinion as to whether he's of unsound mind, as you suggest, but, if he isn't, then it might be better to wish he were in fact insane, since only that could excuse his wild behavior.   **85. use** custom.   **86. blood** passions.   **87. courses . . . denote** actions will reveal.

EMILIA. Never, my lord.
OTHELLO. Nor send you out o' the way?
EMILIA. Never.
OTHELLO. To fetch her fan, her gloves, her mask, nor nothing?   10
EMILIA. Never, my lord.
OTHELLO. That's strange.
EMILIA. I durst, my lord, to wager she is honest.
     Lay down my soul at stake.[1] If you think other,
     Remove your thought: it doth abuse your bosom.[2]   15
     If any wretch have put this in your head,
     Let heaven requite it with the serpent's curse![3]
     For if she be not honest, chaste, and true,
     There's no man happy; the purest of their wives
     Is foul as slander.   20
OTHELLO.   Bid her come hither. Go.

                                    [*Exit* EMILIA.]

     She says enough; yet she's a simple bawd
     That cannot say as much.[4] This[5] is a subtle whore,
     A closet lock and key of villainous secrets,
     And yet she'll kneel and pray; I have seen her do 't.

[*Enter* DESDEMONA *and* EMILIA.]

DESDEMONA. My lord, what is your will?   25
OTHELLO. Pray you, chuck, come hither.
DESDEMONA. What is your pleasure?
OTHELLO.   Let me see your eyes.
     Look in my face.
DESDEMONA.   What horrible fancy's this?
OTHELLO. [*to* EMILIA] Some of your function.[6] mistress,
     Leave procreants[7] alone and shut the door;   30
     Cough or cry "hem" if anybody come.
     Your mystery,[8] your mystery! Nay, dispatch.

                                    [*Exit* EMILIA.]

1. **at stake** as the wager.   2. **abuse ... bosom** deceive you.   3. **serpent's curse** the curse pronounced by God on the serpent for deceiving Eve, just as some man has done to Othello and Desdemona (See Genesis 3.14.).   4. **yet ... much** Any procuress or go-between who couldn't make up as plausible a story as Emilia's would have to be pretty stupid.   5. **This** Desdemona.   6. **function** i.e., practice your chosen profession, that of bawd (by guarding the door).   7. **procreants** mating couples. 8. **mystery** trade.

DESDEMONA. [*kneeling*] Upon my knees, what doth your speech
    import?
    I understand a fury in your words,
    But not the words.   35
OTHELLO. Why, what art thou?
DESDEMONA.   Your wife, my lord, your true
    And loyal wife.
OTHELLO.   Come, swear it, damn thyself,
    Lest, being like one of heaven,[9] the devils themselves
    Should fear to seize thee. Therefore be double damned:
    Swear thou art honest.   40
DESDEMONA.   Heaven doth truly know it.
OTHELLO. Heaven truly knows that thou art false as hell.
DESDEMONA. To whom, my lord? With whom? How am I false?
OTHELLO. [*weeping*] Ah, Desdemon! Away, away, away!
DESDEMONA. Alas the heavy day! Why do you weep?
    Am I the motive[10] of these tears, my lord?   45
    If haply you my father do suspect
    An instrument of this your calling back,
    Lay not your blame on me. If you have lost him,
    I have lost him too.
OTHELLO.   Had it pleased heaven
    To try me with affliction, had they[11] rained   50
    All kinds of sores and shames on my bare head,
    Steeped me in poverty to the very lips,
    Given to captivity me and my utmost hopes,
    I should have found in some place of my soul
    A drop of patience. But, alas, to make me   55
    A fixèd figure for the time of scorn[12]
    To point his[13] slow and moving finger[14] at!
    Yet could I bear that too, well, very well.
    But there where I have garnered[15] up my heart,
    Where either I must live or bear no life,   60
    The fountain[16] from the which my current runs

---

9. Lest . . . heaven looking like an angel. **10. motive** cause. **11. they** i.e. heavenly powers. **12. time of scorn** scornful world. **13. his** its. **14. moving finger** i.e., hour hand of the clock, moving so slowly it seems hardly to move at all. (Othello envisages himself as being eternally pointed at by the scornful world as the numbers on a clock are pointed at by the hour hand.) **15. garnered** stored. **16. fountain** spring.

Or else dries up—to be discarded thence!
Or keep it as a cistern[17] for foul toads
To knot[18] and gender[19] in! Turn thy complexion there.[20]
Patience, thou young and rose-lipped cherubin—   65
Ay, there look grim as hell![21]
DESDEMONA. I hope my noble lord esteems me honest.[22]
OTHELLO. O, ay, as summer flies are in the shambles,[23]
    That quicken[24] even with blowing.[25] O thou weed,
    Who art so lovely fair and smell'st so sweet   70
    That the sense aches at thee, would thou hadst ne'er been
        born!
DESDEMONA. Alas, what ignorant sin[26] have I committed?
OTHELLO. Was this fair paper, this most goodly book,
    Made to write "whore" upon? What committed?
    Committed? O thou public commoner![27]   75
    I should make very forges of my cheeks,
    That would to cinders burn up modesty,
    Did I but speak thy deeds. What committed?
    Heaven stops the nose at it and the moon winks;[28]
    The bawdy[29] wind, that kisses all it meets,   80
    Is hushed within the hollow mine[30] of earth
    And will not hear 't. What committed?
    Impudent strumpet!
DESDEMONA.   By heaven, you do me wrong.
OTHELLO. Are not you a strumpet?
DESDEMONA. No, as I am a Christian.   85
    If to preserve this vessel[31] for my lord
    From any other foul unlawful touch
    Be not to be a strumpet, I am none.
OTHELLO. What, not a whore?
DESDEMONA. No, as I shall be saved.   90
OTHELLO. Is 't possible?

---

17. cistern cesspool.   **18. knot** couple.   **19. gender** engender.   **20. Turn . . .
there** change your color, grow pale, at such a sight.   **21. Patience . . . hell** Even Patience, that rose-lipped cherub, will look grim and pale at this spectacle.
22. honest chaste.   **23. shambles** slaughterhouse.   **24. quicken** come to life.
25. blowing i.e., with the puffing up of something rotten in which maggots are
breeding.   **26. ignorant sin** sin in ignorance.   **27. commoner** prostitute.
28. winks closes her eyes. (The moon symbolizes chastity.)   **29. bawdy** kissing one
and all.   **30. mine** cave (where the winds were thought to dwell).   **31. vessel** body.

DESDEMONA. O, heaven forgive us!
OTHELLO.   I cry you mercy,[32] then.
  I took you for that cunning whore of Venice
  That married with Othello. [*Calling out.*] You, mistress,
  That have the office opposite to Saint Peter   95
  And keep the gate of hell!

  [*Enter* EMILIA.]

                    You, you, ay, you!
  We have done our course.[33] There's money for your pains.
    [*He gives money.*]
  I pray you, turn the key and keep our counsel.   [*Exit.*]
EMILIA. Alas, what does this gentleman conceive?[34]
  How do you, madam? How do you, my good lady?   100
DESDEMONA. Faith, half asleep.[35]
EMILIA. Good madam, what's the matter with my lord?
DESDEMONA. With who?
EMILIA. Why, with my lord, madam.
DESDEMONA. Who is thy lord?   105
EMILIA.   He that is yours, sweet lady.
DESDEMONA. I have none. Do not talk to me, Emilia.
  I cannot weep, nor answers have I none
  But what should go by water.[36] Prithee, tonight
  Lay on my bed my wedding sheets, remember;
  And call thy husband hither.   110
EMILIA. Here's a change indeed!   [*Exit.*]
DESDEMONA. 'Tis meet[37] I should be used so, very meet.
  How have I been behaved, that he might stick[38]
  The small'st opinion[39] on my least misuse?[40]

  [*Enter* IAGO *and* EMILIA.]

IAGO. What is your pleasure, madam? How is 't with you?   115
DESDEMONA. I cannot tell. Those that do teach young babes
  Do it with gentle means and easy tasks.
  He might have chid me so, for, in good faith,

---

32. cry you mercy beg you pardon.   **33. course** business (with an indecent suggestion of "trick," turn at sex).   **34. conceive** suppose.   **35. half asleep** i.e., dazed. **36. go by water** be expressed by tears.   **37. meet** fitting.   **38. stick** attach. **39. opinion** censure.   **40. misuse** misconduct.

I am a child to chiding.

IAGO. What is the matter. lady?   120

EMILIA. Alas. Iago. my lord hath so bewhored her.
    Thrown such despite and heavy terms upon her.
    That true hearts cannot bear it.

DESDEMONA. Am I that name. Iago?

IAGO. What name. fair lady?   125

DESDEMONA. Such as she said my lord did say I was.

EMILIA. He called her whore. A beggar in his drink
    Could not have laid such terms upon his callet.[41]

IAGO. Why did he so?

DESDEMONA. [weeping]
    I do not know. I am sure I am none such.   130

IAGO. Do not weep. do not weep. Alas the day!

EMILIA. Hath she forsook so many noble matches.
    Her father and her country and her friends.
    To be called whore? Would it not make one weep?

DESDEMONA. It is my wretched fortune.   135

IAGO.   Beshrew[42] him for't!
    How comes this trick[43] upon him?

DESDEMONA.   Nay. heaven doth know.

EMILIA. I will be hanged if some eternal[44] villain.
    Some busy and insinuating[45] rogue.
    Some cogging.[46] cozening[47] slave. to get some office.
    Have not devised this slander. I will be hanged else.   140

IAGO. Fie. there is no such man. It is impossible.

DESDEMONA. If any such there be. heaven pardon him!

EMILIA. A halter[48] pardon him! And hell gnaw his bones!
    Why should he call her whore? Who keeps her company?
    What place? What time? What form?[49] What likelihood?   145
    The Moor's abused by some most villainous knave.
    Some base notorious knave. some scurvy fellow.
    O heaven. that such companions thou'dst unfold.[50]
    And put in every honest hand a whip

---

41. **callet** whore. 42. **Beshrew** curse. 43. **trick** delusion. 44. **eternal** inveterate. 45. **insinuating** wheedling. 46. **cogging** cheating. 47. **cozening** defrauding. 48. **halter** hangman's noose. 49. **form** appearance. 50. **that . . . unfold** if only you would expose such fellows.

To lash the rascals naked through the world   150
Even from the east to th' west!

IAGO.   Speak within door.[51]

EMILIA. O, fie upon them! Some such squire[52] he was
That turned your wit the seamy side without[53]
And made you to suspect me with the Moor.

IAGO. You are a fool. Go to.[54]   155

DESDEMONA.   Alas, Iago.
What shall I do to win my lord again?
Good friend, go to him; for, by this light of heaven,
I know not how I lost him. Here I kneel. [*She kneels.*]
If e'er my will did trespass 'gainst his love,
Either in discourse of thought or actual deed,   160
Or that[55] mine eyes, mine ears, or any sense
Delighted them[56] in any other form;
Or that I do not yet,[57] and ever did,
And ever will—though he do shake me off
To beggarly divorcement—love him dearly.   165
Comfort forswear[58] me! Unkindness may do much,
And his unkindness may defeat[59] my life,
But never taint my love. I cannot say "whore."
It does abhor[60] me now I speak the word;
To do the act that might the addition[61] earn   170
Not the world's mass of vanity[62] could make me.

[*She rises.*]

IAGO. I pray you, be content. 'Tis but his humor.[63]
The business of the state does him offense,
And he does chide with you.

DESDEMONA. If 'twere no other—   175

IAGO.   It is but so, I warrant.

        [*Trumpets within.*]
Hark, how these instruments summon you to supper!

---

51. within door not so loud.   **52. squire** fellow.   **53. without** wrong side out.
54. Go to i.e. that's enough.   **55. that** if.   **56. Delighted them** took delight.
57. yet still.   **58. Comfort forswear** May heavenly comfort forsake.   **59. defeat**
destroy.   **60. abhor** fill me with abhorrence. Also, make me whorelike.
61. addition title.   **62. vanity** showy splendor.   **63. humor** mood.

The messengers of Venice stays the meat.[64]
Go in. and weep not. All things shall be well.

[*Exeunt* DESDEMONA *and* EMILIA.]

[*Enter* RODERIGO.]

How now. Roderigo?

RODERIGO. I do not find that thou deal'st justly with me.   180
IAGO. What in the contrary?
RODERIGO. Every day thou daff'st me[65] with some device.[66]
   Iago. and rather, as it seems to me now. keep'st from me all
   conveniency[67] than suppliest me with the least
   advantage[68] of hope. I will indeed no longer endure it. nor   185
   am I yet persuaded to put up[69] in peace what already I
   have foolishly suffered.
IAGO. Will you hear me. Roderigo?
RODERIGO. Faith. I have heard too much. for your words and
   performances are no kin together.   190
IAGO. You charge me most unjustly.
RODERIGO. With naught but truth. I have wasted myself out of
   my means. The jewels you have had from me to deliver[70]
   Desdemona would half have corrupted a votarist.[71] You
   have told me she hath received them and returned me ex-   195
   pectations and comforts of sudden respect[72] and acquaintance. but I find none.
IAGO. Well. go to. very well.
RODERIGO. "Very well"! "Go to"! I cannot go to.[73] man. nor
   'tis not very well. By this hand. I think it is scurvy. and be-   200
   gin to find myself fopped[74] in it.
IAGO. Very well.
RODERIGO. I tell you 'tis not very well.[75] I will make myself
   known to Desdemona. If she will return me my jewels. I

---

64. **stays the meat** wait to dine. 65. **daff'st me** You put me off. 66. **device** excuse. trick. 67. **conveniency** advantage. opportunity. 68. **advantage** increase.
69. **put up** submit to. tolerate. 70. **deliver** deliver to. 71. **votarist** nun.
72. **sudden respect** immediate consideration. 73. **go to** Roderigo changes Iago's
go to. an expression urging patience. to *I cannot go to.* "I have no opportunity for
success in wooing." 74. **fopped** fooled. duped. 75. **I . . . well** Roderigo changes
Iago's *very well.* "all right. then." to *not very well.* "not at all good."

will give over my suit and repent my unlawful solicitation: 205
if not, assure yourself I will seek satisfaction[76] of you.

IAGO. You have said now?[77]

RODERIGO. Ay, and said nothing but what I protest intendment[78] of doing.

IAGO. Why, now I see there's mettle in thee, and even from this   210
instant do build on thee a better opinion than ever before.
Give me thy hand, Roderigo. Thou hast taken against me a
most just exception: but yet I protest I have dealt most directly in thy affair.

RODERIGO. It hath not appeared.   215

IAGO. I grant indeed it hath not appeared, and your suspicion
is not without wit and judgment. But, Roderigo, if thou
hast that in thee indeed which I have greater reason to believe now than ever—I mean purpose, courage, and
valor—this night show it. If thou the next night following   220
enjoy not Desdemona, take me from this world with
treachery and devise engines[79] for my life.

RODERIGO. Well, what is it? Is it within reason and compass?

IAGO. Sir, there is especial commission come from Venice to
depute Cassio in Othello's place.   225

RODERIGO. Is that true? Why, then Othello and Desdemona return again to Venice.

IAGO. O, no: he goes into Mauritania and takes away with him
the fair Desdemona, unless his abode be lingered here by
some accident: wherein none can be so determinate[80] as   230
the removing of Cassio.

RODERIGO. How do you mean, removing of him?

IAGO. Why, by making him uncapable of Othello's place—
knocking out his brains.

RODERIGO. And that you would have me to do?   235

IAGO. Ay, if you dare do yourself a profit and a right. He sups
tonight with a harlotry,[81] and thither will I go to him. He
knows not yet of his honorable fortune. If you will watch

---

76. satisfaction repayment. (The term normally means settling of accounts in a
duel.). **77. You ... now?** Have you finished? **78. intendment** intention.
79. engines plots against. **80. determinate** conclusive. **81. harlotry** slut.

his going thence. which I will fashion to fall out[82] between
twelve and one. you may take him at your pleasure. I will   240
be near to second your attempt. and he shall fall between
us. Come. stand not amazed at it. but go along with me. I
will show you such a necessity in his death that you shall
think yourself bound to put it on him. It is now high[83] sup-
pertime. and the night grows to waste.[84] About it.   245
RODERIGO. I will hear further reason for this.
IAGO. And you shall be satisfied.   *[Exeunt.]*

SCENE 3

[Location: The Citadel. Enter OTHELLO. LODOVICO. DESDEMONA.
EMILIA. *and attendants.]*

LODOVICO. I do beseech you. sir. trouble yourself no further.
OTHELLO. O. pardon me: 'twill do me good to walk.
LODOVICO. Madam. good night. I humbly thank your ladyship.
DESDEMONA. Your honor is most welcome.
OTHELLO.   Will you walk. sir?
   O. Desdemona!   5
DESDEMONA. My lord?
OTHELLO.   Get you to bed on th' instant. I will be returned
forthwith. Dismiss your attendant there. Look 't be done.
DESDEMONA. I will. my lord.

       [Exit OTHELLO. *with* LODOVICO *and attendants.]*

EMILIA. How goes it now? He looks gentler than he did.   10
DESDEMONA. He says he will return incontinent.[1]
   And hath commanded me to go to bed.
   And bid me to dismiss you.
EMILIA.   Dismiss me?
DESDEMONA. It was his bidding. Therefore. good Emilia.
   Give me my nightly wearing. and adieu.   15
   We must not now displease him.
EMILIA. I would you had never seen him!
DESDEMONA. So would not I. My love doth so approve him

---

82. fall out occur.   **83. high** fully.   **84. grows to waste** wastes away.   **1. incontinent** immediately.

That even his stubbornness,[2] his checks,[3] his frowns—
Prithee. unpin me—have grace and favor in them.   20

[EMILIA *prepares* DESDEMONA *for bed.*]

EMILIA. I have laid those sheets you bade me on the bed.
DESDEMONA. All's one.[4] Good faith. how foolish are our minds!
   If I do die before thee. prithee shroud me
   In one of these same sheets.
EMILIA.   Come, come, you talk.[5]
DESDEMONA. My mother had a maid called Barbary.   25
   She was in love. and he she loved proved mad[6]
   And did forsake her. She had a song of "Willow."
   An old thing 'twas. but it expressed her fortune.
   And she died singing it. That song tonight
   Will not go from my mind: I have much to do   30
   But to go hang[7] my head all at one side
   And sing it like poor Barbary. Prithee. dispatch.
EMILIA. Shall I go fetch your nightgown?[8]
DESDEMONA.   No. unpin me here.
   This Lodovico is a proper[9] man.
EMILIA. A very handsome man.   35
DESDEMONA. He speaks well.
EMILIA. I know a lady in Venice would have walked barefoot to
   Palestine for a touch of his nether lip.
DESDEMONA. [*singing*]
  "The poor soul sat sighing by a sycamore tree.
    Sing all a green willow:[10]   40
  Her hand on her bosom. her head on her knee.
    Sing willow. willow. willow.
  The fresh streams ran by her and murmured her moans:
    Sing willow. willow. willow:
  Her salt tears fell from her. and softened the stones—"   45
  Lay by these.
  [*Singing.*] "Sing willow. willow. willow—"

---

2. **stubbornness** roughness.   3. **checks** rebukes.   4. **All's one** All right. It doesn't
really matter.   5. **talk** prattle.   6. **mad** wild.   7. **But . . . hang** I can scarcely keep
myself from hanging.   8. **nightgown** dressing gown.   9. **proper** handsome.
10. **green willow** a conventional emblem of disappointed love.

Prithee. hie thee.[11] He'll come anon.[12]

[*Singing.*] "Sing all a green willow must be my garland.
  Let nobody blame him: his scorn I approve—"   50
Nay. that's not next.—Hark! Who is 't that knocks?
EMILIA. It's the wind.
DESDEMONA. [*singing*]
"I called my love false love: but what said he then?
Sing willow. willow. willow:
  If I court more women. you'll couch with more men."   55
So. get thee gone. Good night. Mine eyes do itch:
Doth that bode weeping?
EMILIA.   'Tis neither here nor there.
DESDEMONA. I have heard it said so. O. these men. these men!
Dost thou in conscience think—tell me. Emilia—
That there be women do abuse[13] their husbands   60
In such gross kind?
EMILIA.   There be some such. no question.
DESDEMONA. Wouldst thou do such a deed for all the world?
EMILIA. Why. would not you?
DESDEMONA.   No. by this heavenly light!
EMILIA. Nor I neither by this heavenly light:
I might do 't as well i' the dark.   65
DESDEMONA. Wouldst thou do such a deed for all the world?
EMILIA. The world's a huge thing. It is a great price
For a small vice.
DESDEMONA. Good troth. I think thou wouldst not.
EMILIA. By my troth. I think I should. and undo 't when I had 70
done. Marry. I would not do such a thing for a joint ring.[14]
nor for measures of lawn.[15] nor for gowns. petticoats. nor
caps. nor any petty exhibition.[16] But for all the whole
world! Uds[17] pity. who would not make her husband a
cuckold to make him a monarch? I should venture purga- 75
tory for 't.
DESDEMONA. Beshrew me if I would do such a wrong
For the whole world.

---

11. **hie thee** hurry. 12. **anon** right away. 13. **abuse** deceive. 14. **joint ring** a
ring made in separate halves. 15. **lawn** fine linen. 16. **exhibition** gift. 17. **Uds**
God's.

EMILIA. Why, the wrong is but a wrong i' the world, and having
    the world for your labor, 'tis a wrong in your own world, and   80
    you might quickly make it right.
DESDEMONA. I do not think there is any such woman.
EMILIA. Yes, a dozen, and as many
    To th' vantage[18] as would store[19] the world they played[20] for.
    But I do think it is their husbands' faults   85
    If wives do fall. Say that they slack their duties[21]
    And pour our treasures into foreign laps.[22]
    Or else break out in peevish jealousies,
    Throwing restraint upon us?[23] Or say they strike us,
    Or scant our former having in despite?[24]   90
    Why, we have galls,[25] and though we have some grace,
    Yet have we some revenge. Let husbands know
    Their wives have sense[26] like them. They see, and smell,
    And have their palates both for sweet and sour,
    As husbands have. What is it that they do   95
    When they change us for others? Is it sport?[27]
    I think it is. And doth affection[28] breed it?
    I think it doth. Is 't frailty that thus errs?
    It is so, too. And have not we affections,
    Desires for sport, and frailty, as men have?   100
    Then let them use us well: else let them know,
    The ills we do, their ills instruct us so.
DESDEMONA. Good night, good night. God me such uses[29] send
    Not to pick bad from bad, but by bad mend[30]

[Exeunt.]

ACT 5
SCENE 1

[Location: A street in Cyprus. Enter IAGO *and* RODERIGO.*]*

18. To th' vantage in addition, to boot.   **19. store** populate.   **20. played** gambled.
Also, sported sexually.   **21. duties** marital duties.   **22. foreign laps** i.e., are unfaithful, give what is rightfully ours (semen) to other women.   **23. Throwing . . . us**
i.e., jealously restricting our freedom to see other men.   **24. Or . . . despite** reduce
our allowance to spite us.   **25. Why . . . galls** are capable of resenting injury and insult.   **26. sense** physical sense.   **27. sport** sexual pastime.   **28. affection** passion.
29. uses practice.   **30. Not . . . mend** Not to learn bad conduct from others' badness
(as Emilia has suggested women learn from men), but to mend my ways by perceiving what badness is, making spiritual benefit out of evil and adversity.

IAGO. Here stand behind this bulk.[1] Straight will he come.
   Wear thy good rapier bare,[2] and put it home.
   Quick, quick! Fear nothing. I'll be at thy elbow.
   It makes us or it mars us. Think on that,
   And fix most firm thy resolution.   5
RODERIGO. Be near at hand. I may miscarry in 't.
IAGO. Here, at thy hand. Be bold, and take thy stand.

   [IAGO *stands aside.* RODERIGO *conceals himself.*]

RODERIGO. I have no great devotion to the deed;
   And yet he hath given me satisfying reasons.
   'Tis but a man gone. Forth, my sword! He dies.   10

   [*He draws.*]

IAGO. I have rubbed this young quat[3] almost to the sense,[4]
   And he grows angry. Now, whether he kill Cassio
   Or Cassio him, or each do kill the other,
   Every way makes my gain. Live Roderigo,[5]
   He calls me to a restitution large   15
   Of gold and jewels that I bobbed[6] from him
   As gifts to Desdemona.
   It must not be. If Cassio do remain,
   He hath a daily beauty in his life
   That makes me ugly; and besides, the Moor   20
   May unfold[7] me to him; there stand I in much peril.
   No, he must die. Be 't so. I hear him coming.

   [*Enter* CASSIO.]

RODERIGO. [*coming forth*] I know his gait, 'tis he.—Villain, thou
      diest!

   [*He attacks* CASSIO.]

CASSIO. That thrust had been mine enemy indeed,
   But that my coat[8] is better than thou know'st.   25

---

1. bulk framework projecting from the front of a shop.   **2. bare** unsheathed.
3. quat pimple.   **4. to the sense** raw.   **5. Live Roderigo** if Roderigo lives.
6. bobbed swindled.   **7. unfold** expose.   **8. coat** possibly a garment of mail under
the outer clothing, or simply a tougher coat than Roderigo expected.

I will make proof[9] of thine.

[*He draws, and wounds* RODERIGO.]

RODERIGO.   O. I am slain! [*He falls.*]

[IAGO, *from behind, wounds* CASSIO *in the leg, and exit.*]

CASSIO. I am maimed forever. Help, ho! Murder! Murder!

[*Enter* OTHELLO.]

OTHELLO. The voice of Cassio! Iago keeps his word.
RODERIGO. O. villain that I am!
OTHELLO.   It is even so.
CASSIO. O. help, ho! Light! A surgeon!   30
OTHELLO. 'Tis he. O brave Iago, honest and just,
    That hast such noble sense of thy friend's wrong!
    Thou teachest me. Minion,[10] your dear lies dead,
    And your unblest fate hies.[11] Strumpet, I come.
    Forth of[12] my heart those charms, thine eyes, are blotted: 35
    Thy bed, lust-stained, shall with lust's blood be spotted.

[*Exit* OTHELLO.]

[*Enter* LODOVICO *and* GRATIANO.]

CASSIO. What ho! No watch? No passage?[13] Murder! Murder!
GRATIANO. 'Tis some mischance. The voice is very direful.
CASSIO. O. help!
LODOVICO. Hark!   40
RODERIGO. O wretched villain!
LODOVICO. Two or three groan. 'Tis heavy[14] night:
    These may be counterfeits. Let's think 't unsafe
    To come in[15] to the cry without more help.

[*They remain near the entrance.*]

RODERIGO. Nobody come? Then shall I bleed to death.   45

[*Enter* IAGO *in his shirtsleeves, with a light.*]

---

9. **proof** a test. **10. Minion** hussy (i.e., Desdemona). **11. hies** hastens on.
12. Forth of from out. **13. passage** passers-by. **14. heavy** thick, dark.
15. come in approach.

LODOVICO. Hark!
GRATIANO Here's one comes in his shirt. with light and weapons.
IAGO. Who's there? Whose noise is this that cries on[16] murder?
LODOVICO. We do not know.
IAGO.   Did not you hear a cry?
CASSIO. Here. here! For heaven's sake. help me!   50
IAGO.   What's the matter?

[*He moves toward* CASSIO.]

GRATIANO. [*to* LODOVICO] This is Othello's ancient. as I take it.
LODOVICO. [*to* GRATIANO] The same indeed. a very valiant fellow.
IAGO. [*to* CASSIO] What[17] are you here that cry so grievously?
CASSIO. Iago? O. I am spoiled.[18] undone by villains!
    Give me some help.   55
IAGO. O me. Lieutenant! What villains have done this?
CASSIO. I think that one of them is hereabout.
    And cannot make[19] away.
IAGO.   O treacherous villains!
    [*To* LODOVICO *and* GRATIANO.] What are you there? Come in.
    and give some help. [*They advance.*]
RODERIGO. O. help me there!   60
CASSIO That's one of them.
IAGO.   O murderous slave! O villain!

[*He stabs* RODERIGO.]

RODERIGO. O damned Iago! O inhuman dog!
IAGO. Kill men i' the dark?—Where be these bloody thieves?—
    How silent is this town!—Ho! Murder. murder!—

[*To* LODOVICO *and* GRATIANO.]

    What may you be? Are you of good or evil?   65
LODOVICO. As you shall prove us. praise[20] us.
IAGO. Signor Lodovico?
LODOVICO. He. sir.
IAGO. I cry you mercy.[21] Here's Cassio hurt by villains.
GRATIANO. Cassio?   70

---

16. cries on cries out. **17. What** who. **18. spoiled** ruined. **19. make** get.
20. praise appraise. **21. I . . . mercy** I beg your pardon.

IAGO. How is 't. brother?

CASSIO. My leg is cut in two.

IAGO. Marry. heaven forbid!
Light. gentlemen! I'll bind it with my shirt.

[*He hands them the light and tends to* CASSIO'S *wound.*]

[*Enter* BIANCA.]

BIANCA. What is the matter. ho? Who is 't that cried?   75

IAGO. Who is 't that cried?

BIANCA.   O my dear Cassio!
My sweet Cassio! O Cassio. Cassio. Cassio!

IAGO. O notable strumpet! Cassio. may you suspect
Who they should be that have thus mangled you?

CASSIO. No.   80

GRATIANO. I am sorry to find you thus. I have been to seek you.

IAGO. Lend me a garter. [*He applies a tourniquet.*] So.—O. for
a chair.²²
To bear him easily hence!

BIANCA. Alas. he faints! O Cassio. Cassio. Cassio!

IAGO. Gentlemen all. I do suspect this trash   85
To be a party in this injury.—
Patience awhile. good Cassio.—Come. come:
Lend me a light. [*He shines the light on* RODERIGO.]
Know we this face or no?
Alas. my friend and my dear countryman   90
Roderigo! No.—Yes. sure.—O heaven! Roderigo!

GRATIANO. What. of Venice?

IAGO. Even he. sir. Did you know him?

GRATIANO. Know him? Ay.

IAGO. Signor Gratiano? I cry your gentle²³ pardon.   95
These bloody accidents²⁴ must excuse my manners
That so neglected you.

GRATIANO.   I am glad to see you.

IAGO. How do you. Cassio? O. a chair. a chair!

GRATIANO. Roderigo!

---

22. chair litter.   **23. gentle** noble.   **24. accidents** sudden events.

IAGO. He. he. 'tis he. [*A litter is brought in.*] O. that's well   100
     said:[25] the chair.
     Some good man bear him carefully from hence;
     I'll fetch the General's surgeon. [*To* BIANCA.] For you. mistress.
     Save you your labor.[26] He that lies slain here. Cassio.
     Was my dear friend. What malice[27] was between you?
CASSIO. None in the world. nor do I know the man.   105
IAGO. [*to* BIANCA.] What. look you pale?—O. bear him out o' th'
     air.[28]

     [*CASSIO and* RODERIGO *are borne off.*]

     Stay you.[29] good gentlemen.—Look you pale. mistress?—
     Do you perceive the gastness[30] of her eye?—
     Nay. if you stare.[31] shall hear more anon.—
     Behold her well: I pray you. look upon her.   110
     Do you see. gentlemen? Nay. guiltiness
     Will speak. though tongues were out of use.

     [*Enter* EMILIA.]

EMILIA. 'Las. what's the matter? What's the matter. husband?
IAGO. Cassio hath here been set on in the dark
     By Roderigo and fellows that are scaped.   115
     He's almost slain. and Roderigo dead.
EMILIA. Alas. good gentleman! Alas. good Cassio!
IAGO. This is the fruits of whoring. Prithee. Emilia.
     Go know[32] of Cassio where he supped tonight.
     [*To* BIANCA.] What. do you shake at that?   120
BIANCA. He supped at my house. but I therefore shake not.
IAGO. O. did he so? I charge you go with me.
EMILIA. O. fie upon thee. strumpet!
BIANCA. I am no strumpet. but of life as honest[33]
     As you that thus abuse me.   125
EMILIA. As I? Faugh! Fie upon thee!

---

25. well said well done.   **26. Save . . . labor** Never you mind tending Cassio.
27. malice enmity.   **28. O . . . air** Fresh air was thought to be dangerous for a
wound.   **29. Stay you** Lodovico and Gratiano are evidently about to leave.
30. gastness terror.   **31. stare** Iago pretends to interpret Bianca's wild looks as an
involuntary confession of guilt.   **32. know** learn.   **33. honest** chaste.

IAGO. Kind gentlemen, let's go see poor Cassio dressed.[34]—
   Come, mistress, you must tell 's another tale.
   Emilia, run you to the citadel
   And tell my lord and lady what hath happed.—   130
   Will you go on afore? [*Aside.*] This is the night
   That either makes me or fordoes[35] me quite.

                                          [*Exeunt.*]

SCENE 2

[*Location: A bedchamber in the citadel.*
Enter OTHELLO *with a light, and* DESDEMONA *in her bed.*][1]

OTHELLO. It is the cause,[2] it is the cause, my soul.
   Let me not name it to you, you chaste stars!
   It is the cause. Yet I'll not shed her blood,
   Nor scar that whiter skin of hers than snow,
   And smooth as monumental alabaster.[3]   5
   Yet she must die, else she'll betray more men.
   Put out the light, and then put out the light.[4]
   If I quench thee, thou flaming minister,[5]
   I can again thy former light restore,
   Should I repent me;[6] but once put out thy light,   10
   Thou cunning'st pattern[7] of excelling nature,
   I know not where is that Promethean heat[8]
   That can thy light relume.[9] When I have plucked thy rose,
   I cannot give it vital growth again;
   It needs must wither. I'll smell thee on the tree.   15

[*He kisses her.*]

   O balmy breath, that dost almost persuade
   Justice to break her sword! One more, one more.

---

34. dressed Cassio's wounds dressed. **35. fordoes** ruins. **1. [Location . . . bed.]**
Either the curtains are drawn back to reveal the bed in a recessed area backstage or
the bed is "thrust out" onstage as the scene begins. **2. cause** cause of justice, the offense itself, which Othello must correct as an agent of justice. **3. alabaster** used in
making tombs and funeral monuments. **4. light** the torch or lamp. . . . Desdemona's
life. **5. minister** torch or lamp that serves me. **6. repent me** change my mind.
7. Thou . . . pattern you skillfully wrought perfect example. **8. Promethean heat**
divine fire (alluding to the theft of fire from heaven by Prometheus). **9. relume**
rekindle.

Be thus when thou art dead, and I will kill thee,
And love thee after. One more, and that's the last.

[*He kisses her.*]

So sweet was ne'er so fatal. I must weep,   20
But they are cruel[10] tears. This sorrow's heavenly:
It strikes where it doth love.[11] She wakes.
DESDEMONA. Who's there? Othello?
OTHELLO. Ay, Desdemona.
DESDEMONA. Will you come to bed, my lord?   25
OTHELLO. Have you prayed tonight, Desdemon?
DESDEMONA. Ay, my lord.
OTHELLO. If you bethink yourself of any crime[12]
  Unreconciled as yet to heaven and grace,
  Solicit[13] for it straight.[14]   30
DESDEMONA. Alack, my lord, what may you mean by that?
OTHELLO. Well, do it, and be brief. I will walk by.
  I would not kill thy unprepared spirit.
  No, heaven forfend![15] I would not kill thy soul.
DESDEMONA. Talk you of killing?   35
OTHELLO.   Ay, I do.
DESDEMONA.   Then heaven
  Have mercy on me!
OTHELLO.   Amen, with all my heart!
DESDEMONA. If you say so, I hope you will not kill me.
OTHELLO. Humh!
DESDEMONA. And yet I fear you; for you're fatal then
  When your eyes roll so. Why I should fear I know not,   40
  Since guiltiness I know not; but yet I feel I fear.
OTHELLO. Think on thy sins.
DESDEMONA.   They are loves I bear to you.[16]
OTHELLO. Ay, and for that thou diest.
DESDEMONA. That death's unnatural that kills for loving.
  Alas, why gnaw you so your nether lip?   45

---

10. cruel unrelenting.   **11. It . . . love** compare Hebrews 12.6: "For whom the Lord
loveth he chasteneth."   **12. crime** sin.   **13. Solicit** pray.   **14. straight** immediately.   **15. forfend** forbid.   **16. They . . . you** If I sinned, it was in loving you more
than my father or more than God.

Some bloody passion shakes your very frame.
These are portents; but yet I hope, I hope,
They do not point on[17] me.

OTHELLO. Peace, and be still!

DESDEMONA. I will so. What's the matter?   50

OTHELLO. That handkerchief which I so loved and gave thee
Thou gav'st to Cassio.

DESDEMONA.   No, by my life and soul!
Send for the man and ask him.

OTHELLO. Sweet soul, take heed, take heed of perjury.
Thou art on thy deathbed.   55

DESDEMONA. Ay, but not yet to die.

OTHELLO.   Yes, presently.[18]
Therefore confess thee freely of thy sin;
For to deny each article with oath
Cannot remove nor choke the strong conception[19]
That I do groan withal.[20] Thou art to die.   60

DESDEMONA. Then Lord have mercy on me!

OTHELLO.   I say, amen.

DESDEMONA. And have you mercy too! I never did
Offend[21] you in my life; never loved Cassio
But with such general warranty[22] of heaven
As I might love. I never gave him token.   65

OTHELLO. By heaven, I saw my handkerchief in 's hand.
O perjured woman! Thou dost stone[23] heart,
And makes me call what I intend to do
A murder, which I thought a sacrifice.
I saw the handkerchief.   70

DESDEMONA.   He found it, then.
I never gave it him. Send for him hither;
Let him confess a truth.

OTHELLO.   He hath confessed.

DESDEMONA. What, my lord?

OTHELLO. That he hath used thee.

---

17. point on point at, predict what is to happen to.   **18. presently** immediately.
19. conception belief in your guilt. Also, plan in my mind.   **20. groan withal**
groan at in sorrow. Also, as in giving birth.   **21. Offend** wrong.   **22. warranty**
sanction.   **23. stone** harden.

DESDEMONA.   How? Unlawfully?
OTHELLO.   Ay.
DESDEMONA. He will not say so.   75
OTHELLO.   No, his mouth is stopped:
    Honest Iago hath ta'en order[24] for 't.
DESDEMONA. O, my fear interprets. What, is he dead?
OTHELLO. Had all his hairs been lives, my great revenge
    Had stomach for them all.
DESDEMONA. Alas, he is betrayed and I undone! [*She weeps.*]   80
OTHELLO. Out, strumpet! Weep'st thou for him to my face?
DESDEMONA. O, banish me, my lord, but kill me not!
OTHELLO. Down, strumpet!
DESDEMONA. Kill me tomorrow; let me live tonight!
OTHELLO. Nay, if you strive—   85
DESDEMONA. But half an hour!
OTHELLO.   Being done,[25] there is no pause.
DESDEMONA. But while I say one prayer!
OTHELLO.   It is too late. [*Smothers
    her.*]
EMILIA. [*at the door*] My lord, my lord! What, ho! My lord, my
    lord!
OTHELLO. What noise is this? Not dead? Not yet quite dead?
    I that am cruel am yet merciful: 90
    I would not have thee linger in thy pain. [*He dispatches her.*]
    So, so.
EMILIA. [*within*] What, ho! My lord, my lord!
OTHELLO.   Who's there?
EMILIA. [*within*] O, good my lord, I would speak a word with
    you!
OTHELLO. Yes, 'tis Emilia.—By and by.—She's dead.   95
    'Tis like[26] she comes to speak of Cassio's death.—
    The noise was here.[27] Ha! No more moving?
    Still as the grave. Shall she come in? Were 't good?—
    I think she stirs again. No. What's best to do?
    If she come in, she'll sure speak to my wife.   100

---

24. ta'en order taken measures.   **25. Being done** since justice has begun its relent-
less course.   **26. like** likely that.   **27. The ... here** The Folio's *high* is possible,
suggesting that the commotion of the attack on Cassio was loud.

My wife! My wife! What wife? I have no wife.
O, insupportable! O heavy hour!
Methinks it should be now a huge eclipse
Of sun and moon, and that th' affrighted globe
Should yawn[28] at alteration.[29]   105
EMILIA. [*within*]   I do beseech you
    That I may speak with you. O, good my lord!
OTHELLO. I had forgot thee. O, come in, Emilia.—
    Soft,[30] by and by. Let me the curtains draw.—

    [*He closes the bed-curtains and opens the door.*]

    Where art thou?

    [*Enter* EMILIA.]

                            What's the matter with thee now?
EMILIA. O, my good lord, yonder's foul murders done!   110
OTHELLO. What, now?
EMILIA. But now, my lord.
OTHELLO. It is the very error[31] of the moon:
    She comes more nearer earth than she was wont,
    And makes men mad.   115
EMILIA. Cassio, my lord, hath killed a young Venetian
    Called Roderigo.
OTHELLO.   Roderigo killed?
    And Cassio killed?
EMILIA.   No, Cassio is not killed.
OTHELLO. Not Cassio killed? Then murder's out of tune,
    And sweet revenge grows harsh.   120
DESDEMONA. O, falsely, falsely murdered!
EMILIA. O Lord, what cry is that?
OTHELLO. That? What?
EMILIA. Out[32] and alas, that was my lady's voice.

    [*She opens the bed-curtains.*]

---

28. yawn gape in amazement, i.e., move in an earthquake. (According to Pliny, earthquakes often happen during eclipses.).   **29. alteration** at these cataclysmic events in nature, well suited to express the horror of Desdemona's death.   **30. Soft** wait a minute.   **31. error** aberration, irregularity.   **32. Out** a cry of dismay, intensifying *alas*.

Help. help. ho. help! O lady. speak again!   125
   Sweet Desdemona! O sweet mistress. speak!
DESDEMONA. A guiltless death I die.
EMILIA. O. who hath done this deed?
DESDEMONA. Nobody: I myself. Farewell.
   Commend me to my kind lord. O. farewell! [*She dies.*]   130
OTHELLO. Why. how should she be murdered?
EMILIA.   Alas. who knows?
OTHELLO. You heard her say herself it was not I.
EMILIA. She said so. I must needs report the truth.
OTHELLO. She's like a liar gone to burning hell!
   'Twas I that killed her.   135
EMILIA.   O. the more angel she.
   And you the blacker devil!
OTHELLO. She turned to folly.³³ and she was a whore.
EMILIA. Thou dost belie³⁴ her. and thou art a devil.
OTHELLO. She was false as water.
EMILIA.   Thou art rash as fire to say
   That she was false. O. she was heavenly true!   140
OTHELLO. Cassio did top her. Ask thy husband else.³⁵
   O. I were damned beneath all depth in hell
   But that I did proceed upon just grounds
   To this extremity. Thy husband knew it all.
EMILIA. My husband?   145
OTHELLO.   Thy husband.
EMILIA.   That she was false to
      wedlock?
OTHELLO. Ay. with Cassio. Nay. had she been true.
   If heaven would make me such another world
   Of one entire and perfect chrysolite.³⁶
   I'd not have sold her for it.
EMILIA. My husband?   150
OTHELLO. Ay. 'twas he that told me on her first.
   An honest man he is. and hates the slime
   That sticks on filthy deeds.
EMILIA. My husband?

---

33. folly i.e.. wantonness. fleshly sin.   **34. belie** slander.   **35. else** i.e.. if you don't believe me.   **36. chrysolite** precious topaz.

OTHELLO. What needs this iterance,[37] woman? I say thy   155
    husband.
EMILIA. O mistress. villainy hath made mocks[38] with love!
    My husband say she was false?
OTHELLO.   He, woman;
    I say thy husband. Dost understand the word?
    My friend. thy husband. honest. honest Iago.
EMILIA. If he say so. may his pernicious soul   160
    Rot half a grain a day! He lies to th' heart.
    She was too fond of her most filthy bargain.
OTHELLO. Ha? [*He draws.*]
EMILIA. Do thy worst!
    This deed of thine is no more worthy heaven   165
    Than thou wast worthy her.
OTHELLO.   Peace. you were best.[39]
EMILIA. Thou hast not half that power to do me harm
    As I have to be hurt.[40] O gull![41] O dolt!
    As ignorant as dirt! Thou hast done a deed—
    I care not for thy sword; I'll make thee known,   170
    Though I lost twenty lives.—Help! Help, ho, help!
    The Moor hath killed my mistress! Murder, murder!

    [*Enter* MONTANO. GRATIANO, *and* IAGO.]

MONTANO. What is the matter? How now. General?
EMILIA. O. are you come. Iago? You have done well.
    That men must lay their murders on your neck.   175
GRATIANO. What is the matter?
EMILIA. [*to* IAGO]
    Disprove this villain. if thou be'st a man.
    He says thou toldst him that his wife was false.
    I know thou didst not; thou'rt not such a villain.
    Speak. for my heart is full.   180
IAGO. I told him what I thought. and told no more
    Than what he found himself was apt[42] and true.
EMILIA. But did you ever tell him she was false?
IAGO. I did.

37. iterance repetition. 38. made mocks made sport. 39. Peace ... best It would be best for you. 40. be hurt to endure hurt. 41. gull dupe. 42. apt plausible.

EMILIA. You told a lie. an odious. damnèd lie!   185
   Upon my soul. a lie. a wicked lie.
   She false with Cassio? Did you say with Cassio?
IAGO. With Cassio. mistress. Go to. charm[43] your tongue.
EMILIA. I will not charm my tongue: I am bound to speak.
   My mistress here lies murdered in her bed—   190
ALL. O heavens forfend!
EMILIA. And your reports have set the murder on.
OTHELLO. Nay. stare not. masters. It is true indeed.
GRATIANO. 'Tis a strange truth.
MONTANO. O monstrous act!   195
EMILIA.   Villainy. villainy. villainy!
   I think upon 't—I think I smell 't! O villainy!
   I thought so then[44]—I'll kill myself for grief—
   O villainy. villainy!
IAGO. What. are you mad? I charge you. get you home.
EMILIA. Good gentlemen. let me have leave to speak.   200
   'Tis proper I obey him. but not now.
   Perchance. Iago. I will ne'er go home.
OTHELLO. O! O! O! [OTHELLO *falls on the bed.*][45]
EMILIA. Nay. lay thee down and roar.
   For thou hast killed the sweetest innocent   205
   That e'er did lift up eye.[46]
OTHELLO. [*rising*]   O. she was foul!
   I scarce did know you. uncle. There lies your niece.
   Whose breath indeed these hands have newly stopped.
   I know this act shows[47] horrible and grim.
GRATIANO. Poor Desdemon! I am glad thy father's dead.   210
   Thy match was mortal to him. and pure grief
   Shore his old thread[48] in twain. Did he live now.
   This sight would make him do a desperate turn.[49]
   Yea. curse his better angel from his side.
   And fall to reprobance.[50]   215

---

43. **charm** keep silent (as though by a magic spell).   **44. then** perhaps in 3.3 and
4.2.   **45. [Othello . . . bed.]** This direction is from the Quarto.   **46. lift up eye** lift
her eyes to heaven.   **47. shows** looks.   **48. Shore . . . thread** sheared the thread of
his old age (as Atropos. one of the three Fates. was thought to do).   **49. turn** deed.
50. reprobance damnation. i.e.. suicide.

OTHELLO. 'Tis pitiful. But yet Iago knows
    That she with Cassio hath the act of shame
    A thousand times committed. Cassio confessed it;
    And she did gratify[51] his amorous works
    With that recognizance[52] and pledge of love   220
    Which I first gave her. I saw it in his hand;
    It was a handkerchief, an antique token
    My father gave my mother.
EMILIA. O God! O heavenly God!
IAGO. Zounds, hold your peace.   225
EMILIA.   'Twill out, 'twill out! I peace?
    No, I will speak as liberal as the north.[53]
    Let heaven and men and devils, let them all,
    All, all, cry shame against me, yet I'll speak.
IAGO. Be wise, and get you home.
EMILIA.   I will not.

    [IAGO *threatens* EMILIA.]

GRATIANO.   Fie.
    Your sword upon a woman?   230
EMILIA. O thou dull Moor! That handkerchief thou speak'st of
    I found by fortune and did give my husband;
    For often, with a solemn earnestness,
    More than indeed belonged[54] to such a trifle,
    He begged of me to steal 't.   235
IAGO.   Villainous whore!
EMILIA. She give it Cassio? No, alas! I found it,
    And I did give 't my husband.
IAGO.   Filth, thou liest!
EMILIA. By heaven, I do not, I do not, gentlemen.
    O murderous coxcomb![55] What should such a fool
    Do with so good a wife?   240
OTHELLO.   Are there no stones[56] in heaven
    But what serves for the thunder?—Precious[57] villain!

---

51. gratify reward. **52. recognizance** token. **53. liberal . . . north** freely as the north wind (blows). **54. belonged** was appropriate. **55. coxcomb** fool (addressed to Othello). **56. stones** bolts, such as those used for thunderbolts. **57. Precious** utter

[He runs at IAGO: MONTANO *disarms* OTHELLO. IAGO. *from behind. stabs* EMILIA.]*[58]*

GRATIANO. The woman falls! Sure he hath killed his wife.
EMILIA. Ay. ay. O. lay me by my mistress' side.

[Exit IAGO.]

GRATIANO. He's gone. but his wife's killed.
MONTANO. 'Tis a notorious villain. Take you this weapon.   245
   Which I have here recovered from the Moor.
   Come. guard the door without. Let him not pass.
   But kill him rather. I'll after that same villain.
   For 'tis a damnèd slave.

[Exit with all but OTHELLO *and* EMILIA.
who has been laid by DESDEMONA'S *side.]*

OTHELLO.   I am not valiant neither.
   But every puny whipster[59] gets my sword.   250
   But why should honor[60] outlive honesty?[61]
   Let it go all.
EMILIA.   What did thy song bode. lady?
   Hark. canst thou hear me? I will play the swan.
   And die in music. *[She sings.]* "Willow. willow. willow."
   Moor. she was chaste. She loved thee. cruel Moor.   255
   So come my soul to bliss as I speak true.
   So speaking as I think. alas. I die. *[She dies.]*
OTHELLO. I have another weapon in this chamber:
   It was a sword of Spain. the ice-brook's temper[62]
   O. here it is. *[He finds a sword.]* Uncle. I must come forth.   260
GRATIANO. *[within]* If thou attempt it. it will cost thee dear.
   Thou hast no weapon. and perforce must suffer.
OTHELLO. Look in upon me then and speak with me.
   Or. naked[63] as I am. I will assault thee.

[Enter GRATIANO.]

---

58. [He . . . Emilia.] The Quarto text reads. "The Moor runs at Iago. Iago kills his wife." The Quarto also specifies the exit of Iago below.   **59. whipster** contemptible fellow (one who is always ready to whip out his sword).   **60. honor** the bravery for which one enjoys a soldier's reputation.   **61. honesty** integrity.   **62. ice-brook's temper** tempered in ice-cold water.   **63. naked** unarmed.

GRATIANO. What is the matter?   265
OTHELLO.   Behold. I have a weapon:
A better never did itself sustain
Upon a soldier's thigh. I have seen the day
That, with this little arm and this good sword,
I have made my way through more impediments
Than twenty times your stop.[64] But O, vain boast!   270
Who can control his fate? 'Tis not so now.
Be not afraid, though you do see me weaponed:
Here is my journey's end. here is my butt[65]
And very seamark[66] of my utmost sail.

[GRATIANO *steps back.*]

Do you go back dismayed? 'Tis a lost[67] fear: 275
Man but a rush[68] against Othello's breast
And he retires. Where should Othello go?

[*He turns to* DESDEMONA.]

Now, how dost thou look now? O ill-starred wench!
Pale as thy smock! When we shall meet at compt,[69]
This look of thine will hurl my soul from heaven.   280
And fiends will snatch at it. Cold, cold, my girl?
Even like thy chastity. O cursèd, cursèd slave![70]
Whip me, ye devils,
From the possession of this heavenly sight!
Blow me about in winds! Roast me in sulfur!   285
Wash me in steep-down gulfs of liquid fire!
O Desdemon! Dead, Desdemon! Dead! O! O!

[*Enter* LODOVICO, CASSIO *(carried in a litter).*[71] MONTANO, *and*
IAGO *(prisoner), with officers.*]

LODOVICO. Where is this rash and most unfortunate man?
OTHELLO. That's he that was Othello. Here I am.
LODOVICO. Where is that viper? Bring the villain forth.   290

[IAGO *is led forward.*]

---

64. stop power (to stop). **65. butt** goal, limit (an archery term). **66. seamark**
beacon (marking his destination or limit). **67. lost** wasted. **68. Man . . . rush**
wield no more than a reed. **69. compt** Judgment Day. **70. slave** Othello himself.
71. [Enter . . . litter) The Quarto specifies that Cassio is "in a chair."

OTHELLO. I look down towards his feet:[72] but that's a fable.
If that thou be'st a devil. I cannot kill thee.

[*He wounds* IAGO.]

LODOVICO. Wrench his sword from him. [OTHELLO *is disarmed.*]
IAGO.   I bleed. sir. but not
    killed.
OTHELLO. I am not sorry neither. I'd have thee live.
    For in my sense[73] 'tis happiness to die.   295
LODOVICO. O thou Othello. that was once so good.
    Fall'n in the practice[74] of a cursèd slave.[75]
    What shall be said to thee?
OTHELLO.   Why. anything.
    An honorable murderer. if you will.
    For naught I did in hate. but all in honor.   300
LODOVICO. This wretch hath part confessed his villainy.
    Did you and he consent[76] in Cassio's death?
OTHELLO. Ay.
CASSIO. Dear General. I never gave you cause.
OTHELLO. I do believe it. and I ask your pardon.   305
    Will you. I pray. demand that demi-devil
    Why he hath thus ensnared my soul and body?
IAGO. Demand me nothing. What you know. you know.
    From this time forth I never will speak word.
LODOVICO. What. not to pray?   310
GRATIANO. Torments[77] will ope your lips.
OTHELLO. Well. thou dost best.
LODOVICO. Sir. you shall understand what hath befall'n.
    Which. as I think. you know not. Here is a letter
    Found in the pocket of the slain Roderigo: 315
    And here another. [*He produces letters.*] The one of them
        imports
    The death of Cassio. to be undertook
    By Roderigo.
OTHELLO. O villain!

---

72. **feet** i.e.. to see if they are cloven. as the devil's are fabled to be.   73. **For . . . sense** to one who feels as I do.   74. **Fall'n . . . practice** through the plotting. into the snare.   75. **slave** villain.   76. **consent** agree.   77. **Torments** torture.

CASSIO.   Most heathenish and most gross!⁷⁸

LODOVICO. [*showing another paper*] Now here's another   320
    discontented paper
  Found in his pocket too. And this, it seems,
  Roderigo meant t' have sent this damnèd villain;
  But that belike⁷⁹ Iago in the interim
  Came in and satisfied him.⁸⁰

OTHELLO. O thou pernicious caitiff!—   325
  How came you, Cassio, by that handkerchief
  That was my wife's?

CASSIO.   I found it in my chamber;
  And he himself confessed but even now
  That there he dropped it for a special purpose
  Which wrought to his desire.⁸¹   330

OTHELLO.   O fool, fool, fool!

CASSIO. There is besides in Roderigo's letter
  How he upbraids Iago, that he made him
  Brave⁸² me upon the watch, whereon it came⁸³
  That I was cast:⁸⁴ and even but now he spake,
  After long seeming dead, Iago hurt him,   335
  Iago set him on.

LODOVICO. [*to* OTHELLO] You must forsake this room and go
    with us.
  Your power and your command is taken off,⁸⁵
  And Cassio rules in Cyprus. For this slave,
  If there be any cunning cruelty   340
  That can torment him much and hold him long,⁸⁶
  It shall be his. You shall close prisoner rest⁸⁷
  Till that the nature of your fault be known
  To the Venetian state.—Come, bring away.

OTHELLO. Soft you:⁸⁸ a word or two before you go.   345
  I have done the state some service, and they know't.
  No more of that. I pray you, in your letters,

---

78. gross monstrous. **79. belike** most likely. **80. Came . . . him** interposed and gave him satisfactory explanation. **81. Which . . . desire** worked out as he wished, fitted in with his plan. **82. Brave** defy. **83. whereon it came** whereof it came about. **84. cast** dismissed. **85. taken off** taken away. **86. That . . . long** Keep him alive a long time (during his torture). **87. rest** remain **88. Soft you** one moment.

When you shall these unlucky[89] deeds relate.
Speak of me as I am: nothing extenuate.
Nor set down aught in malice. Then must you speak   350
Of one that loved not wisely but too well:
Of one not easily jealous but, being wrought.[90]
Perplexed[91] in the extreme: of one whose hand.
Like the base Indian.[92] threw a pearl away
Richer than all his tribe: of one whose subdued[93] eyes.   355
Albeit unusèd to the melting mood.
Drops tears as fast as the Arabian trees
Their medicinable gum.[94] Set you down this:
And say besides that in Aleppo once.
Where a malignant and a turbaned Turk   360
Beat a Venetian and traduced the state.
I took by th' throat the circumcisèd dog
And smote him. thus. [*He stabs himself.*][95]
LODOVICO. O bloody period![96]
GRATIANO.   All that is spoke is marred.
OTHELLO. I kissed thee ere I killed thee. No way but this.   365
    Killing myself. to die upon a kiss.

[*He kisses* DESDEMONA *and dies.*]

CASSIO. This did I fear. but thought he had no weapon:
    For he was great of heart.
LODOVICO. [*to* IAGO]   O Spartan dog.[97]
    More fell[98] than anguish. hunger. or the sea!
    Look on the tragic loading of this bed.   370
    This is thy work. The object poisons sight:
    Let it be hid.[99] Gratiano. keep[100] the house.

[*The bed curtains are drawn*]

89. unlucky unfortunate. **90. wrought** worked upon. worked into a frenzy.
91. Perplexed distraught. **92. base Indian** This reading from the Quarto pictures
an ignorant savage who cannot recognize the value of a precious jewel. The Folio
reading. *Iudean* or *Judean.* i.e.. infidel or disbeliever. may refer to Herod. who slew
Mariam in a fit of jealousy. or to Judas Iscariot. the betrayer of Christ.   **93. subdued**
i.e.. overcome by grief.   **94. medicinable gum** myrrh.   **95. [He . . . himself.]** This
direction is in the Quarto text.   **96. period** end. conclusion.   **97. Spartan dog**
Spartan dogs were noted for their savagery and silence.   **98. fell** cruel.   **99. Let . . .
hid** i.e.. draw the bed curtains. (No stage direction specifies that the dead are to be
carried offstage at the end of the play.).   **100. keep** remain in.

And seize upon the fortunes of the Moor,
For they succeed on you.[101] [*To* CASSIO.] To you, Lord
   Governor,
Remains the censure[102] of this hellish villain.   375
The time, the place, the torture. O, enforce it!
Myself will straight aboard, and to the state
This heavy act with heavy heart relate.   *[Exeunt.]*

Notes

The text of *Othello* is based on the 1623 First Folio (F). The notes below indicate variant readings adopted from the First Quarto (1622), indicated as [Q1]; readings proposed by editors subsequent to the First Folio are indicated as [eds.]. Act and scene numbers indicated below follow those in the first Folio, with the exception of Act 2, Scene 3. The line numbers follow those in this edition. Other abbreviations: s.d. stands for stage direction; s.p. stands for speech prefix.

1.1 1 Tush, never Neuer **4 'Sblood, but** But **16 And, in conclusion** [Q1: not in F] **26 togaed** Tongued **30 other** others **34 God bless** blesse **67 full** fall **thick-lips** Thicks-lips **73 changes** chances **74 [and elsewhere] lose** [eds.] loose **80 Thieves, thieves, thieves** Theeues. Theeues **82 s.d. Brabantio above** [in F, printed as a speech prefix to line 84] **87 Zounds, sir** Sir [also at line 111] **101 bravery** knauerie **117 are now** are **155 pains** apines **157 sign. That** [eds.] signe) that **183 night** might
1.2 34 Duke Dukes **50 carrack** Carract **64 her!** [eds.] her **69 darlings** Deareling **89 I do** do
1.3 1 There is There's **these** this **61 s.p. Duke and Senators** [*All* Q1] *Sen.* **101 maimed** main'd **108 upon** vp on **s.p. Duke** [Q1: not in F] **109 overt** ouer **112 s.p. [and elsewhere] First Senator** *Sen.* **124 till** tell **131 battles** Battaile **fortunes** Fortune **140 travels'** Trauellours **142 rocks, and** Rocks **heads** head **144 other** others **146 Do grow** Grew **148 thence** hence **156 intentively** instinctiuely **160 sighs** kisses **203 Into your favor** [Q1: not in F] **221 ear** eares **226 sovereign** more soueraigne **231 couch** [eds.] Coach [F] Cooch [Q1] **235 These** [eds.] This **242 Nor I, I would not** Nor would I **249 did love** loue **265 me** [eds.] my **271 instruments** Instrument **279 Desdemona. Tonight, my**

---

101. And . . . you Take legal possession of Othello's property, which passes as though by inheritance to you.   **102. censure** sentencing.

lord? Duke. This night [Q1: not in F] **283 With** And **292 s.p. First
Senator** *Sen.* **294 s.d. Exeunt** *Exit* **300 matters** matter **301 the** the
the **325 beam** [eds.] braine [F] ballance [Q1] **329 our unbitted** or
vnbitted **330 scion** [eds.] Seyen [F] syen [Q1] **347 error** errors
347–348 She . . . she must [Q1: not in F] **351 a supersubtle** supersubtle **371–374 Roderigo. What . . . purse** [Q1: not in F] **378 a snipe**
Snpe **381 He's** [Ha's Q1] She ha's **388 ear** eares
2.1 **33 prays** praye **34 heaven** Heauens **40 s.p. Third Gentleman** *Gent.*
42 arrivance Arriuancie **43 this** the **56 s.p. Second Gentleman** *Gent.*
[also at lines 61. 68. and 95] **70 clog** enclogge **82 And . . . comfort**
[Q1: not in F] **88 tell me** tell **92 the sea** Sea **94 their** this **105 list**
leaue **109 doors** doore **155 [and elsewhere]** ne'er neu'r **157 such**
wight *such wightes* **168 gyve** [eds.] giue **173 An** and **173 courtesy**
Curtsie **174 clyster pipes** Cluster-pipes **209 s.d. Exeunt** [eds.] *Exit*
211 hither thither **223 again** a game **232 fortune** Forune **234
compassing** compasse **236 finder out** finder **236–237 occasions**
occasion **has** he's **253 mutualities** mutabilities **288 for wife** for wift
295 rank right **296 nightcap** Night-Cape
2.2 **5 addiction** [eds.] addition **9–10 Heaven bless** Blesse
2.3 **25 stoup** [eds.] stope **34 unfortunate** infortunate **47 lads** else
52 to put put to **56, 65 God** heauen **69 Englishman** Englishmen
83 Then . . . auld [*Then . . . owd* Q1] *And take thy awl'd* **85 'Fore
God** Why **88 God's** heau'ns **96 God forgive** Forgiue **100 speak** I
speake **113 the** his **127 s.d. Cry within: Help! Help** [from Q1:
"Helpe. helpe. within"] **128 Zounds, you** You **138 God's will** Alas
139 Montano—sir *Montano* **142 God's will. Lieutenant. hold** Fie.
fie Lieutenant **144 Zounds. I** I **148 sense of place** [eds.] place of
sense **163 breasts** breastes **170 wont be** wont to be **187 Zounds. If** I
If I once **198 leagued** [eds.] league **204 Thus** This **213 the** then **232
well now** well **236 vile** vil'd **241 God** Heauen **245 thought** had
thought **266 O God** Oh **289 I'll** I **292 denotement** [eds.] deuotement
304 me here me **315 were 't** were **334 s.d. Enter Roderigo** [after line
356 in F] **346 hast** hath **349 By the Mass** Introth **356 on;** [on Q1] on
357 the while [eds.] a while
3.1 **s.d. Musicians** [eds.] *Musicians, and Clowne* **5 s.d. [and at lines 7,
9, and 14]** A Musician *Mus.* **20 s.d. Exeunt** [eds.] *Exit* **21 hear** heare
me **25 General's wife** Generall **29 Cassio. Do, good my friend** [Q1:
not in F] **40 s.d. Exit** at line +1 in F] **50 To . . . front** [Q1: not in F]
3.3 **16 circumstance** Circumstances **40 you** your **52 Yes, faith** sooth
62 or on **74 By' r Lady** Trust me **94 you** he **106 By heaven** Alas **112
In** Of **135 that all** that. All **free to** free **139 But some** Wherein **147 oft**
of **148 wisdom then** wisdome **162 By heaven, I'll** Ile **170 fondly**
[eds.] soundly [F] strongly [Q1] **175 God** Heauen **180 Is once** Is **182
blown** blow'd **185 dances well** Dances **202 God** Heauen **204 keep 't**

[eds.] keepe [Q1] kept [F] **215 I' faith** Trust me **217 my** your **233
disproportion** disproportions **248 to hold** to **258 qualities** Quantities
272 of to **277 O, then heaven mocks** Heauen mock'd **284 Faith** Why
288 s.d. Exit [at line 304 in F] **311 faith** but **328 s.d. Enter Othello**
[after "I did say so" in F] **337 of her** in her **368 remorse;** [remorce.
Q1] remorse **390 see, sir** see **394 supervisor** super-vision **422 then
laid** laid **423 Over** ore **sighed** sigh **kissed** kisse **424 Cried** cry **438
any that was** [eds.] any. it was **450 mind perhaps** minde **453 Ne'er
feels** [eds.] Neu'r keepes
3.4 20 that the **34 It yet** It **52 faith** indeed **72 I' faith** Indeed **74 God**
Heauen **78 Heaven bless** Blesse **83 can, sir** can **89–90 Desdemona. I
pray . . . Cassio. Othello. The handkerchief!** [Q1: not in F] **94 I'
faith** Insooth **95 Zounds** Away **159 that** the **167 I' faith** Indeed **182
friend.** [eds.] friend. **178 absence** [eds.] absence. [Q1] Absence: [F]
183 by my faith in good troth
4.1 32 Faith Why **37 Zounds, that's** that's **44 work** workes **51 No,
forbear** [Q1: not in F] **70 couch** [Coach Q1] Cowch; **76 unsuiting**
[Q1 corrected] vnfitting [Q1 uncorrected] resulting [F] **78 'scuse**
scuses **94 clothes** Cloath **100 conster** conserue **102 you now** you **106
power** dowre **109 a woman** woman **110 i' faith** indeed **117 Do you**
Do ye **118 marry her** marry **121 win** [eds.] winnes. **122 Faith** Why
shall marry marry **129 beckons** becomes **132–133 by this hand, she**
[Q1: not in F] **156 Faith, I I 159 Faith** Yes **206 s.d.** [after line 210 in
F] **209 God save** Saue **230 By my troth** Trust me **240 Truly, an**
Truely **272 denote** denote [F uncorrected] deuote [F corrected]
4.2 32 Nay May **33 knees** knee **35 But not the words** [Q1: not in F] **51
kinds** kind **56 A** The **66 Ay, there** [eds.] I heere **71 ne'er** neuer **83
Impudent strumpet** [Q1: not in F] **96 keep** [eds.] keepes **s.d. Enter
Emilia** [after line 94 in F] **162 them in** [eds.] them: or **174 And . . .
you** [Q1: not inF] **176 you to** to **189 Faith, I I for** and **200 By this
hand** Nay **228 takes** taketh **232 of** [Q1: not in F]
4.3 20 favor in them fauour **22 faith** Father **23 before thee** before **29
sighing** [eds.] *singing* [F corrected] *sining* [F uncorrected] **69 Good
troth** Introth **70 By my troth** Introth **74 Uds pity** why **103 God**
Heauen
5.1 1 bulk Barke **22 Be 't** But **hear** heard **35 Forth** For **49 Did** Do **91 O
heaven** Yes. 'tis **106 out o'** o' **113 'Las, what's . . . What's** Alas. what
is . . . What is **116 dead** quite dead **126 Faugh! Fie** Fie
5.2 34 heaven Heauens **37 say so** say **56 Yes, presently** Presently **61
Then Lord** O Heauen **97 here** high **105 Should** Did **109 s.d. Enter
Emilia** [after line 108 in F] **122 O Lord** Alas **132 heard** heare **146
Nay, had** had **224 O God! O heavenly God** Oh Heauen! oh heauenly
Powres **225 Zounds** Come **246 have here** haue **314 not. Here** [not:
here Q1] not) heere **354 Indian** Iudean

Introduction to Elizabeth Cary and The Tragedy of Mariam, The Fair Queen of Jewry

Elizabeth Cary (1585?–1639)

Elizabeth Cary was the first English woman to write and publish an original play, *The Tragedy of Mariam, The Fair Queen of Jewry*. She was also the first English woman to be the subject of a biography, her daughter's *The Lady Falkland: Her Life*. When we consider that the French poet Louise Labé was called a "common whore" by Calvin because she published her love poems and that Mary Wroth was forced to withdraw her work from publication, we begin to get an idea of how unusual it was for Elizabeth Cary to publish her work. She showed similar independence by separating from her husband, by converting to Catholicism, and by translating controversial theological works. A prodigious scholar, a committed Catholic, and mother of eleven children, Elizabeth Cary was the extraordinary author of an extraordinary play.

Cary's Early Life and Career

Born Elizabeth Tanfield, the daughter of a wealthy lawyer, she had an independent mind and a passion for learning even as a child. Once, when young Elizabeth observed her father hearing a case of witchcraft, she intervened, whispering in his ear the crucial question that exposed the evidence against the accused woman as a fraud. The precocious Elizabeth studied French, Spanish, and Italian, as well as Latin and Hebrew, normally restricted to male students; she even translated some of Seneca's *Epistles* when she was only seven years old. She also translated Abraham Ortelius's *Le Miroir du Monde*, which described such places as China, India, and America.

When Elizabeth was only twelve, the poet Michael Drayton praised her learning in his *Englands Heroicall Epistles*. She was such an avid reader that when her parents forbade her to read at night, she borrowed candles from the servants.

Her family arranged her marriage to Henry Cary in 1602. Master of the Queen's jewels and later made Viscount Falkland, Henry supplied the title and gentry status to the marriage, while Elizabeth supplied the money. Separated by Henry's military duty in the Protestant war against Spain in Holland during the early years of their marriage, they had their first child in 1609. Elizabeth's attempts to aid Henry's career by mortgaging her joint ownership of family property angered her father, who disinherited her.

In 1622 her husband became Lord Deputy of Ireland, and sharp disagreements arose between them. While he directed the colonial administration of Ireland, she studied the Irish language and set up a trade school for poor children in Dublin. Even as her husband attempted to enforce conformity to Protestantism in Catholic Ireland, Elizabeth's own desire to convert to Catholicism strengthened. From childhood she had found Calvinism inimical because of its emphasis on predestination, and she was also critical of Anglicanism. She returned to England at her husband's orders in 1625, and in 1626 she publicly converted to Catholicism. Nonconformity to the official church was dangerous for anyone in early modern England, but Elizabeth's open declaration of it was particularly dangerous for her husband, who was in government service. Henry was outraged and completely distanced himself from her. She complained to King Charles I that her husband did not support her financially; Henry excused himself by charging her with refusing to live "quietly." Their daughter claimed, nevertheless, that her parents were reconciled at Henry's deathbed in 1633.

Elizabeth moved to a small village outside London, where she continued to write until her death in 1639. She lived modestly, giving much of her income to charity. She arranged for her two youngest sons and four daughters, who had also converted, to live in Catholic France, where her daughters became Benedictine nuns. Her son Lucius, made famous by Ben Jonson's ode, remained behind in England. Not sharing his mother's religion, he was able to inherit his grandmother's money. He did, however, share his mother's love of languages and of theological dispute, which she

Portrait of Elizabeth Cary, first Viscountess Falkland, painted by Paul Van Somer, 1621. Courtesy of Sarah Campbell Blaffer Foundation.

continued to pursue. She translated the reply of a French theologian, Jacques Du Perron, to King James I's attack on Catholicism. A comment she made in the preface to her translation shows how thoroughly she rejected the conventional aristocratic and feminine stance of shunning publication: "I will not make use of the worn out form of saying I printed it against my will, moved by the importunity of friends; I was moved to it by my belief that it might make those English that understand not French . . . read Perron." She dedicated this work to the Catholic wife of Charles I, Queen Henrietta Maria. Published on the Continent, this work was immediately confiscated and burned when it was smuggled into England. At the time she died, Elizabeth was translating the Hebrew and Latin writings of the Flemish mystic Blosius.

During the early years of her marriage, Elizabeth Cary wrote a verse life of Tamberlain. Two texts about Edward II are now often attributed to her; one of these, *The History of the Life, Reign, and Death of Edward II*, contains the initials of Elizabeth Falkland on its title page. In addition to her numerous translations, she wrote occasional poetry which circulated in manuscript. Her former tutor Sir John Davies wrote verses praising two of her plays: a lost play set in Greece and *The Tragedy of Mariam*.

Mariam

Though not published until 1613, *Mariam* was probably written sometime between 1604 and 1609. The play portrays Mariam's struggle between her own integrity and her loyalty to her husband Herod when confronted with his tyranny and tragically mistaken jealousy. The play also includes a subplot of political intrigue in which two minor characters, the sons of Baba, attempt to resist King Herod's tyranny. The story is taken from a pair of ancient sources, Josephus's *Jewish War* and *Antiquities of the Jews*, first translated into English in 1602. The dramatic influences may include Shakespeare's *Antony and Cleopatra* and *Othello*, although some would argue that Cary's *Mariam* could have influenced Shakespeare. Cary frequently attended the theater, and though her work was a closet drama—like Seneca's tragedies, meant to be read rather than performed—it is full of high emotion and dramatic action. *Othello* and *Mariam* have much in common. Both concern marriages that defy the expectations of the status quo, a husband's irrational jealousy, and the proper behavior of women. Cary surrounds the chaste yet outspoken Mariam with a range of vivid female characters: Salome, who promotes divorce for women; Graphina, who remains quiet and obedient; and Alexandra, who objects to her daughter's marriage.

Some of the conflicts in *The Tragedy of Mariam* can be related to those in Elizabeth Cary's own life. The disparity between the royal Mariam and her upstart husband may reflect the social and financial disparity between Cary and her husband. The heroine's struggle between obedience to her husband and fidelity to herself may be related to the author's own crisis of conscience. Mariam's questioning of her "public voice" may be read as the text's questioning of the author's publication of her work. More generally, the play illustrates conflicts in the larger social context. The dissent of English Catholics, a long overlooked aspect of early modern English culture, surfaces in the figure of Herod. Catholics saw Herod as an allegorical figure for Henry VIII, because both kings killed their wives and imposed arbitrary dictates on their subjects. Cary's work has further import as a comment on the norms of chastity, silence, and obedience for women of her time. Dramatic tension arises from the contrasts between the conventional pronouncements of the chorus on women's conduct and the perspectives of the female characters.

In her own time Elizabeth Cary was praised by her son's biographer, Edward Clarendon, as "a lady of a most masculine understanding," but she is now appreciated for representing a woman's subjectivity in the genre of tragedy. With its unique blend of popular Shakespearian and learned Senecan tragic style, *Mariam* is an important contribution to the history of English drama. Along with the interracial couple of *Othello*, the mixed marriage of Cary's *Mariam* looks forward to a similar theme in Aphra Behn's *Oroonoko* (1688). For its questioning of power relationships, Elizabeth Cary's *Tragedy of Mariam* is a trenchant comment on perennial problems.

THE TRAGEDY
OF MARIAM,
The Fair Queen of Jewry

[by Elizabeth Cary]

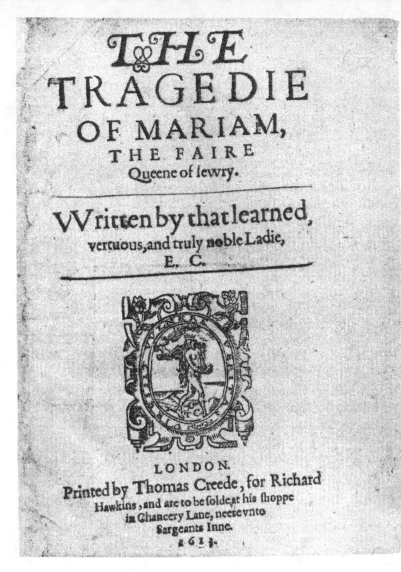

THE TRAGEDIE OF MARIAM, THE FAIRE Queene of Iewry.

Written by that learned, vertuous, and truly noble Ladie, E. C.

LONDON.
Printed by Thomas Creede, for Richard Hawkins, and are to be folde at his shoppe in Chancery Lane, neere vnto Sargeants Inne. 1613.

A copy of the original title page of *The Tragedie of Mariam* (1613). Since it was considered reprehensible for women to publish, Elizabeth Cary's authorship is represented covertly by her initials "E. C." on the title page of the first edition of her work. The leaf that follows the title page (missing from many extant copies of the text) identifies her in the dedicatory sonnet as the sister of the woman to whom she dedicates the play: "my worthy sister, Mistress Elizabeth Cary." Reproduced with permission from *The Tragedy of Mariam 1613*, ed. A.C. Dunstan (Oxford: Malone Society, 1914), revised by Marta Straznicki and Richard Rowland (1992). (British Library Copy C.34.c.9)

The Tragedy of Mariam,
The Fair Queen of Jewry[1]

To Diana's Earthly Deputess
and My Worthy Sister, Mistress Elizabeth Cary[2]

When cheerful Phoebus[3] his full course hath run,
His sister's fainter beams our hearts doth cheer:
So your fair brother is to me the sun,
And you his sister as my moon appear.

You are my next beloved, my second friend,   5
For when my Phoebus' absence makes it night,
Whilst to the Antipodes[4] his beams do bend,
From you my Phoebe,[5] shines my second light.

He like to Sol,[6] clear-sighted, constant, free,
You Luna-like, unspotted, chaste, divine: 10
He shone on Sicily, you destined be,
To illumine the now obscurèd Palestine.
My first[7] was consecrated to Apollo,
My second to Diana now shall follow.

                                         E.C.

---

1. The sole early modern edition of 1613 contains some obvious misprints and inconsistencies in spelling and punctuation, which this edition silently corrects. More problematic errors that have been corrected by modern editors are mentioned in the footnotes.   **2.** Two extant copies of the play contain this sonnet dedicated to the author's sister-in-law. **3. Phoebus** Apollo, the sun god, twin brother of Diana. **4. Antipodes** the opposite end of the earth.   **5. Phoebe** Diana, or Luna, the moon. **6. Sol** the sun.   **7. My first** Cary's first play, which is now lost.

The Names of the Speakers

HEROD. *King of Judea*	PHERORAS. *Herod's brother*
DORIS. *his first wife*	GRAPHINA. *his love*
MARIAM. *his second wife*	BABA'S FIRST SON
SALOME. *Herod's sister*	BABA'S SECOND SON
ANTIPATER. *his son by Doris*	ANANELL. *the high Priest*
ALEXANDRA. *Mariam's mother*	SOHEMUS. *a counselor to Herod*
SILLEUS. *Prince of Arabia*	NUNTIO. *a messenger*
CONSTABARUS. *husband to*	BUTLER. *another messenger*
Salome	CHORUS. *a company of Jews*

THE ARGUMENT

Herod the son of Antipater (an Idumean⁸), having crept by the favor of the Romans into the Jewish monarchy, married Mariam the granddaughter of Hircanus, the rightful king and priest; and for her (besides her high blood, being of singular beauty) he repudiated Doris, his former wife, by whom he had children.

This Mariam had a brother called Aristobolus, and next him and Hircanus his grandfather, Herod in his wife's right had the best title. Therefore to remove them, he charged Hircanus with treason, and put him to death, and drowned Aristobolus under color of sport. Alexandra, daughter to the one and mother to the other, accused him for their deaths before Anthony.⁹

So when he was forced to go answer this accusation at Rome, he left the custody of his wife to Josephus, his uncle that had married his sister Salome, and out of a violent affection (unwilling any should enjoy her after him) he gave strict and private commandment, that if he were slain, she should be put to death. But he returned with much honor, yet found his wife extremely discontented, to whom Josephus had (meaning it for the best, to prove Herod loved her) revealed his charge.

So by Salome's accusation he put Josephus to death, but was reconciled to Mariam, who still bare the death of her friends¹⁰ exceeding hardly.

---

8. Idumean people of Edom, south of Judea, who had converted to Judaism but were not considered fully Jewish.   **9. Anthony** Mark Antony (c. 82–30 BC).   **10. friends** family.

In the meantime Herod was again necessarily to revisit Rome, for Caesar,[11] having overthrown Anthony, his great friend, was likely to make an alteration of Herod's fortune.

In his absence, news came to Jerusalem that Caesar had put him to death. Their willingness it should be so, together with the likelihood, gave this rumor so good credit, as Sohemus that had succeeded Josephus' charge,[12] succeeded him likewise in revealing it. So at Herod's return, which was speedy and unexpected, he found Mariam so far from joy that she showed apparent signs of sorrow. He, still desiring to win her to a better humor, she being very unable to conceal her passion, fell to upbraiding him with her brother's death. As they were thus debating, came in a fellow with a cup of wine, who, hired by Salome, said first, it was a love potion, which Mariam desired to deliver to the king; but afterwards he affirmed that it was a poison and that Sohemus had told her somewhat, which procured the vehement hate in her.

The king, hearing this, more moved with jealousy of Sohemus than with this intent of poison, sent her away; and presently after, by the instigation of Salome, Mariam was beheaded. Which rashness was afterward punished in him, with an intolerable and almost frantic passion for her death.

ACT 1
SCENE 1

[MARIAM *alone.*]

MARIAM. How oft have I with public voice run on
   To censure Rome's last hero for deceit?
   Because he wept when Pompey's life was gone,
   Yet when he lived, he thought his name too great.
   But now I do recant,[1] and, Roman lord,[2]   5
   Excuse too rash a judgment in a woman:
   My sex pleads pardon, pardon then afford.

---

11. **Caesar** Octavius Caesar (63 BC–14 AD), later made emperor Augustus. 12. **that . . . charge** who had taken on Josephus' duties. 1. **recant** renounce my error. 2. **Roman lord** Mariam addresses the absent Julius Caesar ("Rome's last hero"), who was said by Plutarch to have wept when he saw the head of his slain rival Pompey. The characters frequently speak in apostrophe to an imagined or absent figure.

Mistaking is with us, but too too common.
Now do I find by self-experience taught.
One object yields both grief and joy.   10
You wept indeed, when on his worth you thought.
But joyed that slaughter did your foe destroy.
So at his death your eyes true drops did rain.
Whom dead, you did not wish alive again.
When Herod lived, that now is done to death.   15
Oft have I wished that I from him were free:
Oft have I wished that he might lose his breath:
Oft have I wished his carcass dead to see.
Then rage and scorn had put my love to flight.
That love which once on him was firmly set: 20
Hate hid his true affection from my sight.
And kept my heart from paying him his debt.
And blame me not, for Herod's jealousy
Had power even constancy itself to change:
For he, by barring me from liberty.   25
To shun³ my ranging, taught me first to range.
But yet too chaste a scholar was my heart.
To learn to love another than my lord:
To leave his love, my lesson's former part.
I quickly learned, the other I abhorred.   30
But now his death to memory doth call.
The tender love, that he to Mariam bare:⁴
And mine to him, this makes those rivers fall.
Which by another thought unmoistened are.
For Aristobolus the loveliest youth   35
That ever did in angel's shape appear.
The cruel Herod was not moved to ruth:⁵
Then why grieves Mariam Herod's death to hear?
Why joy I not the tongue no more shall speak.
That yielded forth my brother's latest doom: 40
Both youth and beauty might thy⁶ fury break.
And both in him did ill befit a tomb.
And worthy grandsire ill did he requite.⁷

---

3. **shun** prevent. 4. **bare** bore. 5. **ruth** pity.   6. **thy** Herod's. 7. Lines 43–46
are addressed to her dead grandfather Hircanus.

His high assent alone by thee procured.
Except he murdered thee to free the sprite[8]   45
Which still he thought on earth too long immured.[9]
How happy was it that Sohemus' mind
Was moved to pity my distressed estate!
Might Herod's life a trusty servant find,[10]
My death to his had been unseparate.   50
These thoughts have power, his death to make me bear.
Nay more, to wish the news may firmly hold;
Yet cannot this repulse some falling tear.
That will against my will some grief unfold.
And more I owe him for his love to me,   55
The deepest love that ever yet was seen:
Yet had I rather much a milkmaid be,
Than be the monarch of Judea's queen.
It was for naught but love, he wished his end
Might to my death but the vaunt-courier[11] prove: 60
But I had rather still be foe than friend,
To him that saves for hate, and kills for love.[12]
Hard-hearted Mariam, at thy discontent,
What floods of tears have drenched his manly face?
How canst thou then so faintly now lament   65
Thy truest lover's death, a death's disgrace?[13]
Ay, now, mine eyes you do begin to right
The wrongs of your admirer and my lord.[14]
Long since you should have put your smiles to flight,
Ill doth a widowed eye with joy accord.   70
Why now methinks the love I bore him then,
When virgin freedom left me unrestrained,
Doth to my heart begin to creep again,
My passion now is far from being feigned.
But tears fly back, and hide you in your banks,[15]   75
You must not be to Alexandra seen;
For if my moan be spied, but little thanks
Shall Mariam have, from that incensèd queen.

---

8. sprite spirit.   **9. immured** confined.   **10. Might . . . find** If Herod had been
trustworthy while alive.   **11. vaunt-courier** forerunner.   **12. To . . . love** See *Othello*, 5.2.44.   **13. Hard-hearted . . . disgrace** Her lack of grief dishonors his death.
14. my lord Herod.   **15. your banks** her eyes.

SCENE 2

[MARIAM. ALEXANDRA.]

ALEXANDRA. What means these tears? My Mariam doth mistake.
The news we heard did tell the tyrant's end.
What[1] weepst thou for thy brother's murd'rer's sake?
Will ever wight[2] a tear for Herod spend?
My curse pursue his breathless trunk and spirit.   5
Base Edomite the damnèd Esau's heir.
Must he ere Jacob's child the crown inherit?[3]
Must he. vile wretch. be set in David's chair?[4]
No David's soul within the bosom placed
Of our forefather Abram was ashamed   10
To see his seat with such a toad disgraced.
That seat that hath by Judah's race been famed.
Thou fatal enemy to royal blood.[5]
Did not the murder of my boy suffice
To stop thy cruel mouth that gaping stood?   15
But must thou dim the mild Hircanus' eyes?
My gracious father. whose too ready hand
Did lift this Idumean from the dust:[6]
And he ungrateful caitiff[7] did withstand[8]
The man that did in him most friendly trust.   20
What kingdom's right could cruel Herod claim.
Was he not Esau's issue. heir of hell?
Then what succession can he have but shame?
Did not his ancestor his birthright sell?
O yes. he doth from Edom's name derive   25
His cruel nature which with blood is fed.[9]
That made him me of sire and son deprive.
He ever thirsts for blood. and blood is red.
Weep'st thou because his love to thee was bent?
And read'st thou love in crimson characters?   30
Slew he thy friends to work thy heart's content?

1. What why.   **2. wight** a person.   **3. Must ... inherit** The Edomites descended from Esau. who sold his birthright to his brother Jacob (Genesis 25.29–34).
4. chair throne.   **5. blood** Lines 13–16 are addressed to Herod.   **6. Did ... dust** Hircanus raised Herod's station by permitting his marriage to Mariam.   **7. caitiff** wretch.   **8. withstand** oppose.   **9. O ... fed** The root meaning of Edom is "red."

No; hate may justly call that action hers.
He gave the sacred priesthood for thy sake
To Aristobolus, yet doomed him dead;
Before his back the ephod warm could make,   35
And ere the miter settled on his head.[10]
Oh, had he given my boy no less than right,
The double oil should to his forehead bring
A double honor, shining double bright;
His birth anointed him both priest and king,   40
And say my father and my son he slew
To royalize by right your prince-born breath.[11]
Was love the cause, can Mariam deem it true,
That Mariam gave commandment for her death?[12]
I know by fits he showed some signs of love,   45
And yet not love, but raging lunacy:
And this his hate to thee may justly prove,
That sure he hates Hircanus' family.
Who knows if he unconstant wavering lord,
His love to Doris[13] had renewed again?   50
And that he might his bed to her afford,
Perchance he wished that Mariam might be slain.
MARIAM. Doris, alas her time of love was past,
Those coals were raked in embers long ago
Of Mariam's love, and she was now disgraced.[14]   55
Nor did I glory in her overthrow,
He not a whit his first-born son esteemed,
Because as well as his he was not mine:
My children only for his own he deemed,
These boys that did descend from royal line,   60
These did he style his heirs to David's throne,
My Alexander if he live, shall sit
In the majestic seat of Solomon.

---

10. Before ... head The ephod and the miter were Jewish priestly vestments, a brightly colored robe and turban.   **11. And ... breath** to make Mariam's son inherit royal power.   **12. Was ... death** Was it love that gave the order for death to Mariam?   **13. Doris** Herod's first wife.   **14. Of ... disgraced** "If" in the 1613 text is emended to "Of." "Mariam's love" (either Herod's love for Mariam or Mariam's for Herod) covers the coals of Doris's love with ashes.

To will it so. did Herod think it fit.
ALEXANDRA. Why? Who can claim from Alexander's brood[15]   65
That gold-adornèd. lion-guarded chair?
Was Alexander not of David's blood?
And was not Mariam Alexander's heir?
What more than right could Herod then bestow.
And who will think except for more than right.   70
He did not raise them. for they were not low.[16]
But born to wear the crown in his despite.
Then send those tears away that are not sent
To thee by reason. but by passion's power:
Thine eyes to cheer. thy cheeks to smiles be bent.   75
And entertain with joy this happy hour.
Felicity. if when she comes. she finds
A mourning habit and a cheerless look.
Will think she is not welcome to thy mind.
And so perchance her lodging will not brook.[17]   80
Oh. keep her whilst thou hast her: if she go
She will not easily return again.
Full many a year have I endured in woe.
Yet still have sued her presence to obtain:
And did not I to her as presents send   85
A table[18] that best art did beautify
Of two. to whom heaven did best feature lend.
To woo her love by winning Anthony?
For when a prince's favor we do crave.
We first their minions[19] loves do seek to win: 90
So I. that sought felicity to have.
Did with her minion Anthony begin.
With double slight I sought to captivate
The warlike lover. but I did not right:
For if my gift had born but half the rate.   95
The Roman had been overtaken quite.
But now he farèd like a hungry guest.
That to some plenteous festival is gone:

15. Alexander's brood Alexander was Mariam's father.   **16. He ... low** How could Herod grant Mariam's children anything more than what they were already entitled to? Whoever thinks Herod granted them "more than right" should know that "he did not raise them" since "they were not low" in the first place.   **17. brook** put up with.   **18. table** picture.   **19. minions** favorites.

Now this, now that, he deems to eat were best.
Such choice doth make him let them all alone.   100
The boy's large forehead first did fairest seem.
Then glanced his eye upon my Mariam's cheek:
And that without comparison did deem.
What was in either but he most did seek.
And, thus distracted, either's beauty's might   105
Within the other's excellence was drowned:
Too much delight did bare him from delight.
For either's love, the other's did confound.
Where if thy portraiture had only gone,
His life from Herod, Anthony had taken: 110
He would have lovèd thee, and thee alone.
And left the brown Egyptian clean forsaken.
And Cleopatra then to seek had been,[20]
So firm a lover of her wanèd[21] face:
Then great Antonius' fall we had not seen.   115
By her that fled to have him hold the chase.
Then Mariam in a Roman's chariot set.
In place of Cleopatra might have shown:
A mart of beauties in her visage met,
And part in this, that they were all her own.   120
MARIAM. Not to be empress of aspiring Rome,
Would Mariam like to Cleopatra live:
With purest body will I press my tomb,
And wish no favors Anthony could give.[22]
ALEXANDRA. Let us return us, that we may resolve   125
How now to deal in this reversèd state:
Great are the affairs that we must now revolve,
And great affairs must not be taken late.

SCENE 3

[MARIAM, ALEXANDRA, SALOME.]

SALOME. More plotting yet? Why, now you have the thing
For which so oft you spent your suppliant[1] breath:

---

20. And ... been Cleopatra would have been left seeking.   **21. wanèd** dark,
gloomy.   **22. Not ... give.** Mariam disdains Cleopatra's quest for power through her
affairs with Julius Caesar and Mark Antony.   **1. suppliant** humbly begging.

And Mariam hopes to have another king.
Her eyes do sparkle joy for Herod's death.
ALEXANDRA. If she desired another king to have.   5
  She might before she came in Herod's bed
  Have had her wish. More kings than one did crave
  For leave to set a crown upon her head.
  I think with more than reason she laments.
  That she is freed from such a sad annoy: 10
  Who is't will weep to part from discontent.
  And if she joy, she did not causeless joy.[2]
SALOME. You durst not thus have given your tongue the rein.
  If noble Herod still remained in life:
  Your daughter's betters far, I dare maintain.   15
  Might have rejoiced to be my brother's wife.
MARIAM. My betters far! Base woman, 'tis untrue.
  You scarce have ever my superiors seen:
  For Mariam's servants were as good as you.
  Before she came to be Judea's queen.   20
SALOME. Now stirs the tongue that is so quickly moved.
  But more then once your choler[3] have I borne:
  Your fumish[4] words are sooner said than proved.
  And Salome's reply is only scorn.
MARIAM. Scorn those that are for thy companions held.   25
  Though I thy brother's face had never seen.
  My birth, thy baser birth so far excelled.
  I had to both of you the princess been.
  Thou parti-Jew, and parti-Edomite.[5]
  Thou mongrel, issued from rejected race.   30
  Thy ancestors against the heavens did fight.[6]
  And thou like them wilt heavenly birth disgrace.
SALOME. Still twit[7] you me with nothing but my birth.
  What odds betwixt your ancestors and mine?
  Both born of Adam, both were made of earth.   35
  And both did come from holy Abraham's line.

---

2. And ... joy If she were delighted, it would be with good reason.   **3. choler** anger.
4. fumish hot-tempered.   **5. Thou ... parti-Edomite** part Jewish, part Edomite.
6. Thy ... fight In resisting the power of Israel, the Edomites were portrayed as opposing God (Ezekiel 25.13,35).   **7. twit** blame.

MARIAM. I favor thee when nothing else I say.
    With thy black acts I'll not pollute my breath:
    Else to thy charge I might full justly lay
    A shameful life, besides a husband's death.   40
SALOME. 'Tis true indeed, I did the plots reveal,
    That passed betwixt your favorites and you.[8]
    I meant not, I, a traitor to conceal:
    Thus Salome your minion[9] Joseph slew.
MARIAM. Heaven, dost thou mean this infamy to smother?   45
    Let slandered Mariam open thy closèd ear:
    Self-guilt hath ever been suspicion's mother,[10]
    And therefore I this speech with patience bear.
    No, had not Salome's unsteadfast heart,
    In Josephus' stead her Constabarus placed,[11]   50
    To free herself, she had not used the art
    To slander hapless Mariam for unchaste.
ALEXANDRA. Come Mariam, let us go: it is no boot[12]
    To let the head contend against the foot.

SCENE 4

[SALOME *alone.*]

SALOME. Lives Salome, to get so base a style[1]
    As foot, to the proud Mariam? Herod's spirit
    In happy time for her endured exile.[2]
    For did he live she should not miss her merit.[3]
    But he is dead; and though he were my brother,   5
    His death such store of cinders cannot cast
    My coals of love to quench: for though they smother
    The flames a while, yet will they out at last.
    Oh blest Arabia, in best climate placed,
    I by the fruit will censure of the tree: 10

8. 'Tis . . . you Salome accused her first husband, Josephus, and Mariam of adultery.
Herod judged Josephus's telling Mariam about the secret order that she be killed in
the event of Herod's death as proof of Josephus's guilt, and so ordered his execution.
9. minion favorite.   **10. Self-guilt . . . mother** Your own guilt makes you suspicious
of me.   **11. in . . . placed** Mariam claims that she was accused of adultery by Salome because Salome wanted to get rid of her husband so that she could marry Constabarus.   **12. boot** use.   **1. style** name.   **2. exile** separation of the soul from the
body, i.e., death.   **3. For . . . merit** If he were alive, she would get what she deserves.

'Tis not in vain, thy happy name thou hast,
If all Arabians like Silleus⁴ be:
Had not my fate been too too contrary.
When I on Constabarus first did gaze,
Silleus had been object to mine eye,   15
Whose looks and personage must always amaze.
But now ill-fated Salome, thy tongue
To Constabarus by itself is tied:
And now except I do the Hebrew wrong
I cannot be the fair Arabian's bride: 20
What childish lets⁵ are these? Why stand I now
On honorable points? 'Tis long ago
Since shame was written on my tainted brow:⁶
And certain 'tis, that shame is honor's foe,
Had I upon my reputation stood,   25
Had I affected an unspotted life,
Josephus' veins had still been stuffed with blood,
And I to him had lived a sober wife,
Then had I never cast an eye of love
On Constabarus' now detested face,   30
Then had I kept my thoughts without remove
And blushed at motion of the least disgrace.⁷
But shame is gone, and honor wiped away,
And Impudency on my forehead sits:
She bids me work my will without delay,   35
And for my will I will employ my wits.
He loves, I love: what then can be the cause
Keeps me from being the Arabian's wife?
It is the principles of Moses' laws:
For Constabarus still remains in life: 40
If he to me did bear as earnest hate
As I to him, for him there were an ease.
A separating bill⁸ might free his fate
From such a yoke that did so much displease.

---

4. Silleus Salome's lover and minister to King Obodas of Arabia. **5. lets** hindrances. **6. Since . . . brow** since she showed any sign of shame. **7. And . . . disgrace** Compare *Othello*, 1.3.96–98. **8. separating bill** a bill of divorce, which only men could sue for.

Why should such privilege to man be given?   45
Or given to them, why barred from women then?
Are men than we in greater grace with Heaven?
Or cannot women hate as well as men?[9]
I'll be the custom-breaker, and begin
To show my sex the way to freedom's door,   50
And with an offering will I purge my sin.
The law was made for none but who are poor.
If Herod had lived, I might to him accuse
My present lord. But for the future's sake
Then would I tell the king he did refuse   55
The sons of Baba in his power to take.[10]
But now I must divorce him from my bed.
That my Silleus may possess his room.
Had I not begged his life he had been dead.[11]
I curse my tongue the hinderer of his doom: 60
But then my wandering heart to him was fast,
Nor did I dream of change. Silleus said,
He would be here, and see he comes at last,
Had I not named him longer had he stayed.

SCENE 5

[SALOME, SILLEUS.]

SILLEUS. Well found fair Salome, Judea's pride!
    Hath thy innated[1] wisdom found the way
    To make Silleus deem him deified,
    By gaining thee a more than precious prey?
SALOME. I have devised the best I can devise: 5
    A more imperfect means was never found:
    But what cares Salome? It doth suffice
    If our endeavors with their end be crowned.
    In this our land we have an ancient use,

---

9. Or . . . men compare *Othello*, 4.3.91–93.   **10. Then . . . take** Constabarus was supposed to have captured Herod's political enemies, the sons of Baba, but instead hid them on his own estate in hope that they might be useful to him in usurping power. See Josephus, *Antiquities* XV.XI.400–1.   **11. Had . . . dead** When Herod found out that Constabarus, as governor of Idumea, had tried to take over the kingdom, only Salome was able to convince Herod to spare his life.   **1. innated** inborn.

Permitted first by our law-giver's[2] head: 10
Who hates his wife, though for no just abuse,
May with a bill divorce her from his bed,
But in this custom women are not free.
Yet I for once will wrest it: blame not thou
The ill I do, since what I do's for thee,   15
Though others blame, Silleus should allow.
SILLEUS. Thinks Salome, Silleus hath a tongue
To censure her fair actions? Let my blood
Bedash my proper brow,[3] for such a wrong.
The being yours, can make even vices good: 20
Arabia, joy, prepare thy earth with green.
Thou never happy wert indeed 'til now:
Now shall thy ground be trod by beauty's queen.
Her foot is destined to depress thy brow.
Thou shalt fair Salome command as much   25
As if the royal ornament were thine:
The weakness of Arabia's king is such,
The kingdom is not his so much as mine.
My mouth is our Obodas' oracle,
Who thinks not aught but what Silleus will,   30
And thou rare creature, Asia's miracle,
Shalt be to me as it: Obodas' still.[4]
SALOME. 'Tis not for glory I thy love accept,
Judea yields me honor's worthy store:
Had not affection in my bosom crept,   35
My native country should my life deplore.[5]
Were not Silleus he with whom I go,
I would not change my Palestine for Rome:
Much less would I a glorious state to show,
Go far to purchase an Arabian tomb.   40
SILLEUS. Far be it from Silleus so to think,
I know it is thy gratitude requites
The love that is in me, and shall not shrink

---

2. law-giver's Moses'.   **3. Bedash ... brow** splash against my own forehead.
4. The ... still Even though Obodas rules the Kingdom, he follows my judgment as
I follow yours, Salome.   **5. Had ... deplore** If it weren't for love of you, Silleus, I
would regret leaving my country my whole life long.

'Til death do sever me from earth's delights.
SALOME. But whist;[6] methinkes the wolf is in our talk.[7]   45
    Be gone Silleus, who doth here arrive?
    'Tis Constabarus that doth hither walk,
    I'll find a quarrel, him from me to drive.
SILLEUS. Farewell, but were it not for thy command,
    In his despite Silleus here would stand.   50

SCENE 6

[SALOME, CONSTABARUS.]

CONSTABARUS. Oh Salome, how much you wrong your name.
    Your race, your country, and your husband most!
    A stranger's private conference is shame:[1]
    I blush for you, that have your blushing lost.
    Oft have I found, and found you to my grief,   5
    Comforted with this base Arabian here:
    Heaven knows that you have been my comfort chief.
    Then do not now my greater plague appear.
    Now by the stately carved edifice
    That on Mount Sion makes so fair a show,[2]   10
    And by the altar fit for sacrifice,
    I love thee more than thou thyself dost know.
    Oft with a silent sorrow have I heard
    How ill Judea's mouth doth censure thee;
    And did I not thine honor much regard,   15
    Thou shouldst not be exhorted thus for me.
    Didst thou but know the worth of honest fame,
    How much a virtuous woman is esteemed.
    Thou wouldst like hell eschew deservèd shame,
    And seek to be both chaste and chastely deemed.   20
    Our wisest prince did say, and true he said,
    A virtuous woman crowns her husband's head.[3]
SALOME. Did I for this uprear thy low estate?

---

6. whist be silent.   **7. methinkes . . . talk** In discussing our plot for power, we are in danger of being overheard.   **1. A . . . shame** Talking privately with a stranger is shameful.   **2. Now . . . show** the temple of Jerusalem.   **3. A . . . head** Proverbs 12.4; attributed to Solomon.

Did I for this requital beg thy life.
That thou hadst forfeited to hapless fate.   25
To be to such a thankless wretch the wife?
This hand of mine hath lifted up thy head.
Which many a day ago had fall'n full low.
Because the sons of Babas are not dead:
To me thou dost both life and fortune owe.   30
CONSTABARUS. You have my patience often exercised.
  Use make my choler keep within the banks:[4]
  Yet boast no more. but be by me advised.
  A benefit upbraided. forfeits thanks.[5]
  I prithee Salome. dismiss this mood.   35
  Thou dost not know how ill it fits thy place:
  My words were all intended for thy good.
  To raise thine honor and to stop disgrace.
SALOME. To stop disgrace? Take thou no care for me.
  Nay. do thy worst. thy worst I set not by:[6]   40
  No shame of mine is like to light on thee.
  Thy love and admonitions I defy.
  Thou shalt no hour longer call me wife.
  Thy jealousy procures my hate so deep:
  That I from thee do mean to free my life.   45
  By a divorcing bill before I sleep.
CONSTABARUS. Are Hebrew women now transformed to men?
  Why do you not as well our battles fight.
  And wear our armor? Suffer this. and then
  Let all the world be topsy-turvèd[7] quite.   50
  Let fishes graze. beasts. swine. and birds descend.
  Let fire burn downwards whilst the earth aspires:
  Let winter's heat and summer's cold offend.
  Let thistles grow on vines. and grapes on briars.
  Set us to spin or sow. or at the best   55
  Make us wood-hewers. water-bearing wights:
  For sacred service let us take no rest.
  Use us as Joshua did the Gibonites.[8]

---

4. Use . . . banks May habit control my anger. **5. A . . . thanks** If you blame someone for having granted him a benefit. you lose his gratitude. **6. Nay . . . by** I couldn't care less about the worst you could do to me. **7. topsy-turvèd** upside down. **8. Use . . . Gibonites** Joshua enslaved the Gibonites (Joshua 9).

SALOME. Hold on your talk, 'til it be time to end,
  For me I am resolved it shall be so;   60
  Though I be first that to this course do bend,
  I shall not be the last full well I know.
CONSTABARUS. Why then be witness heaven, the judge of sins,
  Be witness spirits that eschew the dark:
  Be witness angels, witness cherubins,   65
  Whose semblance sits upon the holy Ark:
  Be witness earth, be witness Palestine,
  Be witness David's city, if my heart
  Did ever merit such an act of thine;
  Or if the fault be mine that makes us part,   70
  Since mildest Moses, friend unto the Lord,
  Did work his wonders in the land of Ham,[9]
  And slew the first-born babes without a sword,
  In sign whereof we eat the holy lamb;[10]
  'Til now that fourteen hundred years are past,   75
  Since first the Law[11] with us hath been in force:
  You are the first, and will, I hope, be last,
  That ever sought her husband to divorce.
SALOME. I mean not to be led by precedent,
  My will shall be to me instead of Law.   80
CONSTABARUS. I fear me much you will too late repent,
  That you have ever lived so void of awe:
  This is Silleus' love that makes you thus
  Reverse all order: you must next be his.
  But if my thoughts aright the cause discuss,   85
  In winning you, he gains no lasting bliss:
  I was Silleus, and not long ago
  Josephus then was Constabarus now:
  When you became my friend[12] you proved his[13] foe,
  As now for him[14] you break to me your vow.   90
SALOME. If once I loved you, greater is your debt:
  For certain 'tis that you deserve it not,
  And undeserved love we soon forget.

---

9. Ham Egypt. **10. And . . . lamb** During the Passover celebration commemorating the Israelites' deliverance from Egypt (Exodus 12). **11. Law** the law of Moses. **12. friend** lover. **13. his** Josephus's. **14. him** Silleus.

And therefore that to me can be no blot.
But now fare ill my once belovèd lord.   95
Yet never more beloved than now abhorred.
CONSTABARUS. Yet Constabarus biddeth thee farewell.
   Farewell light creature. Heaven forgive thy sin:
   My prophesying spirit doth foretell
   Thy wavering thoughts do yet but new begin.   100
   Yet I have better 'scaped than Joseph did:
   But if our Herod's death had been delayed.
   The valiant youths[15] that I so long have hid.
   Had been by her. and I for them betrayed.
   Therefore in happy hour did Caesar give   105
   The fatal blow to wanton Anthony:
   For had he lived. our Herod then should live.
   But great Anthonius' death made Herod die.
   Had he enjoyed his breath. not I alone
   Had been in danger of a deadly fall: 110
   But Mariam had the way of peril gone.
   Though by the tyrant most beloved of all.
   The sweet-faced Mariam as free from guilt
   As heaven from spots. yet had her lord come back
   Her purest blood had been unjustly spilt.   115
   And Salome it was would work her wrack.[16]
   Though all Judea yield her innocent.
   She often hath been near to punishment.   *[Exit.]*

CHORUS. Those minds that wholly dote upon delight.
   Except[17] they only joy in inward good.   120
   Still hope at last to hop upon the right.[18]
   And so from sand they leap in loathsome mud.
   Fond wretches. seeking what they cannot find.
   For no content attends a wavering mind.

   If wealth they do desire. and wealth attain.   125
   Then wondrous fain[19] would they to honor leap:
   Of mean degree they do in honor gain.

---

15. **youths** Baba's sons. 16. **wrack** destruction. 17. **Except** unless. 18. **Still . . . right** To hop on to land on the right side meant to achieve a good outcome. 19. **fain** gladly.

They would but wish a little higher step.
Thus step to step, and wealth to wealth they add,
Yet cannot all their plenty make them glad.   130

Yet oft we see that some in humble state,
Are cheerful, pleasant, happy, and content:
When those indeed that are of higher state,
With vain additions do their thoughts torment.
Th' one would to his mind his fortune bind,   135
Th' other to his fortune frames his mind.

To wish variety is sign of grief,
For if you like your state as now it is,
Why should an alteration bring relief?
Nay change would then be feared as loss of bliss.   140
That man is only happy in his fate,
That is delighted in a settled state.

Still Mariam wished she from her lord were free,
For expectation of variety:
Yet now she sees her wishes prosperous be,   145
She grieves, because her lord so soon did die.
Who can those vast imaginations feed,
Where in a property contempt doth breed?[20]

Were Herod now perchance to love again,
She would again as much be grieved at that: 150
All that she may,[21] she ever doth disdain,
Her wishes guide her to she knows not what,
And sad must be their looks, their honor sour,
That care for nothing being in their power.

ACT 2
SCENE 1

[PHERORAS *and* GRAPHINA.][1]

PHERORAS. 'Tis true Graphina, now the time draws nigh

---

20. Where . . . breed where what is possessed is despised.   **21. All . . . may** All that she may have or do.   **1. Graphina** From the minor figure of a nameless slave girl in Josephus's *Jewish War*, Cary created Graphina, derived from *graphesis*, the Greek word for writing.

Wherein the holy priest with hallowed right.
The happy long-desired knot shall tie.
Pheroras and Graphina to unite:
How oft have I with lifted hands implored   5
This blessed hour, 'til now implored in vain.
Which hath my wished liberty restored.
And made my subject self my own again.
Thy love, fair maid, upon mine eye doth sit.
Whose nature hot doth dry the moisture all.   10
Which were in nature, and in reason fit
For my monarchal brother's death to fall:
Had Herod lived, he would have plucked my hand
From fair Graphina's palm perforce. and tied
The same in hateful and despisèd band.   15
For I had had a baby to my bride:[2]
Scarce can her infant tongue with easy voice
Her name distinguish to another's ear:[3]
Yet had he lived, his power, and not my choice
Had made me solemnly the contract swear.   20
Have I not cause in such a change to joy?
What? Though she be my niece, a princess born:
Near-blood's without respect: high birth a toy.
Since love can teach us blood and kindred's scorn.
What booted it[4] that he did raise my head.   25
To be his realm's copartner. kingdom's mate?
Withall. he kept Graphina from my bed.
More wished by me than thrice Judea's state.
Oh. could not he be skilful judge in love.
That doted so upon his Mariam's face?   30
He, for his passion. Doris did remove:
I needed not a lawful wife displace.
It could not be but he had power to judge.
But he that never grudged a kingdom's share.
This well-known happiness to me did grudge.   35

2. For . . . bride Herod would have ordered a marriage between his oldest daughter ("a baby") and Pheroras. 3. Scarce . . . ear She is so young she can hardly say her own name clearly: "infant" from Latin *infans*. speechless. 4. What . . . it What use was it?

And meant to be therein without compare.
Else had I been his equal in love's host.[5]
For though the diadem on Mariam's head
Corrupt the vulgar judgments, I will boast
Graphina's brow's as white, her cheeks as red.   40
Why speaks thou not fair creature? Move thy tongue,
For silence is a sign of discontent:
It were to both our loves too great a wrong
If now this hour do find thee sadly bent.

GRAPHINA. Mistake me not my lord, too oft have I   45
Desired this time to come with wingèd feet,
To be enwrapped with grief when 'tis too nigh.
You know my wishes ever yours did meet.
If I be silent, 'tis no more but fear
That I should say too little when I speak: 50
But since you will my imperfections bear,
In spite of doubt I will my silence break.
Yet might amazement tie my moving tongue,
But that I know before Pheroras' mind,
I have admirèd[6] your affection long,   55
And cannot yet therein a reason find.
Your hand hath lifted me from lowest state,
To highest eminency's wondrous grace,
And me your handmaid have you made your mate,
Though all but you alone do count me base.   60
You have preserved me pure at my request,
Though you so weak a vassal[7] might constrain
To yield to your high will; then last not best
In my respect a princess you disdain;
Then need not all these favors study crave,   65
To be requited by a simple maid?[8]
And study still you know must silence have.
Then be my cause for silence justly weighed,
But study cannot boot nor I requite,

---

5. **host** army.   6. **admirèd** marvelled at.   7. **vassal** The feudal relation between lord and subordinate with a pun on "vessel," as in woman as "the weaker vessel" (1 Peter 3.7).   8. **Then . . . maid** All these favors will require effort for a simple maid to repay them.

Except your lowly handmaid's steadfast love   70
And fast obedience may your mind delight.
I will not promise more then I can prove.
PHERORAS. That study needs not let Graphina smile.
And I desire no greater recompense:
I cannot vaunt[9] me in a glorious style.   75
Nor show my love in far-fetched eloquence:
But this believe me, never Herod's heart
Hath held his prince-born beauty-famèd wife
In nearer place than thou, fair virgin, art.
To him that holds the glory of his life.   80
Should Herod's body leave the sepulcher.
And entertain the severed ghost again.[10]
He should not be my nuptial hinderer.
Except he hindered it with dying pain.
Come fair Graphina, let us go in state.   85
This wish-endearèd time to celebrate.

SCENE 2

[CONSTABARUS *and* BABA'S SONS.]

FIRST SON. Now valiant friend you have our lives redeemed.
      Which lives as saved by you, to you are due.
      Command and you shall see yourself esteemed:
      Our lives and liberties belong to you.
      This twice six years with hazard of your life.   5
      You have concealed us from the tyrant's sword:
      Though cruel Herod's sister were your wife.
      You durst in scorn of fear this grace afford.
      In recompense we know not what to say.
      A poor reward were thanks for such a merit.[1]   10
      Our truest friendship at your feet we lay.
      The best requital to a noble spirit.
CONSTABARUS. Oh how you wrong our friendship valiant youth!
      With friends there is not such a word as debt.

9. vaunt boast, proclaim.   10. And . . . again The spirit separated from the body.
an image of death.   1. A . . . merit Thanks would be a poor reward for your saving
our lives.

Where amity is tied with bond of truth,   15
All benefits are therein common set.
Then is the golden age with them renewed,
All names of properties are banished quite:[2]
Division and distinction are eschewed:
Each hath to what belongs to other's right.[3]   20
And 'tis not sure so full a benefit,
Freely to give, as freely to require:
A bounteous act hath glory following it,
They cause the glory that the act desire.
All friendship should the pattern imitate,   25
Of Jesse's son and valiant Jonathan:[4]
For neither sovereign's nor father's hate,
A friendship fixed on virtue sever can.
Too much of this, 'tis written in the heart,
And need no amplifying with the tongue: 30
Now may you from your living tomb depart,
Where Herod's life hath kept you overlong,
Too great an injury to a noble mind,
To be quick buried:[5] you had purchased fame,
Some years ago, but that you were confined,   35
While thousand meaner did advance their name,
Your best of life the prime of all your years,
Your time of action is from you bereft,
Twelve winters have you overpassed in fears:
Yet if you use it well, enough is left,   40
And who can doubt but you will use it well?
The sons of Babas have it by descent:
In all their thoughts each action to excel,
Boldly to act, and wisely to invent.
SECOND SON. Had it not like the hateful cuckoo been,   45
Whose riper age his infant nurse doth kill.[6]
So long we had not kept ourselves unseen,

---

2. All . . . quite All individual ownership is forbidden.   **3. Each . . . right** Each one
has a right to what belongs to the other.   **4. Of . . . Jonathan** See 1 Samuel 20 for
how David (Jesse's son) was saved by Jonathan (Saul's son) from death at the hands
of King Saul.   **5. quick buried** buried alive.   **6. Had . . . kill** The cuckoo lays its
eggs in other birds' nests, and when grown the chicks kill their foster parents.

But Constabarus safely crossed our will:
For had the tyrant fixed his cruel eye.
On our concealèd faces wrath had swayed   50
His justice so. that he had forced us die.
And dearer price than life we should have paid:
For you our truest friend had fallen with us.
And we much like a house on pillars set.
Had clean depressed our prop. and therefore thus   55
Our ready will with our concealment met.
But now that you. fair lord. are dangerless.
The sons of Babas shall their rigor show:
And prove it was not baseness did oppress
Our hearts so long. but honor kept them low.   60
FIRST SON. Yet do I fear this tale of Herod's death.
At last will prove a very tale indeed:
It gives me strongly in my mind. his breath
Will be preserved to make a number bleed.
I wish not therefore to be set at large.   65
Yet peril to myself I do not fear:
Let us for some days longer be your charge.[7]
'Til we of Herod's state the truth do hear.
CONSTABARUS. What art thou turned a coward. noble youth.
That thou beginn'st to doubt undoubted truth?   70
FIRST SON. Were it my brother's tongue that cast this doubt
I from his heart would have the question out
With this keen falchion.[8] but 'tis you my lord
Against whose head I must not lift a sword:
I am so tied in gratitude.   75
CONSTABARUS.   Believe
You have no cause to take it ill.
If any word of mine your heart did grieve.
The word descended from the speakers's will:
I know it was not fear the doubt begun.
But rather valor and your care of me: 80
A coward could not be your father's son.
Yet know I doubts unnecessary be:

---

7. **charge** care.   8. **falchion** curved sword.

For who can think that in Anthonius' fall,
Herod his bosom friend should 'scape unbruised.[9]
Then, Caesar, we might thee an idiot call,   85
If thou by him should'st be so far abused.
SECOND SON. Lord Constabarus, let me tell you this,
Upon submission Caesar will forgive:
And therefore though the tyrant did amiss,
It may fall out that he will let him live.   90
Not many years agone it is since I
Directed thither by my father's care,
In famous Rome for twice twelve months did live,
My life from Hebrew's cruelty to spare.
There though I were but yet of boyish age,   95
I bent mine eye to mark, mine ears to hear,
Where I did see Octavius then a page,
When first he did to Julius' sight appear:[10]
Methought I saw such mildness in his face,
And such a sweetness in his looks did grow,   100
Withall, commixed with so majestic grace,
His phis'nomy his fortune did foreshow:[11]
For this I am indebted to mine eye,
But then mine ear received more evidence,
How he with hottest choler[12] could dispense.   105
CONSTABARUS. But we have more than barely heard the news,
It hath been twice confirmed, And though some tongue
Might be so false, with false report t'abuse,
A false report hath never lasted long.
But be it so that Herod have his life,   110
Concealment would not then a whit avail:
For certain 'tis, that she that was my wife,
Would not to set her accusation fail.
And therefore now as good the venture give,
And free ourselves from blot of cowardice.   115

---

9. For . . . unbruised The victory of Octavius Caesar over Anthony and Cleopatra in
the battle of Actium made it seem unlikely that Herod would remain in power.
10. Where . . . appear Octavius (63 B.C.–A.D. 14), Julius Caesar's great-nephew
and adopted heir, later became Augustus Caesar.   **11. His . . . foreshow** Octavius'
courteous manners and graceful appearance (physiognomy) foretold his greatness.
12. choler anger.

As show a pitiful desire to live.
For, who can pity but they must despise?
FIRST SON. I yield, but to necessity I yield:
　I dare upon this doubt engage mine arm:[13]
　That Herod shall again this kingdom wield,　　　　　　　120
　And prove his death to be a false alarm.
SECOND SON. I doubt[14] it too. God grant it be an error.
　'Tis best without a cause to be in terror;
　And rather had I, though my soul be mine,
　My soul should lie, than prove a true divine.[15]　　　　125
CONSTABARUS. Come, come, let fear go seek a dastard's nest.
　Undaunted courage lies in noble breast.

SCENE 3

[DORIS *and* ANTIPATER.]

DORIS. You royal buildings bow your lofty side,
　And stoop to her that is by right your queen:
　Let your humility upbraid the pride
　Of those in whom no due respect is seen.
　Nine times have we with trumpets' haughty sound,　　　5
　And banishing sour leaven from our taste,
　Observed the feast that takes the fruit from ground.[1]
　Since I, fair city, did behold thee last,
　So long it is since Mariam's purer cheek
　Did rob from mine the glory.[2] And so long　　　　　　10
　Since I returned my native town to seek,
　And with me nothing but the sense of wrong.
　And thee my boy, whose birth though great it were,
　Yet have thy after fortunes proved but poor;
　When thou wert born how little did I fear　　　　　　　15
　Thou shouldst be thrust from forth thy father's door.
　Art thou not Herod's right begotten son?

13. I . . . arm I am willing to take up arms on the suspicion that Herod is still alive and will return to power.　**14. doubt** fear.　**15. And . . . divine** I would rather that my suspicions be found false than that I be confirmed as a prophet.　**1. Observed . . . ground** The feast of first fruits was observed each year on the day after Passover (the feast of unleavened bread).　**2. So . . . glory** It had been nine years since Herod's divorce of Doris.

Was not the hapless Doris, Herod's wife?
Yes: ere he had the Hebrew kingdom won,
I was companion to his private life.   20
Was I not fair enough to be a queen?
Why, ere thou wert to me false monarch tied,
My lake of beauty might as well be seen,
As after I had lived five years thy bride,
Yet then thine oath came powering like the rain,   25
Which all affirmed my face without compare,
And that if thou might'st Doris love obtain,
For all the world besides thou didst not care,
Then was I young, and rich, and nobly borne,
And therefore worthy to be Herod's mate: 30
Yet thou ungrateful cast me off with scorn,
When heaven's purpose raised your meaner fate.
Oft have I begged for vengeance for this fact,[3]
And with dejected[4] knees, aspiring hands
Have prayed the highest power to enact   35
The fall of her that on my trophy[5] stands.
Revenge I have according to my will,
Yet where I wished this vengeance did not light.
I wished it should high-hearted Mariam kill,
But it against my whilom[6] lord did fight.   40
With thee, sweet boy, I came, and came to try
If thou before his bastards might be placed
In Herod's royal seat and dignity.
But Mariam's infants here are only graced,
And now for us there doth no hope remain: 45
Yet we will not return 'til Herod's end
Be more confirmed, perchance he is not slain.
So glorious fortunes may my boy attend,
For if he[7] live, he'll think it doth suffice,
That he to Doris shows such cruelty: 50
For as he did my wretched life despise,
So do I know I shall despisèd die.
Let him but prove as natural to thee.

3. fact action.   **4. dejected** bent down.   **5. my trophy** the spoils of my defeat.
6. whilom former.   **7. he** Herod.

As cruel to thy miserable mother:
His cruelty shall not upbraided be   55
But in thy fortunes.[8] His faults will smother.
ANTIPATER. Each mouth within the city loudly cries
That Herod's death is certain. Therefore we
Had best some subtle hidden plot devise.
That Mariam's children might subverted be.   60
By poisons drink. or else by murderous knife.
So we may be advanced. it skills not[9] how:
They are but bastards. you were Herod's wife.
And foul adultery blotteth Mariam's brow.
DORIS. They are too strong to be by us removed.   65
Or else revenge's foulest spotted face:
By our detested wrongs might be approved.
But weakness must to greater power give place.
But let us now retire to grieve alone.
For solitariness best fitteth moan.   [*They exit.*]

SCENE 4

[SILLEUS *and* CONSTABARUS.]

SILLEUS. Well met Judean lord. the only wight[1]
Silleus wished to see. I am to call
Thy tongue to strict account.
CONSTABARUS.   For what despite
I ready am to hear. and answer all.
But if directly at the cause I guess   5
That breeds this challenge. you must pardon me:[2]
And now some other ground of fight profess.
For I have vowed. vows must unbroken be.
SILLEUS. What may be your exception? Let me know.[3]
CONSTABARUS. Why? Aught concerning Salome. my sword   10
Shall not be wielded for a cause so low:
A blow for her my arm will scorn t'afford.

---

8. His ... fortunes I won't criticize his cruelty except in so far as it affects your fortunes.   **9. skills not** makes no difference.   **1. wight** person.   **2. But ... me** If I am right in guessing why you want to fight me. you'll have to excuse me from responding to your challenge.   **3. What ... know** "Expectation" in the 1613 text has been emended "exception." the reason why you will not fight.

SILLEUS. It is for slandering her unspotted name.[4]
   And I will make thee in thy vows despite.
   Suck up the breath that did my mistress blame.   15
   And swallow it again to do her right.
CONSTABARUS. I prithee give some other quarrel ground
   To find beginning. rail against my name:
   Or strike me first. or let some scarlet wound
   Inflame my courage. give me words of shame: 20
   Do thou our Moses' sacred laws disgrace.
   Deprave our nation, do me some despite:
   I'm apt enough to fight in any case.
   But yet for Salome I will not fight.
SILLEUS. Nor I for aught but Salome. My sword   25
   That owes his service to her sacred name
   Will not an edge for other cause afford:
   In other fight I am not sure of fame.
CONSTABARUS. For her.[5] I pity thee enough already.
   For her. I therefore will not mangle thee: 30
   A woman with a heart so most unsteady.
   Will of herself sufficient torture be.
   I cannot envy for so light a gain.
   Her mind with such inconstancy doth run:
   As with a word thou didst her love obtain.   35
   So with a word she will from thee be won.
   So light as her possessions for most day
   Is her affections lost, to me 'tis known:[6]
   As good go hold the wind as make her stay.
   She never loves. but 'til she call her own.[7]   40
   She merely is a painted sepulcher.[8]
   That is both fair. and vilely foul at once:
   Though on her outside graces garnish her.
   Her mind is filled with worse than rotten bones.
   And ever ready lifted is her hand.   45
   To aim destruction at a husband's throat:

---

4. It . . . name I challenge you because you have slandered Salome. **5. For her** because of her. **6. So . . . known** You value her affection so little when you have it that it is a light loss when you lose it. **7. She . . . own** She loves only up to the point when she gets what she wants. **8. painted sepulcher** See Matthew 23.27: "Woe unto you. scribes and Pharisees. hypocrites! for ye are like unto whited sepulchers."

For proofs. Josephus and myself do stand.
Though once on both of us she seemed to dote.
Her mouth though serpentlike it never hisses.
Yet like a serpent. poisons where it kisses.   50
SILLEUS. Well Hebrew well. thou bark'st. but wilt not bite.
CONSTABARUS. I tell thee still for her I will not fight.
SILLEUS. Why then I call thee coward.
CONSTABARUS.   From my heart
I give thee thanks. A coward's hateful name.
Cannot to valiant minds a blot impart.   55
And therefore I with joy receive the same.
Thou know'st I am no coward. Thou wert by
At the Arabian battle th'other day.
And saw'st my sword with daring valiancy
Amongst the faint Arabians cut my way.   60
The blood of foes no more could let it shine.
And 'twas enameled with some of thine.
But now have at thee:[9] not for Salome
I fight. but to discharge a coward's style:[10]
Here 'gins the fight that shall not parted be.   65
Before a soul or two endure exile. [*They fight.*]
SILLEUS. Thy sword hath made some windows for my blood.
To show a horrid crimson phis'nomy:[11]
To breathe[12] for both of us methinks 'twere good.
The day will give us time enough to die.   70
CONSTABARUS. With all my heart take breath. thou shalt have
    time.
And if thou list[13] a twelve month: let us end.
Into thy cheeks there doth a paleness climb:
Thou canst not from my sword thyself defend.
What needest thou for Salome to fight?   75
Thou hast her. and may'st keep her. none strives for her:
I willingly to thee resign my right.
For in my very soul I do abhor her.
Thou seest that I am fresh. unwounded yet.
Then not for fear I do this offer make: 80

9. **But . . . thee** I'll fight you.   10. **style** name.   11. **phis'nomy** face.   12. **breathe** catch breath.   13. **list** wish.

Thou art with loss of blood, to fight unfit.
For here is one, and there another take.[14]

SILLEUS. I will not leave, as long as breath remains
    Within my wounded body. Spare your words.
    My heart in blood's stead, courage entertains.   85
    Salome's love no place for fear affords.

CONSTABARUS. Oh, could thy soul but prophesy like mine,
    I would not wonder thou should'st long to die:
    For Salome, if I aright divine,
    Will be than death a greater misery.   90

SILLEUS. Then list, I'll breathe no longer.[15]

CONSTABARUS.   Do thy will.
    I hateless fight, and charitably kill. [*They fight.*] Aye, aye,
    Pity thyself Silleus, let not death
    Intrude before his time into thy heart:
    Alas it is too late to fear, his breath   95
    Is from his body now about to part.
    How farest thou brave Arabian?

SILLEUS.   Very well.
    My leg is hurt, I can no longer fight:
    It only grieves me, that so soon I fell,
    Before fair Salom's wrongs[16] I came to right.   100

CONSTABARUS. Thy wounds are less than mortal. Never fear.
    Thou shalt a safe and quick recovery find:
    Come, I will thee unto my lodging bear.
    I hate thy body, but I love thy mind.

SILLEUS. Thanks, noble Jew, I see a courteous foe,   105
    Stern enmity to friendship can no art:[17]
    Had not my heart and tongue engaged me so,
    I would from thee no foe, but friend depart.
    My heart to Salome is tied too fast
    To leave her love for friendship, yet my skill   110
    Shall be employed to make your favor last,
    And I will honor Constabarus still.

CONSTABARUS. I ope my bosom to thee, and will take

---

14. For ... take In this fight, each of us gives and takes.   **15. Then ... longer**
Then listen, I won't pause or live any longer.   **16. Salom's wrongs** the wrong done
to Salome.   **17. Stern ... art** No art can turn enmity into friendship.

Thee in. as friend. and grieve for thy complaint:
But if we do not expedition make.   115
Thy loss of blood I fear will make thee faint.

[*They exit.*]

CHORUS. To hear a tale with ears prejudicate.[18]
    It spoils the judgment and corrupts the sense:
    That human error given to every state.
    Is greater enemy to innocence.[19]   120
    It makes us foolish. heady. rash. unjust:
    It makes us never try before we trust.[20]

It will confound the meaning. change the words.
For it our sense of hearing much deceives:
Besides no time to judgment it affords.   125
To weigh the circumstance our ear receives.
The ground of accidents[21] it never tries.
But makes us take for truth ten thousand lies.

Our ears and hearts are apt to hold for good.
That we ourselves do most desire to be: 130
And then we drown objections in the flood
Of partiality. 'tis that[22] we see
That makes false rumors long with credit passed.
Though they like rumors must conclude at last.

The greatest part of us prejudicate.[23]   135
With wishing Herod's death do hold it true:
The being once deluded doth not bate.[24]
The credit to a better likelihood due.[25]
Those few that wish it not. the multitude
Do carry headlong. so they doubts conclude.[26]   140

They[27] not object the weak uncertain ground.
Whereon they built this tale of Herod's end:

---

18. **prejudicate** prejudiced.   19. **That . . . innocence** The naïve are more vulnerable to human error.   20. **It . . . trust** It makes us never try to find out the truth before we trust what we have heard.   21. **ground of accidents** basis or cause of appearances.   22. **that** partiality.   23. **prejudicate** judge too soon.   24. **bate** lessen. 25. **The . . . due** Having been deceived before about Herod's death doesn't lessen the belief that it might be true this time.   26. **Those . . . conclude** Those who do not wish for Herod's death are swayed by the majority and so stop doubting.   27. **They** the few.

Whereof the author scarcely can be found.
And all because their wishes that way bend.
They think not of the peril that ensu'th.[28]   145
If this should prove the contrary to truth.

On this same doubt. on this so light a breath.
They pawn their lives and fortunes. For they all
Behave them as the news of Herod's death.
They did of most undoubted credit call;   150
But if their actions now do rightly hit.[29]
Let them commend their fortune. not their wit.

ACT 3
SCENE 1

[PHERORAS. SALOME.]

PHERORAS. Urge me no more Graphina to forsake.
    Not twelve hours since I married her for love:
    And do you think a sister's power can make
    A resolute decree, so soon remove?
SALOME. Poor minds they are that honor not affects.   5
PHERORAS. Who hunts for honor. happiness neglects.
SALOME. You might have been both of felicity
    And honor too in equal measure seized.
PHERORAS. It is not you can tell so well as I.
    What 'tis can make me happy. or displeased.   10
SALOME. To match for neither beauty nor respects
    One mean of birth. but yet of meaner mind.
    A woman full of natural defects.
    I wonder what your eye in her could find.
PHERORAS. Mine eye found loveliness. mine ear found wit.   15
    To please the one. and to enchant the other;
    Grace on her eye. mirth on her tongue doth sit.
    In looks a child. in wisdom's house a mother.
SALOME. But say you thought her fair. as none thinks else.
    Knows not Pheroras. beauty is a blast:[1]   20
    Much like this flower which today excels.
    But longer than a day it will not last.

---

28. ensu'th comes about.   **29. hit** succeed.   **1. blast** brief gust of wind.

PHERORAS. Her wit exceeds her beauty.
SALOME.   Wit may show
     The way to ill as well as good you know.
PHERORAS. But wisdom is the porter of her head.   25
     And bars all wicked words from issuing thence.
SALOME. But of a porter. better were you sped.[2]
     If she against their entrance made defense.[3]
PHERORAS. But wherefore comes the sacred Ananell.[4]
     That hitherward his hasty steps doth bend?   30
     Great sacrificer y'are arrived well.
     Ill news from holy mouth I not attend.[5]

                              SCENE 2

[PHERORAS. SALOME. ANANELL.]

ANANELL. My lips. my son. with peaceful tidings bless'd.
     Shall utter honey to your list'ning ear:
     A word of death comes not from priestly breast.
     I speak of life: in life there is no fear.
     And for the news I did the Heavens salute.   5
     And filled the temple with my thankful voice:
     For though that mourning may not me pollute.[1]
     At pleasing accidents I may rejoice.
PHERORAS. Is Herod then revived from certain death?
SALOME. What? Can your news restore my brother's breath?   10
ANANELL. Both so. and so. the king is safe and sound.
     And did such grace in royal Caesar meet:
     That he with larger style than ever crowned.
     Within this hour Jerusalem will greet.
     I did but come to tell you. and must back   15
     To make preparatives for sacrifice:
     I knew his death. your hearts like mine did rack.
     Though to conceal it. proved you wise.   [Exit.]
SALOME. How can my joy sufficiently appear?

2. sped provided.   3. If . . . defense See *Othello*. 3.3.136–41.   4. Ananell Herod
first had made Ananelus high priest. but then. he gave the position to Mariam's
brother Aristobolus. After a year. jealous of Aristobulus' popularity. Herod had him
killed and made Ananelus high priest again.   5. attend expect.   1. For . . . pollute
Priests had to avoid ritually defiling contact with corpses in mourning rites (Leviticus
21.1–2).

PHERORAS. A heavier tale did never pierce mine ear.   20
SALOME. Now Salome of happiness may boast.
PHERORAS. But now Pheroras is in danger most.
SALOME. I shall enjoy the comfort of my life.
PHERORAS. And I shall lose it, losing of my wife.
SALOME. Joy heart, for Constabarus shall be slain.   25
PHERORAS. Grieve soul, Graphina shall from me be ta'en.
SALOME. Smile, cheeks, the fair Silleus shall be mine.
PHERORAS. Weep, eyes, for I must with a child combine.
SALOME. Well, brother, cease your moans, on one condition
    I'll undertake to win the King's consent;   30
    Graphina still shall be in your tuition.[2]
    And her with you be ne'er the less content.
PHERORAS. What's the condition? Let me quickly know,
    That I as quickly your command may act;
    Were it to see what herbs in Ophir grow,   35
    Or that the lofty Tyrus might be sacked.[3]
SALOME. 'Tis not so hard a task; it is no more,
    But tell the king that Constabarus hid
    The sons of Baba, done to death before;[4]
    And 'tis no more than Constabarus did,   40
    And tell him more that he for Herod's sake,
    Not able to endure his brother's foe,
    Did with a bill our separation make,
    Though loath from Constabarus else to go.
PHERORAS. Believe this tale for told, I'll go from hence,   45
    In Herod's ear the Hebrew to deface;
    And I that never studied eloquence,
    Do mean with eloquence this tale to grace.   *[Exit.]*
SALOME. This will be Constabarus' quick dispatch,
    Which from my mouth would lesser credit find;   50
    Yet shall he not decease without a match,
    For Mariam shall not linger long behind.
    First, jealousy, if that avail not, fear
    Shall be my minister to work her end.
    A common error moves not Herod's ear,   55

---

2. **tuition** care.   3. **Were . . . sacked** Ophir, on the west coast of Arabia or India,
was a source of gold. Tyre, on the coast of Lebanon, was the greatest city of ancient
Phoenicia.   4. **done . . . before** assumed to have been put to death.

Which doth so firmly to his Mariam bend.
She shall be charged with so horrid crime.
As Herod's fear shall turn his love to hate:
I'll make some swear that she desires to climb.
And seeks to poison him for his estate.[5]   60
I scorn that she should love my birth t'upbraid.
To call me base and hungry Edomite:
With patient show her choler I betrayed.[6]
And watched the time to be revenged by slight.
Now tongue of mine with scandal load her name.   65
Turn hers to fountains. Herod's eyes to flame.
Yet first I will begin Pheroras' suit.
That he my earnest business may effect:
And I of Mariam will keep me mute.
'Till first some other doth her name detect.[7]   70
Who's there. Silleus' man? How fares your lord
That your aspects do bear the badge of sorrow?
SILLEUS' MAN. He hath the marks of Constabarus' sword.
    And for a while desires your sight to borrow.
SALOME. My heavy curse the hateful sword pursue: 75
    My heavier curse on the more hateful arm
    That wounded my Silleus. But renew
    Your tale again. Hath he no mortal harm?
SILLEUS' MAN. No sign of danger doth in him appear.
    Nor are his wounds in place of peril seen.   80
    He bids you be assured you need not fear:
    He hopes to make you yet Arabia's queen.
SALOME. Commend my heart to be Silleus' charge.
    Tell him my brother's sudden coming now
    Will give my foot no room to walk at large.   85
    But I will see him yet ere night I vow.

SCENE 3

[MARIAM *and* SOHEMUS.]

MARIAM. Sohemus. tell me what the news may be

---

5. estate royal position.   **6. With . . . betrayed** By pretending patience. I provoked
her to anger.   **7. detect** accuse.

That makes your eyes so full, your cheeks so blue?
SOHEMUS. I know not how to call them. Ill for me
    'Tis sure they are; not so, I hope, for you.
    Herod—   5
MARIAM.   Oh what of Herod?
SOHEMUS.   Herod lives.
MARIAM. How! Lives? What, in some cave or forest hid?
SOHEMUS. Nay, back returned with honor. Caesar gives
    Him greater grace than ere Anthonius did.
MARIAM. Foretell the ruin of my family,
    Tell me that I shall see our city burned,   10
    Tell me I shall a death disgraceful die,
    But tell me not that Herod is returned.
SOHEMUS. Be not impatient madam, be but mild,
    His love to you again will soon be bred.
MARIAM. I will not to his love be reconciled,   15
    With solemn vows I have forsworn his bed.
SOHEMUS. But you must break those vows.
MARIAM.   I'll rather break
    The heart of Mariam. Cursed is my fate,
    But speak no more to me, in vain ye speak[1]
    To live with him I so profoundly hate.   20
SOHEMUS. Great Queen, you must to me your pardon give,
    Sohemus cannot now your will obey:
    If your command should me to silence drive,
    It were not to obey, but to betray.
    Reject and slight my speeches, mock my faith,   25
    Scorn my observance, call my counsel nought
    Though you regard not what Sohemus saith,
    Yet will I ever freely speak my thought.
    I fear ere long I shall fair Mariam see
    In woeful state and by herself undone: 30
    Yet for your issue's sake more temp'rate be,
    The heart by affability is won.
MARIAM. And must I to my prison turn again?
    Oh, now I see I was an hypocrite:

---

1. speak tell me.

I did this morning for his death complain.   35
And yet do mourn, because he lives ere night.
When I his death believed, compassion wrought.
And was the stickler[2] 'twixt my heart and him:
But now that curtain's drawn from off my thought.
Hate doth appear again with visage grim.   40
And paints the face of Herod in my heart.
In horrid colors with detested look.
Then fear would come, but scorn doth play her part.
And saith that scorn with fear can never brook.[3]
I know I could enchain him with a smile.   45
And lead him captive with a gentle word:
I scorn my look should ever man beguile.
Or other speech, than meaning[4] to afford.
Else Salome in vain might spend her wind.
In vain might Herod's mother whet her tongue.   50
In vain had they complotted and combined.
For I could overthrow them all ere long.
Oh what a shelter is mine innocence.
To shield me from the pangs of inward grief.
'Gainst all mishaps it is my fair defense.   55
And to my sorrows yields a large relief.
To be commandress of the triple earth.
And sit in safety from a fall secure:
To have all nations celebrate my birth.
I would not that my spirit were impure.   60
Let my distressèd state unpitied be.
Mine innocence is hope enough for me.   [*Exit.*]
SOHEMUS. Poor guiltless Queen. Oh that my wish might place
    A little temper[5] now about thy heart:
    Unbridled speech is Mariam's worst disgrace.   65
    And will endanger her without desert.[6]
    I am in greater hazard. O'er my head.
    The fatal ax doth hang unsteadily:
    My disobedience once discovered
    Will shake it down: Sohemus so shall die.   70

---

2. **stickler** mediator.   3. **brook** put up with.   4. **meaning** what I mean.
5. **temper** moderation.   6. **without desert** without her deserving it.

For when the king shall find we thought his death
Had been as certain as we see his life,
And marks withall I slighted so his breath.[7]
As to preserve alive his matchless wife.
Nay more, to give to Alexander's hand[8]   75
The regal dignity. The sovereign power.
How I had yielded up at her command
The strength of all the city. David's Tower.
What more than common death may I expect,
Since I too well do know his cruelty?   80
'Twere death, a word of Herod's to neglect,
What then to do directly contrary?
Yet life I quit thee with a willing spirit,
And think thou could'st not better be employed:
I forfeit thee for her that more doth merit.   85
Ten such[9] were better dead than she destroyed.
But fare thee well chaste Queen, well may I see
The darkness palpable and rivers part,
The sun stand still, nay more, retorted[10] be,
But never woman with so pure a heart.   90
Thine eyes' grave majesty keeps all in awe,
And cuts the wings of every loose desire.
Thy brow is table[11] to the modest law,
Yet though we dare not love, we may admire.
And if I die, it shall my soul content,   95
My breath in Mariam's service shall be spent.

CHORUS. 'Tis not enough for one that is a wife
       To keep her spotless from an act of ill:
       But from suspicion she should free her life,[12]
       And bare herself of power as well as will.   100
       'Tis not so glorious for her to be free,
       As by her proper[13] self restrained to be.

       When she hath spacious ground to walk upon,
       Why on the ridge should she desire to go?

---

7. **breath** order. 8. **Alexander's hand** to Mariam's son. 9. **such** such as I.
10. **retorted** turned backward. 11. **table** tablet. 12. **But . . . life** Conduct books
for women stressed that they should be pure not only in deed but also in reputation.
13. **proper** own.

It is no glory to forebear alone[14]   105
Those things that may her honor overthrow.
But 'tis thank-worthy, if she will not take
All lawful liberties for honor's sake.

That wife her hand against her fame doth rear.
That more than to her lord alone will give   110
A private word to any second ear.
And though she may with reputation live.
Yet though most chaste. she doth her glory blot.
And wounds her honor. though she kills it not.

When to their husbands they themselves do bind.   115
Do they not wholly give themselves away?
Or give they but their body not their mind.
Reserving that though best. for other's prey?
No sure. their thoughts no more can be their own.
And therefore should to none but one be known.   120

Then she usurps upon another's right.
That seeks to be by public language graced:
And though her thoughts reflect with purest light.
Her mind if not peculiar[15] is not chaste.
For in a wife it is no worse to find.   125
A common[16] body. than a common mind.

And every mind though free from thought of ill.
That out of glory[17] seeks a worth to show.
When any's ears but one therewith they fill.
Doth in a sort her pureness overthrow.   130
Now Mariam had (but that to this she bent)[18]
Been free from fear. as well as innocent.

ACT 4
SCENE 1

[*Enter* HEROD *and his attendants.*]

HEROD. Hail happy city. happy in thy store.[1]

---

14. alone only.   **15. peculiar** kept private.   **16. common** shared. public.   **17. out of glory** out of a desire for glory.   **18. Now . . . bent** Except that she wanted to speak about herself to more than one person.   **1. store** abundance.

And happy that thy buildings such we see;
More happy in the temple where w'adore,
But most of all that Mariam loves in thee. [*Enter* NUNTIO.]
Art thou returned? How fares my Mariam? How?[2]   5

NUNTIO. She's well my Lord, and will anon be here
    As you commanded.

HEROD.   Muffle up thy brow,
    Thou day's dark taper.[3] Mariam will appear,
    And where she shines, we need not thy dim light.
    Oh haste thy steps rare creature, speed thy pace,   10
    And let thy presence make the day more bright,
    And cheer the heart of Herod with thy face.
    It is an age since I from Mariam went,
    Methinks our parting was in David's days;[4]
    The hours are so increased by discontent,   15
    Deep sorrow, Joshua-like the season stays:[5]
    But when I am with Mariam, time runs on,
    Her sight can make months minutes, days of weeks:
    An hour is then no sooner come than gone,
    When in her face mine eye for wonders seeks.   20
    You world-commanding city, Europe's grace,
    Twice hath my curious eye your streets surveyed,
    And I have seen the statue-filled place,
    That once if not for grief had been betrayed.
    I all your Roman beauties have beheld,   25
    And seen the shows your ediles[6] did prepare:
    I saw the sum of what in you excelled,
    Yet saw no miracle like Mariam rare.
    The fair and famous Livia,[7] Caesar's love,
    The world's commanding mistress did I see,   30
    Whose beauties both the world and Rome approve,
    Yet Mariam, Livia is not like to thee,
    Be patient but a little, while mine eyes

---

2. **How?** Modern editors have added "How?" to correct the rhyme scheme.
3. **day's ... taper** candle, "day's dark taper," as a metaphor for the sun.
4. **David's days** a thousand years before.   5. **Joshua-like ... stays** Joshua ordered the sun to keep shining so the Israelites could finish a battle (Joshua 10.12–14).
6. **ediles** Roman magistrates.   7. **Livia** wife of the Emperor Augustus.

Within your compassed limits be contained:
That object straight shall your desires suffice.   35
From which you were so long a while restrained.
How wisely Mariam doth the time delay.
Least sudden joy my sense should suffocate:
I am prepared. thou needst no longer stay.
Who's there. my Mariam. more than happy fate?   40
Oh no. it is Pheroras. welcome brother.
Now for a while. I must my passion smother.

                                SCENE 2

[HEROD. PHERORAS.]

PHERORAS. All health and safety wait upon my Lord.
    And may you long in prosperous fortunes live
    With Rome-commanding Caesar at accord.
    And have all honors that the world can give.
HEROD. Oh brother. now thou speakst not from thy heart: 5
    No. thou hast struck a blow at Herod's love
    That cannot quickly from my memory part.
    Though Salome did me to pardon move.
    Valiant Phasaelus.[1] now to thee farewell.
    Thou wert my kind and honorable brother: 10
    Oh hapless hour. when you self-stricken fell.
    Thou father's image. glory of thy mother.
    Had I desired a greater suit of thee
    Than to withhold thee from a harlot's bed.
    Thou shouldst have granted it: but now I see   15
    All are not like that in a womb are bred.
    Thou wouldst not. hadst thou heard of Herod's death.
    Have made his burial time. thy bridal hour:
    Thou wouldst with clamors. not with joyful breath.
    Have showed the news to be not sweet but sour.   20
PHERORAS. Phasaelus' great worth I know did stain
    Pheroras' petty valor: but they lie

_____

1. Phasaelus Herod's brother Phasaelus killed himself to escape the disgrace of being executed by his enemies, who captured him in the war against Herod's rival. Antigonus.

(Excepting you yourself) that dare maintain
That he did honor Herod more than I.
For what I showed, love's power constrained me show,   25
And pardon loving faults[2] for Mariam's sake.
HEROD. Mariam, where is she?
PHERORAS.   Nay, I do not know,
But absent use of her fair name I make:
You have forgiven greater faults than this,
For Constabarus that against your will   30
Preserved the sons of Baba, lives in bliss,
Though you commanded him the youths to kill.
HEROD. Go, take a present order for his death,
And let those traitors feel the worst of fears:
Now Salome will whine to beg his breath,   35
But I'll be deaf to prayers and blind to tears.
PHERORAS. He is my lord from Salome divorced,
Though her affection did to leave him grieve:
Yet was she by her love to you enforced
To leave the man that would your foes relieve.   35
HEROD. Then haste them to their death. I will requite
Thee gentle Mariam—Salome, I mean—
The thought of Mariam doth so steal my spirit,
My mouth from speech of her I cannot wean.   [*Exit.*]

SCENE 3

[HEROD, MARIAM.]

HEROD. And here she comes indeed. Happily met
My best and dearest half. What ails my dear?
Thou dost the difference certainly forget
'Twixt dusky habits and a time so clear.[1]
MARIAM. My lord, I suit my garment to my mind,   5
And there no cheerful colors can I find.
HEROD. Is this my welcome? Have I longed so much
To see my dearest Mariam discontent?
What is't that is the cause thy heart to touch?

---

2. loving faults errors motivated by love.   **1. Thou . . . clear** You have forgotten
how inappropriate dark clothes are for such a bright and joyful day.

Oh speak. that I thy sorrow may prevent.   10
Art thou not Jewry's queen and Herod's too?
Be my commandress. be my sovereign guide:
To be by thee directed I will woo.
For in thy pleasure lies my highest pride.
Or if thou think Judea's narrow bound   15
Too strict a limit for thy great command.
Thou shalt be Empress of Arabia crowned.
For thou shalt rule. and I will win the land.
I'll rob the holy David's sepulcher
To give thee wealth. if thou for wealth do care: 20
Thou shalt have all they did with him inter.
And I for thee will make the temple bare.
MARIAM. I neither have of power nor riches want.
  I have enough. nor do I wish for more:
  Your offers to my heart no ease can grant.   25
  Except they could my brother's life restore.
  No. had you wished the wretched Mariam glad.
  Or had your love to her been truly tied.
  Nay. had you not desired to make her sad.
  My brother nor my grandsire had not died.   30
HEROD. Wilt thou believe no oaths to clear thy lord?
  How oft have I with execration[2] sworn
  Thou art by me beloved. by me adored:
  Yet are my protestations heard with scorn.
  Hircanus plotted to deprive my head   35
  Of this long-settled honor that I wear.
  And therefore I did justly doom him dead.
  To rid the realm from peril. me from fear.
  Yet I for Mariam's sake do so repent
  The death of one whose blood she did inherit: 40
  I wish I had a kingdom's treasure spent.
  So I had ne'er expelled Hircanus' spirit.
  As I affected that same noble youth.[3]
  In lasting infamy my name enroll.

---

2. **execration** curses. 3. **As . . . youth** Since I was fond of Aristobolus ("that same
noble youth"). Mariam's young brother. whom Herod had murdered. There may be
a missing line just before this one. since the rhyme scheme is interrupted here.

    If I not mourned his death with hearty truth.   45
    Did I not show to him my earnest love.
    When I to him the priesthood did restore?
    And did for him a living priest remove.
    Which never had been done but once before.
MARIAM. I know that moved by importunity.   50
    You made him priest. and shortly after die.
HEROD. I will not speak. unless to be believed.
    This froward[4] humor will not do you good:
    It hath too much already Herod grieved.
    To think that you on terms of hate have stood.   55
    Yet smile my dearest Mariam. do but smile.
    And I will all unkind conceits[5] exile.
MARIAM. I cannot frame disguise. nor never taught
    My face a look dissenting from my thought.
HEROD. By heaven. you vex me. build not on my love.   60
MARIAM. I will not build on so unstable ground.
HEROD. Nought is so fixed. but peevishness may move.
MARIAM. 'Tis better slightest cause than none were found.
HEROD. Be judge yourself. if ever Herod sought
    Or would be moved a cause of change to find: 65
    Yet let your look declare a milder thought.
    My heart again you shall to Mariam bind.
    How oft did I for you my mother chide.
    Revile my sister. and my brother 'rate.[6]
    And tell them all my Mariam they belied?[7]   70
    Distrust me still. if these be signs of hate.

SCENE 4

[*Enter* BUTLER.]

HEROD. What hast thou here?
BUTLER.   A drink procuring love
    The queen desired me to deliver it.
MARIAM. Did I? Some hateful practice[1] this will prove.

---

4. froward perverse.   **5. conceits** thoughts.   **6. 'rate** berate.   **7. belied** told lies about.   **1. practice** intrigue.

Yet can it be no worse than heaven's permit.
HEROD. [*To the* BUTLER.] Confess the truth thou wicked   5
    instrument
    To her outrageous will. 'tis poison sure:[2]
    Tell true. and thou shalt 'scape the punishment.
    Which. if thou do conceal. thou shalt endure.
BUTLER. I know not. but I doubt it be no less.
    Long since the hate of you her heart did seize.   10
HEROD. Know'st thou the cause thereof?
BUTLER.   My Lord I guess
    Sohemus told the tale that did displease.
HEROD. Oh heaven! Sohemus false! Go let him die.
    Stay not to suffer him to speak a word:
    Oh damned villain. did he falsify   15
    The oath he swore ev'n of his own accord?
    Now did I know thy falsehood. painted devil.
    Thou white enchantress.[3] Oh thou art so foul
    That hyssop[4] cannot cleanse thee. worst of evil.
    A beauteous body hides a loathsome soul.   20
    Your love Sohemus moved by his affection.
    Though he have ever heretofore been true
    Did blab forsooth. that I did give direction.
    If we were put to death to slaughter you.
    And you in black revenge attended[5] now   25
    To add a murther to your breach of vow.
MARIAM. Is this a dream?
HEROD.   Oh heaven. that 'twere no more
    I'll give my realm to who can prove it so:
    I would I were like any beggar poor.
    So I for false my Mariam did not know.   30
    Foul pith contained in the fairest rind.
    That ever graced a cedar. Oh thine eye
    Is pure as heaven. but impure thy mind.

---

2. poison sure The text reads "passion." but editors have emended this to "poison" to make sense of the plot and to follow Cary's source. Josephus's *Antiquities*. **3. white enchantress** "white." appearing to be good. with a possible allusion to the Renaissance notion of a "white devil." a hypocritical woman.   **4. hyssop** an herb used to treat lepers.   **5. attended** waited.

And for impurity shall Mariam die.
Why didst thou love Sohemus?   35
MARIAM.   They can tell
   That say I loved him. Mariam says not so.
HEROD. Oh cannot impudence the coals expel,
   That for thy love in Herod's bosom glow?
   It is as plain as water, and denial
   Makes of thy falsehood but a greater trial.   40
   Hast thou beheld thyself, and couldst thou stain
   So rare perfection. Even for love of thee
   I do profoundly hate thee. Wert thou plain,
   Thou shouldst the wonder of Judea be.
   But oh thou art not. Hell itself lies hid   45
   Beneath thy heavenly show. Yet never wert thou chaste:
   Thou might'st exalt, pull down, command, forbid,
   And be above the wheel of fortune placed.[6]
   Hadst thou complotted Herod's massacre,
   That so thy son a monarch might be styled,   50
   Not half so grievous such an action were,
   As once to think, that Mariam is defiled.
   Bright workmanship of nature sullied o'er,
   With pitched darkness now thine end shall be.
   Thou shalt not live fair fiend to cozen[7] more,   55
   With heavy[8] semblance, as thou cozenest me.
   Yet must I love thee in despite of death,
   And thou shalt die in the despite of love:
   For neither shall my love prolong thy breath,
   Nor shall thy loss of breath my love remove.   60
   I might have seen thy falsehood in thy face,
   Where couldst thou get thy stars that served for eyes?
   Except by theft, and theft is foul disgrace,
   This had appeared before were Herod wise,
   But I'm a sot,[9] a very sot, no better: 65
   My wisdom long ago a-wandering fell,
   Thy face encountering it, my wit did fetter,
   And made me for delight my freedom sell.

---

6. **And ... placed** free from reversals of fortune.   7. **cozen** trick.   8. **heavy** perhaps an error for "heavenly."   9. **sot** fool.

Give me my heart, false creature. 'Tis a wrong.
My guiltless heart should now with thine be slain.   70
Thou hadst no right to lock it up so long.
And with usurper's name I Mariam stain.

 [*Enter* BUTLER.]

HEROD. Have you designed Sohemus to his end?
BUTLER. I have my Lord.
HEROD.   Then call our royal guard
 To do as much for Mariam. [*Exit* BUTLER.] They offend 75
 Leave[10] ill unblamed, or good without reward.
  [*Enter soldiers.*]
 Here, take her to her death. Come back, come back.
 What meant I to deprive the world of light:
 To muffle Jewry in the foulest black.
 That ever was an opposite to white?   80
 Why whither would you carry her?
SOLDIER.   You bade
 We should conduct her to her death my Lord.
HEROD. Why, sure I did not. Herod was not mad.
 Why should she feel the fury of the sword?
 Oh now the grief returns into my heart.   85
 And pulls me piecemeal. Love and hate do fight.
 And now hath love acquired the greater part.
 Yet now hath hate affection conquered quite.
 And therefore bear her hence: and, Hebrew, why
 Seize you with lion's paws the fairest lamb   90
 Of all the flock? She must not, shall not, die.
 Without her I most miserable am.
 And with her more than most. Away, away!
 But bear her but to prison not to death.
 And is she gone indeed? Stay, villains, stay!   95
 Her looks alone preserved your sovereign's breath.
 Well, let her go, but yet she shall not die.
 I cannot think she meant to poison me:
 But certain 'tis she lived too wantonly.
 And therefore shall she never more be free. [*They exit.*]

10. Leave who leave.

SCENE 5

BUTLER. Foul villain, can thy pitchy-colored soul
    Permit thine ear to hear her causeless doom?[1]
    And not enforce thy tongue that tale control.[2]
    That must unjustly bring her to her tomb?
    Oh Salome thou hast thyself repaid   5
    For all the benefits that thou hast done:
    Thou art the cause I have the queen betrayed,
    Thou hast my heart to darkest falsehood won.
    I am condemned. Heav'n gave me not my tongue
    To slander innocents, to lie, deceive,   10
    To be that hateful instrument to wrong,
    The earth of greatest glory to bereave.
    My sin ascends and doth to Heav'n cry.
    It is the blackest deed that ever was,
    And there doth fit an angel notary,   15
    That doth record it down in leaves of brass.
    Oh how my heart doth quake. Achitophel,
    Thou founds[3] a means thyself from shame to free:[4]
    And sure my soul approves[5] thou didst not well.
    All follow some, and I will follow thee.   *[He exits.]*

SCENE 6

[CONSTABARUS, BABAS' SONS, *and their guard.*]

CONSTABARUS. Now here we step our last, the way to death:
    We must not tread this way a second time.
    Yet let us resolutely yield our breath.
    Death is the only ladder, heaven to climb.
FIRST SON. With willing mind I could myself resign,   5
    But yet it grieves me with a grief untold:
    Our death should be accompanied with thine,
    Our friendship we to thee have dearly sold.
CONSTABARUS. Still wilt thou wrong the sacred name of friend?

---

1. **doom** fate. 2. **And . . . control** and not compel your tongue to hold back the tale. 3. **founds** foundest. 4. **Achitophel . . . free** When King David's son Absalom rebelled against his father, his counselor Achitophel urged a decisive quick strike. Absalom rejected this advice; knowing their cause would be doomed by delay, Achitophel went home and hanged himself. 5. **approves** judges.

Then shouldst thou never style it friendship more.   10
But base mechanic traffic[1] that doth lend:
Yet will be sure they shall the debt restore.
I could with needless complement return.
'Tis for thy ceremony I could say:
Tis I that made the fire your house to burn.   15
For but for me she would not you betray.
Had not the damned woman sought mine end.
You had not been the subject of her hate.
You never did her hateful mind offend.
Nor could your deaths have freed her nuptial fate.   20
Therefore fair friends. though you were still unborn.
Some other subtlety devised should be.
Whereby my life. though guiltless should be torn:
Thus have I proved. 'tis you that die for me.
And therefore should I weakly now lament.   25
You have but done your duties: friends should die
Alone their friends' disaster to prevent.[2]
Though not compelled by strong necessity.
But now farewell. fair city. never more
Shall I behold your beauty shining bright: 30
Farewell. of Jewish men the worthy store.
But no farewell to any female wight.[3]
You wavering crew: my curse to you I leave.
You had but one to give you any grace:
And you yourselves will Mariam's life bereave.   35
Your commonwealth doth innocency chase.[4]
You creatures made to be the human curse.
You tigers. lionesses. hungry bears.
Tear massacring hyenas:[5] nay far worse.
For they for prey do shed their feigned tears.   40
But you will weep. (you creatures cross[6] to good)
For your unquenchèd thirst of human blood.

---

1. Base … traffic base business: "mechanics" are manual laborers. "traffic" is the exchange of goods or services.   **2. friends … prevent** Friends should be willing to die to save their friends' lives.   **3. wight** creature.   **4. chase** drive out.   **5. Tear … hyenas** Hyenas were said to pretend to weep over their victims as they tore them to shreds. (See Pliny. *Natural History*. 8.44).   **6. cross** opposed.

You were the angels cast from Heav'n for pride.
And still do keep your angel's outward show.
But none of you are inly[7] beautified,   45
For still your heaven-depriving pride doth grow.
Did not the sins of man[8] require a scourge,
Your place on earth had been by this withstood:[9]
But since a flood no more the world must purge,
You stayed in office of a second flood.[10]   50
You giddy creatures, sowers of debate,
You'll love today, and for no other cause,
But for you yesterday did deeply hate.
You are the wreck of order, breach of laws.
Your best are foolish, froward,[11] wanton, vain,   55
Your worst adulterous, murderous, cunning, proud:
And Salome attends[12] the latter train,[13]
Or rather she their leader is allowed.
I do the sottishness[14] of men bewail,
That do with following you enhance your pride: 60
'Twere better that the human race should fail,
Than be by such a mischief multiplied.
Cham's servile curse to all your sex was given,
Because in Paradise you did offend.[15]
Then do we not resist the will of Heaven,   65
When on your wills like servants we attend?
You are to nothing constant but to ill,
You are with nought but wickedness indued:[16]
Your loves are set on nothing but your will.
And thus my censure I of you conclude,   70
You are the least of goods, the worst of evils,
Your best are worse than men; your worst than devils.
SECOND SON. Come, let us to our death: are we not bless'd?

---

7. inly inwardly.   **8. man** The text reads "many," but as Weller and Ferguson point out, both the meter and the meaning of the line call for the emendation to "man." **9. by . . . withstood** by this time denied.   **10. But . . . flood** As God promised never to send another worldwide flood, women had to perform the function of "scourge" to mankind.   **11. froward** perverse.   **12. attends** follows.   **13. train** set.   **14. sottishness** foolishness.   **15. 'Twere . . . offend** A combination of the pain of childbirth, the curse upon Eve after the fall (Genesis 3), with slavery, the curse upon Canaan (the son of Cham or Ham) after Ham brought his brothers to see their father Noah's nakedness. (Genesis 9).   **16. indued** endowed.

Our death will freedom from these creatures give:
Those trouble-quiet[17] sowers of unrest.   75
And this I vow that had I leave to live.
I would for ever lead a single life.
And never venture[18] on a devilish wife.

SCENE 7

[HEROD *and* SALOME.]

HEROD. Nay. she shall die.
SALOME.   Die quoth you?
HEROD.   That she shall.
But for the means. The means! Methinks 'tis hard
To find a means to murther her withall.
Therefore I am resolved she shall be spared.
SALOME. Why? Let her be beheaded.   5
HEROD.   That were well.
Think you that swords are miracles like you?
Her skin will ev'ry curtlax[1] edge refell.[2]
And then your enterprise you well may rue.
What if the fierce Arabian notice take
Of this your wretched weaponless estate: 10
They[3] answer when we bid resistance make.
That Mariam's skin their falchions[4] did rebate.[5]
Beware of this. you make a goodly hand.
If you of weapons do deprive our land.
SALOME. Why. drown her then.   15
HEROD.   Indeed. a sweet device.
Why? Would not ev'ry river turn her course
Rather than do her beauty prejudice?[6]
And be reverted[7] to the proper source?
So not a drop of water should be found
In all Judea's quondam[8] fertile ground.   20
SALOME. Then let the fire devour her.
HEROD.   'Twill not be.

---

17. **trouble-quiet** peace-disturbing.   18. **venture** take a risk.   1. **curtlax** heavy
sword.   2. **refell** repel.   3. **They** the people of Jerusalem.   4. **falchions**
broadswords.   5. **rebate** blunt.   6. **prejudice** harm.   7. **reverted** driven back.
8. **quondam** once.

Flame is from her derived[9] into my heart.
Thou nursest flame, flame will not murther thee.
My fairest Mariam, fullest of desert.
SALOME. Then let her live for me.[10]   25
HEROD.   Nay, she shall die.
    But can you live without her?
SALOME.   Doubt you that?
HEROD. I'm sure I cannot: I beseech you try.
    I have experience but I know not what.[11]
SALOME. How should I try?
HEROD.   Why, let my love be slain.
    But if we cannot live without her sight   30
    You'll find the means to make her breathe again.
    Or else you will bereave my comfort quite.
SALOME. Oh I, I warrant[12] you.   [*Exit.*]
HEROD.   What is she gone?
    And gone to bid the world be overthrown?
    What? Is her heart's composure hardest stone?   35
    To what a pass are cruel women grown? [*Re-enter* SALOME.]
    She is returned already: have you done?
    Is't possible you can command so soon
    A creature's heart to quench the flaming sun,
    Or from the sky to wipe away the moon?   40
SALOME. If Mariam be the sun and moon, it is:
    For I already have commanded this.
HEROD. But have you seen her cheek?
SALOME.   A thousand times.
HEROD. But did you mark it too?
SALOME.   Aye, very well.
HEROD. What is't?   45
SALOME.   A crimson bush, that ever limes[13]
    The soul whose foresight doth not much excel.
HEROD. Send word she shall not die. Her cheek a bush,
    Nay, then I see indeed you marked it not.
SALOME. 'Tis very fair, but yet will never blush,

---

9. **derived** drawn off.   10. **Then . . . me** as far as I am concerned.   11. **I . . . what**
I know not either what to do in this instance or what to do in the event of Mariam's
death.   12. **warrant** assure.   13. **limes** entraps.

Though foul dishonors do her forehead blot.   50
HEROD. Then let her die. 'tis very true indeed.
And for this fault alone shall Mariam bleed.
SALOME. What fault my Lord?
HEROD.   What fault is't? You that ask.
  If you be ignorant I know of none.
  To call her back from death shall be your task.   55
  I'm glad that she for innocent is known.
  For on the brow of Mariam hangs a fleece.
  Whose slenderest twine is strong enough to bind
  The hearts of kings. the pride and shame of Greece.
  Troy-flaming Helen's not so fairly shined.[14]   60
SALOME. 'Tis true indeed. she lays them[15] out for nets.
  To catch the hearts that do not shun a bait.
  'Tis time to speak: for Herod sure forgets
  That Mariam's very tresses hide deceit.
HEROD. Oh do they so? Nay. then you do but well.   65
  In sooth I thought it had been hair.
  Nets call you then? Lord. how they do excel.
  I never saw a net that showed so fair.
  But have you heard her speak?
SALOME.   You know I have.
HEROD. And were you not amazed?   70
SALOME.   No. not a whit.
HEROD. Then 'twas not her you heard: her life I'll save.
  For Mariam hath a world-amazing wit.
SALOME. She speaks a beauteous language. but within
  Her heart is false as powder. and her tongue
  Doth but allure the auditors to sin.   75
  And is the instrument to do you wrong.
HEROD. It may be so. Nay. 'tis so! she's unchaste!
  Her mouth will ope[16] to ev'ry stranger's ear.
  Then let the executioner make haste.
  Lest she enchant him. if her words he hear.   80
  Let him be deaf. lest she do him surprise

---

14. For . . . shined Mariam's hair is compared to the golden fleece. sought by Jason and the Argonauts. and the hair of Helen. the great beauty whose abduction was the cause of the Trojan War.   **15. them** strands of her hair.   **16. ope** open.

That shall to free her spirit be assigned.
Yet what boots deafness if he have his eyes,
Her murtherer must be both deaf and blind.
For if he see, he needs must see the stars   85
That shine on either side of Mariam's face,
Whose sweet aspect will terminate the wars,
Wherewith he should a soul so precious chase.
Her eyes can speak, and in their speaking move:
Oft did my heart with reverence receive   90
The world's mandates. Pretty tales of love
They utter, which can humane bondage weave.
But shall I let this Heaven's model die?
Which for a small self-portraiture she[17] drew?
Her eyes like stars, her forehead like the sky,   95
She is like Heaven, and must be heavenly true.
SALOME. Your thoughts do rave with doting on the queen.
Her eyes are ebon-hued,[18] and you'll confess,
A sable star hath been but seldom seen:
Then speak of reason more, of Mariam less.   100
HEROD. Yourself are held a goodly creature here,
Yet so unlike my Mariam in your shape
That when to her you have approached near,
Myself hath often ta'en you for an ape.
And yet you prate of beauty: go your ways,   105
You are to her a sun-burnt blackamoor![19]
Your paintings[20] cannot equal Mariam's praise:
Her nature is so rich, you are so poor.
Let her be stayed from death, for if she die,
We do we know not what to stop her breath.[21]   110
A world cannot another Mariam buy.
Why stay you lingering? Countermand her death.
SALOME. Then you'll no more remember what hath past,
Sohemus' love, and hers shall be forgot:

---

17. **she** Heaven.   18. **ebon-hued** dark black.   19. **blackamoor** Female vice was often portrayed in terms of blackness. The Moors were thought of as black in the medieval and early modern periods.   20. **your paintings** your face made up with cosmetics.   21. **We . . . breath** Compare with Luke 23.34, when Christ says of his executioners "they know not what they do."

'Tis well in truth, that fault may be her last.   115
And she may mend, though yet she love you not.
HEROD. Oh God, 'tis true. Sohemus! Earth and heaven.
Why did you both conspire to make me cursed,
In coz'ning[22] me with shows and proofs unev'n?[23]
She showed the best, and yet did prove the worst.   120
Her show was such as had our singing king,
The holy David, Mariam's beauty seen,
The Hittite had then felt no deadly sting,
Nor Bathsheba had never been a queen.[24]
Or had his son the wisest man of men,   125
Whose fond delight did most consist in change,[25]
Beheld her face, he had been stayed again:
No creature having her, can wish to range.
Had Asuerus seen my Mariam's brow,
The humble Jew, she might have walked alone.[26]   130
Her beauteous virtue should have stayed below,
Whiles Mariam mounted to the Persian throne.
But what avails it all? For in the weight[27]
She is deceitful, light as vanity.
Oh, she was made for nothing but a bait,   135
To train[28] some hapless man to misery.
I am the hapless man that have been trained
To endless bondage. I will see her yet:
Methinks I should discern her if she feigned:
Can human eyes be dazed by woman's wit?   140
Once more these eyes of mine with hers shall meet,
Before the headsman[29] do her life bereave.
Shall I forever part from thee, my sweet,
Without the taking of my latest leave?
SALOME. You had as good resolve to save her now,   145
I'll stay her death, 'tis well determined:

---

22. coz'ning tricking. **23. unev'n** unjust. **24. Bathsheba ... queen** When Bathsheba became pregnant by David, he ordered her husband Uriah the Hittite to go to war, where he would be killed in battle (2 Samuel 11). **25. Or ... change** David's son Solomon was known for his wisdom and his many concubines (1 Kings 4.11). **26. humble ... alone** See Esther 2 for how Ahasuerus made Esther (the humble Jew) queen. **27. weight** balance. **28. train** mislead. **29. headsman** executioner.

For sure she nevermore will break her vow.
Sohemus and Josephus both are dead.
HEROD. She shall not live, nor will I see her face.
    A long-healed wound, a second time doth bleed!   150
    With Joseph I remember her disgrace.
    A shameful end ensues[30] a shameful deed.
    Oh that I had not called to mind anew
    The discontent of Mariam's wavering heart!
    'Twas you, you foul-mouthed Até,[31] none but you,   155
    That did the thought hereof to me impart.
    Hence from my sight, my black tormenter hence.
    For hadst not thou made Herod unsecure
    I had not doubted Mariam's innocence,
    But still had held her in my heart for pure.   160
SALOME. I'll leave you to your passion: 'tis no time
    To purge me now, though of a guiltless crime.   *[Exit.]*
HEROD. Destruction take thee: thou hast made my heart
    As heavy as revenge. I am so dull,
    Methinks I am not sensible of smart.   165
    Though hideous horrors at my bosom pull.
    My head weighs downwards; therefore will I go
    To try if I can sleep away my woe.   *[Exit.]*

SCENE 8

[MARIAM.]

MARIAM. Am I the Mariam that presumed so much,
    And deemed my face must needs preserve my breath?
    Ay, I it was that thought my beauty such,
    As it alone could countermand my death.
    Now death will teach me: he can pale as well   5
    A cheek of roses as a cheek less bright,
    And dim an eye whose shine doth most excel,
    As soon as one that casts a meaner light.
    Had not myself against myself conspired,
    No plot, no adversary from without   10

30. ensues follows.   **31. Até** "Até" in Greek means blindness or delusion and is goddess of discord.

Could Herod's love from Mariam have retired.
Or from his heart have thrust my semblance out.
The wanton queen that never loved for love.
False Cleopatra. wholly set on gain.
With all her flights did prove. yet vainly prove.[1]   15
For her the love of Herod to obtain.
Yet her allurements. all her courtly guile.
Her smiles. her favors. and her smooth deceit
Could not my face from Herod's mind exile.
But were with him of less than little weight.   20
That face and person that in Asia late
For beauty's goddess. Paphos' queen[2] was ta'en.
That face that did captive[3] great Julius'[4] fate.
That very face that was Anthonius'[5] bane.[6]
That face that to be Egypt's pride was born.   25
That face that all the world esteemed so rare.
Did Herod hate. despise. neglect. and scorn
When with the same. he Mariam's did compare?
This made that I improvidently wrought.
And on the wager even my life did pawn.   30
Because I thought. and yet but truly thought.
That Herod's love could not from me be drawn.
But now. though out of time. I plainly see
It could be drawn. though never drawn from me:
Had I but with humility been graced   35
As well as fair. I might have proved me wise:
But I did think because I knew me chaste.
One virtue for a woman might suffice.
That mind for glory of our sex might stand.
Wherein humility and chastity   40
Doth march with equal paces. hand in hand.
But one if single seen. who setteth by?[7]
And I had singly one. but 'tis my joy.
That I was ever innocent. though sour.
And therefore can they but my life destroy: 45

1. **prove** try. 2. **Paphos' queen** Aphrodite or Venus. 3. **captive** capture.
4. **Julius'** Julius Caesar. 5. **Anthonius'** Mark Antony. 6. **bane** ruin. 7. **setteth
by** values.

My soul is free from adversary's power. [*Enter* DORIS.]
You princes great in power and high in birth.
Be great and high. I envy not your hap;[8]
Your birth must be from dust, your power on earth.
In heaven shall Mariam sit in Sarah's lap.[9]   50
DORIS. In heaven! Your beauty cannot bring you thither.
    Your soul is black and spotted, full of sin:
    You in adult'ry lived nine year together.
    And Heav'n will never let adult'ry in.[10]
MARIAM. What art thou that dost poor Mariam pursue?   55
    Some spirit sent to drive me to despair.
    Who sees for truth that Mariam is untrue?
    If fair she be, she is as chaste as fair.
DORIS. I am that Doris that was once beloved.
    Beloved by Herod. Herod's lawful wife.   60
    'Twas you that Doris from his side removed.
    And robbed from me the glory of my life.
MARIAM. Was that adult'ry? Did not Moses say.
    That he that being matched did deadly hate
    Might by permission put his wife away   65
    And take a more beloved to be his mate?
DORIS. What did he hate me for: for simple truth?
    For bringing[11] beauteous babes for love to him.
    For riches, noble birth, or tender youth?
    Or for no stain did Doris' honor dim?   70
    Oh tell me Mariam, tell me if you know,
    Which fault of these made Herod Doris' foe?
    These thrice three years have I with hands held up.
    And bowèd knees fast nailed to the ground.
    Besought for thee the dregs of that same cup.   75
    That cup of wrath that is for sinners found.
    And now thou art to drink it: Doris' curse
    Upon thyself did all this while attend.
    But now it shall pursue thy children worse.

---

8. hap fortune.   **9. Sarah's lap** with the wife of Abraham.   **10. adult'ry in** The charge of adultery against Mariam makes her analogous to Anne Boleyn, who was seen as an adulteress by some who objected to Henry VIII's divorce.   **11. bringing** giving birth to.

MARIAM. Oh. Doris. now to thee my knees I bend.   80
    That heart that never bowed to thee doth bow.
    Curse not mine infants. let it thee suffice.
    That Heav'n doth punishment to me allow.
    Thy curse is cause that guiltless Mariam dies.
DORIS. Had I ten thousand tongues. and ev'ry tongue   85
    Inflamed with poison's power and steeped in gall.
    My curses would not answer for my wrong.
    Though I in cursing thee employed them all.
    Hear thou that didst mount Gerizim[12] command.
    To be a place whereon with cause to curse: 90
    Stretch thy revenging arm. thrust forth thy hand.
    And plague the mother much. the children worse.
    Throw flaming fire upon the base-born heads
    That were begotten in unlawful[13] beds.
    But let them live 'til they have sense to know   95
    What 'tis to be in miserable state:
    Then be their nearest friends their overthrow.
    Attended be they by suspicious hate.
    And. Mariam. I do hope this boy of mine
    Shall one day come to be the death of thine.[14]   *[Exit.]*
MARIAM. Oh! Heaven forbid. I hope the world shall see.
    This curse of thine shall be returned on thee.
    Now earth farewell. though I be yet but young:
    Yet I. methinks. have known thee too too long.   *[Exit.]*

CHORUS. The fairest action of our human life   105
    Is scorning to revenge an injury:
    For who forgives without a further strife.
    His adversary's heart to him doth tie.
    And 'tis a firmer conquest truly said.
    To win the heart than overthrow the head.   110

    If we a worthy enemy do find.
    To yield to worth. it must be nobly done:[15]
    But if of baser metal be his mind.

12. Gerizim Weller and Ferguson emend Gerarim to Gerizim. named as the place of blessing in Deuteronomy 11. here confused with the twin mountain Ebal. a place of cursing. **13. unlawful** outside of marriage. **14. I . . . thine** Doris foretells the future. in which her son Antipater turns Herod against Mariam's sons. **15. To . . . done** We act nobly when we concede victory to a worthy enemy.

In base revenge there is no honor won.
Who would a worthy courage overthrow,   115
And who would wrestle with a worthless foe?

We say our hearts are great and cannot yield;
Because they cannot yield it proves them poor;
Great hearts are tasked beyond their power, but seld.[16]
The weakest lion will the loudest roar.   120
Truths schooled for certain doth this same allow.
High-heartedness doth sometimes teach to bow.

A noble heart doth teach a virtuous scorn.
To scorn to owe a duty over-long.[17]
To scorn to be for benefits foreborn.[18]   125
To scorn to lie, to scorn to do a wrong.
To scorn to bear an injury in mind.
To scorn a free-born heart slave-like to bind.

But if for wrongs we needs revenge must have,
Then be our vengeance of the noblest kind:[19]   130
Do we his body from our fury save,
And let our hate prevail against our mind?[20]
What can 'gainst him a greater vengeance be,
Then make his foe more worthy far than he?

Had Mariam scorned to leave a due unpaid,   135
She would to Herod then have paid her love,
And not have been by sullen passion swayed.
To fix her thoughts all injury above
Is virtuous pride. Had Mariam thus been proved,[21]
Long, famous life to her had been allowed.   140

ACT 5
SCENE 1

[NUNTIO.]

NUNTIO. When, sweetest friend, did I so far offend

---

16. **seld** seldom.   17. **To ... over-long** to delay in fulfilling an obligation.
18. **To ... foreborn** not being required to fulfill an obligation because of previous
good deeds.   19. **noblest kind** forgiveness.   20. **Do ... mind** Do we allow our enemy to escape injury from our anger but then turn that anger against ourselves by
holding a grudge?.   21. **Had ... proved** had Mariam proved to be virtuously proud.

Your heavenly self. that you my fault to quit
Have made me now relator of your end.
The end of beauty. chastity and wit?[1]
Was none so hapless in the fatal place.   5
But I. most wretched. for the queen t' choose.
'Tis certain I have some ill-boding face
That made me culled[2] to tell this luckless news.
And yet no news to Herod: were it new.
To him unhappy it had not been at all:[3]   10
Yet do I long to come within his view.
That he may know his wife did guiltless fall.
And here he comes. Your Mariam greets you well.

[*Enter* HEROD.]

HEROD. What? Lives my Mariam? Joy. exceeding joy.
She shall not die.   15
NUNTIO.   Heaven doth your will repel.
HEROD. Oh. do not with thy words my life destroy.
  I prithee tell no dying-tale. Thine eye
  Without thy tongue doth tell but too too much.
  Yet let thy tongue's addition make me die.
  Death welcome. comes to him whose grief is such.   20
NUNTIO. I went amongst the curious gazing troop.
  To see the last of her that was the best:
  To see if death had heart to make her stoop.
  To see the sun admiring phoenix'[4] nest.
  When there I came. upon the way I saw   25
  The stately Mariam not debased by fear:
  Her look did seem to keep the world in awe.
  Yet mildly did her face this fortune bear.
HEROD. Thou dost usurp my right. my tongue was framed
  To be the instrument of Mariam's praise: 30
  Yet speak: she cannot be too often famed.
  All tongues suffice not her sweet name to raise.

---

1. **When ... wit** These lines are addressed to Mariam. **2. culled** picked.
3. And ... all If Herod had been ignorant of (and not responsible for) Mariam's
death. the news of it would not be tragic to him. **4. To ... phoenix** A mythical
bird. which burnt itself every 500 years only to emerge from its ashes renewed. The
phoenix symbolized Christ's resurrection.

NUNTIO. But as she came she Alexandra met,
 Who did her death (sweet queen) no whit bewail,
 But as if nature she did quite forget,   35
 She did upon her daughter loudly rail.[5]
HEROD. Why stopped you not her mouth? Where had she words
 To darken that, that heaven made so bright?
 Our sacred tongue no epithet affords
 To call her other than the world's delight.   40
NUNTIO. She told her that her death was too too good,
 And that already she had lived too long:
 She said, she shamed to have a part in blood
 Of her that did the princely Herod wrong.
HEROD. Base pick-thank[6] devil. Shame, 'twas all her glory   45
 That she to noble Mariam was the mother:
 But never shall it live in any story—
 Her name, except to infamy I'll smother.
 What answer did her princely daughter make?
NUNTIO. She made no answer, but she looked the while,   50
 As if thereof she scarce did notice take,
 Yet smiled, a dutiful, though scornful smile.
HEROD. Sweet creature, I that look to mind do call,
 Full oft hath Herod been amazed withall.
 Go on.   55
NUNTIO. She came unmoved with pleasant grace,
 As if to triumph her arrival were,
 In stately habit, and with cheerful face:
 Yet ev'ry eye was moist, but Mariam's there.
 When justly opposite to me she came,
 She picked me out from all the crew;   60
 She beckoned to me, called me by my name,
 For she my name, my birth, and fortune knew.
HEROD. What, did she name thee? Happy, happy man.
 Wilt thou not ever love that name the better?
 But what sweet tune did this fair dying swan[7]   65
 Afford thine ear? Tell all, omit no letter.
NUNTIO. Tell thou my Lord, said she.

---

5. rail utter abuse.   **6. pick-thank** flattering.   **7. dying swan** The swan was said to sing at its death. See *Othello*, 5.2.253–57.

HEROD.   Me, meant she me?
  Is't true, the more my shame: I was her lord:
  Were I not mad, her lord I still should be:
  But now her name must be by me adored.   70
  Oh say, what said she more? Each word she said
  Shall be the food whereon my heart is fed.
NUNTIO. "Tell thou my Lord thou saw'st me loose[8] my breath."
HEROD. Oh that I could that sentence now control![9]
NUNTIO. If guiltily eternal be my death.   75
HEROD. I hold her chaste ev'n in my inmost soul.
NUNTIO. By three days hence if wishes could revive.
  I know himself would make me oft alive.[10]
HEROD. Three days, three hours, three minutes, not so much.
  A minute in a thousand parts divided.   80
  My penitency for her death is such.
  As in the first[11] I wished she had not died.
  But forward in thy tale.
NUNTIO.   Why on she went.
  And after she some silent prayer had said.
  She did as if to die she were content.   85
  And thus to Heav'n her heavenly soul is fled.
HEROD. But art thou sure there doth no life remain?
  Is't possible my Mariam should be dead?
  Is there no trick to make her breathe again?
NUNTIO. Her body is divided from her head.   90
HEROD. Why, yet methinks there might be found by art
  Strange ways of cure, 'tis sure rare things are done
  By an inventive head and willing heart.
NUNTIO. Let not, my Lord, your fancies idly run.
  It is as possible it should be seen   95
  That we should make the holy Abraham live.
  Though he entombed two thousand years had been.
  As breath again to slaughtered Mariam give.
  But now for more assaults prepare your ears.
HEROD. There cannot be a further cause of moan: 100

8. **loose** meaning "let go of" or "lose.".   9. **Oh . . . control!** If only I could overturn her death sentence.   10. **By . . . alive** The "three days" may allude to the time between Christ's death and resurrection.   11. **first** the first thousandth of a minute.

This accident shall shelter me from fears.
What can I fear? Already Mariam's gone.
Yet tell ev'n what you will.
NUNTIO.   As I came by,
  From Mariam's death I saw upon a tree
  A man that to his neck a cord did tie.   105
  Which cord he had designed his end to be.
  When me he once discerned, he downward bowed,
  And thus with fearful voice, he cried aloud:
  "Go tell the king he trusted ere he tried,[12]
  I am the cause that Mariam causeless died."   110
HEROD. Damnation take him, for it was the slave
  That said she meant with poison's deadly force
  To end my life that she the crown might have.[13]
  Which tale did Mariam from herself divorce.
  Oh pardon me thou pure unspotted ghost,   115
  My punishment must needs sufficient be,
  In missing that content I valued most,
  Which was thy admirable face to see.
  I had but one inestimable jewel,[14]
  Yet one I had no monarch had the like.   120
  And therefore may I curse myself as cruel.
  'Twas broken by a blow myself did strike.
  I gazed thereon and never thought me blessed,
  But when on it my dazzled eye might rest,
  A precious mirror made by wonderous art,   125
  I prized it ten times dearer than my crown,
  And laid it up fast-folded in my heart,
  Yet I in sudden choler cast it down,
  And pashed[15] it all to pieces. 'Twas no foe
  That robbed me of it: no Arabian host,   130
  Nor no Armenian guide hath used me so:
  But Herod's wretched self hath Herod crossed.

---

12. Go . . . tried This line echoes the Chorus' words at 2.4.122.   **13. To . . . have**
The Butler's accusation that Mariam was attempting to take over the throne is not in
Cary's source, Josephus's *Antiquities.*   **14. I . . . jewel** See *Othello,* 5.2.353–55:
"one whose hand / Like the base Indian, threw a pearl away / Richer than all his
tribe." The Folio text reads "Judean" for "Indian" and thus may allude to Herod.
15. pashed smashed.

She was my graceful moiety:[16] me accursed.
To slay my better half and save my worst.
But sure she is not dead. you did but jest.   135
To put me in perplexity a while:
'Twere well indeed if I could so be dressed:[17]
I see she is alive. methinks you smile.
NUNTIO. If sainted Abel yet deceased be.[18]
'Tis certain Mariam is as dead as he.   140
HEROD. Why then go call her to me. bid her now
Put on fair habit. stately ornament.
And let no frown o'ershade her smoothest brow:
In her doth Herod place his whole content.
NUNTIO. She'll come in stately weeds[19] to please your sense. 145
If now she come attired in robe of Heav'n.
Remember you yourself did send her hence.
And now to you she can no more be given.
HEROD. She's dead! Hell take her murderers! She was fair.
Oh what a hand she had. it was so white.   150
It did the whiteness of the snow impair.
I never more shall see so sweet a sight.
NUNTIO. 'Tis true. her hand was rare.
HEROD.   Her hand? Her hands.
She had not singly one of beauty rare.
But such a pair as here where Herod stands: 155
He dares the world to make to both compare.[20]
Accursed Salome. hadst thou been still.[21]
My Mariam had been breathing by my side.
Oh never had I. had I had my will.
Sent forth command that Mariam should have died!   160
But Salome thou didst with envy vex.
To see thyself out-matchèd in thy sex.
Upon your sex's forehead Mariam sat.
To grace you all like an imperial crown:
But you. fond fool. have rudely pushed thereat.   165

16. moiety half.   17. dressed treated.   18. If . . . be The death of innocent Abel in Genesis 4 was read as a prefiguration of Christ's death in the New Testament. 19. weeds clothes.   20. He . . . compare to find a pair of hands as beautiful as Mariam's.   21. still silent.

And proudly pulled your proper glory down.
One smile of hers—nay—not so much—a look
Was worth a hundred thousand such as you.
Judea how canst thou the wretches brook.[22]
That robbed from thee the fairest of the crew?   170
You dwellers in the now deprived land.
Wherein the matchless Mariam was bred.
Why grasp not each of you a sword in hand.
To aim at me our cruel sovereign's head?
Oh. when you think of Herod as your king.   175
And owner of the pride of Palestine.
This act to your remembrance likewise bring.
'Tis I have overthrown your royal line.
Within her purer veins the blood did run.
That from her grandam Sarah she derived.   180
Whose beldam[23] age the love of kings hath won:
Oh that her issue had as long been lived.
But can her eye be made by death obscure?[24]
I cannot think but it must sparkle still.
Foul sacrilege to rob those lights so pure.   185
From out a temple made by heavenly skill.
I am the villain that have done the deed.
The cruel deed. though by another's hand:
My word though not my sword made Mariam bleed.
Hircanus' grandchild did at my command—   190
That Mariam that I once did love so dear.
The partner of my now detested bed.
Why shine you sun with an aspect so clear?
I tell you once again my Mariam's dead.
You could but shine, if some Egyptian blowse   195
Or Ethiopian dowdy lose her life;[25]
This was—then wherefore bend you not your brows?—
The King of Jewry's fair and spotless wife.
Deny thy beams. and moon refuse thy light.
Let all the stars be dark, let Jewry's eye   200

---

22. brook put up with.   **23. beldam** old woman's.   **24. obscure** dull.   **25. You . . .
life** A "blowse" was a beggar's prostitute; a "dowdy" was a shabbily dressed woman.
"Egyptian" here probably refers to Cleopatra.

No more distinguish which is day and night.
Since her best birth did in her bosom die.
Those fond idolaters. the men of Greece.
Maintain these orbs are falsely governèd.[26]
That each within themselves have gods a piece   205
By whom their steadfast course is justly led.
But were it so. as so it cannot be.
They all would put their mourning garments on:
Not one of them would yield a light to me.
To me that is the cause that Mariam's gone.   210
For though they feign their Saturn melancholy.
Of sour behaviors and of angry mood.
They feign him likewise to be just and holy.
And justice needs must seek revenge for blood.
Their Jove. if Jove he were. would sure desire.   215
To punish him that slew so fair a lass:
For Leda's beauty set his heart on fire.[27]
Yet she not half so fair as Mariam was.
And Mars would deem his Venus had been slain.[28]
Sol[29] to recover her would never stick:[30]   220
For if he want the power her life to gain.
Then physic's god is but an empiric.[31]
The Queen of Love would storm for beauty's sake.
And Hermes too. since he bestowed her wit:
The night's pale light for angry grief would shake.   225
To see chaste Mariam die in age unfit.
But. oh. I am deceived. she pass'd[32] them all
In every gift. in every property.[33]
Her excellencies wrought her timeless fall.
And they rejoiced. not grieved to see her die.   230
The Paphian goddess did repent her waste[34]

---

26. Maintain . . . governèd In Ptolemaic astronomy the orbs are the hollow spheres
that surround the earth and within which the planets revolve around the earth. Each
was thought to be governed by one of the gods. each of whom embodied human qualities.   **27. For . . . fire** Jove (or Jupiter) turned himself into a swan to rape Leda.
28. And . . . slain Mars. the god of war. was the lover of Venus. goddess of love and
beauty.   **29. Sol** Sol. or Apollo. was the god of the sun and of medicine.   **30. stick**
hesitate.   **31. empiric** quack.   **32. pass'd** surpassed.   **33. property** quality.
34. The . . . waste The "Paphian goddess." Venus. would have regretted having
given so much beauty to Mariam.

When she to one such beauty did allow:
Mercurius thought her wit his wit surpassed.
And Cynthia envied Mariam's brighter brow.[35]
But these are fictions, they are void of sense: 235
The Greeks but dream, and dreaming falsehoods tell.
They neither can offend nor give defense.
And not by them it was my Mariam fell.
If she had been like an Egyptian black[36]
And not so fair, she had been longer lived: 240
Her overflow of beauty turned back,
And drowned the spring from whence it was derived.
Her heavenly beauty 'twas that made me think
That it with chastity could never dwell:
But now I see that heaven in her did link   245
A spirit and a person[37] to excel.
I'll muffle up myself in endless night,
And never let mine eyes behold the light.
Retire thyself vile monster, worse than he
That stained the virgin earth with brother's blood:[38]   250
Still in some vault or den enclosèd be,
Where with thy tears thou mayst beget a flood,
Which flood in time may drown thee. Happy day
When thou at once shalt die and find a grave.
A stone upon the vault, someone shall lay,   255
Which monument shall an inscription have,
And these shall be the words it shall contain:
"Here Herod lies, that hath his Mariam slain."

                                                        [*Exit.*]

CHORUS. Who ever hath beheld with steadfast eye
          The strange events of this one only day?[39]   260
          How many were deceived? How many die,
          That once today did grounds of safety lay?
          It will from them all certainty bereave,
          Since twice six hours so many can deceive.

---

35. And ... brow Cynthia, or Diana, goddess of chastity and of the moon.
36. Egyptian black another allusion to Cleopatra.   **37. person** appearance.
38. That ... blood Herod compares himself to Cain, who murdered Abel.   **39. only day** The play follows the unity of time, "one day," as required by neoclassical critics.

This morning Herod held for surely dead.   265
And all the Jews on Mariam did attend:
And Constabarus rise from Salom's bed.
And neither dreamed of a divorce or end.
Pheroras joyed that he might have his wife.
And Babas' sons for safety of their life.   270

Tonight our Herod doth alive remain.
The guiltless Mariam is deprived of breath:
Stout Constabarus both divorced and slain.
The valiant sons of Babas have their death.
Pheroras sure his love to be bereft.   275
If Salome her suit unmade had left.[40]

Herod this morning did expect with joy
To see his Mariam's much belovèd face:
And yet ere night he did her life destroy.
And surely thought she did her name disgrace.   280
Yet now again so short do humors last.
He both repents her death and knows her chaste.

Had he with wisdom now her death delayed.
He at his pleasure might command her death:
But now he hath his power so much betrayed.   285
As all his woes cannot restore her breath.
Now doth he strangely lunaticly rave.
Because his Mariam's life he cannot save.

This day's events were certainly ordained.
To be the warning to posterity: 290
So many changes are therein contained.
So admirably strange variety.
This day alone. our sagest Hebrews shall
In after-times the school of wisdom call.

---

40. Pheroras . . . left Pheroras would have lost Graphina if Salome had not interceded on his behalf with Herod.

CONTEXTS

Narrative Sources
for Othello *and*
The Tragedy of Mariam

In the early modern period, writers frequently reinterpreted stories inherited from literary tradition and ancient history as the basis of their own original work. Both Shakespeare and Cary take works that are not tragedies and reshape them into that genre. In the selections by Geraldi Cinthio and Flavius Josephus, there are key differences in these works as compared to Shakespeare's *Othello* and Cary's *Mariam*, particularly in regard to the shape and details of plot and delineation of character. Although Story 7 of the Third Decade of Cinthio's *Hecatommithi* is not a tragedy, it is a moral fable. Shakespeare's recreation of the story as a tragedy changes the ethics of the story. Greater individual detail and psychological complexity in the presentation of character in *Othello* also strikingly alter the stereotypical representations of race and gender from what they are in the Italian source. Similarly, Josephus's *Antiquities of the Jews* and *Wars of the Jews* provide a story in the form of a narrative history, focusing on the fate of an entire people, whereas Elizabeth Cary condenses and reorganizes this material in order to highlight the individual struggles of Herod in his mistaken jealousy and Mariam in her proud chastity and indignant innocence. Both tragedies address the way individuals are subjected to and struggle with structures of power and ethical norms.

Giambattista Giraldi Cinthio (1504–1573)

Giraldi, also called Cinthio, was an Italian writer and professor of rhetoric at the University of Ferrara. He wrote poems, plays, and prose short stories. His Hecatommithi *(1565) imitated the structure of Boccaccio's* Decameron *with its frame of an outer narrative in which the storytellers discussed the tales that they told. The stories of the Third Decade are about marital infidelity.*

The chief source for Shakespeare's Othello *is Story 7 about a "Moorish captain" and a "Venetian lady," unjustly accused of adultery by her husband's Ensign. There was no English translation of the story printed during Shakespeare's lifetime; so, he must have read it in a now-lost English manuscript, the French translation of Chappuys (1585), or the original Italian.*

Shakespeare follows many elements of Cinthio's plot and echoes his language. The notes point out some of these parallels but hardly exhaust them. Also noted, but not exhausted, are the innovations in the action, among the most remarkable of which are the double plot of Roderigo, the highly erotic and ritualized execution of Desdemona's murder, and the overall contraction of time. Even more remarkable is the far greater complexity of Shakespeare's major characters, whose motives and errors cannot be singly or simply explained the way they are in Cinthio's tale.

A comparison of Cinthio's tale to Othello *shows how a melodrama was transformed into a tragedy. The text that follows here was translated by Geoffrey Bullough in his* Narrative and Dramatic Sources of Shakespeare *(London: Routledge and Kegan Paul, 1975).*

from *Gli Hecatommithi*
The Third Decade. Story 7

A Moorish Captain takes to wife a Venetian lady, and his Ensign accuses her to her husband of adultery: he desires the Ensign to kill the man whom he believes to be the adulterer: the Captain kills his wife and is accused by the Ensign. The Moor does not confess, but on clear indications of his guilt he is banished: and the scoundrelly Ensign, thinking to injure others, brings a miserable end on himself.

The ladies would have had great pity for the fate of the Florentine woman had her adultery not made her appear worthy of the severest punishment: and it seemed to them that the gentleman's patience had been unusually great. Indeed they declared that it would be hard to find any other man who, discovering his wife in such a compromising situation, would not have slain both of the sinners outright. The more they thought about it the more prudently they considered him to have behaved.

From *Narrative and Dramatic Sources of Shakespeare*, Volume VII, edited by Geoffrey Bullough. Copyright 1973 by Columbia University Press. Reprinted with permission of the publisher.

After this discussion. Curzio, on whom all eyes were turned as they waited for him to begin his story, said: I do not believe that either men or women are free to avoid amorous passion, for human nature is so disposed to it that even against our will it makes itself powerfully felt in our souls.[1] Nevertheless, I believe that a virtuous lady has the power, when she feels herself burning with such a desire, to resolve rather to die than through dishonourable lust to stain that modesty which ladies should preserve as untainted as white ermine. And I believe that they err less who, free from the holy bonds of matrimony, offer their bodies to the delight of every man, than does a married woman who commits adultery with one person only. But as this woman suffered well-deserved punishment for her fault, so it sometimes happens that without any fault at all, a faithful and loving lady, through the insidious plots (*tesele*) of a villainous mind, and the frailty of one who believes more than he need, is murdered by her faithful husband[2] as you will clearly perceive by what I am about to relate to you.

There was once in Venice a Moor, a very gallant man, who, because he was personally valiant and had given proof in warfare of great prudence and skilful energy, was very dear to the Signoria, who in rewarding virtuous actions ever advance the interests of the Republic. It happened that a virtuous Lady of wondrous beauty called Disdemona, impelled not by female appetite but by the Moor's good qualities, fell in love with him, and he, vanquished by the Lady's beauty and noble mind, likewise was enamoured of her.[3] So propitious was their mutual love that, although the Lady's relatives did all they could to make her take another husband: they were united in marriage and lived together in such concord and tranquility while they remained in Venice, that never a word passed between them that was not loving.

It happened that the Venetian lords made a change in the forces that they used to maintain in Cyprus: and they chose the Moor as

---

[1] Contrast with Iago at 1.3.318–27. Othello claims that, for great men, being cuckolded is "destiny unshunnable, like death" (3.3.274).

[2] "And many worthy and chaste dames even thus, / All guiltless, meet reproach" (4.1.45–6).

[3] "not / To please the palate of my appetite / . . . But to be free and bounteous to her mind" (1.3.262–3, 266).

MORO DI
CONDI-
TIONE.

The figure of "A Moor" from Cesare Vecellio's *Degli habiti*
(Venice, 1590). By permission of the Folger Shakespeare Library.

Commandant of the soldiers whom they sent there.[4] Although he was pleased by the honor offered him (for such high rank and dignity is given only to noble and loyal men who have proved themselves most valiant), yet his happiness was lessened when he considered the length and dangers of the voyage, thinking that Disdemona would be much troubled by it. The Lady, who had no other happiness on earth but the Moor, and was very pleased with the recognition of his merits that her husband had received from so noble and powerful a Republic, could hardly wait for the hour when he would set off with his men, and she would accompany him to that honorable post. It grieved her greatly to see the Moor troubled; and, not knowing the reason for it, one day while they were dining together she said to him: "Why is it, my Moor, that after being given such an honorable rank by the Signoria, you are so melancholy?"

The Moor said to Disdemona: "The love I bear you spoils my pleasure at the honour I have received, because I see that one of two things must happen: either I must take you with me in peril by sea, or, so as not to cause you this hardship, I must leave you in Venice. The first alternative must inevitably weigh heavily on me, since every fatigue you endured and every danger we met would give me extreme anxiety. The second, having to leave you behind, would be hateful to me, since, parting from you I should be leaving my very life behind."[5]

"Alas, husband," said Disdemona, hearing this, "What thoughts are these passing through your mind? Why do you let such ideas perturb you? I want to come with you wherever you go, even if it meant walking through fire in my shift instead of, as it will be, crossing the water with you in a safe, well-furnished galley. If there really are to be dangers and fatigues, I wish to share them with you; and I should consider myself very little beloved if, rather than have my company on the sea, you were to leave me in Venice, or persuaded yourself that I would rather stay here in safety than be in the same danger as yourself.[6] Get ready then for the voyage in the cheerfulness that befits the high rank you hold."

Then the Moor joyously threw his arms round his wife's neck and said, with a loving kiss: "God keep us long in this love, my dear

---

[4]Cinthio omits the Turkish military threat.

[5]At first, Othello attempts to make provision for Desdemona to remain safely in Venice (1.3.237–40).

[6]Desdemona asks that she be allowed to go with him to Cyprus (1.3.260).

wife!" Shortly afterwards, having donned his armour and made all
ready for the journey, he embarked in the galley with his lady and
all his train: then, hoisting sail, they set off, and with a sea of the utmost tranquility arrived safely in Cyprus.[7]

The Moor had in his company an Ensign of handsome presence
but the most scoundrelly nature in the world. He was in high favor
with the Moor, who had no suspicion of his wickedness: for although
he had the basest of minds, he so cloaked the vileness hidden in his
heart[8] with high sounding and noble words, and by his manner, that
he showed himself in the likeness of a Hector or an Achilles. This
false man had likewise taken to Cyprus his wife, a fair and honest
young woman. Being an Italian she was much loved by the Moor's
wife, and spent the greater part of the day with her.

In the same company there was also a Corporal who was very
dear to the Moor. This man went frequently to the Moor's house and
often dined with him and his wife. The Lady, knowing him so well
liked by her husband, gave him proofs of the greatest kindness, and
this was much appreciated by the Moor.

The wicked Ensign, taking no account of the faith he had
pledged to his wife, and of the friendship, loyalty and obligations he
owed the Moor, fell ardently in love with Disdemona[9] and bent all
his thoughts to see if he could manage to enjoy her:[10] but he did not
dare openly show his passion, fearing that if the Moor perceived it
he might straightway kill him. He sought therefore in various ways,
as deviously as he could, to make the Lady aware that he desired
her. But she, whose every thought was for the Moor, never gave a
thought to the Ensign or anybody else. And all the things he did to
arouse her feelings for him had no more effect than if he had not
tried them. Whereupon he imagined that this was because she was
in love with the Corporal,[11] and he wondered how he might remove
the latter from her sight. Not only did he turn his mind to this, but
the love which he had felt for the Lady now changed to the bitterest
hate, and he gave himself up to studying how to bring it about that,

---

[7]Contrast with the storm at 2.1.1–19.

[8]"Utter my thoughts? Why, say they are file and false." (Iago at 3.3.136).

[9]Iago says, "Now, I do love her too / . . . But partly led to diet my revenge" (2.1.280,
283).

[10]Iago claims to Roderigo, "thou shalt enjoy her" (1.3.353).

[11]Iago observes, "That she loves him, 'tis apt" (2.1.276).

once the Corporal were killed, if he himself could not enjoy the Lady, then the Moor should not have her either. Turning over in his mind divers schemes, all wicked and treacherous, in the end he determined to accuse her of adultery, and to make her husband believe that the Corporal was the adulterer.[12] But knowing the singular love of the Moor for Disdemona,[13] and his friendship for the Corporal, he recognized that, unless he could deceive the Moor with some clever trick, it would be impossible to make him believe either charge. Wherefore he set himself to wait until time and place opened a way for him to start his wicked enterprise.

Not long afterwards the Moor deprived the Corporal of his rank for having drawn his sword and wounded a soldier while on guard-duty.[14] Disdemona was grieved by this and tried many times to reconcile the Moor with him. Whereupon the Moor told the rascally Ensign that his wife importuned him so much for the Corporal that he feared he would be obliged to reinstate him. The evil man saw in this a hint for setting in train the deceits he had planned, and said: "Perhaps Disdemona has good cause to look on him so favourably!" "Why is that?" asked the Moor. "I do not wish," said the Ensign, "to come between man and wife, but if you keep your eyes open you will see for yourself."[15] Nor for all the Moor's inquiries would the Ensign go beyond this: nonetheless his words left such a sharp thorn in the Moor's mind, that he gave himself up to pondering intensely what they could mean. He became quite melancholy, and one day, when his wife was trying to soften his anger towards the Corporal, begging him not to condemn to oblivion the loyal service and friendship of many years just for one small fault, especially since the Corporal had been reconciled to the man he had struck, the Moor burst out in anger and said to her, "There must be a very powerful reason why you take such trouble for this fellow, for he is not your brother, nor even a kinsman, yet you have him so much at heart!"

The lady, all courtesy and modesty, replied: "I should not like you to be angry with me. Nothing else makes me do it but sorrow to see you deprived of so dear a friend as you have shown that the

---

[12]See 2.1.287–300.

[13]See 2.1.277–79.

[14]Shakespeare's Iago portrays Cassio's action as manipulated by Iago's plying him with drink and setting Roderigo on him (2.3.140 & ff.).

[15]"Look to your wife, observe her well" (3.3.197).

Corporal was to you. He has not committed so serious an offence as to deserve such hostility.[16] But you Moors are so hot by nature that any little thing moves you to anger and revenge."

Still more enraged by these words the Moor answered: "Anyone who does not believe that may easily have proof of it! I shall take such revenge for any wrongs done to me as will more than satisfy me!" The lady was terrified by these words, and seeing her husband angry with her, quite against his habit,[17] she said humbly: "Only a very good purpose made me speak to you about this, but rather than have you angry with me I shall never say another word on the subject."

The Moor, however, seeing the earnestness with which his wife had again pleaded for the Corporal, guessed that the Ensign's words had been intended to suggest that Disdemona was in love with the Corporal, and he went in deep depression to the scoundrel and urged him to speak more openly. The Ensign, intent on injuring this unfortunate lady, after pretending not to wish to say anything that might displease the Moor,[18] appeared to be overcome by his entreaties and said: "I must confess that it grieves me greatly to have to tell you something that must be in the highest degree painful to you; but since you wish me to tell you, and the regard that I must have of your honor as my master spurs me on, I shall not fail in my duty to answer your request. You must know therefore that it is hard for your Lady to see the Corporal in disgrace for the simple reason that she takes her pleasure with him whenever he comes to your house. The woman has come to dislike your blackness."[19]

These words struck the Moor's heart to its core; but in order to learn more (although he believed what the Ensign had said to be true, through the suspicion already sown in his mind) he said, with a fierce look: "I do not know what holds me back from cutting out that outrageous tongue of yours which has dared to speak such insults against my Lady!"[20] Then the Ensign: "Captain," he said, "I did not expect any other reward for my loving service; but since my duty and my care for your honor have carried me so far, I repeat

---

[16]See 3.3.41–83; 3.4.45–92, for Desdemona's defense of Cassio to Othello.

[17]"My lord is not my lord; nor should I know him" (3.4.121).

[18]Iago claims, "I do not like the office" (3.3.409).

[19]Othello fears that his wife has become repulsed by his age and blackness (3.3.262–6).

[20]See 3.3.364–6, where Othello threatens Iago.

that the matter stands exactly as you have just heard it, and if your Lady, with a false show of love for you, has so blinded your eyes that you have not seen what you ought to have seen, that does not mean that I am not speaking the truth. For this Corporal has told me all, like one whose happiness does not seem complete until he has made someone else acquainted with it."[21] And he added: "If I had not feared your wrath, I should, when he told me, have given him the punishment he deserved by killing him. But since letting you know what concerns you more than anyone else brings me so undeserved a reward, I wish that I had kept silent, for by doing so I should not have fallen into your displeasure."

Then the Moor, in the utmost anguish, said, "If you do not make me see with my own eyes[22] what you have told me, be assured, I shall make you realize that it would have been better for you had you been born dumb."[23] "To prove it would have been easy," replied the villain, "when he used to come to your house; but now when, not as it should have been, but for the most trivial cause, you have driven him away, it cannot but be difficult for me, for although I fancy that he still enjoys Disdemona whenever you give him the opportunity, he must do it much more cautiously than he did before, now that he knows you have turned against him. Yet I do not lose hope of being able to show you what you do not wish to believe." And with these words they parted.

The wretched Moor, as if struck by the sharpest of darts, went home to wait for the day when the Ensign would make him see that which must make him miserable for ever. But no less trouble did the Ensign suffer by his knowledge of the Lady's chastity, for it did not seem possible to find a way of making the Moor believe what he had falsely told him, till, his thoughts twisting and turning in all directions, the scoundrel thought of a new piece of mischief.

The Moor's wife often went, as I have said, to the house of the Ensign's wife, and stayed with her a good part of the day: wherefore seeing that she sometimes carried with her a handkerchief embroidered most delicately in the Moorish fashion, which the Moor had given her and which was treasured by the Lady and her husband

---

[21] Iago's story of Cassio's dream of being in bed with Desdemona is added by Shakespeare.

[22] "Give me the ocular proof" (3.3.359).

[23] "Thou hadst been better to have been born a dog" (3.3.361).

too, the Ensign planned to take it from her secretly, and thereby prepare her final ruin. He had a little girl of three years old, much loved by Disdemona. One day, when the unfortunate Lady had gone to pass some time at the villain's house, he took the child in his arms and carried her to the Lady, who took her and pressed her to her breast. The deceiver, who had great sleight of hand, lifted the handkerchief from her girdle so warily that she did not notice it; and he took his leave of her in great joy.[24]

Disdemona, knowing nothing of it, went back home and, being occupied with other thoughts, did not miss the handkerchief. But a few days later, she looked for it, and not finding it she became afraid that the Moor might ask for it, as he often did. The wicked Ensign, seizing a suitable opportunity, went to the Corporal's room, and with cunning malice left the handkerchief at the head of his bed.[25] The Corporal did not notice it till the next morning when, getting out of bed, he put his foot upon the handkerchief, which had fallen to the floor. Not being able to imagine how it had come into his house, and knowing that it was Disdemona's, he determined to give it back to her. So he waited till the Moor had gone out, then went to the back door and knocked. Fortune, it seems, had conspired with the Ensign to bring about the death of the unhappy lady; for just then the Moor came home, and hearing a knock on the door went to the window and shouted angrily: "Who is knocking?" The Corporal, hearing the Moor's voice and fearing that he might come down and attack him, fled without answering. The Moor ran down the stairs, and opening the outside door went out into the street and looked around, but could see nobody. Then returning full of evil passion, he asked his wife who had knocked on the door below.

The Lady replied truthfully that she did not know. The Moor then said, "It looked to me like the Corporal." "I do not know," she said, "whether it was he or somebody else." The Moor restrained his fury, though he was consumed with rage. He did not want to do anything before consulting the Ensign, to whom he went at once and told him what had occurred, praying him to find out from the Corporal all that he could about it. Delighted with what had

---

[24]There is no mention of the child; instead, Shakespeare has Emilia pick up the handkerchief which Desdemona has dropped (3.3.285–90).

[25]Iago plots to plant the handkerchief in Cassio's room (3.3.320–1).

happened, the Ensign promised to do so. Accordingly he spoke to the Corporal one day while the Moor was standing where he could see them as they talked; and chatting of quite other matters than the Lady,[26] he laughed heartily and, displaying great surprise, he moved his head about and gestured with his hands, acting as if he were listening to marvels. As soon as the Moor saw them separate he went to the Ensign to learn what the other had told him; and the Ensign, after making him entreat him for a long time, finally declared: "He has hidden nothing from me. He tells me that he has enjoyed your wife every time you have given them the chance by your absence. And on the last occasion she gave him the handkerchief which you gave her as a present when you married her."[27] The Moor thanked the Ensign and it seemed obvious to him that if he found that the Lady no longer had the handkerchief, then all must be as the Ensign claimed.

Wherefore one day after dinner, while chatting with the Lady on various matters, he asked her for the handkerchief. The unhappy woman, who had greatly feared this, grew red in the face at the request, and to hide her blushes (which the Moor well noted), she ran to the chest, pretending to look for it. After much search, "I do not know," she said, "why I cannot find it; perhaps you have had it?" "If I had had it," said he, "why should I ask for it? But you will look more successfully another time."[28]

Leaving her the Moor began to think how he might kill his wife, and the Corporal too, in such a way that he would not be blamed for it.[29] And since he was obsessed with this, day and night, the Lady inevitably noticed that he was not the same towards her as he was formerly. Many times she said to him, "What is the matter with you? What is troubling you? Whereas you used to be the gayest of men, you are now the most melancholy man alive!"

The Moor invented various excuses, but she was not at all satisfied, and although she knew no act of hers which could have so per-

---

[26]See the conversation of Iago with Cassio about Bianca, that Iago easily convinces Othello is about Desdemona (4.1.107–40).

[27]Iago tells Othello that the handkerchief, which he has seen Bianca return to Cassio, was originally given to him by Desdemona (4.1.166–70).

[28]Shakespeare makes Othello much more insistent and furious about the handkerchief (3.4.49–93).

[29]Othello and Iago discuss how Othello will kill Desdemona (4.1.174–201).

turbed the Moor, she nevertheless feared that through the abundance of lovemaking which he had with her he might have become
tired of her. Sometimes she would say to the Ensign's wife. "I do not
know what to make of the Moor. He used to be all love towards me.
but in the last few days he has become quite another man. and I fear
greatly that I shall be a warning to young girls not to marry against
their parents' wishes: and Italian ladies will learn by my example
not to tie themselves to a man whom Nature. Heaven. and manner
of life separate from us. But because I know that he is very friendly
with your husband. and confides in him. I beg you. if you have
learned anything from him which you can tell me. that you will not
fail to help me." She wept bitterly as she spoke.[30]

The Ensign's wife. who knew everything (for her husband had
wished to use her as an instrument in causing the Lady's death. but
she had never been willing to consent). did not dare. for fear of her
husband. to tell her anything. She said only: "Take care not to give
your husband any reason for suspicion. and try your hardest to
make him realize your love and loyalty."[31] "That indeed I do." said
Disdemona. "but it does not help."

In the meantime the Moor sought in every way to get more proof
of that which he did not wish to discover. and prayed the Ensign to
contrive to let him see the handkerchief in the Corporal's possession:
and although that was difficult for the villain. he promised nonetheless to make every effort to give him this testimony.

The Corporal had a woman at home who worked the most wonderful embroidery on lawn. and seeing the handkerchief and learning that it belonged to the Moor's wife. and that it was to be returned to her. she began to make a similar one before it went
back.[32] While she was doing so. the Ensign noticed that she was
working near a window where she could be seen by whoever passed
by on the street. So he brought the Moor and made him see her. and
the latter now regarded it as certain that the most virtuous Lady
was indeed an adulteress. He arranged with the Ensign to kill her
and the Corporal. and they discussed how it might be done. The
Moor begged the Ensign to kill the Corporal. promising to remain

[30]Desdemona asks Iago for help (4.2.155–8).

[31]Emilia remarks on Othello's jealousy to Desdemona (3.4.26) and protests to him
that Desdemona is honest (4.2.13–20).

[32]Cassio asks Bianca to copy the embroidery of the handkerchief (3.4.185–7).

eternally grateful to him. The Ensign refused to undertake such a thing, as being too difficult and dangerous, for the Corporal was as skilful as he was courageous; but after much entreaty, and being given a large sum of money, he was persuaded to say that he would tempt Fortune.[33]

Soon after they had resolved on this, the Corporal, issuing one dark night from the house of a courtesan with whom he used to amuse himself, was accosted by the Ensign, sword in hand, who directed a blow at his legs to make him fall down; and he cut the right leg entirely through, so that the wretched man fell.[34] The Ensign was immediately on him to finish him off, but the Corporal, who was valiant and used to blood and death, had drawn his sword, and wounded as he was he set about defending himself, while shouting in a loud voice: "I am being murdered!"[35]

At that the Ensign, hearing people come running, including some of the soldiers who were quartered thereabouts, began to flee, so as not to be caught there; then, turning back he pretended to have run up on hearing the noise. Mingling with the others, and seeing the leg cut off, he judged that if the Corporal were not already dead, he soon would die of the wound, and although he rejoiced inwardly, he outwardly grieved for the Corporal as if he had been his own brother.[36]

In the morning, news of the affray was spread throughout the city and reached the ears of Disdemona: whereupon, being tender-hearted and not thinking that evil would come to her by it, she showed the utmost sorrow at the occurrence. On this the Moor put the worst possible construction.[37] Seeking out the Ensign, he said to him: "Do you know, my imbecile of a wife is in such grief about the Corporal's accident that she is nearly out of her mind!" "How could you expect anything else?" said the other, "since he is her very life and soul?"

"Soul indeed!" replied the Moor, "I'll drag the soul from her body, for I couldn't think myself a man if I didn't rid the world of such a wicked creature."

---

[33]Iago volunteers to kill Cassio (4.1.202).

[34]Having manipulated Roderigo to attack Cassio, Iago ends up stabbing Cassio (5.1.1–27).

[35]Help! ho! murder! murder! (5.1.27).

[36]Iago pretends to lament Cassio's wounding (5.1.69–102).

[37]"Out, strumpet, weep'st thou for him to my face!" (5.2.81).

They were discussing whether the Lady should perish by poison or the dagger. and not deciding on either of them. when the Ensign said: "A method has come into my head that will satisfy you and that nobody will suspect. It is this: the house where you are staying is very old. and the ceiling of your room has many cracks in it. I suggest that we beat Disdemona with a stocking filled with sand until she dies. Thus there will not appear on her any sign of the blows. When she is dead. we shall make part of the ceiling fall; and we'll break the Lady's head. making it seem that a rafter has injured it in falling. and killed her. In this way nobody will feel any suspicion of you. for everyone will think that she died accidentally."[38]

The cruel plan pleased the Moor. and they waited for a suitable opportunity. One night the Moor concealed the Ensign in a closet which opened off the bedchamber. and when the husband and wife were in bed. the Ensign. in accordance with their plan. made some sort of noise. Hearing it the Moor said to his wife:

> "Did you hear that noise?"
> "Yes. I heard it." she replied.
> "Get up." said the Moor. "and see what it is."

The unfortunate Disdemona got out of bed. and as soon as she was near the closet. the Ensign came out and. being strong and muscular. he gave her a frightful blow in the small of her back. which made the Lady fall down at once. scarcely able to draw her breath. With the little voice she had she called on the Moor to help her. But he. jumping out of bed. said to her. "You wicked woman.[39] you are having the reward of your infidelity. This is how women are treated who. pretending to love their husbands. put horns on their heads."

The wretched Lady. hearing this and feeling herself near to death (for the Ensign had given her another blow). called on Divine Justice to witness to her fidelity.[40] since earthly justice failed: and as she called on God to help her. a third blow struck her. and she lay still. slain by the impious Ensign. Then. placing her in the bed. and breaking her skull. he and the Moor made the ceiling fall as they

[38]Shakespeare has Othello propose to poison Desdemona and Iago to strangle her. Othello is not concerned with being found out.

[39]"O perjured woman" (5.2.67).

[40]"By heaven. you do me wrong" (4.2.83): "A guiltless death I die" (5.2.127).

had previously planned, and the Moor began to call for help, that the house was falling. Hearing his cries the neighbours ran in and found the bed, and the Lady dead under the rafters—which made everyone grieve, for they knew what a good life she had led.[41]

Next day Disdemona was buried, amid the universal mourning of the people. But God, the just observer of men's hearts, did not intend such vile wickedness to go without proper punishment. He ordained that the Moor, who had loved the Lady more than his life,[42] on finding himself deprived of her should feel such longing that he went about like one beside himself, searching for her in every part of the house.[43] Realizing now that the Ensign was the cause of his losing his Lady and all joy in life, he held the villain in such abhorrence that he could not bear even to see him; and if he had not been afraid of the inviolable justice of the Venetian lords, he would have slain him openly. Not being able to do this with safety, he took away his rank and would not have him in his company, whereupon such a bitter hatred sprang up between them that no greater or more deadly feud could be imagined.

The Ensign, that worst of all scoundrels, therefore set all his mind to injuring the Moor, and seeking out the Corporal, who had now recovered and went about with a wooden leg instead of the one that had been cut off, he said to him, "It is time you got your revenge for the leg you lost. If you will come to Venice with me, I shall tell you who the miscreant was, for here I dare not tell you, for many reasons; and I am willing to bear witness for you in court."

The Corporal who felt himself deeply wronged but did not know the real truth, thanked the Ensign and came with him to Venice. When they arrived there the Ensign told him that it was the Moor who had cut off his leg because of a suspicion he had formed that he was Disdemona's lover, and that for the same reason he had murdered her, and afterwards made it known that the fallen ceiling had killed her. Hearing this, the Corporal accused the Moor to the Signoria, both of cutting off his leg and of causing the Lady's death, and called as witness the Ensign, who said that both accusations were true, for the Moor had approached him and tried to induce

---

[41]"Thou hast killed the sweetest innocent" (5.2.205).

[42]"My life upon her faith" (1.3.295).

[43]See Othello's moaning and falling on the bed (5.2.203) and violence (5.2.241–3).

him to commit both crimes; and that, having then killed his wife through the bestial jealousy that he had conceived in his mind, he had told him how he had killed her.

When the Signoria learned of the cruelty inflicted by the Barbarian[++] upon a citizen of Venice, they ordered the Moor to be apprehended in Cyprus and to be brought to Venice, where with many tortures they tried to discover the truth. But enduring with great steadfastness of mind every torment, he denied everything so firmly that nothing could be extorted from him. Although by his constancy he escaped death, he was, however, after many days in prison, condemned to perpetual exile, in which he was finally slain by Disdemona's relatives, as he richly deserved.

The Ensign returned to his own country; and not giving up his accustomed behaviour, he accused one of his companions, saying that the latter had sought to have him murder one of his enemies, who was a nobleman. The accused man was arrested and put to the torture, and when he denied that what his accuser said was true, the Ensign too was tortured, to compare their stories; and he was tortured so fiercely that his inner organs were ruptured.[45] Afterwards he was let out of prison and taken home, where he died miserably. Thus did God avenge the innocence of Disdemona. And all these events were told after his death by the Ensign's wife, who knew the facts, as I have told them to you.[46]

[Story 8 is (as usual) prefaced by a linking passage commenting on the tale just heard:]

It appeared marvellous to everybody that such malignity could have been discovered in a human heart; and the fate of the unhappy Lady was lamented, with some blame for her father, who had given her a name of unlucky augury.[47] And the party decided that since a name is the first gift of a father to his child, he ought to bestow one that is grand and fortunate, as if he wished to foretell success and greatness. No less was the Moor blamed, who had believed too foolishly. But all praised God because the criminals had had suitable punishment.

[++]"an erring barbarian" (1.3.351).

[45]Gratiano foretells the tortures that will befall Iago: "Torments will ope your lips" (5.2.311).

[46]See Emilia's speeches at 5.2.177 & ff.

[47]Desdemona is Greek for "unfortunate."

Flavius Josephus (c. 37–c.100)
Author

One of the foremost historians of Jewish history, Josephus, originally named Joseph Ben Matthias, was a controversial figure, in no small part because of his adoption of apparently contradictory political positions. As a strictly religious observant Pharisee, he at first opposed the Jewish revolt against Roman imperial rule in 66 AD, but later accepted an appointment as military commander of the Jewish resistance in Galilee. When the Romans quelled the revolt in Galilee, Josephus survived only to surrender, while his compatriots preferred to die rather than to accept defeat. He managed to endure imprisonment and to regain his fortune by presenting himself as a prophet to the emperor Vespasian.

Taking the emperor's family name "Flavius" as his own, Josephus went to work for the Romans. They employed him to act as an intermediary between Roman and Jewish forces at the siege of Jerusalem in 70. Not entirely trusted by either side, he was unsuccessful in his attempts to bring about a truce.

After the fall of Jerusalem, Josephus went to live in Rome, where he wrote History of the Jewish War *(75–79)*, an account of the great revolt against Rome in 66–70, and his greatest work, The Antiquities of the Jews *(93)*, a narrative of events from the creation of the world to the eve of the Jewish rebellion. The original Aramaic versions of his writings are lost, but the Greek texts whose production he oversaw remain. Josephus makes history as fascinating as a novel with his quickly moving narrative of historical events and his emotionally moving character portrayal of historical figures. His work was of great interest in the early modern period, with a Latin translation printed at Augsburg in 1470 followed by translations into French, German, Italian and English.

Thomas Lodge (c. 1557–1625)
Translator

Thomas Lodge was a law student at Lincoln's Inn, a doctor, and a writer. He wrote poems, plays, and prose romances, the most famous of which is Rosalynd, the chief source for Shakespeare's As You Like It. With his sharp satirical wit, Lodge was also an immensely erudite translator of French, Italian, and Latin texts.

He was the first English translator of Josephus, from whose Works Elizabeth Cary took the story of Mariam. The evidence of the Stationer's Register suggests that Lodge began work on his translation of Josephus as early as 1591. The Famous and Memorable Works of Josephus, a Man of Much Honor and Learning among the Jewes, Faithfully translated out of the Latin and French, by Tho. Lodge, Doctor in Physicke *was first printed in 1602, and was so well received that it was reprinted in 1609, 1620, 1632, 1640, 1655, 1670, 1685, and 1693.*

Dunstan and Greg, in their edition of The Tragedy of Mariam *(1914), were the first to point out the verbal echoes of Lodge's translation in Cary's play, and Stephanie Hodgson-Wright, in her edition (2000), notes further parallels. As the verbal echoes and parallels that have been noted suggest, Lodge's* Josephus *clarifies Cary's interpretation of this source for her dramatic purposes.*

It is likely that Elizabeth Cary knew Lodge in person as well, for he was prominent in recusant Catholic circles. He converted to Catholicism in 1597, and after the Gunpowder Plot in 1605, he sought refuge in Brussels in order to escape being apprehended as a Catholic traitor. Barry Weller and Margaret Ferguson note in the introduction to their edition of The Tragedy of Mariam *(1994), that English Roman Catholics read the story of Herod as analogous to the life of Henry VIII, regarding both as tyrants. Lodge's introductory letter to his translation, "To the Courteous Reader," encourages this kind of practical and topical interpretation. He stresses the relevance of history for moral self-understanding and practical guidance in public affairs, a sentiment echoed by Cary's Chorus at the end of the play: "This day's events were certainly ordained,/To be the warning to posterity."*

The excerpts reproduced here are from the University of Michigan microfilm of the 1620 edition in the Huntington Library.

from The Famous and Memorable Works of Josephus (1620)

Second edition of the 1602 translation by Thomas Lodge

The Antiquities of the Jews
BOOK XV. CHAPTER IIII. 387–88

[Marginal notes indicate that the events of this chapter occurred "before Christ's nativity 33" and "32."]

Cleopatra thirsting after the kingdom of Arabia and Jewry. laboreth to beg a part of them at Anthony's hands.

But none of all these things could either move or mollify Alexandra. but that daily more and more she increased her sorrow. and in the heart of her tears kindled her wrath and heat with a desire of revenge. She therefore certified Cleopatra by her private letters of Herod's treasons. and her son's most miserable and untimely death. Cleopatra long before that time desirous to assist her. and having compassion of her misery. undertook the matter. and ceased not to incite Anthony to revenge Aristobolus' death. telling him that it was an unpardonable error, that Herod being created king in such a state, whereunto he had no right, should be suffered to practice such conspiracies against the true and lawful kings. Anthony persuaded by these her words (as soon as he came unto Laodicea) sent for Herod, to the end that making his appearance he might answer that which might be objected against him, as touching Aristobolus' death. For he disliked the act, notwithstanding that Herod himself had attempted it. But although Herod was afraid of this accusation, and did not a little suspect Cleopatra's displeasure (for that she ceased not continually to provoke Anthony against him) yet obeyed he this commandment, and transported himself thither (the rather for that he durst not otherwise do), notwithstanding he left his uncle Joseph behind him, committing the government both of the kingdom and his private estate unto him, giving him secret introductions to kill Mariam, if so be that Anthony should happen to do him any mischief. For he loved her so extremely by reason of her beauty, that he supposed himself injured, if after his decease she should be beloved by any other; and he openly declared that all that misery which befell him proceeded from Anthony's passion and entire affection, and admiration of her beauty, whereof he had before time heard some report. As soon therefore as he had in this sort disposed his affairs, notwithstanding he had little hope of good hap, yet repaired he to Anthony.

But Joseph governing the kingdom that was committed to his hands, conversed diverse times upon this occasion with Mariam, and communicated oftentimes with her, not only for public profit sake, but also to do her that honor which so great a princess deserved. At such time therefore as he secretly devised with her, as touching the friendship and ardent affection which Herod bare unto her, his speeches were jested at after the manner of Ladies, but especially flouted at by Alexandra. For which cause Joseph, being over-forward to express the King's goodwill towards her, proceeded so far that he discovered[1] the commandment that was given him: thereby to make manifest that it was not possible for Herod to live without her, and that if any inconvenience should happen unto him, he would not in death also be disjoined from her. This discourse of Joseph's was not interpreted by the Ladies as a demonstration of his

[1]Revealed.

goodwill, but rather as a manifestation of Herod's malignity: who dying, desired also that they should perish, and interpreted that which he had spoken, as the testimony of his tyrannous and malicious heart. At that time there was a rumor spread in the city of Jerusalem by Herod's maligners, that Anthony had in such sort tormented him, that he was dead.[2] Whereupon all those of the King's house were troubled, and in especial the Ladies: so that Alexandra incited Joseph to forsake the palace, and take the Ladies, and to retire himself under the ensigns of the Roman legion, who at that time were about the city for the security of the kingdom, under the conduct of the Tribune Julius, to the end first of all, that if any trouble should happen in the King's house, they might be by this means in safety, having the Romans to friend; and afterwards, for that they hoped that if Anthony should see Mariam, she might obtain all things at his hands whatsoever she desired, assuring him that he would restore the kingdom unto her, and deprive her of nothing that concerned, or was answerable to her royal estate.

But whilst they were distracted with these deliberations, there came letters from Herod, contrary to some few men's report, and all men's expectation. For as soon as he came unto Anthony, he compassed his favor by his many presents, which he had brought with him to that intent from Jerusalem, and suddenly debating the matter with him, he appeased him in such sort, as he was no more displeased against him. And from that time forward, Cleopatra's speeches were but coldly conceived of in regard of his so ample satisfaction. For Anthony said, that there was no reason that a King should be answerable for that which he had done in his kingdom: for that in so doing he should no more be King: but that when the honor is once given him, he hath the authority likewise left him, to use his regal power: urging further, that it concerned Cleopatra likewise herself, not to search too curiously into the affairs and government of kingdoms. Herod certified all this by his letters, and signified further what other honors he had received at Anthony's hands in assemblies and feasts, to which he invited him always: notwithstanding that Cleopatra seemed to be displeased therewith, detract-

---

[2]Cary changes the story so that the false report of Herod's death occurs not during his first absence from Judaea, when he visits Anthony, but during his second absence, when he visits Caesar.

ing him: and being desirous to get the kingdom of Jewry into her hands, strove by all means possible to put him to death: but that he had found Anthony always an upright man, and feared not henceforward that any evil should befall him. And returning presently upon this, he brought with him a more ample testimony of Anthony's most assured affection, both in respect of his own kingdom, as of his particular affairs. And as touching Cleopatra, she pretended not to seek any further than that which she had, because that Anthony had given her Coelesyria instead of that which she had demanded, forbearing thence forward to mention Jewry any more, because that Anthony wholly rejected those suits.

After these letters came unto their hands, the trouble and disturbance wherein they were, and their desire to retire unto the Romans, as if Herod had been dead, was wholly extinguished. Yet was not this their resolution hidden from the King: but that Herod after he had brought Anthony on his way (who at that time set forward in his wars against the Parthians) he returned into Jewry. Upon his arrival, his sister Salome, and his mother certified him exactly of Alexandra's intent, and the determination of her friends. Salome likewise spake against Joseph her husband, and slandered him, objecting against him that he had Mariam's company. All which she speaketh through the malice she had long time conceived against him, for that in a certain debate Mariam had in her rage despitefully hit them in the teeth with their obscure birth.[3] Herod (who was always inflamed with the earnest affection which he bare unto his wife Mariam) was suddenly troubled hereat: and although jealousy pressed him forward, yet love restrained him and kept him from doing anything rashly, through passion or affection: for which cause he called Mariam aside, and demanded of her in secret, what familiar company she had kept with Joseph. She by solemn oaths and by all possible allegations in her own defense appeased the King by little and little, and pacified his choler. For in such sort was he transported with the love that he bare unto his wife, that he believed she had sufficiently purged herself of those slanders that had been enforced against her: yielding her most hearty thanks for her honest affection towards him, and declaring unto her openly the great esteem and love that he bare unto her. Finally (as it often falleth out

[3]See 1.3.25–32, where Mariam upbraids Salome for her "baser birth."

amongst lovers) they fell to tears. and embraced each other with great affection: for that she gave him no credit. he endeavored the more to draw her to belief. Whereupon Mariam said unto him: "It is not the act of a lover to have given commandment. that if anything should befall thee otherways than well with Anthony. I should presently be done to death with thee: notwithstanding I have no ways offended thee." No sooner were these words out of her mouth. but the King entered into a strange passion, and giving over his embraces he cried out with a loud voice and tore his hair. saying that he had a most evident proof that Joseph had committed adultery with her: for that he would not have discovered those things which had been spoken to him in secret. except they had greatly trusted the one the other: and in this emotion or rage of jealousy hardly contained he himself from killing his wife. But the force of love overcame him so much. that he bridled his rage notwithstanding it were irksome and grievous unto him. Yet gave he order that Joseph should be slain without either audience or justification of his innocence:[4] and as touching Alexandra. who was the cause of all these troubles. he kept her prisoner.

The Antiquities of the Jews
BOOK XV. CHAPTER XI. 396–99

> [Marginal notes indicate the date of the events for this chapter as "before Christ's nativity 29" and "28."]

But as soon as he returned into his kingdom. he found all his household troubled. and both his wife Mariam and her mother Alexandra grievously displeased with him. For they both supposed (and not without cause) that they were not shut up in that Castle for their security's sake. but as it were in a prison: so that in as much as they neither might make use of other men's. nor enjoy their own goods. they were highly discontented. Mariam also supposed that her husband did but dissemble his love. rather for his own profit and commodity. than for any entire affection he bare towards her. But nothing more grieved her. than that she had not any hope to live after him. if so be he should happen to die. especially for the order he had

---

[4]Cary represents Salome as accusing Mariam of adultery with Josephus in order to get rid of her husband and marry Constabarus (1.3.41–44).

left concerning her: neither could she ever forget what commandment before that time he had left with Joseph: so that by all means
possible, she labored to win the affections of those that had the
charge of her, and especially Sohemus, knowing very well that her
safety depended wholly on his hands, who in the beginning behaved
himself very wisely and faithfully, containing himself very circum-
spectly within the bounds of his commission. But after these Ladies
had with pretty presents and feminine flatteries mollified and
wrought him by little and little,[1] at last he blabbed out all that
which the King had commanded him: especially, for that he hoped
not that he should return with the same power and authority, which
before he had: and for that cause he thought thus in himself, that
without incurring any danger in regard of Herod, he might greatly
gratify the Ladies, who in all likelihood should not be deprived of
that dignity wherein they were at that time; but would return them
the like kindness when Mariam should be Queen, or next unto the
King. Furthermore, he hoped that if Herod also should return with
all things answerable to his desires, that he would perform nothing
without his wife's consent: or upbraid him with the act, if she contradicted. For he knew too well that the King loved her in such sort,
as it was impossible to equal or express his affections: and for these
causes he disclosed the trust that was committed unto him. But
Mariam was very sore displeased to hear that there was no end of
her miseries, but they were altogether united and tied to the dangers
of Herod. And she oftentimes wished that he might never more return again in safety, supposing that her life with him should be very
intolerable. All which she afterwards dissembled not, but openly
confessed that which afflicted her with discontent. For whenas
Herod beyond all expectation arrived in his country, being adorned
with mighty fortune, he first of all, as it became him certified his
wife of his good tidings and happy success, whom only amongst all
other his friends and wives, he embraced and saluted, for the pleasing conversation and affection that was in her. But she, whilst he repeated unto her these fortunate events of his affairs, rather entertained the same with a displeasant attention, than applauding joy.
And these affections of hers likewise she could not conceal. For at

---

[1]Cary omits any mention of Mariam's attempts to ingratiate herself with and to manipulate Sohemus.

such time as he folded his arms about her neck, she unfolded her sorrow in her sighs: so simple and unfeigned were her affections: and seemed rather to be displeased than appeased by his narrations. Whereupon Herod was sore troubled, perceiving these things not only suspected, but also fully manifest: but above all things he was distracted, when he considered the incredible and apparent hatred that his wife had conceived against him, which in such sort incensed him that he could not resist the love that had attainted him: so that he neither could continue in wrath, nor listen long to peace: and being unresolved in himself, he now was attempted by this, straight distracted by a contrary affection: so much was his mind travailed between love and hatred, that when as oftentimes he desired to punish the woman's pride, his heart by love's mediation failed him in the enterprise. For nothing did more torment him than his fear, least executing his displeasure against her, he should by this means more grievously wound himself, through the desire he bare unto his deceased delight. Whilst thus he was sweltered and devoured in his passions, and conceived sinister opinions against Mariam his wife, Salome his sister and his mother having an inkling of his discontents, thought that they had gotten a fit opportunity to express and execute their hatred towards Mariam: for which cause they conferred with Herod, and whetted his spleen and displeasure with variety of slanders, sufficient at one assault to engender hatred, and kindle his jealousy against her. To these reproaches of theirs, he lent no unwilling ears: yet he had not the heart to attempt anything against his wife, or to give free credit to their report: notwithstanding his displeasure increased, and was inflamed more and more against her, for that neither she could color her cares and discontents, nor he contain himself from exchanging his love into hatred. And perhaps at that time he had published some fatal doom against her, had not a happy messenger brought him word, that Anthony and Cleopatra being dead, Caesar was become Lord of Egypt: for which cause hastening forward to meet and entertain him, he left his family to that present estate. Upon his departure he recommended Mariam to Sohemus, giving him great thanks for the care he had had of her, and granted him in way of gratuity a part of Jewry to govern.

When Herod was arrived in Egypt, and had friendly and familiarly conferred with Caesar, he was highly honored by him: for Caesar gave him those four hundred Frenchmen that were of Cleopatra's guard; and restored that part of his country unto him again. which was taken away and spoiled by her. He annexed also unto his kingdom Gadara. Hippon. Samaria. and on the sea coasts the Cities of Gaza. Anthedon. Joppe, with the tower of Straton: which when he had obtained, he grew more mighty than before. And after he had accompanied Caesar as far as Antioch, he returned into his own country. Upon his arrival, he found that fortune which was favorable unto him abroad. too froward[2] at home. especially in regard of his wife. in whose affection before time he seemed to be most happy. For he was inwardly touched with the lawful love of Mariam. as any other of whom the Histories make report: and as touching her. she was both chaste. and faithful unto him: yet she had a certain womanly imperfection and natural frowardness.[3] which was the cause that she presumed too much upon the entire affection wherewith her husband was entangled:[4] for that without regard of his person. who had power and authority over others. she entertained him oftentimes very outrageously. All which he endured patiently. without any show of discontent. But Mariam upbraided and publicly reproached both the King's mother and sister. telling them that they were but abjectly and basely born.

Whereupon there grew a great enmity and unrecoverable hatred between the Ladies; and from thence also there arose an occasion of greater accusations and calumniation then before. These suspicions were nourished amongst them. for the space of one whole year after Herod's return from Caesar; and finally this long contrived and fore-imagined hatred at last brake out violently upon this occasion that ensueth.[5] When as about mid-day the King had withdrawn himself into his chamber to take his rest. he called Mariam unto him to sport with her. being incited thereunto by the great affection that he bare unto her. Upon this his command she came unto him: yet would she not lie with him. nor entertain his courtings with friendly acceptance. but upbraided him bitterly with her father's and brother's death. The King took these reproachful words in very evil

---

[2]Contrary.

[3]Obstinacy. rebellious independence of mind.

[4]Compare with 4.8.1: "Am I the Mariam that presumed so much."

[5]Cary contracts the time frame in her tragedy.

part, and was almost ready to strike her: but his sister, hearing a greater stir and noise within than was usual, sent in the Butler,[6] who long before that time was suborned by her, whom she commanded to tell the king that Mariam had prepared a drink for him to incite and quicken him unto love: willing him that if the King should be moved thereat, and should demand what he meant, he should certify him that Mariam having prepared a poison for his grace, had dealt with him to deliver it to his Majesty. Charging him moreover, that if the King in hearing him speak of this potion, should seem to be moved therewith, that then he should proceed no further in his discourse. He therefore (being in this manner beforehand instructed what he ought to do) at that very instant was sent in to discover his treachery unto the King: for which cause with a sober and stayed countenance he entered in unto him, being seriously and well prepared to discourse, and told him that Mariam had bribed him to present his Majesty with an amorous cup of drink. Now when he perceived that the King was troubled with these words, he prosecuted his discourse, alleging that the potion was a certain medicine which Mariam had given him, the virtue whereof he knew not, which he had received according as he had told him, knowing that it concerned both his own security, and the King's safety.

Herod, who before this was highly displeased, hearing these words, was so much the more incensed: for which cause he presently commanded Mariam's most faithful servant to be examined by torments, as concerning the poison, supposing that it was impossible for her to undertake anything whatever without his privity.[7] He being tried and tormented after this cruel manner, confessed nothing of that for which he was tortured: but declared unto the King that the hatred which his wife had conceived against him proceeded from certain words that Sohemus had told her. Scarcely had he finished these words, but that the King cried out with a loud voice, saying that Sohemus, who before time had been most faithful both to him and his kingdom, would not have declared these his privy commands, except there had been some more inward familiarity and secrecy betwixt him and Mariam: for which cause he presently

---

[6]Cary includes the character of the Butler, rendered as Bu. in the 1613 edition, thus following Lodge's translation for *pincernam*.

[7]His knowledge, being privy to information.

commanded his ministers to lay hands on Sohemus, and to put him to death. As for his wife, he drew her to her trial,[8] and to this effect, he assembled his most familiar friends, before whom he began to accuse her with great spite and spleen, as touching these potions and poisons aforesaid: wherein he used intemperate and unseemly speeches, and such as for their bitterness did ill become him in cause of justice: so that in the end, the assistants, seeing the but and bent of his desire, pronounced sentence of death against her: which being past, both he, and all other the assistants were of this opinion, that she should not so speedily be executed, but that she should be kept close prisoner in some sure place of the Palace. But by Salome's solicitations Herod was incited to hasten her death, for that she alleged that the King ought to fear, least some sedition should be raised amongst the people, if he should keep her alive in prison. And by this means Mariam was led unto her death.[9]

Alexandra, her mother, considering the estate of the time, and fearing no less mischief from Herod's hands than her daughter was assured of: she undecently changed her mind, and abjectly laid aside her former courage and magnanimity. For intending to make it known that she was neither party nor privy to those crimes wherewith Mariam was charged, she went out to meet her daughter, and entertained her injuriously, protesting publicly that she was a wicked woman, and ungrateful towards her husband: and that she well deserved the punishment that was adjudged her, for that she durst be so bold to attempt so heinous a fact, neglecting to requite her husband's entire love, with her unfeigned loyalty.[10] Whilst thus dishonestly she counterfeited her displeasure, and was ready to pull Mariam by the hair, the assistants according to her defect, condemned her generally for her shameful hypocrisy: but she that was led to be punished, convicted by her mild behavior. For first of all, she gave her no answer: neither was any ways altered by her reproaches, neither would so much as cast her eyes upon her: making it appear that she discreetly concealed and covered her mother's

[8]In Cary's play there is no trial of Mariam..

[9]A marginal note at this point in the text comments: "Mariam by Salome's instigations is led to execution" which is echoed in Cary's "Argument": "presently after by the instigation of Salome, [Mariam] was beheaded."

[10]See 5.1.33-52.

imperfections, and was aggrieved that she had so openly showed so great indignity: expressing for her own part a constant behavior: and going to her death without change of color, so that those that beheld her, perceived in her a kind of manifest courage and nobility, even in her utmost extremity. Thus died Mariam, having been a woman that excelled both in continence and courage: notwithstanding that she defaulted somewhat in affability and impatience of nature: for the rest of her parts, she was an admirable and pleasing beauty, and of such a carriage in those companies wherein she was entertained, that it was impossible to express the same, in that she surpassed all those of her time, which was the principal cause that she lived not so graciously and contentedly with the King. For being entertained by him, who entirely loved her, and from whom she received nothing that might discontent her, she presumed upon a great and intemperate liberty in her discourse. She digested also the loss of her friends very hardly,[11] according as in open terms she made it known unto the King: whereby also it came to pass, that both Herod's mother, and sister, and himself likewise grew at odds with her, and in especial her husband, from whom only she expected no hard measure.

After her death the King began more powerfully to be inflamed in his affections: who before times, as we have declared, was already miserably distracted. For neither did he love after the common manner of married folk: but whereas almost even unto madness he nourished this his desire, he could not be induced by the too unbridled manners of his wife [12] to allay the heat of his affections, but that daily more and more by doting on her, he increased the same. And all that time especially he supposed that God was displeased with him, for the death of Mariam his wife. Oftentimes did he invocate her name, and more often undecently lamented he her. And notwithstanding he devised all kind of delights and sports that might be imagined, by preparing banquets, and inviting guests with princely hospitality, to pass away the time: yet all those profited him nothing. For which cause he gave over the charge and administration of his kingdom. And in such sort was he overwhelmed with

---

[11]Compare with "The Argument": "Mariam, who still bore the death of her friends exceeding hardly."

[12]Compare with 3.3.65: "Unbridled speech is Mariam's worst disgrace."

grief, that oftentimes he commanded his ministers to call his wife, Mariam, as if as yet she had been alive. Whilst thus he was affected: there befell a pestilence within the city, that consumed a great sort of people, and the better part of the nobility, and each man interpreted that this punishment was inflicted by God upon men, for the unjust death of the Queen. Thus the King's discontents being by this means increased, he at last hid himself in a solitary wilderness, under pretext of hunting: where afflicting himself incessantly, at last he fell into a most grievous sickness. This disease of his was an inflammation or pain in the neck: he seemed also in some sort to rave and wax mad: neither could any remedies relieve him of his agony: but when as the sickness seemed rather to increase, all men at last grew almost desperate of his recovery. For which cause his Physician, partly in respect of the contumacy[13] of his disease, partly because in so great a danger there was not any free election of diet, they gave him leave to taste whatsoever best pleased his appetite, committing the uncertain event of his health to the hands of fortune.

The Antiquities of the Jews
BOOK XV, CHAPTER XI, 400–01

> [A marginal note indicates that the events of this chapter took place in the year "before Christ's nativity, 28."]

Costabarus was an Idumean, and one of the greatest account amongst his countrymen, who was descended from the Priests of Cozas, whom the Idumeans esteem for a God. Now after that Hircanus had drawn the policy of the Idumeans to the reformed customs of the Jews, Herod was made King of the Jews, and appointed Costabarus to be governor in Idumea and Gaza, giving him Salome his sister to wife, after he had put Joseph to death, to whom she had been married before time, as we have heretofore declared. Costabarus seeing himself in this estate beyond his expectation, grew more elate and proud than his good fortune required, and in a little time forgot himself so far, that he thought himself dishonored if he should perform that which Herod commanded him, and scorned that the Idumeans should be under the Jews' subjection, notwithstanding they had received their manner of government

---

[13]Rebellious stubbornness, obstinate resistance.

from them. He therefore sent messengers unto Cleopatra, giving her to understand that Idumea had always been under her ancestors' subjection, and for that cause she ought upon just cause to demand and beg that country at Antonius' hands, and that in respect of himself he was ready to become her servant. All which he practiced, not to gratify Cleopatra in any sort whatsoever, but to the intent that if Herod's fortunes should be any ways weakened, he might more easily by this means both enlarge and obtain the kingdom of Idumea. And with these foolish hopes was he transported in regard of his birth and riches, which he had heaped together, by such dishonest means, as he continually practiced as he that intended no small matters. But notwithstanding Cleopatra's often and earnest petition to obtain this sovereignty, yet could she not obtain it at Antonius' hands. When Herod had notice of these covert and cunning practices, he was ready to kill Costabarus, but upon the earnest supplications of his sister and her mother, he dismissed and pardoned him, yet held him always in suspicion, by reason of this his practice. Not long after, it happened, that Salome fell at debate with Costabarus, for which cause she sent a libel of divorce to her husband, notwithstanding it were against the laws and ordinary customs of the Jews. For according to our ordinances, it is only lawful for the husband to do the same and as touching the wife, notwithstanding she were separated, yet is it not lawful for her to marry again, except her husband first give her license. But Salome without respect of the laws of the country, grounding herself too much upon her own authority, forsook her husband, saying that she separated herself from her husband, by reason of the great friendship which she bore unto her brother, for that she had received some notice that Costabarus practiced some innovation with Antipater, Lysimachus, and Dositheus. And this accusation of hers confirmed she by Baba's children, whom he had already kept with him in all security for the space of twelve years. All which was true, and at the time beyond all men's expectation wonderfully troubled Herod, as soon as he heard it. For as touching Baba's sons, he had heretofore resolved to cut them off, for that they had been always badly affected towards him and all his enterprises, but all that time he had let them pass, because by continuance they were grown out of his remembrance. Now the cause of this enmity and hatred which he bore towards them, was gathered from this ground. At such time as Antigonus enjoyed the sovereignty, and Herod besieged the city of Jerusalem with an army; now those incommodities and necessities that ordinarily happen unto those that are besieged were the cause that divers acknowledged Herod. and fixed their hopes upon him. But Baba's sons being in authority. and besides that. attended by a great number of men. persevered in their faithful observation of Antigonus. and blamed Herod continually. encouraging the inhabitants to continue the kingdom in those to whom in appertained by descent. and they themselves followed that course. which in their opinion was most profitably for the commonwealth. But after that the city was surprised by Herod. and he grew master of the estate. Costabarus. who was appointed to keep the city gates. and to lie in wait that none of those who were accused to have forsaken the King's side should escape. knowing that the sons of Baba were greatly esteemed and honored among the people. and foreseeing that their safety might be no small furtherance to himself. if at any time there might befortune any alteration:[1] he discharged and hid them within his own possessions: and notwithstanding that at that time he had protested to Herod by an oath. that he knew not what was become of them; yet though suspected of perjury. he concealed them. And afterwards when the king had by proclamation promised a reward to him that should discover them. and sought for them by all means. neither then also would he confess the fact. For being afraid least he should be punished for his first denial, he continued through concealment. being not only now driven thereunto by friendship. but also by necessity.

The Antiquities of the Jews
BOOK XVI. CHAPTER XI. 425

> [A marginal note indicates that the events of this chapter took place in the year "before Christ's nativity. 7."]

After this contention. Salome was hardly thought of. because she was judged to be the author of this ill report. The King's wives wished evil unto her. because they knew her to be of strange qualities and hard to please. and so variable. that according to the time. one while she would profess friendship. and presently after hatred. Wherefore they still had something to inform Herod of

---

[1]Whereas Cary's Constabarus conceals Baba's sons out of concern for them. Josephus's Costabarus conceals them to protect his own interests.

against her, taking occasion happening by chance, which was this.
There was a King of the Arabians, named Obodas, a slothful man,
and one given to idleness; and there was one Syllaeus that did govern all his affairs; this man was a crafty fellow, and in the prime of
his youth, and very beautiful. This Syllaeus coming unto Herod
about some business, and viewing Salome, who then sat at supper
with him, began to set his mind upon her; and finding she was a
widow, he entered into talk with her; and she finding of her
brother now not so friendly unto her as before he had been, and
also entangled with the beauty of this young man, did not greatly
deny to marry him; and many feasts being made at the time, they
showed evident signs of their mutual consent, and love one unto
another. The King's wives told the King of this in scoffing sort:
Herod herewith not contented, demanded of Pheroras how the
matter stood, and willed him at supper time to note if he could
espy any tokens of familiarity betwixt them. And Pheroras told
him that by signs and mutual viewing one another, they sufficiently showed their intents. After this the Arabian being suspected, departed into his own country. But two or three months after he came again into Judaea, only for this purpose, and talked
with Herod touching this matter, requesting him to let Salome be
his wife; affirming that that affinity would be profitable unto him
for the traffic between his people and the Arabians, whose Prince
he was to be, and did already enjoy a great part of the dominion.
Herod told all this unto his sister, and asked her if she would
marry him; and she answered, she would. Then they requested
that Syllaeus should become a Jew in religion, or else it was not
lawful for him to marry her. He would not condescend hereunto,
affirming that he should be stoned to death by his people, if he did
it; and so he departed without obtaining his purpose. From that
time forth, Pheroras, and especially the King's wives accused Salome of intemperancy, affirming that she had had the company of
the Arabian.

The Wars of the Jews
BOOK I. CHAPTER XVII. 589–90

But his private and domestical sorrows seemed to envy him his
public felicity, and most adverse fortune befell him through the

means of a woman, whom he loved as himself. For being now made
King, he put away his wife, which he first married (which was a
Lady born in Jerusalem, whose name was Doris), and married
Mariam, the daughter of Alexander, who was Aristobolus' son,
which caused troubles in his house, both before, but especially after
he returned from Rome. For he banished his eldest son Antipater,
whom he had by Doris, out of the city, only for his children's sake
that he had by Mariam, licensing him only at festival times to come
unto the city in regard of some suspicion of treason intended
against him. And afterward he slew Hircanus, his wife's uncle
(notwithstanding that he returned out of Parthia unto him), because after he suspected that he intended some treason against him:
whom Barzapharnes, after he had taken all Syria, took away prisoner with him. But his own countrymen that dwelt beyond Eu-
phrates, in commiseration redeemed him from thralldom: and had
he been counseled by them and not come unto Herod, he had not
been killed. But the marriage of his niece caused his death: for
that cause, and especially for the love of his native soil, he came
thither. That which moved Herod to kill him was, not for that he
sought the kingdom: but because he had right unto the kingdom.
Herod had five children by Mariam, two daughters, and three sons.
The youngest was sent to Rome to study, where he died. The other
two he brought up like Princes, both for their mother's nobility
sake, and for that they were born after he was King. But that which
above all was most forcible, was the love he bare to Mariam, which
from day to day tormented him more violently, in such sort, that he
felt not any part of those griefs which this his best beloved enforced
against him. For Mariam hated him as much as he loved her, and
having a just cause and color of discontent, moreover being em-
boldened by the love which he bore her, she every day upbraided
him with that which he had done unto Hircanus her uncle, and
unto her brother Aristobolus. For Herod spared him not although
he was a child, but after he had made him High Priest in the seventeenth year of his age, he presently put him to death after he had so
honored him, who when he came to the altar clothed in the sacred
attire upon a festival day, all the people wept, and the same night
he was sent into Jericho and drowned in like by the Galatheans,
who had received commission to perform the murder. These things
did Mariam daily cast in Herod's teeth, and upbraided both his

mother and sister, with very sharp reproachful words: yet he so loved her, that notwithstanding all this he held his peace. But the women were set on fire, and that they might the rather move Herod against her, they accused her of adultery, and of many other things which bore a show of truth, objecting against her that she had sent her portraiture into Egypt unto Antonius: and that through immoderate lust, she did what she could to make herself known unto him, who doted upon women's love, and was of sufficient power to do what wrong he pleased.

Hereat Herod was sore moved, especially for that he was jealous of her whom he loved, bethinking himself upon the cruelty of Cleopatra, for whose sake King Lysania and Malichius, King of Arabia, were put to death. And now he measured not the danger by the loss of his wife, but by his own death which he feared: for which cause being drawn by his affairs into the country, he gave secret commandment unto Joseph, his sister Salome's husband (whom he knew to be trusty, and one who for affinity was his well wisher) to kill his wife Mariam, if so be Antonius should have killed him. But Joseph, not maliciously, but simply to show her how greatly the King loved her, disclosed that secret unto her: and she when Herod was returned, and amongst other talk with many oaths swore that he never loved woman but her. "Indeed" (quoth she) "it may be well known how greatly you love me by the commandment you gave to Joseph, whom you charged to kill me." Herod hearing this which he thought to be secret, was like a madman, and presently persuaded himself Joseph would never have disclosed that commandment of his, except he had abused her. So that hereupon he became furious, and leaping out of his bed, he walked up and down the palace: whereupon his sister Salome having fit opportunity, confirmed his suspicion of Joseph. For which cause Herod growing now raging mad with jealousy commanded both of them to be killed. Which done, his wrath was seconded by repentance and after his anger ceased, the affection of love was presently renewed. Yea, so great was the power of his affection that he would not believe she was dead, but spake unto her as though she was alive, until in process of time being ascertained of her funeral, he equaled the affection he bore her during her life, by the vehemence of his passion for her death.

The Wars of the Jews
BOOK I. CHAPTER XVII. 592–93

. . . Pheroras, who was fellow with his brother of all, saving only the crown, and had his own revenues amounting to a hundred talents a year, and received all fruits of the whole country beyond Jordan, which was given him by his brother. Herod also had obtained of Caesar, to make him Tetrarch, and bestowed upon him a Princess for his wife, despousing unto him his wife's sister, after whose decease he despoused unto him his eldest daughter, and gave him three hundred talents with her for a dowry. But Pheroras fell in love with his maid, and forsook a Princess: whereat Herod being angry married his daughter unto his brother's son, who was afterwards slain by the Parthians: but Herod presently pardoned Pheroras' offence. Divers before this time were of opinion that in the lifetime of the Queen, he would have poisoned Herod: and Herod although he loved his brother very well, yet because many who had access unto him told him so, he began to misdoubt: and so examining many that were suspected, lastly he came to Pheroras' friends, and none of them confessed it. Yet they confessed that he was determined to fly unto the Parthians with her whom he was so in love withal, and that Costabarus, Salome's husband, was privy thereunto, unto whom the King married her after her first husband for suspicion of adultery was put to death. Salome herself also was not free from accusation, for Pheroras accused her that she had contracted matrimony with Syllaeus, who was procurator to Oboda, King of Arabia, who was a great enemy of the King's: and she being convinced both of this and all things else, whereof her brother Pheroras accused her, yet obtained pardon, as likewise Pheroras did: so the whole tempest of all their family was turned against Alexander, and light upon his head.

Othello *in Context*

Ethnography in the Literature of Travel and Colonization

What would Shakespeare's audience have thought of the description of Othello as "the Moor"? Both the play and the literature on Africa available in English in the early modern period show that "Moor" was often a synonym for "Negro." Two kinds of accounts of the Moors and North Africans were available to Shakespeare's audience: mythical travel literature inherited from such classical authors as Herodotus, Pliny, and Diodorus Siculus and more recent eyewitness accounts by seamen and traders who had traveled to Africa. While there were still many completely fantastical notions about non-European peoples such as Moors, Africans, and Turks, Leo Africanus's *History of Africa* enlightened sixteenth- and seventeenth-century European and English audiences about the peoples and customs of Africa.

This kind of writing, describing the physical features and social customs of a people, is called ethnography, a word derived from two Greek roots: *ethnos* ("nation") and *graphia* ("writing"). Rather than stressing the history of a people through time, ethnography reads as a timeless description of a people in geographical space. Not surprisingly, ethnography was deployed mainly to describe cultural "others," from the Scythians (the wild Northern Europeans of Book Four of Herodotus' *Histories*) to the "Ethiopes" of Philemon Holland's *History of the World*. Even within the British Isles, Spenser and other authors portrayed the Irish as barbarians because their language, customs, and religion were different from those of the English, who settled as colonists in Ireland.

Ethnography was also used to describe the people of the Caribbean. Columbus's description of the Caribes, or Canibes, gave rise to the word "cannibal." At the same time that Europeans traveled to and colonized the Americas, they also embarked on trade and took slaves in Africa. With the explorations of Portuguese navigators of the African coast came the exploitation of Africans as slaves in the plantations of the Caribbean. The British brought the first African slaves to Virginia in 1619. Leo Africanus himself was taken as a slave by Italian pirates. He was a learned man and was able to win his freedom through conversion, which he later recanted. His accounts and those of eyewitnesses began to change the view of Africa as a place of such fantastical creatures as "men whose heads / Do grow beneath their shoulders" (*Othello* 1.3.145–46) to a place of prosperous kings and traders.

Peter Martyr (1457?–1526)
Author

Italian humanist Peter Martyr (Pietro Martire d'Anghiera) came to the court of Isabella and Ferdinand of Spain some time after 1480. Martyr became part of an intellectual movement that celebrated the consolidation of the monarchy's power over Spain and their conquests in the Americas. Although Martyr deplored the interventions of the French in Italy, he celebrated Spanish exploration and colonization around the world in De Orbe Novo Decades *(1530). The style of this book reflects the tradition of travel writing and ethnography going back to Book 4 of Herodotus's* Histories *as well as Italian humanist letter writing as a method of disseminating information. Martyr himself never traveled beyond Europe, basing his accounts upon the reports of eyewitnesses.*

Richard Eden (1521?–1576)
Translator

Like Martyr, his English translator Richard Eden had a humanist education. Studying at Cambridge with Sir Thomas Smith prepared Eden for a life in government, in which he used his scholarship. He served as private secretary to Sir William Cecil in 1552 and gained a position in the English treasury of the Prince of Spain in 1554.

Eden added two eyewitness accounts of English voyages to Africa to his English translation of Martyr's work, Decades of the New World *(1555). Although two papal bulls had given a monopoly over the West African coast to the Portuguese, two English seamen defied the ban: Thomas Windham voyaged to Guinea in 1553 and John Lok to Mina (Elmina) in 1554–1555. The account of Windham's voyage is the source for the first excerpt here, a description of the court of Benin, a kingdom in what is now Nigeria. Eden introduces these two accounts with his own "brief description of Africa" and interjects his comments throughout the eyewitness reports, as in the next excerpted passage taken from "Second Voyage." Eden mixes his informants' observations with fanciful fables about the mythical Christian king of Ethiopia, Prester John, derived from medieval legend, and outlandish and bizarre ethnographic fictions, from Pliny's* Historia Naturalis. *Eden's accounts of Africa were later republished in Richard Hakluyt's monumental* Principal Navigations *(1589).*

from *Decades of the New World*

[The Court of Benin]

When they came they were brought with a great company to the presence of the king [of Benin]. who being a black Moor[1] (although not so black as the rest) sat in a great huge hall. long and wide. the walls made of earth without windows. the roof of thin boards. open in sundry places. like unto louvers to let in the air.

And here to speak of the great reverence they give to their king being such that if we would give as much to our Savior Jesus Christ. we should remove from our heads many plagues which we daily deserve for our contempt and impiety.

* * *

And now to speak somewhat of the communication that was between the king and our men. you shall first understand that he himself could speak the Portugal tongue. which he had learned of a child. Therefore after that he had commanded our men to stand up and demanded of them the cause of their coming into that country.

---

[1] Inhabitants of northwestern Africa (Morocco and Algeria). who were Islamic. From the Middle Ages to the 17th century. Europeans thought of the Moors primarily as blacks. and so the word became a synonym for Negro: hence the term "Blackamoor."

they answered by Pinteado[2] that they were merchants traveling into those parts for the commodities of his country for exchange of wares which they had brought from their countries, being such as should be no less commodious for him and his people.

[The People of Africa]

Now therefore I will speak somewhat of the people and their manners and manner of living, with also another brief description of Africa. It is to understand that the people which now inhabit the regions of the coast of Guinea, and the mid parts of Africa, as Libya the inner, and Nubia,[3] with diverse other great and large regions about the same, were in old time called Ethiopes and Nigrite, which we now call Moors, Moorens, or Negros, a people of beastly living, without a god, law, religion, or commonwealth, and so scorched and vexed with the heat of the sun, that in many places they curse it when it riseth.[4]

* * *

But to speak somewhat more of Ethiopia. Although there are many nations of people so named, yet is Ethiopia chiefly divided into two parts, whereof the one is called Ethiopia under Egypt, a great and rich region. To this pertaineth the Island of Meroe, embraced round about with the streams of the river Nilus.[5] In this island women reigned in old time. Josephus writeth, that it was

[2]Captain Antonianes Pinteado was a Portuguese mariner and guide whom Windham used as translator. Once a member of the King of Portugal's household, Pinteado was "forced by poverty" into England. Eden portrays Pinteado as "a man worthy to serve any prince most vilely used." Both Windham and the crew derisively called him "a Jew," and after Windham's death, Pinteado was made a prisoner and died on board ship.

[3]Nubia is in northeastern Africa. At its height the kingdom stretched from the first cataract of the Nile in Egypt to Khartoum in Sudan. During the time of the Roman Emperor Diocletian, the Negro tribe the Nobatae settled in Nubia. The Nubian kingdom was converted to Christianity in the 6th century. After the Moslems moved into Nubia in 1366, Nubia was divided into smaller states.

[4]Many Greek and Roman as well as early modern authors believed that Africans had black skin because of the intense heat of the sun. Sir Thomas Browne was one of the first to show this "common opinion" was an "error" in *Pseudodoxia Epidemica* (1646); see 6:10: "Of the Blackness of Negroes."

[5]When the Nubians were expelled from Egypt in the 7th century B.C., they moved their capital to Meroe, which the Ethiopians conquered in A.D. 350. The site of ancient pyramids, Meroe, is on the Nile in Northern Sudan.

sometime called Saba. and that the queen of Saba came from thence to Jerusalem to hear the wisdom of Solomon.[6] From hence toward the East reigneth the said Christian Emperor Prester John.[7] whom some call Papa Johannes. and others say that he is called Pean Juan (that is) great John. whose empire reacheth far beyond Nilus and is extended to the coasts of the Red Sea and Indian Sea. The middle of the region is almost in the 66 degrees of longitude. and 12 degrees of latitude. About this region inhabit the people called Clodii. Risophagi. Babilonii. Axiunite. Mosili. and Molibe. After these is the region called Trogloditica. whose inhabitants dwell in caves and dens. for these are their houses. and the flesh of serpents their meat. as writeth Pliny and Diodorus Siculus.[8] They have no speech. but rather a grinning and chattering. There are also people without heads. called Blemines. having their eyes and mouth in their breast. Likewise Strucophagi. and naked Ganphasantes: Satyrs also. which have nothing of men but only shape. Moreover Oripei. great hunters. Mennones also. and the region of Smyrnophara. which bringeth forth myrrh. After these is the region of Azania. in the which many elephants are found. A great part of the other regions of Africa that are beyond the equinoctial line. are now ascribed to the kingdom of Melinde.[9] whose inhabitants are accustomed to traffic with the nations of Arabie. and their kind is joined in friendship with the king of Portugal. and payeth tribute to Prester John.

The other Ethiope. called Ethiopia Interior (that is) the inner Ethiope. is not yet known for the greatness thereof. but only by the seacoasts. Yet is it described in this manner. First from the equinoctial toward the south is a great region of Ethiopians. which bringeth forth white elephants. tigers. and the beasts called Rhinocerontes.

---

[6]For the visit of the Queen of Sheba (Saba) to Solomon. see 1 Kings 10. See also *Antiquities of the Jews* by the Jewish historian Flavius Josephus (c. 37–c.100).

[7]The medieval legend of Prester John placed this Christian king in either Asia or Africa. Marco Polo said that Prester John ruled over the Tartars. and some European writers thought of him as King of a Christian kingdom in either Ethiopia or India.

[8]For Pliny. see *The History of the World* below. Diodorus Siculus (d. 21 B.C.) was a Sicilian author of a world history. including Ethiopia and North Africa. which is today considered unreliable.

[9]Said to be in Arabia. 90 miles from Persia (Introduction to Martyr's *Decades*).

Also a region that bringeth forth plenty of cinnamon, lying between the branches of Nilus. Also the kingdom of Habech or Habassia,[10] a region of Christian men, lying both on this side and beyond Nilus. Here are also the Ethiopians, called Ichthiophagi (that is) such as live only by fish, and were sometimes subdued by the wars of great Alexander. Furthermore the Ethiopians calleth Rhapsii, and Anthropophagi, that are accustomed to man's flesh, inhabit the regions near unto the mountains called Montes Lunae (that is) the Mountains of the Moon.[11] Gazatia is under the Tropic of Capricorn.[12] After this followeth the front of Africa, the Cape of Buena Speranza, or Caput Bonae Spei (that is) the Cape of Good Hope,[13] by the which they pass that sail from Spain to Calicut. But by what names the capes and gulfs are called, for as much as the same are in every globe and card, it were here superfluous to rehearse them.

Pliny the Elder (A.D. 23–79)

Pliny the Elder (Caius Plinius Secundus, A.D. 23–79) was a Roman naturalist from Cisalpine Gaul. His sole remaining work, the Historia Naturalis, *is an encyclopedia of natural science, divided into 37 books, dealing with everything from the nature of the universe to geography, anthropology, and a history of the arts. Like the Greek historian Herodotus, Pliny knew more about Egypt than he did about the rest of Africa and had to rely on stories and legends for his accounts. The European view of Africa and Africans as wild, exotic, and unnatural derives from such accounts as the following from Book 6 of* The History of the World *(1601), the English translation of Pliny by Philemon Holland. This passage was Shakespeare's source for Othello's description of the "Anthropophagi" (man-eaters) in* Othello *1.3.144–46.*

[10]Possibly Abyssinia, another name for Ethiopia. In the 4th century the king of Northern Ethiopia was converted to Coptic Christianity, but later, in 451, the Alexandrian patriarch refused to recognize the Ethiopian Christians as part of the Church. They believe that Christ has one nature in which his humanity is subsumed under his divinity.

[11]This fantastical passage comes from Pliny.

[12]The Southern Tropic.

[13]The southern tip of Africa, around which the Portuguese sailed to India.

from *The History of the World*

All Ethiopia in general was in old time called Aetheria, afterwards Atlantia, and finally of Vulcan's son Aethops, it took the name Ethiopia. No wonder it is, that about the coasts thereof there be found both men and beasts of strange and monstrous shapes, considering the agility of the sun's fiery heat, so strong and powerful in those countries, which is able to frame bodies artificially of sundry proportions, and to imprint and grave[1] in them diverse forms. Certes, reported it is, that far within the country eastward there are a kind of people without any nose at all on their face, having their visage all plain and flat. Others again without any upper lip, and some tongueless. Moreover, there is a kind of them that want a mouth, framed apart from their nostrils, and at one and the same hole, and no more, taketh in breath, receiveth drink by drawing it in with an oaten straw: yea, and after the same manner feed themselves with the grains of oats, growing of their own accord without man's labor and tillage, for their only food. And others there be, who instead of speech and words, make signs, as well with nodding their heads, as moving their other members. There are also among them, that before the time of Ptolomaeus Lathyrus king of Egypt,[2] knew no use at all of fire.

Furthermore, writers there be, who have reported, that in the country near unto the mires and marshes from whence Nilus issueth, there inhabit those little dwarves called Pygmies *** But then he [Dalion, the historian] telleth fabulous and incredible tales of those countries. Namely, that westward there are people called Nigroi, whose king hath but one eye, and that in the midst of his forehead. Also he talketh of the Agriophagi, who live most of panthers' and lions' flesh. Likewise of the Pomphagi, who eat all things whatsoever. Moreover, of the Anthropophagi, that feed on man's flesh. Furthermore, of the Cynamolgi[3] who have heads like dogs. Over and besides, the Artabatites who wander and go up and down in the forests like four-footed savage beasts. Beyond whom, as he saith, be the Hesperioi and Perorsi, who, as we said before, were

[1] Engrave.

[2] Ptolomeus Lathyrus (d. 81 B.C.), King of Ancient Egypt of the Macedonian dynasty.

[3] Dog-milkers.

planted in the confines of Mauritania. In certain parts also of
Ethiopia the people live off locusts only, which they powder with
salt and hang up in smoke to harden, for their yearly provision, and
these live not above 40 years at the most.

Leo Africanus (1488?–1552)

*Born in Moorish Granada in the late 1480s and educated in Fez, to which his
Moslem family fled in 1497, Al Hassan Ibn Mohammed (Leo Africanus) was
the first to write accurately about the interior of Africa. Captured by Italian pirates in the Mediterranean, he was at first enslaved and then presented to Pope
Leo X, who freed him once he had converted to Christianity. In Rome, Leo
Africanus learned Latin and taught Arabic. He wrote his history of Africa in
1526, but it was published in Venice only in 1550, when, according to one contemporary, Leo was living in Tunis, where he returned to his Moslem faith.*

*Encouraged by Richard Haklyut, who called Leo's work "the very best," John
Pory first translated it into English as A Geographical History of Africa in
1600. Leo's history, which first appeared in Italian, was already known in England through Latin and French editions. Sir Thomas Smith owned a French
translation, and Ben Jonson mentions Leo's work as a source for his Masque
of Blackness. According to Lois Whitney and Eldred Jones, strong circumstantial evidence suggests that Shakespeare knew Leo's Geographical History and that it provided the background material for references to Africa in
Othello and Antony and Cleopatra.*

*Pory prefaced his translation with Leo's biography, excerpted here, which
makes for fascinating reading. There are some parallels between Leo's life and
Othello's. A North African Moor, Leo had visited many parts of Africa but lived
much of his life in Italy. Leo was not only a scholar and traveler but also a soldier; as Pory relates, Leo "did . . . personally serve king Mahumet of Fez in his
wars." Like Leo who often recited poems and stories, Othello told his "travel's
history." Both Leo and many of the African kingdoms that he describes emerge
from his work as civilized, learned, and prosperous in contrast to the stereotyped
ethnographies, which had portrayed Africans as barbarous, ignorant, and poor.
While Leo's account of Africa was well known to Shakespeare's generation and
even the generation that followed, subsequent scholarship chose either to misrep-
resent it, as in Peter Heylyn's highly selective choice of uncomplimentary pas-*

*sages, or to ignore it, as in Samuel Coleridge's false assertion that "at that time
. . . negroes were not known except as slaves."*

from The History and Description of Africa
from John Pory's Preface

Give me leave (gentle readers) if not to present unto your knowledge, because some perhaps may as well be informed as myself: yet, to call to your remembrance, some few particulars, concerning this geographical history and John Leo the author thereof.

Who albeit by birth a Moor, and by religion for many years a Mahumetan: yet if you consider his parentage, wit, education, learning, employments, travels, and his conversion to Christianity, you shall find him not altogether unfit to undertake such an enterprise, not unworthy to be regarded.

First therefore his parentage seemeth not to have been ignoble, seeing (as in his second book himself testifieth) an uncle of his was so honorable a person and so excellent an orator and poet, that he was sent as a principal ambassador, from the king of Fez to the king of Tombuto.[1]

And whether this our author were born at Granada in Spain (as it is most likely) or in some part of Africa,[2] certain it is, that in natural sharpness and vivacity of wit, he most lively resembled those great and classical authors, Pomponius Mela, Justinus Historicus, Columella, Seneca, Quintilian, Orosius, Prudentius, Martial, Juvenal, Avicen, etc., reputed all for Spanish writers, as likewise Terentius Afer, Tertullian, Saint Augustine, Victor, Optatus, etc, known to be writers of Africa.[3] But amongst great variety which are to be found in the process of this notable discourse, I

---

[1] Timbuktu, near the Niger, with the Sahara to the north. Settled in 1087. Timbuktu was a center for trade and Moslem culture.

[2] Pory's hesitation is due to a passage in the Latin translation (Antwerp 1556) that can be translated as "Africa, unto which country I stand indebted for my birth." But in the original Italian edition, this passage simply states that Africa was his "nurse," where he spent the early part of his life.

[3] Pomponius Mela . . . Juvenal: Roman historians and rhetoricians: Avicen: the Arabic translator of Aristotle; Terentius Afer: a Roman writer of comedies, born in Carthage; Tertullian, Saint Augustine: the Church Fathers of late antiquity: Victorinus: a Neoplatonist convert to Christianity.

will here lay before your view our only pattern of his surpassing wit. In his second book therefore, if you peruse the description of Mount Teneves, you shall there find the learned and sweet Arabian verses of John Leo, not being then fully sixteen years of age, so highly esteemed by the prince of the same mountain that in recompense thereof, after bountiful entertainment, he dismissed him with gifts of great value.

Neither wanted he the best education that all Barbary could afford. For being even from his tender years trained up at the University of Fez, in grammar, poetry, rhetoric, philosophy, history, Cabala, astronomy, and other ingenuous sciences,[4] and having so great acquaintance and conversation in the king's court, how could he choose but prove in his kind a most accomplished and absolute man? So as I may justly say (if the comparison be tolerable) that as Moses was learned in all the wisdom of the Egyptians, so likewise was Leo, in that of the Arabians and Moors.

And that he was not meanly, but extraordinarily learned: let me keep silence, that the admirable fruits of his rare learning and this geographical history among the rest may bear record. Besides which, he wrote an Arabian grammar, highly commended by a great linguist of Italy who had the sight and examination thereof, as likewise a book of the lives of the Arabian philosophers and a discourse of the religion of Mahumet, with diverse excellent poems and other monuments of his industry, which are not come to light.

Now as concerning his employments, were they not such as might well beseem a man of good worth? For (to omit how many courts and camps of princes he had frequented) did not he, as himself in his third book witnesseth, personally serve king Mahumet of Fez in his wars against Arzilla?[5] And was he not at another time, as appeareth out of his second book, in service and honorable place under the same king of Fez, and sent ambassador by him to the king of Morocco? Yea, how often in regard of his singular knowledge and

---

[4]The University of Fez dated from the 13th-century Merinid dynasty. The Cabala, or Kabbala, was a system of occult wisdom and mystical interpretation of the Scriptures.

[5]Leo served the Sultan Mohammed VI, who reigned in Fez (1508–1527), both in war and in diplomacy.

judgment in the laws of those countries, was he appointed and sometimes constrained at diverse strange cities and towns through which he traveled, to become a judge and arbiter in matters of greatest moment?

Moreover as touching his exceeding great travels, had he not at the first been a Moor and a Mahumetan in religion, and most skillful in the languages and customs of the Arabians and Africans, and for the most part traveled in caravans or under the authority, safe conduct, and commendation of great princes? I marvel much how ever he should have escaped so many thousands of imminent dangers. And (all the former notwithstanding) I marvel much more, how ever he escaped them. For how many desolate cold mountains and huge, dry, and barren deserts passed he? How often was he in hazard to have been captived or to have had his throat cut by the prowling Arabians and wild Moors? And how hardly many times escaped he the lion's greedy mouth and the devouring jaws of the crocodile? But if you will needs have a brief journal of his travels, you may see in the end of his eighth book, what he writeth for himself. Wherefore (saith he) if it shall please God to vouchsafe me longer life, I purpose to describe all the regions of Asia which I have traveled—to wit, Arabia Deserta, Arabia Petrea, Arabia Felix,[6] the Asian part of Egypt, Armenia, and some part of Tartaria—all which countries I saw and passed through in the time of my youth. Likewise I will describe my last voyages from Constantinople to Egypt and from thence unto Italy, etc. Besides all which places he had also been at Tauris in Persia; and of his own country and other African regions adjoining and remote, he was so diligent a traveler that there was no kingdom, province, signory, or city, or scarcely any town, village, mountain, valley, river, or forest, etc. which he left unvisited. And so much the more credit and commendation deserveth this worthy history of his, in that it is (except the antiquities and certain other incidents) nothing else but a large itinerarium or journal of his African voyages, neither describeth he almost any one particular place, where himself had not sometime been an eyewitness.

---

[6]The ancients divided Arabia into three parts based on its principal location Petra, the desert, and the fertile area.

But, not to forget his conversion to Christianity, amidst all these his busy and dangerous travels, it pleased the divine providence, for the discovery and manifestation of God's wonderful works and of his dreadful and just judgments performed in Africa (which before the time of John Leo, were either utterly concealed or unperfectly and fabulously reported both by ancient and late writers) to deliver this author of ours, and this present geographical history into the hands of certain Italian pirates about the isle of Gerbi, situated in the Gulf of Capes, between the cities of Tunis and Tripolis in Barbary. Being thus taken, the pirates presented him and his book unto Pope Leo the Tenth, who, esteeming of him as of a most rich and invaluable prize, greatly rejoiced at his arrival and gave him most kind entertainment and liberal maintenance, til such time as he had won him to be baptized in the name of Christ, and to be called John Leo, after the Pope's own name. And so during his abode in Italy, learning the Italian tongue, he translated this book thereinto, being before written in Arabic. Thus much of John Leo.

[On the Customs of the African People in Libya]

Those five kinds of people before rehearsed, to wit, the people of Zenega, of Gansiga, of Terga, of Leuta, and of Bardeoa, are called of the Latins Numidae;[7] and they live all after one manner, that is to say, without all law and civility. Their garment is a narrow and base piece of cloth, wherewith scarce half their body is covered. Some of them wrap their heads in a kind of black cloth, as it were with a scarf, such as the Turks use, which is commonly called a turbant.[8] Such as well be discerned from the common sort, for gentlemen wear a jacket made of blue cotton with wide sleeves. And cotton cloth is brought unto them by certain merchants from the land of negros. They have no beasts fit to ride upon except their camels, unto whom nature, between the bunch standing upon the hinder part of their backs and their necks, hath allotted a place, which may

---

[7]Numidia, an ancient kingdom in North Africa, north of the Sahara, was at one time a province of the Roman Empire. Leo here gives a description of the Tuareg, a pastoral people on the western and central Sahara, now located in Algeria, Mali, and Niger. The alphabet of the Tuareg is related to ancient Phoenician script.

[8]Tuareg men traditionally wore dark blue robes and turbans.

fitly serve to ride upon, instead of a saddle. Their manner of riding
is most ridiculous. For sometimes they lay their legs across upon the
camel's neck, and sometimes again (having no knowledge nor regard of stirrups) they rest their feet upon a rope, which is cast over
his shoulders. Instead of spurs they use a truncheon of a cubit's
length, having at the one end thereof a goad, wherewith they prick
only the shoulders of their camels. Those camels which they use to
ride upon have a hole bored through the gristles of their nose, in the
which a ring of leather is fastened, whereby as with a bit, they are
more easily curbed and mastered, after which manner I have seen
buffles[9] used in Italy. For beds, they lie upon mats made of sedge
and bulrushes. Their tents are covered for the most part with coarse
chamlet[10] or with a harsh kind of wool which commonly groweth
upon the boughs of their date trees. As for their manner of living, it
would seem to any man incredible what hunger and scarcity this nation will endure. Bread they have none at all, neither use they any
seething or roasting: their food is camel's milk only, and they desire
no other dainties. For their breakfast they drink off a great cup of
camel's milk: for supper they have certain dried flesh steeped in but-
ter and milk, whereof each man, taking his share, eateth it out of his
fist. And that this their meat may not stay long undigested in their
stomachs, they sup off the foresaid broth wherein their flesh was
steeped: for which purpose they use the palms of their hands as a
most fit instrument framed by nature to the same end. After that,
each one drinks his cup of milk, & so their supper hath an end.
These Numidians, while they have any store of milk, regard water
nothing at all, which for the most part happeneth in the spring of
the year, all which time you shall find some among them that will
neither wash their hands nor their faces. Which seemeth not altogether to be unlikely: for (as we said before) while their milk
lasteth, they frequent not those places where water is common: yea,
and their camels, so long as they may feed upon grass, will drink no
water at all. They spend their whole days in hunting and thieving:
for all their endeavor and exercise is to drive away the camels of
their enemies: neither will they remain above three days in one
place, by reason that they have not pasture any longer for the suste-

[9]Buffaloes.

[10]Chamlet, a fabric made from a mixture of silk and camel's hair.

nance of their camels. And albeit (as is aforesaid) they have no civility at all, nor any laws prescribed unto them, yet have they a certain governor or prince placed over them, unto whom they render
obedience and due honor, as unto their king. They are not only ignorant of all good learning and liberal sciences, but are likewise altogether careless and destitute of virtue, insomuch that you shall
find scarce one amongst them all which is a man of judgment or
counsel. And if any injured party will go to the law with his adversary, he must ride continually five or six days before he can come to
the speech of any judge. This nation hath all learning and good dis-
ciplines in such contempt that they will not once vouchsafe to go out
of their deserts for the study and attaining thereof; neither, if any
learned man shall chance to come among them, can they love his
company and conversation, in regard of their most rude and de-
testable behavior. Howbeit, if they can find any judge, which can
frame himself to live and continue among them, to him they give [a]
most large yearly allowance. Some allow their judge a thousand
ducats yearly, some more, and some less, according as themselves
think good. They that will seem to be accounted of the better sort,
cover their heads (as I said before) with a piece of black cloth, part
whereof, like a vizard or mask, reacheth down over their faces, covering all their countenance except their eyes; and this is their daily
kind of attire. And so often as they put meat into their mouths they
remove the said mask, which being done, they forthwith cover their
mouths again, alleging this fond reason: for (say they) as it is unseemly for a man, after he hath received meat into his stomach, to
vomit it out of his mouth again and to cast it upon the earth; even so
it is an undecent part to eat meat with a man's mouth uncovered.

The women of this nation be gross, corpulent, and of a swart[11]
complexion. They are fattest upon their breast and paps, but slen-
der about the girdle-stead.[12] Very civil they are, after their manner,
both in speech and gestures. Sometimes they will accept of a kiss;
but whoso tempteth them farther, putteth his own life in hazard. For
by reason of jealousy you may see them daily one to be the death
and destruction of another, and that in such savage and brutish
manner that in this case they will show no compassion at all. And

[11]Dark.
[12]Waist.

they seem to be more wise in this behalf than diverse of our people, for they will by no means match themselves unto a harlot.

The liberality of this people hath at all times been exceeding great. And when any travelers may pass through their dry and desert territories, they will never repair unto their tents, neither will they themselves travel upon the common highway. And if any caravan or multitude of merchants will pass those deserts, they are bound to pay certain custom unto the prince of the said people, namely, for every camel's load a piece of cloth worth a ducat. Upon a time I remember that traveling in the company of certain merchants over the desert called by them Araoan, it was our chance there to meet with the prince of Zanaga: who, after he had received his due custom, invited the said company of merchants, for their recreation, to go and abide with him in his tents four or five days. Howbeit, because his tents were too far out of our way, and for that we should have wandered farther than we thought good, esteeming it more convenient for us to hold on our direct course, we refused his gentle offer, and for his courtesy gave him great thanks. But not being satisfied therewith, he commanded that our camels should proceed on forward, but the merchants he carried along with him and gave them very sumptuous entertainment at his place of abode. Where we were no sooner arrived but this good prince caused camels of all kinds and ostriches, which he had hunted and taken by the way, to be killed for his household provision. Howbeit we requested him not to make such daily slaughters of his camels, affirming moreover that we never used to eat the flesh of a gelt[13] camel, but when all other victuals failed us. Whereunto he answered that he should deal uncivilly, if he welcomed so worthy and so seldom seen guests with the killing of small cattle only. Wherefore he wished us to fall to such provision as was set before us. Here might you have seen great plenty of roasted and sudden flesh. Their roasted ostriches were brought to the table in wicker platters, being seasoned with sundry kinds of herbs and spices. Their bread made of mill and panick[14] was of a most savory and pleasant taste: and always at the end of dinner or supper we had plenty of dates and great store of milk served in. Yea, this bountiful and noble prince,

---

[13]Gelded, castrated.

[14]Varieties of millet, or grain.

that he might sufficiently show how welcome we were unto him, would together with his nobility always bear us company; howbeit we ever dined and supped apart by ourselves. Moreover he caused certain religious and most learned men to come unto our banquet, who, all the time we remained with the said prince, used not to eat any bread at all, but fed only upon flesh and milk. Whereat we being somewhat amazed, the good prince gently told us that they all were born in such places whereas no kind of grain would grow, howbeit that himself, for the entertainment of strangers, had great plenty of corn laid up in store. Wherefore he bade us to be of good cheer, saying that he would eat only of such things as his own native soil afforded, affirming moreover, that bread was yet in use among them at their feast of passover, and at other feasts also, whereupon they used to offer sacrifice. And thus we remained with him for the space of two days, all which time, what wonderful and magnificent cheer we had made us, would seem incredible to report. But the third day, being desirous to take our leave, the prince accompanied us to that place where we overtook our camels and company sent before. And this I dare most deeply take mine oath on, that we spent the said prince ten times more than our custom which he received came to.[15] We thought it not amiss here to set down this history to declare in some sort the courtesy and liberality of the said nation. Neither could the prince aforesaid understand our language nor we his, but all our speech to and fro was made by an interpreter. And this which we have here recorded as touching this nation is likewise to be understood of the other four nations above mentioned, which are dispersed over the residue of the Numidian deserts.

---

[15]Leo is saying that the prince gave them much more than they paid in tribute.

Edmund Spenser (1552?–1599)

In addition to writing some of the greatest English poetry, Edmund Spenser wrote a colonialist tract promoting England's subjugation of Ireland. Spenser first came to Ireland as secretary to Lord Grey de Wilton, Lord Deputy of Ireland, in 1580. Through government service, Spenser acquired his land and house in Kilcoman, property confiscated from Sir John of Desmond, an "Old English" aristocrat who had rebelled against English rule. The Old English had been Anglo-Normans who settled in Ireland in the twelfth century. In A View of the Present State of Ireland, Spenser writes about the customs of the Irish, among whom he finds the Old English to be the most troublesome because they have gone native and become "more Irish than O'Hanlon's breech." Drawing heavily on the ethnographic stereotypes of the medieval Topography of Ireland by Gerald of Wales, Spenser wrote his text as a dialogue between Irenius ("Peaceful"), a veteran of English service in Ireland, and Eudoxus ("Of good opinion"), a younger man who questions why English policy in Ireland has not worked. In the 1590s, when Spenser was writing this text, another Irish rebellion had broken out under the command of Hugh O'Neill. Spenser and his family were driven out of Kilcoman. Creating a view of the Irish as a separate race, Spenser compares Irish customs with those of Africans and Moors. The description of the Irish as barbarous prepares for the conclusion of the text in which he recommends a military solution to the colonization of Ireland. Though not published until 1633, A View of the Present State of Ireland was entered in the Stationer's Register in 1598 and circulated widely in manuscript.

from *A View of the Present State of Ireland*

EUDOXUS. Believe me, this observation of yours, Irenius,[1] is very good and delightful: far beyond the blind conceit of some, who (I remember) have upon the same word *Farragh*, made a very blunt conjecture, as namely Master Stanyhurst,[2] who though he be the same countryman born, that should search more nearly into the secret of these things, yet hath strayed from the truth all the heavens wide (as they say), for he thereupon groundeth a very gross imagi-

---

[1] Irenius, who has greater experience of Ireland than Eudoxus, has just asserted that the Irish battle cry "Ferragh" is from the Scottish word "Fergus," which means that the Irish are Scots. The 17th-century Irish language historian Geoffrey Keating points out in his *History of Ireland* that the Irish etymology of "Ferragh" is "faire ó" or "ó faire" ("take care").

[2] Richard Stanyhurst (1547–1618), a Dubliner and Catholic, wrote *Description of Ireland* in Holinshed's *Chronicles*, as well as *De rebus in Hibernia gestis*, in which he dismisses the Egyptian origin of the Irish war cry.

nation, that the Irish should descend from the Egyptians which came into that island, first under the leading of one Scota the daughter of Pharaoh, whereupon they use (saith he) in all their battles to call upon the name of Pharaoh, crying Ferragh, Ferragh.[3] Surely he shoots wide on the bow hand and very far from the mark. For I would first know of him what ancient ground of authority he hath for such a senseless fable, and if he have any of the rude Irish books, as it may be he hath, yet (me seems) that a man of his learning should not so lightly have been carried away with old wives' tales, from approvance of his own reason: for whether it be a smack of any learned judgment to say that Scota is like an Egyptian word, let the learned judge. But his Scota rather comes of the Greek *scotos*, that is, darkness, which hath not let him see the light of the truth.

IRENIUS. You know not, Eudoxus, how well Master Stanyhurst could see in the dark: perhaps he hath owls' or cats' eyes. But well I wot he seeth not well the very light in matters of more weight. * * * There be other sorts of cries also used among the Irish, which savor greatly of the Scythian barbarism,[4] as their lamentations at their burials, with despairful outcries, and immoderate wailings, the which Master Stanyhurst might also have used for an argument to prove them Egyptians. For so in scripture it is mentioned, that the Egyptians lamented for the death of Joseph.[5] Others think this custom to come from the Spaniards, for that they do immeasurably likewise bewail their dead. But the same is not proper Spanish, but altogether heathenish, brought in thither first either by the Scythians, or the Moors that were Africans and long possessed that country. For it is the manner of all pagans and infidels to be intemperate in their wailings of their dead, for that they had no faith nor hope of salvation. And this ill custom also is specially noted by Diodorus Siculus,[6] to have been in the Scythians, and is yet amongst the Northern Scots at this day, as you may read in their chronicles.

[3]The notion that the Irish were descended from the Egyptian Scota dates back to the 8th-century life of St. Abban and is repeated in the medieval Irish *Book of Invasions (Leabhar gabhála)*.

[4]Spenser claims both Irish and Scots are descended from the Scythians, described by Herodotus as a nomadic, barbarous people to the northwest of Greece.

[5]Jacob, not Joseph (see Genesis 50.3).

[6]Diodorus Siculus (d. 21 B.C.), a Sicilian author of a world history in Greek.

EUDOXUS. This is sure an ill custom also, but yet doth not so much concern civil reformation, as abuse in religion.[7]

* * *

EUDOXUS. It seemeth strange to me that the English should take more delight to speak that language than their own, whereas they should (me thinks) rather take scorn to acquaint their tongues thereto. For it hath ever been the use of the conqueror to despise the language of the conquered and to force him by all means to learn his. So did the Romans always use, insomuch that there is almost no nation in the world but is sprinkled with their language. It were good therefore (me seems) to search out the original cause of this evil: for, the same being discovered, a redress thereof will the more easily be provided. For I think: it very strange that the English being so many, and the Irish so few, as they then were left, the fewer should draw the more unto their use.

IRENIUS. I suppose that the chief cause of bringing in the Irish language amongst them was especially their fostering[8] and marrying with the Irish, the which are two most dangerous infections: for first the child that sucketh the milk of the nurse must of necessity learn his first speech of her, the which being the first inured to his tongue, is ever after most pleasing unto him insomuch as though he afterwards be taught English, yet the smack of the first will always abide with him, and not only of speech but also of the manners and conditions. For besides that young children be like apes, which will affect and imitate what they see done before them, especially by their nurses whom they love so well, they moreover draw into themselves together with their suck even the nature and disposition of their nurses: for the mind followeth much the temperature of the body, and also the words are the image of the mind, so as they proceeding from the mind, the mind must needs be affected with the words. So that the speech being Irish, the heart must needs be Irish: for out of the abundance of the heart the tongue speaketh. The next is the marrying with the Irish, which how dangerous a thing it is in all

---

[7] Irenius continues to discuss the Scythian, i.e., barbarous, character of Irish customs including going into battle naked, wearing glibs (masses of hair), and the women riding horses facing right in the "old Spanish and as some say African" fashion, drinking blood and speaking the Irish language.

[8] Gaelic custom of having children raised by clients, friends, or relatives to cement alliances.

commonwealths, appeareth to every simplest sense. And though some great ones have perhaps used such matches with their vassals and have of them nevertheless raised worthy issue, as Telamon did with Tecmissa, Alexander the Great with Roxanne, and Julius Caesar with Cleopatra,[9] yet the example is so perilous, as it is not to be adventured: for instead of those few good, I could count unto them infinite many evil. And indeed how can such matching but bring forth an evil race, seeing that commonly the child taketh most of his nature of the mother, besides speech, manners, and inclination, which are (for the most part) agreeable to the conditions of their mothers: for by them they are first framed and fashioned, so as what they receive once from them, they will hardly ever after forgo. Therefore are these evil customs of fostering and marrying with the Irish most carefully to be restrained: for of them two, the third evil, that is the custom of language (which I spake of), chiefly proceedeth.

Sir John Smith (1580–1631)

Sir John Smith (1580–1631) spent his youth as a merchant's apprentice and then, at his father's death, set off to travel. He fought against the Turks in eastern Europe and was enslaved for a time in Turkey. On returning to England, he invested in the Virginia Company in 1606 and was appointed a member of the government council for the Jamestown settlement. He is probably best known for the much romanticized story of his being rescued from captivity by Pocahontas, the Indian princess and daughter of King Powhatan. After years of sea voyaging, warfare, and exploration, Smith returned to England. Among his many works of travel writing are A Map of Virginia *(1612),* A Description of New England *(1616), and* The Generall Historie of Virginia, New England and the Summer Isles *(1624), from which the following passage describing the Barbary Coast (Tunisia and Morocco) is taken. Note Smith's mention of "that most excellent statesman, John de Leo"—further evidence of how well known Leo Africanus' history of Africa was in early modern England.*

---

[9]All examples of interracial or cross-cultural marriages: the Phrygian Tecmessa with Greek Ajax, the Bactrian Roxana with the Macedonian Alexander, the Egyptian Cleopatra with the Roman Caesar.

from *The General History of Virginia, New England and the Summer Isles*

Being thus satisfied with Europe and Asia, understanding of the wars in Barbary, he went from Gibraltar to Guta and Tanger, thence to Safee,[1] where growing into acquaintance with a French man-of-war:[2] the captain and some twelve more went to Morocco, to see the ancient monuments of that large renowned city. It was once the principal city in Barbary, situated in a goodly plain country, 14 miles from the great Mount Atlas and sixty miles from the Atlantic Sea, but now little remaining but the king's palace, which is like a city of itself, and the Christian church, on whose flat square steeple is a great brooch of iron, whereon is placed the three golden balls of Africa. The first is near three ells[3] in circumference, the next above it somewhat less, the uppermost the least over them, as it were, an half ball, and over all a pretty gilded pyramid. Against those golden balls hath been shot many a shot, their weight is recorded 700 weight of pure gold, hollow within, yet no shot did ever hit them, nor could ever any conspirator attain that honor as to get them down. They report the prince of Morocco betrothed himself to the king's daughter of Ethiopia, he dying before their marriage, she caused those three golden balls to be set up for his monument, and vowed virginity all her life. The Alfantica is also a place of note because it is environed with a great wall, wherein lie the goods of all the merchants securely guarded. The Juderea is also (as it were) a city of itself, where dwell the Jews. The rest for the most part is defaced, but by the many pinnacles and towers, with balls on their tops, hath much appearance of much sumptuousness and curiosity. There have been many famous universities, which are now but stables for fowls and beasts, and the houses in most parts lie tumbled one above another: the walls of earth are with the great fresh floods washed to the ground, nor is there any village in it, but tents for strangers, Larbes and Moors. Strange tales they will tell of a great garden, wherein were all sorts of birds, fishes, beasts, fruits and fountains, which for beauty, art and pleasure, exceeded any place

[1] From Gibraltar at the southern tip of Spain to Tangier in Morocco.
[2] A large sailing ship equipped for warfare.
[3] Twelve feet.

known in the world, though now nothing but dunghills, pigeon houses, shrubs and bushes. There are yet many excellent fountains adorned with marble, and many arches, pillars, towers, ports and temples, but most only relics of lamentable ruins and sad desolation.

When Mully Hamet[+] reigned in Barbary he had three sons, Mully Sheck, Mully Sidan, and Mully Befferes—he, a most good and noble king that governed well with peace and plenty, til his empress, more cruel than any beast in Africa, poisoned him, her own daughter, Mully Sheck his eldest son born of a Portugal Lady, and his daughter, to bring Mully Sidan to the crown now reigning, which was the cause of all those brawls and wars that followed betwixt those brothers, their children, and a saint that start up, but he played the Devil.[5]

King Mully Hamet was not black, as many suppose, but Molata, or tawny, as are the most of his subjects, in every way noble, kind and friendly, very rich and pompous in state and majesty, though he sitteth not upon a throne nor chair of estate, but cross-legged upon a rich carpet, as doth the Turk, whose religion of Mahomet, with an incredible miserable curiosity they observe. His ordinary guard is at least 5,000 but in progress he goeth not with less than 20,000 horsemen, himself as rich in all his equipage as any prince in Christendom, and yet a contributor to the Turk. In all his kingdom were so few good artificers that he entertained from England, goldsmiths, plumbers, carvers and polishers of stone, and watchmakers, so much he delighted in the reformation of workmanship he allowed each of them ten shillings a day standing fee, linen, woolen, silks, and what they would for diet and apparel, and custom-free to transport or import what they would; for there were scarce any of those qualities in his kingdoms, but those of which there are diverse of them living at this present in London. Amongst the rest, one Mr. Henry Archer, a watchmaker, walking in Morocco from the Alfantica to the Juderea, the way being very foul, met a great priest, or a

---

[+]Sultan of Morocco.

[5]A reference to the "battle of the three kings" (1578) in Alcazarquivir, in which the Moroccan sultan (whose army was victorious), his Portuguese-supported rival, and Sebastian of Portugal (a religiously fervent prince who led an army of mercenaries to disaster) all perished.

Sante (as they call all great clergymen) who would have thrust him into the dirt for the way. But Archer, not knowing what he was, gave him a box on the ear: presently he was apprehended and condemned to have his tongue cut out and his hand cut off: but no sooner it was known at the king's court but 300 of his guard came and broke open the prison and delivered him, although the fact was next degree to treason. * * *

Fez also is a most large and plentiful country, the chief city is called Fez, divided into two parts, old Fez, containing about 80 thousand households, the other 4,000 pleasantly situated upon a river in the heart of Barbary, part upon hills, part upon plains, full of people and all sorts of merchandise. The great temple is called Carucer, in breadth seventeen arches, in length 120 born up with 2,500 white marble pillars. Under the chief arch, where the tribunal is kept, hangeth a most huge lamp, compassed with 110 lesser: under the other also hang great lamps, and about some are burning fifteen hundred lights. They say they were all made of the bells the Arabians brought from Spain. It hath three gates of notable height, priests and officers so many that the circuit of the church, the yard, and other houses is little less than a mile and an half in compass. There are in this city 200 schools, 200 inns, 400 water mills, 600 water conduits, 700 temples and oratories, but fifty of them most stately and richly furnished. Their Alcazer or Burse is walled about: it hath twelve gates and fifteen walks covered with tents to keep the sun from the merchants and them that come there. The king's palace, both for strength and beauty is excellent, and the citizens have many great privileges. Those two countries of Fez and Morocco are the best part of Barbary, abounding with people, cattle, and all good necessaries for man's use. For the rest, as the Larbes, or Mountainers, the kingdoms of Cocow, Algier, Tripoly, Tunis, and Egypt, there are so many large histories of them in diverse languages, especially that writ by that most excellent statesman, John de Leo [Africanus], who afterward turned Christian. The unknown countries of Ginny and Binne[6] this six and twenty years have been frequented with a few English ships only to trade, especially the river of Senega, by Captain Brimstead, Captain Brockit, Mr. Crump, and

---

[6]Guinea and Benin, on the west coast of Africa.

diverse others. Also the great river of Gambra, by Captain Jobson, who is returned in thither again in the year 1626 with Mr. William Grent and thirteen or fourteen others, to stay in the country, to discover some way to those rich mines of Gago or Tumbatu,[7] from whence is supposed the Moors of Barbary have their gold, and the certainty of those supposed descriptions and relations of those interior parts, which daily the more they are sought into, the more they are corrected. For surely, those interior parts of Africa are little known to either English, French, or Dutch, though they use much the coast; therefore we will make a little bold with the observations of the Portugals.

---

[7]Timbuktu, near the Niger with the Sahara to the north, a center of trade and Moslem culture.

Othello
and The Tragedy
of Mariam *in Context*

Tracts on Marriage

The selection of texts on marriage for this Longman Cultural Edition are representative of a variety of genres. drawing on both biblical and humanist traditions. and emanating from a variety of institutions. The selection from the *Second Tome of Homilies* (1563) is a sermon that was read as part of the marriage ceremony in the Church of England. Largely based on St. Paul's letter to the Ephesians. the sermon expresses the Pauline concept of the husband as the head of his wife. analogous to Christ as head of the Church. This theological text contrasts in interesting ways with the humanist dialogue by Edmund Tilney. *The Flower of Friendship* (1568). in which the hierarchical relationship between man and woman is debated by a number of interlocutors. The Puritan author William Perkins' *Christian Economy* (1609) puts forward the notion of marriage as a matter of mutual responsibilities in a new Protestant ideal of companionate marriage. While sexuality is not condemned as an inferior state to celibacy. as it had been at times by the Roman Catholic Church. it is still fraught with dangers. even within marriage: as he writes: "even in wedlock excess in lust is no better than plain adultery." *A Bride-Bush* (1617) of William Whatley. like all of these texts. turns to the issue of the need for the wife to obey her husband. Such cultural preconceptions as the proper conduct of wives. the place of sexuality within marriage. and the relative power of husband and wife in marriage are all crucial in understanding both *Othello* and *Mariam*.

Secon∂ Tome of Homilie∂ (1563)

The full title of The Second Tome of Homilies *points to important details about the publication history, status, and use of this text in early modern England: "of such matters as were provided and entitled in the former part of homilies, set out by the authority of the Queen's Majesty. And to be read in every parish Church agreeably." This text was a continuation of* Certain Sermons, *or* Homilies *(1547), composed in the wake of Henry VIII's break with the Roman Catholic Church and published at the start of his son Edward VI's reign.*

The Church of England required all of its churches to keep a copy of this text along with the Bible and The Book of Common Prayer. *The Sunday service, at which attendance was mandatory right up until the English Civil War (1640s), included a reading from the* Homilies. *The* Second Tome of Homilies *was compiled under the direction of Archbishop John Jewel, the leading figure in the English Church in the early part of Elizabeth I's reign. Both books of homilies were used to enforce conformity to church doctrine, and to instruct both clergy and laity in everyday morality.*

This homily, or sermon, on marriage was read following the pledging of vows in the marriage ceremony. Widely known through church ritual, this text shows how the popular marriage tracts of the later sixteenth and early seventeenth centuries reinforce and sometimes modify the view of marriage promulgated by the Church of England.

from *The Second Tome of Homilies* (1563)
"The Sermon of the State of Matrimony."

The word of Almighty God doth testify and declare, whence the original beginning of matrimony cometh, and why it is ordained. It is instituted of God, to the intent that man and woman should live lawfully in a perpetual friendly fellowship, to bring forth fruit, and to avoid fornication, by which means, a good conscience might be preserved on both parties, in bridling the corrupt inclinations of the flesh, within the limits of honesty. For God hath straightly forbidden all whoredom and uncleanness, and hath from time to time taken grievous punishments[1] of this inordinate lust, as all stories and ages hath declared. Furthermore, it is also ordained that the Church of God and his kingdom might, by this kind of life, be conserved and enlarged, not only in that God giveth children by his blessing, but

---

[1] Has seriously punished.

also that they be brought up by the parents godly in the knowledge
of God's word. that this the knowledge of God and true religion.
might be delivered by the succession from one to another. that finally. many might enjoy that everlasting immortality. Wherefore.
forasmuch as matrimony serveth as well to avoid sin and offence as
to increase the kingdom of God. you. as all other which enter that
state. must acknowledge this benefit of God. with pure and thankful
minds. for that he hath so ruled your hearts. that ye follow not the
example of the wicked world. who set their delight in filthiness of
sin. where both of you stand in the fear of God. and abhor all filthiness. . .

Learn thou therefore. if thou desirest to be void of all these miseries. if thou desirest to live peaceably and comfortably in wedlock.
how to make thy earnest prayer to God. that he would govern both
your hearts by the holy spirit. to restrain the devil's power. whereby
your concord may remain perpetually. But to this prayer. must be
joined a singular diligence. whereof St. Peter giveth his precept saying: "You husbands deal with your wives according to knowledge.
giving honor to the wife. as unto the weaker vessel. and as unto
them that are heirs also of the grace of life. that your prayers be not
hindered.[2] This precept doth peculiarly pertain to the husband. For
he ought to be the leader and author of love. in cherishing and increasing concord. which then shall take place if he will use measurableness and not tyranny. and if he yield some things to the woman.
For the woman is a weak creature. not endued with like strength
and constancy of mind. therefore they be the sooner disquieted. and
they be the more prone to all weak affections and dispositions of
mind. more than men be. and lighter they be. and more vain in their
fantasies and opinions. These things must be considered of[3] the
man. that he be not too stiff. so that he ought to wink at some
things. and must gently expound all things. and to forbear. Howbeit. the common sort of men doth judge. that such moderation
should not become a man. For they say. that it is a token of woman-
ish cowardness. and therefore they think that it is a man's part to
fume in anger. to fight with fist and staff. Howbeit. howsoever they

---

[2] 1 Peter 3:7.
[3] On the part of. by.

imagine, undoubtedly St. Peter doth better judge what should be seeming to a man, and what he should most reasonably perform. For he saith, reasoning should be used, and not fighting. Yea, he saith more, that the woman ought to have a certain honor attributed to her, that is to say, she must be spared and born with, the rather for that she is the weaker vessel, of a frail heart, inconstant and, with a word, soon stirred to wrath. And therefore considering these her frailties, she is to be the rather spared. By this means, thou shalt not only nourish concord, but shalt have her heart in thy power and will. For honest natures will sooner be retained to do their duty, rather by gentle words, than by stripes. But he which will do all things with extremity and severity, and doth use always rigor in words, and stripes, what will that avail in the conclusion? Merely nothing, but that he thereby setteth forward the devil's work, he banisheth away concord, charity, and sweet amity, and bringeth in dissension, hatred, and irksomness, the greatest griefs that can be in the mutual love and fellowship of man's life. . .

Now as concerning the wife's duty, what shall become her? Shall she abuse the gentleness and humanity of her husband? And at her pleasure turn all things upside down? No, surely, for that is far repugnant against God's commandment. For thus does St. Peter preach to them: Ye wives be ye in subjection to obey your own husband.[4] To obey is another thing than to control or command, which they may do to their children and to their family. But as for their husbands, them must they obey, and cease from commanding, and perform subjection. For this utterly doth nourish concord very much, when she will apply herself to his will, when she endeavoreth herself to seek his contentation,[5] and to do him pleasure, when she will eschew all things that might offend him. For thus will most truly be verified by the saying of the poet: "A good wife by obeying her husband, shall bear the rule,"[6] so that he shall have a delight and a gladness, the sooner at all times to return home to her. But on the contrary part, when the wives be stubborn, froward, and

---

[4] 1 Peter 3:1.

[5] Contentment, happiness.

[6] According to John Griffiths, editor of *The Two Books of Homilies* (Oxford, 1859), the "poet" referred to may well be Erasmus, who makes a similar comment in his *Christiani Matrimonii Institutio* (Institution of Christian Marriage).

malapert.[7] their husbands are compelled thereby to abhor and flee from their own houses, even as they should have battle with their enemies. Howbeit, it can scantly[8] be, but that some offences shall sometime chance betwixt them. For no man doth live without fault, specially for that the woman is the more frail part. Therefore let them beware that they stand not in their faults and willfulness, but rather let them acknowledge their follies and say: "My husband, so it is, that by my anger I was compelled to do this or that, forgive it me, I hereafter will take better heed." Thus ought women the more readily to do, the more they be ready to offend. And they shall not do this only to avoid strife and debate, but rather in the respect of the commandment of God, as St. Paul expresseth it in this form of words: "Let women be subject to their husbands as to the Lord. For the husband is the head of the woman, as Christ is the head of the Church."[9]

Edmund Tilney (d.1610)
The Flower of Friendship

The Flower of Friendship *was one of the most popular Elizabethan texts on marriage, appearing in no less than seven editions between 1568 and 1587. The author presents contrasting views of marriage in the form of a lively dialogue imitating Castiglione's* The Courtier, *an Italian courtesy book (trans. Hoby, 1561). Tilney's dialogue occurs on two days, each devoted to the proper conduct of husbands and wives.*

The main sources are two humanist dialogues, Pedro di Luxan's Coloquios matrimoniales *(1550) and Erasmus'* Conjugiam, *translated as* A Mery Dialogue, declaring the propertyes of shrowde shrews, and honest wyves *(1557). These humanist authors provide the names for characters Master Pedro and Erasmus. Lady Julia represents the dominant view of marriage at*

[7] Intractable, contentious, disrespectful.
[8] Scarcely, hardly.
[9] Ephesians 5:22–23.

Reprinted from Edmund Tilney, Valerie Wayne (ed.), *The Flower of Friendship: A Renaissance Dialogue Contesting Marriage.* Copyright 1992 by Cornell University. Used by permission of the publisher, Cornell University Press.

the time, and her name derives appropriately from Eulalia, the "pleasantly speaking" ideal wife in Erasmus's text.

By 1559, the Pope had placed the works of Erasmus, a Catholic writer, on the Index of Prohibited Books. *One element that aroused the ire of theologians was his stance on the equality of married and celibate states.*

Tilney incorporates this humanist view along with another view of humanist origin, the value of companionate marriage. He contrasts these views with a number of dissonant perspectives, for example, the tradition of misogyny in Gualter, who complains about the shortcomings of women, and whose name may derive from the cruel husband of Chaucer's Clerk's Tale. *In Aloisa, an alternative medieval view is represented: skepticism about the possibility of passionate love in marriage. This character is based on Eloise, the medieval nun who espoused such views in her letters to her former teacher and lover Abelard. In the character of Isabella (Spanish for Elizabeth), who speaks about how women are as capable as men, Tilney may have presented a compliment to the Queen.*

Tilney was a remote cousin of Elizabeth I, to whom he dedicated The Flower of Friendship. *From 1557 to 1610, he was the Master of Revels, responsible for overseeing, censoring, approving and at times prohibiting the performance of plays. He did not marry until he was forty-seven, and then seems to have acted more on practicality rather than passion, choosing a wealthy and noble widow, Dame Mary Bray. In his dialogue, Tilney claims that wealth is far less important than virtue in the choice of a wife. In any event, his wife's wealth was ultimately of little help to him, since during her life and after her death he was unable to gain control of her property.*

from *A Brief and Pleasant Discourse of Duties in Marriage, called The Flower of Friendship* (London, 1568)

[Master Pedro speaks about the husband's duties in marriage]

And as I said before, the better to nourish, and maintain this Flower, there are certain delicate herbs that must of force be cherished, which be these. First to be advised in speech, courteous, and gentle in conversation, trusty, and secret in that, wherein he is trusted, wise in giving counsel, careful in providing for his house, diligent in looking to that which is his, sufferable of the importunities[1] of his wife, dangerous,[2] and circumspect in matters touching his honesty, and jealous in the education of his children. . . .

---

[1] Pestering annoyances.
[2] Chary, cautious, careful.

The sixth is that the married man accompany no defamed persons, and in any case, that he harbor them not. For many men blame their wives for ill life, when they themselves are the causers thereof for maintaining such companions, whereby he himself doth hardly escape infamy, and these good fellows do seek to creep into greatest friendship with the husband, to the intent they may have better opportunity with his wife. Yet may he use his tried friend, or near kinsman familiarly as well in his own house, as elsewhere, having always heard the old saying, that a man may show his wife, and his sword to his friend, but not too far to trust them. For if thereby grow unto him any infamy, let him not blame his wife, but his own negligence. . .

The eighth is to be circumspect in matters, that concern his honesty, and not to be jealous of his wife. The Stoic philosophers say that jealousy is a certain care of man's mind, lest another should possess the thing, which he alone would enjoy. There is no greater torment than the vexation of a jealous mind, which, even as the moth fretteth the cloth, doth consume the heart that is vexed therewith. Two kinds of persons are commonly sore sick in this disease, either those that are evil themselves, or they that in their youth have gone astray, supposing that as other men's wives have done towards them, so will theirs do towards others, which is vanity to think, more folly to suspect, and greatest foolishness to speak of. For as some lewd women be dissolute: so likewise women there be, honest, and very circumspect. If the wife be to be suspected, let the man work as secretly, and closely as he can to reprehend her, yet all will not peradventure avail. For, trust me, no wisdom, no craft, no conscience, no strength, no subtlety, yea, no patience sufficeth to enforce a woman, to be true to her husband, if she otherwise determine. Therefore I conclude to be jealous either needeth not, or booteth[3] not . . .

[From the second day: Lady Julia speaks about "the office, or duty, of the married woman."]

It is sure, quoth the Lady Julia, a hard matter for a virtuous wife to live with a vicious husband. For an honest woman to love a dissolute man, or a wise spouse to accept a foolish mate. Yet notwith-

---

[3]Helps or avails.

standing, how much more the husband be evil, and out of order, so much more is it the woman's praise, if she love him. And you men, as intractable as you be, yet is it not possible, if your wives do lovingly embrace you, though you cannot enforce your evil inclinations to repay love for love again, yet can ye not well hate them, which is no small matter. I could recite diverse worthy examples as well of Roman, as Grecian Ladies, that have so entirely affected their linked mates, that not only have they endangered themselves in great perils for their sakes, but have willingly spent their blood to die with them . . .

I could occupy you, quoth the Lady Julia, till tomorrow this time, with like stories of worthy women. But these may suffice, to show the love of the wife to her husband, and to let you understand also, Master Gualter, that there hath been always women as loving as men.

No doubt Madam, quoth he, ye love passingly,[4] when ye do love, and you hate as extremely, when you do hate. Wherefore it were a goodly matter, if you could bring your married women unto a mean.

Not so, quoth Lady Julia, I will have no mean in love. And when the woman hath thus grounded the perfect roots of love, and planted this *Friendly Flower*, in a faithful heart, she must be as curious as Master Pedro's good husband in preserving it against all tempestuous storms, and from all venomous weeds. The greatest help whereto is shamefastness, which is of such power, and virtue, that it sufficeth alone to defend it against all weathers. And if so be that there were but one only virtue in a woman, it might well be shamefastness. For as in a creature void of shame, there is nothing found worthy of commendation, so in the woman indued with that virtue is not anything worthy of reprehension,[5] and there is the root of godliness, where springeth the branch of shamefastness, which is the only defense that nature hath given to women, to keep their reputation, to preserve their chastity, to maintain their honor, and to advance their praise. How far are ye men overseen[6] when you only inquire of their beauty, substance, and parentage, leaving virtue beside, and the most excellent gift of shamefastness, which is the

---

[4] "Passingly" can mean both temporarily and exceedingly.
[5] Rebuke, reprimand, reproof.
[6] Deceived, deluded.

chiefest dowry, greatest inheritance, and the preciousest Jewel that a woman can bring with her.

There is another maintainer of this *Flower*, and that is the goodly grace of obedience. For reason it is that we obey our husbands. God commandeth it. and we are bound to do so.

I know not, quoth the Lady Isabella, what we are bound to do, but as meet it is, that the husband obey the wife, as the wife the husband, or at the least there be no superiority between them, as the ancient philosophers have defended. For women have souls as well as men, they have wit as well as men, and more apt for procreation than men. What reason is it then, that they be bound, whom nature hath made free? Nay, among the Achaians.[7] women had such sovereignty, that whatsoever they commanded their husbands obeyed. Yet Plutarch saith, that the man swept the house, dressed the meat, and did all other necessaries. where the women governing the house, and keeping the money. answered all matters, and which worse was, they corrected them at their discretion.

What did she, quoth Master Gualter, and might she beat him too? Mary lo. Here is the matter, that some of our Dames in this Country take so much upon them. They think belike that they be in Achaia. But sure if I had been amongst such women—

You would have done, quoth the Lady Isabella, as they did. For Dogs bark boldly at their own master's door.

Believe not daughter, quoth Lady Julia, neither those ignorant philosophers. nor these fond customs. For contrary also to this, the Parthians, and Thracians accounted not their wives, more than of slaves. so that after they had born them a dozen children, or more, they sold the mothers at the common markets, or exchanged them for younger.

Fye upon that law. quoth the Lady Isabella. But what say you to the custom which Dionysius Alicarnasseus, writeth of the Numidians, and Lydians.[8] where the women commanded within doors, and the men without.

---

[7]People of Ancient Greece

[8]Greek rhetorician and historian in Rome. Dionysius Halicarnassus died c. 7 B.C. In ancient times, the Numidians inhabited a country in North Africa, roughly the territory of modern Algeria; the ancient kingdom of the Lydians was in West Asia Minor.

Yea marie. quoth the Lady Aloisa, that was a just law, where the commanding was equal.

Not so. quoth the Lady Julia. For though it were better than the other two; yet not tolerable amongst us, neither was the sovereignty so equally divided, as you think. For if the woman keep always her house, as duty is, the man standeth ever at her commandment. For as long as she is within, though he command her without, this law bindeth her not to obey. Wherefore in my opinion all those Barbarian customs are to be disanulled, and contemned of Christians.[9]

Ye say well, Madam, quoth Master Erasmus. For in deed both divine and human laws in our religion giveth the man absolute authority over the woman in all places.

And. quoth the Lady Julia, as I said before, reason doth either confirm the same, the man being as he is, most apt for the sovereignty being in government, not only skill and experience to be required, but also capacity to comprehend, wisdom to understand, strength to execute, solicitude to prosecute, patience to suffer, means to sustain, and above all a great courage to accomplish, all which are commonly in a man, but in a woman very rare. Then what blame deserve those men that do permit their wives to rule all, and suffer themselves to be commanded for company.

A hard adventure, quote Master Gualter, hapneth to that man, which is matched with a masterly shrew. For she being once past shame, not only blabbeth out all, that she knoweth, but thundereth out that also, which her mad head conceiveth, or her fantastical brain dreameth of, and yet will she maintain that she is never angry, or speaketh without great cause.

There be, quoth the Lady Julia, some such women, but I do utterly condemn them. For this married woman, whom I have taken upon me to describe, must of duty be unto her husband in all things obedient, and therefore if he, sometimes moved, do chance to chide her, she must forbear. In doing whereof he shall neither eat the more at his dinner, nor she have the less appetite to her supper. The wise woman must consider that her husband chideth either without reason, or hath good cause. If reason move him, then of duty she is bound to obey, if otherwise, it is her part to dissemble the matter. For in nothing can a wife show a greater wisdom than

---

[9]Abolished and despised by Christians.

in dissembling with an importunate husband. Her honesty, her good
nature, and her praise is shown in nothing more than in tolerating
of an undiscreet[10] man, and to conclude, as the woman ought not
to command the man but to be always obedient, so ought he not to
suffer himself to be commanded of his wife.

Robert Cleaver, (1561 or 2–1614)

from *A Godly Form of Household Government: for the ordering of private families, according to the direction of God's word* (1598)

(STC 5387). 1: 189–92; 220–22

A household, is as it were, a little commonwealth, by the good government whereof, God's glory may be advanced, the commonwealth
which standeth of several families benefited, and all that live in that
family may receive much comfort and commodity. . .

In the days of Moses, husbands were easily and soon entreated
to forsake their wives, by giving them a Bill of divorce: yet so far
was this course from being lawful, that contrariwise, Jesus Christ
saith that it was tolerated only in respect of the hardness of the husband's hearts, who otherwise would have vexed their wives, and entreated them cruelly.[1]

And this libel, containing the cause of divorce, and putting away
of the woman, did justify her, and condemn the man. For seeing it
was never given in case of adultery (which was punished with
death),[2] all other causes alleged in the libel, tended to justify the

[10]Indiscreet.

[1]Matthew 19:8: "He saith unto them: Moses because of the hardness of your hearts
suffered you to put away your wives: but from the beginning it was not so."

[2]Leviticus 20:10: "And the man that committeth adultery with another man's wife,
even he that committeth adultery with his neighbor's wife, the adulterer and the
adulteress shall surely be put to death." Contrast this with John 8:4–7: "They say
unto him, Master, this woman was taken in adultery, in the very act. Now Moses in
the law commanded us, that such should be stoned: but what sayest thou? This they
said, tempting him, that they might have to accuse him. But Jesus stooped down, and
with his finger wrote on the ground, as though he heard them not. So when they continued asking him he lifted up himself, and said unto them, He that is without sin
among you, let him first cast a stone at her."

woman, and declare, that she was wrongfully divorced, and so condemn the husband, as one that contraried the first institution of marriage. Whereto Jesus Christ condemning this corruption, doth return the saying: It was not so from the beginning, and therefore whosoever shall put away his wife, except it be for whoredom, and marrieth another, commit adultery; and whosoever marrieth her, which is divorced, doth commit adultery with her,[3] so straight is the bond of marriage.

Hereof it followeth, that notwithstanding, whatsoever difficulties that may arise between the husband and the wife, whether it be long, tedious, and incurable sickness of either party; whether natural and contrary humors, that breed debate, wrangling, or strife, about household affairs; whether it be any vice, as the husband to be a drunkard, or the wife to be a slothful, idle or unthrifty huswife; whether either party forsake the truth, and profession of religion, do fall to idolatry or heresy. Yet still the bond of marriage remaineth steadfast, and not to be dissolved. Neither may they be separated, even by their own mutual consent. For as the Holy Ghost that pronounced: "That which God hath joined together, let no man put asunder."[4]

As the Church should depend upon the wisdom, discretion and will of Christ, and not follow what itself listeth, so must the wife also submit and apply herself to the discretion and will of her husband, even as the government and conduct of everything resteth in the head, not in the body.[5] Moses writeth that the serpent was wise above all beasts of the field,[6] and that he did declare in assaulting the woman, that when he had seduced her, she might also seduce and deceive her husband. St. Paul noting this, among other causes of the woman's subjection, doth sufficiently show, that for the

---

[3]Matthew 19:9: "And I say unto you, Whosoever shall put away his wife, except it be for fornication, and shall marry another, committeth adultery; and whoso marrieth her which is put away doth commit adultery."

[4]Matthew 19:6: "Wherefore they are no more twain, but one flesh. What therefore God hath joined together, let not man put asunder."

[5]Ephesians 5:22–24: "Wives submit yourselves unto your own husbands, as unto the Lord. For the husband is the head of the wife, even as Christ is the head of the church; and he is the savior of the body. Therefore as the church is subject unto Christ, so let the wives be to their own husbands in every thing."

[6]Genesis 3:1: "Now as the serpent was more subtle that any beast of the field which the Lord God had made. And he said unto the woman, Yea, hath God said, Ye shall not eat of every tree of the garden."

avoiding of like inconveniences, it is God's will, that she should be subject to her husband, so that she shall have no other discretion or will, but what may depend upon her head.[7] As also the same Moses saith: "Thy desire shall be subject to thy husband and he shall rule over thee."[8] This dominion over the wife's will doth manifestly appear in this, that God in old time ordained, that if the woman had vowed anything unto God, it should notwithstanding rest in her husband to disavow it.[9]

So much is the wife's will subject to her husband, yet it is not meant, that the wife should not employ her knowledge and discretion, which God hath given her, in the help and for the good of her husband. But always as it must be with condition to submit herself unto him, acknowledging him to be her head, that finally they may agree in one, as the conjunction of marriage doth require. Yet as when in a lute, or other musical instrument, two strings concurring in one tune, the sound nevertheless is imputed to the strongest and highest, so in a well ordered household, there must be a communication, and consent of counsel and will, between the husband and the wife, yet such, as the counsel and commandment may rest in the husband.

True it is that some women are wiser and more discreet than their husbands, As Abigail the wife of Naball, and others. Whereupon Solomon saith: "A wise woman buildeth up the house, and blessed is the man, that hath a discreet wife."[10] Yet still a great part of the discretion of such women, shall rest in acknowledging their husbands to be their heads, and so using the graces that they have received of the Lord, that their husbands may be honored, not contemned, neither of them, nor of others, which falleth out contrary, when the wife will seem wiser than her husband.

[7] 1 Timothy 2:14: "And Adam was not deceived, but the woman being deceived was in the transgression."

[8] Genesis 3:16: "Unto the woman he said, I will greatly multiply thy sorrow and thy conception; in sorrow thou shalt bring forth children; and thy desire shall be to thy husband, and he shall rule over thee."

[9] Numbers 30:13: "Every vow, and every binding oath to afflict the soul, her husband may establish it, or her husband may make it void."

[10] Proverbs 14:1: "Every wise woman buildeth her house; but the foolish plucketh it down with her hands." 19:14: "House and riches are the inheritance of fathers; and a prudent wife is from the Lord." 31:10: "Who can find a virtuous woman? For her price is far above rubies."

So that this modesty and government ought to be in a wife:
namely, that she should not speak but to her husband, or by her
husband. And as the voice of him that soundeth a trumpet, is not so
loud as the sound it yieldeth: so is the wisdom and word of a
woman, of greater virtue and efficacy, when all that she knoweth,
and can do is, as it were said and done by her husband.

William Perkins (1558–1602)

*William Perkins was a prolific Puritan author whose influence continued to be
felt long after his death in 1602. Educated at Christ's College, Cambridge, where
he was an active participant in theological controversies, he took a strongly Puritan line on matters of both ritual and morality, anxious to rid the English
practice of religion from the influence of Roman Catholicism. His* Christian
Economy, or A Short Survey of the Right Manner of Erecting and
Ordering a Family, According to the Scriptures *was written in Latin in
the 1590s and translated into English in 1609 by Thomas Pickering. The*
Christian Economy *was included in the three-volume edition of Perkins'*
Works *which appeared in no less than ten editions between 1609 and 1635. His
treatise on marriage is divided into separate topics, which are in turn examined
in terms of particular "cases" followed by "answers." That this form follows the
structure of texts of legal interpretation—for both canon and common law—in-
dicates that Perkins saw his work as analogous to, and even challenging, both
the institutions of church and secular law. In contrast to both forms of law, he
maintains that divorce can be sought on grounds other than adultery, including
not only desertion but even the spouses' hateful mistreatment of one another. His
wider interpretation of the grounds for divorce influenced the practice of the Puri-
tans in New England, where both men and women did seek divorce on such
grounds as desertion and cruelty.*

*While at times Perkins seems to promote an enlightened and egalitarian view
of marriage, at other times his positions are harshly authoritarian. Although he
values companionate marriage, he insists that its validity requires parental consent. On the one hand, he views sex in marriage for purposes other than procreation as morally neutral; on the other, he argues that "even in marriage excess in
lust is no better than plain adultery." And while he claims that men and women
are "equally bound to each other and have the same interest in one another's bodies," the "rejoicing and delight" of the body is "more permitted to the man than to
the woman."*

from *Christian Economy; or, A Short Survey of the Right Manner of Erecting and Ordering a Family; According to the Scriptures.*

[Translated by Thomas Pickering. London. 1609.]

Of the Communion of Married Folks, and of Due Benevolence
CHAPTER 10

The communion of man and wife is that duty whereby they do mutually and willingly communicate both their persons and goods each to other for their mutual help, necessity, and comfort.[1] Due benevolence must be shewed with a singular and entire affection one towards another, and that three ways principally. First by the right and lawful use of their bodies or of the marriage-bed, which is indeed an essential duty of marriage. The marriage-bed signifieth that solitary and secret society that is between man and wife alone. And it is a thing of its own nature indifferent, neither good nor bad.[2] Wherefore the Church of Rome erreth two contrary ways. First in that it maketh marriage to be a sacrament and so every action of it to be of its own nature good. Secondly in that they prohibit marriage of certain parties and the reason of the prohibition may seem to be this, that they think this secret coming together of man and wife to be filthiness[3] . . .

This coming together of man and wife, although it be indifferent, yet by the holy usage thereof, it is made a holy and undefiled action.[4] The word of God giveth direction to married folks in two ways. First by giving them warrant that they may lawfully do this action, because whatsoever is not done of faith (which faith must be grounded on God's word) is a sin. Secondly, by prescribing the right

---

[1] 1 Corinthians 7:3: "Let the husband render unto the wife due benevolence; and likewise also the wife unto the husband." Ephesians 5:33: "Let every one of you in particular so love his wife even as himself; and the wife see that she reverence her husband."

[2] Sexual intercourse.

[3] Priests and nuns took vows of celibacy. The Roman Catholic Church proclaimed at the Council of Trent (1563) that the celibate state was superior to the married state and to claim otherwise was wrong.

[4] Hebrews 13:4: "Marriage is honorable in all, and the bed undefiled; but whoremongers and adulterers God will judge."

and holy manner of doing the same. The holy manner stands in these particulars. First, that it be done in moderation. For even in wedlock excess in lusts is no better than plain adultery before God . . . Secondly, that it be used in an holy abstinence . . . while the woman is in her flowers:[5] secondly, in the time of a solemn fast, when some grievous calamity is imminent . . . Next unto the word, this action may be sanctified by prayer, and a blessing upon it.

Children are the gift of God, and therefore married folks are not only to use means but also to pray for the obtaining of them. Now the fruits, which are reaped and enjoyed by this holy usage of the marriage bed are three: I. The having of a blessed seed.[6] II. The preservation of the body in cleanness, that it may be a fit temple for the Holy Ghost to dwell in.[7] III. The holy estate of marriage is a lively type of Christ and his church, and this communion of married persons is also a figure of the conjunction that is between him and the faithful.[8]

Here some questions are to be resolved. Case I. Whether may marriage be dissolved in the case of barrenness? Answer: No. For barrenness is an hidden infirmity for the most part and which God hath many times cured, even when it seemed to be desperate, as in Sarah. Again, the fruit of the womb is God's blessing, and wholly dependeth upon him. He therefore that in want of children rejecteth his wife whom he hath received at the hands of God, offereth wrong even to God himself.

Case II. What if either of the married folks commit fornication or any sin of the same kind greater than fornication, as incest, sodomy, lying with beasts or such like. Answer: Adultery and fornication are most grievous and therefore when they are certainly

---

[5]The married couple is to refrain from intercourse when the wife is having her period.

[6]The text cites Deuteronomy 28:1, but the reference is actually to 28:4: "Blessed shall be the fruit of thy body."

[7]1 Thessalonians 4:3–4: "For this is the will of God, even your sanctification, that ye should abstain from fornication. That every one of you should know how to possess his vessel in sanctification and honor."

[8]Ephesians 5:23: "For the husband is the head of the wife, even as Christ is the head of the church: and he is the savior of the body." Hosea 2:19: "And I will betroth thee unto me for ever: yea, I will betroth thee unto me in righteousness, and in judgment, and in loving kindness, and in mercies."

known by such persons. they are at no hand to be winked at. but the
magistrate is presently to be informed of them. Howbeit. if the innocent party be willing to receive the adulterer again in regard of his
repentance. lest he should seem to favor and maintain sin. and to be
himself a practicer of uncleanness. he is to repair to the congrega-
tion. and declare the whole matter to the minister. that he may understand the party's repentance and desire of forgiveness. And if the
adulteress hath conceived and is in travail. the husband. to avoid
the imputation of having an heir in bastardy. is to make relation to
the church of the repentance of the adulteress or to acquaint some
certain persons therewith not to the end that she should be punished
for the fact. but that they may take notice of a child conceived in
adultery. whom afterwards he may lawfully put off. as none of his.
The matter being known. the innocent party may require a divorcement. For adultery is such a sin as doth quite break off not only the
use but the bond and covenant of marriage.[9] And yet the same bond
may be continued and grow up again by the good will and consent
of the party innocent and consequently they may be reconciled and
dwell together still.

Now in requiring a divorce. there is an equal right and power in
both parties. so as the woman may require it as well as the man: and
he as well as she. The reason is because they are equally bound each
to other and have also the same interest in one another's body. provided always that the man is to maintain his superiority and the
woman to observe that modesty which beseemeth her towards the
man. . .

So much for the first way of performance of due benevolence.
The second way is by cherishing one another. The cherishing is the
performing of any duties that tend to the preserving of the lives one
of another. Wherefore they are freely to communicate their goods.
their counsel. their labors each to other. for the good of themselves
and theirs.

The third way is by an holy kind of rejoicing and solacing themselves each with other in a mutual declaration of the signs and to-

[9]Matthew 19:9: "And I say to you whoever shall put away his wife. except it be for
fornication. and shall marry another committeth adultery: and whoso marrieth her
which is put away doth commit adultery."

kens of love and kindness.[10] This rejoicing and delight is more permitted to the man than to the woman; and to them both, more in their young years than in their old age.

William Whatley (1583–1639)
from *A Bride-Bush*

William Whatley, a vicar of strong Puritan leaning, called "the Roaring Boy of Banbury" for his indefatigable style of preaching, wrote a dozen tracts on moral and religious topics. A Bride-Bush *(1617), the most famous, raised controversy in the church for arguing that adultery and desertion dissolve the bond of marriage. He later disavowed this position, retracting it before the high commission in 1621, and making amends with a subsequent tract on marriage entitled* A Care-Cloth *(1624). This passage from* A Bride-Bush *spells out just how far women have to go in obeying their husbands.*

from *A Bride-Bush,* or
A Wedding Sermon: compendiously describing the duties of married persons (1617)
STC 25296. 42–43.

Let the wife be subject to her husband in all things, in the Lord [Ephesians 5:22]. What need we further proof? Why is she his wife, if she will not obey? And how can she require obedience of the children and servants, if she will not yield to the husband? Doth not she exact it in his name, and as his deputy? But the thing will not be so much questioned, as the measure: not whether she must obey, but how far. Wherefore we must extend it as far as the Apostle, to a generality of thing, to all things, so it be in the Lord. In whatsoever thing obeying of him doth not disobey God, she must obey: and if not in all things, it were as good as nothing. It is a thankless service

---

[10]Genesis 26:8: "And it came to pass, when he had been there a long time, that Abimelech king of the Philistines looked out at a window, and saw, and, behold, Isaac was sporting with Rebekah his wife." Proverbs 5:18–19: "Let thy fountain be blessed: and rejoice with the wife of thy youth. Let her be as the loving hind and the pleasant roe; let her breasts satisfy thee at all times; and be thou always ravished with her love."

if not general. To yield alone in things that please herself, is not to
obey him, but her own affections. The trial of obedience is when it
crossesth her desires. To do that which he bids, when she would
have done without his bidding, what praise is it? But this declares
conscionable submission, when she chooseth to do what herself
would not, because her husband wills it. And seeing she requireth
the like largesse of duty in his name from the servants, herself shall
be judge against herself, if she give not what she looks to receive.
But it sufficeth not that her obedience reach to all things that are
lawful, unless it be also willing, ready, without brawling, contend-
ing, thwarting, sourness. A good work may be marred in the manner of doing. And as good stuff is spilt by bad making, so doth the
wife disgrace and disfigure her obedience if she hang off and con-
tend, and be impatient, and will not, till she cannot choose. Needs
must, needs shall, we say in the proverb. Such kind of yielding declares no reverence, deserves no praise. Then it is laudable, com-
mendable, a note of a virtuous woman, a dutiful wife, when she
submits herself with quietness, cheerfully, even as a well-broken
horse turns at the least turning, stands at the least check of the
rider's bridle, readily going and standing as he wishes that sits upon
his back. If you will have your obedience worth anything, make no
tumult about it outwardly, allow none within.

An Excerpt from the First Biography of Elizabeth Cary

The Lady Falkland: Her Life is the first known biography of an Englishwoman by a woman. The text survives in a manuscript located in the Archives of the Départment du Nord in Lille, France, a collection that contains documents from the Benedictine monastery of Our Blessed Lady of Consolation in Cambray, where four of Elizabeth Cary's six daughters became Benedictine nuns. Heather Wolfe, editor of the most recent critical edition of the *Life* (2001), has discerned four different hands in the manuscript—those of Anne, Mary, Elizabeth, and Lucy Cary. This collaborative work was composed in 1645. Later in 1649, their brother Patrick added his own emendations to the text.

The passage reprinted here, from the first half of the biography, highlights Elizabeth Cary's intellectual precociousness, theological questioning, obedience to her husband, devotion to her children, and, above all, her strong spiritual life despite her many trials. One of the most palpable expressions of Cary's spirituality was her philanthropy in Ireland. When her husband was Lord Deputy there (1622–29), Elizabeth set up a trade school to help poor children. In a characteristically seventeenth-century God-centered view of life, Cary, according to her daughter, viewed the failure of the enterprise as God's punishment for the forced conversion of the children from Catholicism to Protestantism. Although the selection here stops short of Cary's own conversion from Protestantism to Catholicism, her daughter writes from the perspective of that change as the defining event of her mother's spiritual life.

from *The Lady Falkland Her Life*

Her mother's name was Elizabeth Symondes. She was their only child. She was christened Elizabeth. She learnt to read very soon and loved it much. When she was but four or five year old they put her to learn French, which she did about five weeks and, not profiting at all, gave it over. After, of herself, without a teacher, whilst she was a child, she learnt French, Spanish, Italian, which she always understood very perfectly. She learnt Latin in the same manner (without being taught) and understood it perfectly when she was young, and translated the Epistles of Seneca out of it into English: after having long discontinued it, she was much more imperfect in it, so as a little afore her death, translating some (intending to have done it all had she lived) of Blosius[1] out of Latin, she was fain to help herself somewhat with the Spanish translation. Hebrew she likewise, about the same time, learnt with very little teaching: but for many year neglecting it, she lost it much: yet not long before her death, she again beginning to use it, could in the Bible understand well, in which she was most perfectly well read. She then learnt also, of a Transylvanian, his language, but never finding any use of it, forgot it entirely. She was skilful and curious in working,[2] ⟨but⟩ never having been helped by anybody: those that knew her would never have believed she knew how to hold a needle unless they had seen it.

Being once present when she was ⟨about⟩ ten year old, when a poor old woman was brought before her father for a witch, and, being accused for having bewitched two or 3 to death, the witness not being found convincing, her father asked the woman what she said for herself? She falling down before him trembling and weeping confessed all to be true, desiring him to be good to her and she

---

[1] Louis de Blois (1506–66). Benedictine mystic and author of devotional works such as *Institutio Spiritualis* ("Spiritual Instruction") and *Consolatio Pusillanimium* ("Comfort for the Fainthearted").

[2] Needleworking. In the next phrase and onward, angle brackets indicate likely readings of illegible words in the manuscript.

would mend. Then he asking her particularly, did you bewitch such a one to death? she answered yes. He asked her how she did it? One of her accusers, preventing her, said, "Did not you send your familiar in the shape of a black dog, a hare or a ⟨toad?⟩ cat, and he finding him asleep, licked his hand, or breathed on him, or stepped over him, and he presently came home sick and languished away?" She, quaking, begging pardon, acknowledged all, and the same of each particular accusation, with a several manner of doing it. Then the standers-by said, what would they have more than her own confession? But the child, seeing the poor woman in so terrible a fear, and in so simple a manner confess all, thought fear had made her idle,[3] so she whispered her father and desired him to ask her whether she had bewitched to death Mr John Symondes of such a place (her uncle that was one of the standers-by). He did so, to which she said yes, just as she had done to the rest, promising to do so no more if they would have pity on her. He asked how she did it? She told one of her former stories; then (all the company laughing) he asked her what she ailed to say so? told her the man was alive, and stood there. She cried, "Alas, sir, I knew him not, I said so because you asked me." Then he, "Are you no witch then?" ⟨(says he)⟩ "No, God knows," says she. "I know no more what belongs to it than the child newborn." "Nor did you never see the devil?" She answered, "No, God bless me, never in all my life." Then he examined her what she meant to confess all this, if it were false? She answered they had threatened her if she would not confess, and said, if she would, she should have mercy showed her—which she said with such simplicity that (the witness brought against her being of little force, and her own confession appearing now to be of less) she was easily believed innocent, and [ac]quitted.

She having neither brother nor sister, nor other companion of her age, spent her whole time in reading: to which she gave herself so much that she frequently read all night: so as her mother was fain to forbid her servants to let her have candles, which command they turned to their own profit, and let themselves be hired by her to let her have them, selling them to her at half a crown apiece, so was she bent to reading: and she not having money so free, was to owe it them, and in this fashion was she in debt a hundred pound afore she

[3]Delirious.

was twelve year old. which with two hundred more ⟨afore⟩ for the like bargains and promises she paid on her wedding day: this will not seem strange to those that knew her well. When she was twelve year old. her father (who loved much to have her read. and she as much to please him) gave her Calvin's *Institutions*[4] and bid her read it. against which she made so many objections. and found in him so many contradictions. and with all of them she still went to her father. that he said. "This girl hath a spirit averse from Calvin."

At fifteen year old. her father married her to one Sir Harry Cary (son to Sir Edward Cary of Barkhamsteed in Harfordshire). then Master of the Jewel House to Queen Elizabeth. He married her only for being an heir. for he had no acquaintance with her (she scarce ever having spoke to him) and she was nothing handsome. though then very fair. The first year or more she lived at her own father's: her husband about that time went into Holland. leaving her ⟨there⟩ still with her own friends.[5] He. in the time they had been married. had been for the most part at the court or his father's house. from her. and ⟨so⟩ had heard her speak little. and those letters he had received from her had been indited by others. by her mother's appointment. so he knew her then very little.

Soon after his being gone. his mother must needs have her to her. and. her friends not being able to satisfy the mother-in-law with any excuse. were fain to send her: though her husband had left her with them till his return. knowing his own mother well. and desiring (though he did not care for his wife) to have her be where she should be best content. Her mother-in-law having her. and being one that loved much to be humored. and finding her not to apply herself to it. used her very hardly. so far. as at last. to confine her to her chamber: which seeing she little cared for. but entertained herself with reading. the mother-in-law took away all her books. with command to have no more brought her: then she set herself to make verses. There was only two in the whole house (besides her own servants) that ever came to see her. which they did by stealth: one of her husband's sisters and a gentlewoman that waited on her mother-in-law. (To the first of them. she always. all her life after.

---

[4]*Institutes of the Christian Religion* (1536) defines the central doctrines of Calvinist theology. including moral election and predestination for redemption.
[5]Relatives.

showed herself a very true friend in all occasions wheresoever she was able ⟨to⟩: of the other (being gone from her mother-in-law's service) she never gave over to take care till she died, she [the gentlewoman] having continual recourse to her when she had need, who ever provided her places with her children or friends, and helped her in the meantime.) But her husband returning (who had been taken prisoner in the Low Countries by the Spaniards, and carried prisoner into Spain, where he was kept a year whilst his father was raising his ransom),[6] all this was soon at an end, he being much displeased to see her so used.

In his absence he had received some letters from her, since she came from her mother, which seemed to him to be in a very different style from the former, which he had thought to have been her own. These he liked much, but believed some other did them, till, having examined her about it and found the contrary, he grew better acquainted with her and esteemed her more. From this time she writ many things for her private recreation, on several subjects, and occasions, all in verse (out of which she scarce even writ anything that was not translations). One of them was after stolen out of that sister-in-law's (her friend's) chamber and printed, but by her own procurement was called in. Of all she then writ, that which was said to be the best was the life of Tamberlaine in verse.[7]

She continued to read much, and when she was about twenty year old, through reading, she grew into much doubt of her religion. The first occasion of it was reading a Protestant book much esteemed, called Hooker's *Ecclesiastical Polity*:[8] It seemed to her, he left her hanging in the air, for having brought her so far (which she thought he did very reasonably), she saw not how, nor at what, she could stop, till she returned to the church from whence they were come. This was more confirmed in her by a brother of her husband's returning out of Italy, with a good opinion of Catholic religion. His wit, judgment and ⟨company⟩ conversation she was much pleased withal. He was a great reader of the Fathers, especially

[6]Spanish troops captured Henry Cary in October 1605, when he was fighting with a joint English-Dutch force.

[7]Tamerlane (1336–1405), the Mongol military leader whose conquests are the subject of Christopher Marlowe's *Tamberlaine the Great*, Parts I and II (1587–1588).

[8]Richard Hooker wrote *Of the Laws of Ecclesiastical Polity* (Books 1–4, 1593; Book 5, 1597) to defend the bishops of the Church of England.

St Augustine, whom he affirmed to be of the religion of the Church of Rome. He persuaded her to read the Fathers also (what she had read till then having been for the most part poetry and history, except Seneca, and some other such, whose Epistles it is probable she translated afore she left her father's house, because the only copy of it was found by her son in her father's study)—which she did upon his persuasion, all that she could meet with in French, Spanish or Italian. It may be she might then read some in Latin, but for many year only in the others.

Her distrust of her religion increased by reading them, so far as that at two several times she refused to go to church for a long while together. The first time she satisfied herself she might continue as she was, having a great mind to do so. The second time, going much to the house of a Protestant bishop,[9] which was frequented by many of the learnedest of their divines (out of the number of whose chaplains, those of the King's were frequently chosen, and some of their greatest bishops), she there grew acquaint[ed] with many of them, making great account of them, and using them with much respect (being ever more inclined to do so to any for their learning and worth, than for their greatness of quality, and she had learnt in the Fathers, and histories of former Christian times to bear a high reverence to the dignity they pretended to). By them she was persuaded she might lawfully remain as she was, she never making question for all that but that to be in the Roman Church were infinitely better and securer. Thus (from the first) she remained about two and twenty year, flattering herself with good intentions. She was in the house of the same bishop divers times present at the examination of such beginners, or receivers, of new opinions, as were by them esteemed heretics, where some (strangers to her), wondering to see her, asked the bishop how he durst trust that young lady to be there? who answered, he would warrant she would never be in danger to be an heretic, so much honor and adherence did she ever render to authority, where she (conceived) imagined it to be, much more where she knew it to be.

She was married seven year without any child; after, had eleven born alive.[10] When she had some children, she and her husband

---

[9]Richard Neile, dean of Westminster (1605) and archbishop of York (1631).

[10]She had five sons and six daughters.

went to keep house by themselves, where she, taking the care of her family, which at first was but little, did seem to show herself capable of what she would apply herself to. She was very careful and diligent in the disposition of the affairs of her house of all sorts; and she herself would work hard, together with her women and her maids, curious pieces of work, teaching them and directing all herself; nor was her care of her children less, to whom she was so much a mother that she nursed them all herself, but only her eldest son[11] (whom her father took from her to live with him from his birth), and she taught 3 or 4 of the eldest. After, having other occasions to divert her, she left that to others, of whose care long experience might make her confident, for she never changed her servants about them, and whilst she was with them she was careful nothing in that kind might be wanting.

Her first care was (whether by herself or others) to have them soon inclined to the knowledge, love, and esteem of all moral virtue; and to have them according to their capacities instructed in the principles of Christianity, not in manner of a catechism (which would have instructed them in the particular Protestant doctrines, of the truth of which she was little satisfied), but in a manner more apt to make an impression in them (than things learnt by rote and not understood), as letting them know, when they loved anything, that they were to love God more than it; that he made it, and them, and all things; they must love him, and honor him, more than their father; he gave them their father, he sent them every good thing, and made it for them; the King was his servant, he made all kings, and gave them their kingdom[s?].***

Being once like to die, whilst she had but two or 3 children, and those very little, that her care of them might not die with her, she writ (directed to her two eldest, a daughter and a son) a letter of some sheets of paper (to be given them when they were come to a more capable age), full of such moral precepts as she judged most proper for them, and such effect had this care of hers in the mind of her eldest daughter (for the forming of whose spirit and her instruction (though she were of a good nature) she had taken extraordinary pains, and ever found her again the most dutiful and best loving of

[11]Lucius Cary (1610–1643), second Viscount Falkland, about whom Ben Jonson wrote in the *Cary-Morison Ode.*

all her children), that being married afore she was thirteen year old, and going then to live in the house of her mother-in-law (in which she yielded a great obedience to her father's will) where she lived till her death (which was between sixteen and seventeen year old, in childbed of her first child), she being exceedingly beloved by her mother-in-law and all her family, her own mother asked her what she had done to gain all their affections in so great a degree? She said, indeed, she knew not anything that she did, unless that she had been careful to observe, as exactly as she could, the rule she had given her, when she took her leave of her at her first going from her: that wheresoever conscience and reason would permit her, she should prefer the will of another before her own.

Neither did she neglect to have those that were of a bigness capable of it (whilst she was with them) learn all those things that might be fit for them. She always thought it a most misbecoming thing in a mother to make herself more her business than her children and, whilst she had care of herself, to neglect them. Her doing was most contrary to this, being excessive in all that concerned their clothes or recreation, and she that never (not in her youth) could take care or delight in her own fineness, could apply herself to have too much care and take pleasure in theirs.

To her husband she bore so much respect that she taught her children, as a duty, to love him better than herself: and, though she saw it was a lesson they could learn without teaching, and that all but her eldest son did it in a very high degree, it never lessened her love or kindness to any of them. He was very absolute, and though she had a strong will, she had learnt to make it obey his. The desire to please him ⟨would⟩ had power to make her do that, that others would have scarce believed possible for her: as taking care of her house in all things (to which she could have no inclination but what his will gave her): the applying herself to use and love work:[12] and, being most fearful of a horse, both before and after, she did (he loving hunting and desiring to have her a good horsewoman) for many year ride so much, and so desperately, as if she had no fear but much delight in it: and so she had, to see him pleased, and did really make herself love it as long as that lasted. But after (as before) she neither had the courage, nor the skill, to sit upon a horse: ⟨and he

[12] Needlework.

left to desire it. after her having had a fall from her horse (leaping a hedge and ditch being with child of her fourth child. when she was taken up for dead though both she and her child did well). she being continually after as long as she lived with him either with child or giving suck).

Dressing was all her life a torture to her. yet because he would have it so. she willingly supported it. all the while she lived with him. in her younger days. even to tediousness: but all that ever she could do towards it. was to have those about her that could do it well. and to take order that it should be done. and then endure the trouble: for though she was very careful it should be so, she was not able to attend to it all. nor ever was her mind the least engaged in it. but her women were fain to walk round the room after her (which was her custom) while she was seriously thinking on some other business. and pin on her things and braid her hair: and while she writ or read. curl her hair and dress her head; and it did sufficiently appear how alone for his will she did undergo the trouble by the extraordinary great carelessness she had of herself after he was angry with her. from which time she never went out of plain black. frieze or coarse stuff. or cloth.

Where his interest was concerned. she seemed not able to have any consideration of her own: which amongst other things. she showed in this: a considerable part of her jointure[13] (which upon her marriage had been made sufficiently good) having been reassumed to the crown. to which it had formerly belonged. a greater part of it (being all that remained. but some very small thing) she did on his occasions consent to have mortgaged: which act of hers did so displease her own father that he disinherited her upon it. putting before her. her two eldest (and then only) sons. tying his estate on the eldest and. in case he failed.[14] on the second. She showed herself always no less ready to avoid whatsoever might displease him. Of this all her life she gave many proofs: and after she was a Catholic. when he would neither speak to her nor see her. she forbore things most ordinarily done by all. and which she did much delight in. for hearing from some other that he seemed to dislike it: and where she did but apprehend it would not please him. she

---

[13]The holding of property for a wife to be granted her in widowhood.
[14]Died without a male heir.

would not do the least thing, though on good occasion: so as she
seemed to prefer nothing but religion and her duty to God before his
will. The rules which she did, in some things she writ (and in her
opinions), seem to think fit to be held in this, did displease many as
overstrict. She did always much disapprove ⟨a⟩ the practice ⟨with⟩ of
satisfying oneself with their conscience being free from fault, not
forbearing all that might have the least show, ⟨of unfit⟩ or suspicion,
of uncomeliness, or unfitness: what she thought to be required in
this she expressed in this motto (which she caused [to be inscribed]
in her daughter's wedding ring): be and seem.

In this time she had some occasions of trouble, which afflicted
her so much as twice to put her into so deep melancholy ⟨(while she
was with child of her 2d and 4th child) that she lost the perfect use
of her reason, and was in much danger of her life. She had ground
for the beginning of her apprehensions, but she giving full way to
them (which were always apt to go as far as she would let them),
they arrived so far as to be plain distractedness. It is like she at first
gave the more way to it at those times, thinking her husband would
then be most sensible of her trouble, knowing he was extraordinary
careful of her when she was with child or gave suck, as being a most
tenderly loving father.⟩ One of these times for fourteen days together
she eat nor drunk nothing in the world, but only a little beer with a
toast, yet without touching the toast, so as being great with child
and quick, the child left to stir, and she became as flat as if she had
not been with child at all. Yet after, coming out of her melancholy,
the child and she did well.

From this time she seemed so far to have overcome all sadness
that she was scarce ever subject to it on any occasion (but only
once), but always looked on the best side of everything, and what
good every accident brought with it. Her greatest sign of sadness
(after) was sleeping, which she was used to say she could do when
she would, and then had most will to when she had occasion to have
sad thoughts waking: which she much sought to avoid, and it
seemed could (for the most part) do it, when she gave herself to it;
and she could well divert others in occasions of trouble, having
sometimes with her conversation much lightened the grief of some,
suddenly, in that which touched them nearliest. This occasion of her
own trouble being past, she did so far pardon the causers of it as to
some of them she showed herself a most faithful and constant

friend, to others so careful a provider and reliever in their necessities that she was by some (that knew her but afar off, and were not witness of what she had suffered) thought almost guilty of their faults.

She continued the care of her house till, her husband being made Controller of the King's Household, she came to live frequently at his lodgings at court; and her father-in-law dying, their family being increased, she put it into the hands of others. She continued her opinion of religion, and bore a great and high reverence to our Blessed Lady, to whom, being with child of her last daughter[15] (and still a Protestant) she offered up that child, promising if it were a girl it should (in devotion to her) bear her name, and that as much as was in her power, she would endeavor to have it be a nun. Whilst she yet gave suck to the same child, she went into Ireland,[16] with her lord and all her children, except her eldest daughter (who, just before her going, was married into Scotland). Being there, she had much affection to that nation, and was very desirous to have made use of ⟨her⟩ what power she had on any occasion in their behalf, as also in that of any Catholics. She there learnt to read Irish in an Irish Bible; but it being very hard (so as she could scarce find one that could teach it) and few books in it, she quickly lost what she had learnt.

Here chiefly the desire of the benefit and commodity of that nation set her upon a great design. It was to bring up the use of all trades in that country, which is fain to be beholding to others for the smallest commodities. To this end she procured some of each kind to come from those other places where those trades are exercised (as several sorts of linen and woolen weavers, dyers, all sorts of spinners, and knitters, hatters, lace makers, and many other trades) at the very beginning; and for this purpose she took of beggar children (with which that country swarms) more than 8 score prentices, refusing none above seven year old, and taking some less. These were disposed to their several masters and mistresses to learn those trades they were thought most fit for, the least amongst them being set to something, as making points, tags, buttons, or lace, or some other

---

[15]Mary Cary, born c. 1621.

[16]Henry Cary's tenure as Lord Deputy of Ireland (1622–1629) was characterized by such policies as the suppression of the Roman Catholic clergy and continued colonization.

thing. They were parted in their several rooms and houses, where they exercised their trades, many rooms being filled with little boys or girls, sitting all round at work: besides those that were bigger, for trades needing more understanding and strength. She brought it to that pass that they there made broadcloth so fine and good (of Irish wool, and spun and weaved and dyed and dressed there) that her Lord, being Deputy, wore it.

Yet it came to nothing: which she imputed to a judgment of God on her, because the overseers made all those poor children go to church: and she had great losses by fire and water (which she judged extraordinary, others but casual).[17] Her workhouse, with all that was in it, much cloth and much materials, was burnt: her fulling mills carried away: and much of her things spoiled with water—all which when she was a Catholic she took to be the punishment of God for the children's going to church, and that therefore her business did not succeed. But others thought it rather that she was better at contriving than executing, and that too many things were undertaken at the very first, and that she was fain (having little choice) to employ either those that had little skill in the matters they dealt in, or less honesty, and so she was extremely cozened,[18] which she was most easily, though she were not a little suspicious in her nature: but chiefly the ill order she took for paying money in this (as in all other occasions). Having the worst memory, in such things, in the world, and wholly trusting to it (or them she dealt with), and never keeping any account of what she did, she was most subject to pay the same thing often (as she hath had it confessed to her, by some, that they have (in a small matter) made her pay them the same thing five times in five days). Neither would she suffer herself to be undeceived by them that stood by and saw her do it frequently: rather suspecting they said it out of dislike of her designs, and to divert her from them: and the same unwillingness she had to see she was cozened, in all things on which she was set with such violence (as she was on all the things she undertook, which were many), which violence in all occasions made her ever subject to necessities (even when she had most), and made her continually pawn

---

[17]She thought these events were due to God's anger while others saw them as accidents.

[18]Tricked or deceived.

and sell anything she had (though it were a thing she should need (almost) within an hour after) to procure what she had a mind to at the present: the same violence made her subject to make great promises to those that assisted her in those things which, being many, could not always be performed. It made her, too, to acknowledge small things, done at the instants she desired them, so great (and without regarding to whom it was) that, if it chanced to be to such as would claim a requital according to the acknowledgment (and not the worth of the thing), at a greater distance, looking on it with truer eyes, what she had said could not always be stood to.

About these works, after the beginning of them, her lord seemed often displeased with her: yet rather with the manner of ordering it than the thing itself, which she knew not how to mend. It would have been in his power easily to have made her give over: but she conceived what he showed in it was rather not to engage his own credit in the success of it, than that he desired to have her leave it: and in this she after saw herself not deceived: for, some letters of his, to others, came after to her hands, where she saw he highly praised that for which he had often chidden her, and that he affirmed it would have been to the exceeding great benefit of that kingdom, could it have been well prosecuted.

Further Reading

On Elizabeth Cary and *Mariam:*

Beilin, Elaine. "Elizabeth Cary and *The Tragedie of Mariam.*" *Papers on Language and Literature*. 16 (1980): 45–64.

Callaghan, Dympna. "Re-reading *The Tragedie of Mariam, the Faire Queene of Jewry.*" In *Women, "Race," and Writing in the Early Modern Period*. Eds. Margo Hendricks and Patricia Parker. Routledge, 1994. 163–77.

Ferguson, Margaret. "Running on With Almost Public Voice: The Case of 'E.C.'" In *Tradition and the Talents of Women*. Ed. Florence Howe. University of Illinois Press, 1991. 37–67.

_____. "The Spectre of Resistance: *The Tragedy of Mariam* (1613)." *Staging the Renaissance: Representations of Elizabethan and Jacobean Drama*. Eds. David Kastan and Peter Stallybrass. Routledge, 1991. 235–50.

Fischer, Sandra K. "Elizabeth Cary and Tyranny, Domestic and Religious." In *Silent But for the Word: Tudor Women as Patrons, Translators, and Writers of Religious Works*. Ed. Margaret Hannay. Kent State University Press, 1985. 225–37.

Kaul, Mythili, ed. Othello: *New Essays by Black Writers*. Howard University Press, 1996.

Kemp, Theresa D. "The Family Is a Little Commonwealth: Teaching *Mariam* and *Othello* in a Special-Topics Course on Domestic England." *Shakespeare Quarterly* 47 (1996): 451–60.

Kolin, Philip C., ed. Othello: *New Critical Essays*. Taylor & Francis, Inc., 2002.

Krontiris, Tina. *Oppositional Voices: Women as Writers and Translators of Literature in the English Renaissance*. Routledge, 1992.

_____. "Reading with the Author's Sex: A Comparison of Two Seventeenth-Century Texts." *Gramma: Journal of Theory and Criticism* 1 (1993): 123–36.

Newman, Karen. "Feminity and the Monstrous." In *Shakespeare Reproduced: The Text in History and Ideology*. Eds. Jean E. Howard and Marion F. O'Connor. Methuen, 1987. 141–62.

Pechter, Edward. Othello *and Interpretive Traditions*. University of Iowa Press, 1999.

Quilligan, Maureen. "Staging Gender: William Shakespeare and Elizabeth Cary." In *Sexuality and Gender in Early Modern Europe: Institutions,*

Texts. Images. Ed. James Grantham Turner. Cambridge University Press. 1993. 208–32.

Raber. Karen L. "Gender and the Political Subject in *Tragedy of Mariam.*" *Studies in English Literature, 1500–1900:* 35 (1995): 321–43.

Shannon. Laurie J. "*The Tragedie of Mariam:* Cary's Critique of the Terms of Founding Social Discourses." *ELR* 24 (1994): 135–53.

Straznicky. Marta "'Profane and Stoical Paradoxes': *The Tragedie of Mariam* and Sidnean Closet Drama." *ELR* 24 (1994): 104–34.

Travitsky. Betty. "The *Femme Couvert* in Elizabeth Cary's *Mariam.*" In *Ambiguous Realities: Women in the Middle Ages and Renaissance.* Eds. Carole Levin and Jeanie Watson. Wayne State University Press. 1987. 184–96.

——. "Husband-Murder and Petty Treason in English Renaissance Tragedy." *Renaissance Drama* 21 (1990): 171–98.

Wolfe. Heather. *Elizabeth Cary: Lady Falkland: Life and Letters.* RTM Publications. 2001.

Zimmerman. Shari. "Disaffection. Dissimulation and the Uncertain Ground of Silent Dismission: Juxtaposing John Milton and Elizabeth Cary." *ELH* 66 (1999): 553–89.

On William Shakespeare and *Othello:*

Aubrey. James R. "Race and the Spectacle of the Monstrous in Othello." *Clio* 22 (1993): 221–38.

Bayley. John. "Love and Identity." *The Characters of Love: A Study in the Literature of Personality.* Collier Books. 1963. 111–74.

Bartheley. Anthony Gerard. ed. *Critical Essays on Shakespeare's Othello.* Macmillan Library Reference. 1994.

Boose. Lynda E. "Othello's Handkerchief: 'The Recognizance and Pledge of Love'" *English Literary Renaissance* 5 (1975): 360–74.

Bradley. A. C. "Othello" in *Shakespearean Tragedy.* St. Martin's Press. 1992.

Burton. Jonathan. "'A Most Wily Bird': Leo Africanus. Othello and the Trafficking in Difference." In *Post-Colonial Shakespeares.* Ed. Marin Orkin. Routledge. 1998. 43–63.

Cavell. Stanley. "Literature as Knowledge of the Outsider." *The Claim of Reason: Wittgenstein, Scepticism, Morality and Tragedy.* Oxford University Press. 1999. 476–96.

Granville-Barker. Harley. "Preface to Othello." *Prefaces to Shakespeare.* Vol. IV. Princeton University Press. 1965. 120–266.

Greenblatt. Stephen. "The Improvisation of Power." *Renaissance Self-Fashioning.* University of Chicago Press. 1980. 222–54.

Fernie. Ewan. "Shame in Othello." *Cambridge Quarterly* 28 (1999): 19–45.

Habib. Imtiaz. "Othello. Sir Peter Negro. and the Blacks of Early Modern England: Colonial Inscription and Postcolonial Excavation." *Literature* 9 (1998): 15–30.

Hall, Kim. "Beauty and the Beast of Whiteness: Teaching Race and Gender." *Shakespeare Quarterly* 47 (1996): 461-75.

Honan, Park. *Shakespeare: A Life*. Oxford University Press. 2000.

Kastan, David Scott. *A Companion to Shakespeare*. Blackwell Publishers. 2000.

Matz, Robert "Slander. Renaissance Discourses of Sodomy and *Othello*." *ELH* 66 (1999): 261-76.

Neely, Carol Thomas. "Women and Men in Othello: What Should Such a Fool / Do with So Good a Woman!" In *The Woman's Part: Feminist Criticism of Shakespeare*. Eds. Carolyn Ruth Swift Lenz, Gayle Green, and Carol Thomas Neely. University of Illinois Press. 1980. 211–39.

Newman, Karen. *Fashioning Feminity and English Renaissance Drama*. University of Chicago Press, 1991.

Nostbakken, Faith. *Understanding* Othello, *A Student Casebook to Issues, Sources, and Historical Documents*. Greenwood Press, 2000.

Orkin, Martin. "Othello and the Plain Face of Racism." *Shakespeare Quarterly* 38 (1987): 166–88.

Rosenberg, Marvin. *The Masks of Othello: The Search for the Identity of Othello, Iago and Desdemona by Three Centuries of Actors and Critics*. University of California Press, 1961.

Vaughan, Virginia Mason. Othello: *A Contextual History*. Cambridge University Press, 1997.

On Ethnography:

Bartels, Emily C. "Making More of the Moor: Aaron, Othello, and Renaissance Refashioning of Race." *Shakespeare Quarterly* 41 (1990): 433–54.

Hall, Kim. *Things of Darkness: Economies of Race and Gender in Early Modern England*. Cornell University Press, 1995.

Hendricks, Margo and Patricia Parker, eds. *Women, Race, and Writing in the Early Modern Period*. Routledge, 1994.

Johnson, Rosalind R. "Parallels between Othello and the Historical Leo Africanus." *Bim* 18, (1986): 9-34.

Jones, Eldred D. *The Elizabethan Image of Africa*. Folger Books, 1971.

———. *Othello's Countrymen: The African in English Renaissance Drama*. Oxford University Press, 1965.

Levin, Carole. "Backgrounds and Echoes of *Othello*: From Leo Africanus to Ignatius Sancho." *Lamar Journal of the Humanities* 22 (1996): 45–68.

On the Tracts on Marriage:

Emerson, Everett H. *English Puritanism from John Hooper to John Milton*. Duke University Press. 1968.

Jordan, Constance. *Renaissance Feminism: Literary Texts and Political Models*. Cornell University Press, 1990.

Klein. Joan Larsen. *Daughters. Wires and Widows: Writings by Men about Women and Marriage in England. 1500–1640.* University of Illinois Press. 1992.

Merrill.Thomas F.. ed. *William Perkins. 1558–1602: English Puritanist.* Nieuwkoop. 1966.

Orlin. Lena Cowen. *Private Matters and Public Culture in Post-Reformation England.* Cornell University Press. 1994.

_____. *Elizabethan Households: An Anthology.* University of Washington Press. 1995.

Stone. Lawrence. *The Family Sex, and Marriage in England. 1500–1800.* HarperCollins Publishers. 1986.

Tilney. Edmund. *The Flower of Friendship: A Renaissance Dialogue Contesting Marriage.* Edited with an introduction by Valerie Wayne. Cornell University Press. 1992.

Woodbridge. Linda. *Women and the English Renaissance: Literature and the Nature of Womankind. 1540–1640.* University of Illinois. 1984.

On the Textual Problems of *Othello:*

Honigmann. E. A. J. *The Texts of Othello and Shakespearean Revision.* Routledge. 1996.

McMillin. Scott. ed. *The First Quarto of Othello.* Cambridge University Press. 2001.

Videos and Films of *Othello:*

1952   *The Tragedy of Othello: the Moor of Venice.* Directed and produced by Orson Welles.

1984   *The Tragedy of Othello: the Moor of Venice.* Bard Productions Limited. Directed by Franklin Melton. produced by Jack Nakano. distributed by Century Home Video. c. 1984.

1988   *Othello.* BBC/Time-Life Television. Directed by Jonathan Miller. produced by Cedric Messina. Jonathan Miller. Ambrose Video Publications.

1990   *Othello.* Rockbottom Productions. Directed by Ted Lange. screenplay adaptation by Ted Lange. produced by James M. Swain and Katherine A. Kaspar.

1990   *Othello.* Primetime Television Ltd. BBC. Directed by Trevor Nunn. produced by Greg Smith.

1995   *Othello.* Coloumbia TriStar Home Video. Drected by Oliver Parker. produced by Luc Roeg and David Barron.